Cromwell as a Soldier

Cromwell as a Soldier
The Military Career of Oliver Cromwell during the
English Civil War and Other Conflicts
ILLUSTRATED EDITION

T S Baldock

Cromwell as a Soldier
The Military Career of Oliver Cromwell during the English Civil War and Other Conflicts
by T S Baldock

ILLUSTRATED

First published under the title
Cromwell as a Soldier

Leonaur is an imprint of Oakpast Ltd
Copyright in this form © 2017 Oakpast Ltd

ISBN: 978-1-78282-656-9 (hardcover)
ISBN: 978-1-78282-657-6 (softcover)

http://www.leonaur.com

Publisher's Notes

The views expressed in this book are not necessarily those of the publisher.

Contents

Preface	7
Outbreak of Civil War	7
Military organisation of England before the Civil War	16
Battle of Edgehill	36
Origin of the Ironsides	50
Cromwell's activity in the Eastern Association	63
Battle of Gainsborough	76
Sir T. Fairfax Joins Cromwell	91
Cromwell in the Midlands	105
Marston Moor	116
Royalists march to Oxford	134
Cromwell's charge against Manchester	150
Cromwell's Raid Round Oxford	170
Cromwell and Fairfax	207
Cromwell at Winchester and Basing	218
The End of the First Civil War	235
Flight of the King	246
Cromwell in South Wales	257

Cromwell Joins Lambert	267
Cromwell advances to Argyle's Assistance	289
Cromwell's Plan of Campaign	303
Cromwell before Waterford	314
Cromwell Returns to England	330
Cromwell Crosses the Border	341
Cromwell's Preparations for Battle	355
Edinburgh Castle Surrenders	370
Cromwell Decides to Cross the Forth	380
Cromwell's Pursuit	393
His Claims to be Ranked among the Greatest Commanders	412

CROMWELL AS A SOLDIER

Preface

That Cromwell was a great military genius is universally admitted, but the grounds on which rest his claims to be one of England's foremost soldiers are not always well understood.

The stories of the battles and campaigns in which he took part have been told again and again, but always as part of the general history of the period, or as incidents in a career that has many other important aspects—political, social, and religious. Their continuity is therefore lost, and it becomes difficult to follow the purely military development. The aim of this work is to give a succinct account of Cromwell's life as a soldier, pointing out how his genius taught him to reject one after the other the principal military errors of his day, and how, under his guidance, a crude untrained militia developed in a few years into the most perfect regular army of that period.

The narrative is founded on contemporaneous accounts which are fairly sufficient; though more information as to the tactical formations would often be highly valuable. This is specially the case in connection with the movements and pace of the cavalry, for Cromwell fought in the days when it was still the most important arm, and was himself, probably, the finest cavalry leader England ever produced.

It is, however, hoped that the following pages will serve to put before Englishmen the military career of one of their greatest soldiers.

T. S. Baldock, Lieut.-Col., R.A.

Outbreak of Civil War

Of Oliver Cromwell's early life little need be said here. Little, indeed, is known. He was born in April, 1599, of a good family, his father being one of the younger sons of a very wealthy Huntingdonshire squire, Sir Henry Cromwell, of Hinchinbrook. Originally the

family appears to have come from South Wales, and to have borne the name of Williams. One of them married the sister of Thomas Cromwell, Earl of Essex, and his son adopted the surname of Cromwell.

Oliver's mother was a Steward, a family which, like the Cromwells, had grown rich on the spoils of the monasteries. Both families were, therefore, zealously Protestant, and Oliver was educated strictly in the doctrine of that faith. Both at school and college Puritan influences surrounded him and were readily absorbed by his stern but passionate nature.

In 1617, when Oliver was only eighteen, his father died, and, as the only surviving son, he was thus early associated with his mother in the management of a moderate estate. He is said to have studied the law for some months, in order probably to fit himself for the duties of a magistrate. He married in 1620 and settled down into the peaceful life of a country gentleman. He farmed, sat on the bench of magistrates, interested himself in the schemes for draining the fens, started just then by the Earl of Bedford, and sat in Parliament in 1626 as member for Huntingdon. His pursuits were entirely peaceful in a period of profound peace. He appears to have had no military training whatever beyond such exercises in the use of his weapons as then formed part of the education of every gentleman. Possibly he may have been an officer of the local trained bands, though it is nowhere said that he was, and at any rate the training these local forces received was exceedingly scanty.

Yet in a few years this same peaceful country squire developed into the most brilliant warrior in Europe, a consummate tactician, a reorganiser of armies, who, in an uninterrupted career of victory, defeated veterans trained in the schools of Gustavus Adolphus and William of Orange. By him the art of war was revolutionised, old pedantries were crumbled into dust, and a new spirit was infused into the organisation and leading of armies. Yet it was not till 1642, when he was forty-three years old, that Cromwell unwillingly assumed the role of a soldier. To every thinking soldier his career is of the deepest interest, and is worthy of the closest study. At this period, the storm of civil strife which had long been threatening burst.

Already in 1639, the first rumblings of the thunder had been heard. The Scots had finally rejected Laud's scheme of episcopal hierarchy, and refused to submit to the authority of the bishops. Charles, without calling a Parliament, managed somehow, by illegal means, to raise an army in order to enforce his decrees. The Scots flew to arms. Thousands of war-worn veterans streamed back to defend in their native land the religious tenets for which they had spilt their blood on the continent. When Charles arrived at the Border in May, 1639, he found them encamped on Dunoe Law ready to oppose him. A mere glance at the two armies was enough. On the king's side an undisciplined rabble, a confused medley of courtiers, adventurers, jail-birds, and pressed men—on the other, a well-organised, well-disciplined army, led by veteran officers, and inspired by deep religious enthusiasm. A slight skirmish or two only accentuated the difference between the armies, and Charles was forced to patch up the best peace he was able, at the risk of seeing England invaded and its northern counties in the hands of his enemies.

The peace, however, did not last many months, and Charles, with an empty treasury and war staring him in the face, reluctantly summoned a Parliament, which met on 13th April, 1640. In this Parliament Cromwell sat as member for Cambridge. Instead of voting supplies to carry on the Scotch war, Parliament proceeded to discuss grievances. Charles, in a rage, dissolved it on 5th May. Again, he had recourse to illegal means of levying men and money. An army was raised with difficulty, the rendezvous was appointed at York, but the service was most unpopular.

Only the courtiers and the episcopal clergy responded warmly to the king's call. The country gentlemen hung back, the soldiers pressed into the ranks, were positively hostile to the cause. In common with most of the lower orders, they were Puritans at heart, and sympathized with the Scots in their opposition to the bishops. They mutinied continually, and even shot their officers. (Carlyle, People's edition, vol. i.) The only hope of success for Charles lay in the presence of Strafford, a man of iron will and a first-rate soldier, who was associated with the Earl of Northampton and Lord Conway in the command. But even Strafford could do nothing with such materials.

The Scots, who saw that a passive attitude only encouraged Charles, crossed the Tweed on 20th August, at Coldstream. The Earl of Leven was in command; under him, amongst others, was the famous Marquis of Montrose, afterwards the organiser of victories for the king. Their army was excellent, well led, well fed, well disciplined. Against such leaders and such troops Charles could do nothing.

On 29th August, the Scots forced the passage of the Tyne at Newburn, and overran Northumberland and Durham. They appealed to their co-religionists in England to assist rather than oppose them. The

Puritans looked upon them as deliverers; the whole English nation was clamouring for peace and a Parliament. Charles turned to Strafford for advice, and at his suggestion summoned a Council of Peers. This council, which met at York, petitioned the king to assemble a Parliament, and the necessary writs were then issued. At the same time a treaty was opened with the Scots at Ripon, on October 1st.

This Parliament, the famous "Long Parliament," met for the first time on 3rd November, 1640. Cromwell sat in it again as member for Cambridge. A man of strong convictions, and of an energetic, passionate nature, he threw himself heart and soul into the party, which, led by Pym, attacked the illegalities of the Star Chamber, the encroachments of the royal prerogative, and denounced the bishops. The story of the Long Parliament, and of the part which Cromwell played as a member of it, are outside the scope of this work; only one or two points will be touched on which affect, or help to explain, his career as a soldier.

One of his first acts after taking his seat was to present the petition of John Lilburne, who, in accordance with a sentence of the Star Chamber, had received 200 lashes. Lilburne had been clerk to Prynne, who, for publishing a work displeasing to Laud, had been put in pillory and his ears cut off. Lilburne was a truculent sort of fellow, who gave Cromwell much trouble afterwards, but on this occasion the latter supported his petition with vehemence. Sir Philip Warwick, a Royalist, gives an oft quoted sketch of him on this occasion. He says:—

> I came into the House one morning well clad; and perceived a gentleman speaking, whom I knew not, very ordinarily apparelled; for it was a plain cloth suit, which seemed to have been made by an ill country tailor; his linen was plain, and not very clean; and I remember a speck or two of blood on his little band which was not much larger than his collar. His hat was without a hatband. His stature was a good size, his sword stuck close to his side, his countenance swollen and reddish, his voice sharp and untuneable, and his eloquence full of fervour. For the subject matter would not bear much of reason; it being on behalf of a servant of Mr. Prynne's who had dispersed libels. I sincerely profess it lessened much my reverence as to that Great Council, for this gentleman was very much hearkened unto.— Carlyle, vol. i

Whilst Parliament was receiving petitions, discussing grievances, contending against illegal courts, denouncing bishops, and impeaching Strafford, the treaty with the Scots lingered on. The scene of the negotiation had been transferred to London, whither the Scottish Commissioners had proceeded. Meanwhile their army lay quartered in Northumberland and Durham, and opposite them, in Yorkshire, lay the mutinous army of the king. Parliament was in no hurry to conclude the treaty.

Pym and his party looked on the Scottish Army as a safeguard against any attempt on the part of the monarch to use force against them. Until more certain of their own power they were by no means anxious that the Scots should go. Parliament allowed the latter £850 a day, (Carlyle), as a subsidy, and on these terms, they were willing enough to keep their army on foot. Not till July, 1641, was the treaty completed, and their army withdrawn. At the same time the king's forces were disbanded by Parliament, which now began to have confidence in its own strength.

Meanwhile the war of words waxed hotter and hotter at Westminster. Strafford had been beheaded, Laud imprisoned, yet the Puritans were not appeased. Then in November, 1641, came the news of the terrible Irish Rebellion to add fresh fuel to the flames. Charles was accused of having instigated the rising, and of intending to employ Irish Catholics to suppress the Puritans in England. There were but few troops in Ireland, and those holding on for dear life in Dublin. Reinforcements were voted to be raised, not by the king, but by Parliament. Then followed the "Grand Petition and Remonstrance," and the memorable debate during which the heated orators drew their swords on each other in the House itself, and were only prevented from fighting out the quarrel there and then by Hampden's tact and influence. Riots in the streets followed violence in the House.

The bishops were prevented taking their seats in the Lords. The confusion increased daily. At last Charles took the decisive step in his quarrel with the majority in Parliament. On the 4th January, 1642, he went down to the House with a following of three or four hundred armed men and attempted to seize five of the members—Pym, Hampden, Hazlerigg, Holies, and Strode—in their places. The scheme failed, the House having been warned, and the members sent for safety into the City. Both parties now felt that the die was cast, and that the quarrel must henceforth be fought out with the sword.

On the 10th, the king quitted London, sending the queen to Holland to pawn the crown jewels, borrow money, and buy arms; he,

ENGLAND IN THE CIVIL WAR (1642)

with a very small following, repaired to York, where he began to concert measures for raising troops. Parliament, on its side, did not delay. Troops were being levied, nominally to suppress the Irish Rebellion, but their chance of reaching Ireland was remote. Funds were rapidly raised. Cromwell subscribed £500, Hampden £1000.

Hull was one of the most important ports in the north, and contained a well-furnished magazine. On the 23rd April, 1642, Charles appeared before it, but found the gates shut. He summoned the governor, Sir John Hotham, to open them, but the latter refused. Charles, having no means to enforce his commands, was obliged to turn away. It was the first act of open rebellion. Henceforth, Hull was to become the rock against which all the campaigns of the king's forces in the north were wrecked.

Still, both parties were loath to commit an open act of war; indeed, the forces as yet available were insignificant. Negotiations, therefore, were carried on, whilst both sides continued to arm. Active members of the House used their local influence in raising troops. Foremost amongst these was Cromwell, who, in July, obtained permission to raise two companies of volunteers in Cambridge, and journeyed down there for that purpose. Arrived there he found Royalist tendencies prevalent, especially amongst the university authorities. He promptly seized the castle, with its magazine, and, overawing the university, he secured its plate, which had been intended for the king, for the use of the Parliament. Prompt and energetic in all his actions, he had, whilst in London, spent £100 in arms, which he had sent down into Cambridge, and already by the end of July he had men enrolled and piquets watching the roads. (Chief Justice Bramston's sons were stopped by Cromwell's musketeers, Carlyle vol. 1.)

On the 27th July, the king again appeared before Hull at the head of a small force, hoping Hotham would be induced to open the gates. He found the surrounding country flooded and the garrison reinforced. A skirmish ensued, in which the king's troops were worsted and lost their ammunition. The king, finding no prospect of obtaining the town by force or negotiations, withdrew on 30th July. (Warburton, *Prince Rupert and the Cavaliers*, vol. i.) A similar attempt on Coventry on the 20th August failed in a similar way, and on the 22nd, Charles set up his standard at Nottingham, and called upon all his faithful subjects to gather round it and assist him in reducing his rebellious Parliament to obedience.

This was indeed tantamount to a declaration of war. But Charles' forces were very weak; the foot at Nottingham were only 300 strong, the horse at Leicester some 800. Rupert had joined him and had been given command of the horse; the Earl of Lindsay, an experienced veteran, commanded in chief; Sir Jacob Astley was major-general of the foot. In July, Parliament had voted that an army should be raised for the protection of "King and Parliament" against the traitors who had misled the king and induced him to take up arms against his faithful subjects. It was to consist of twenty regiments of foot each 1000 strong, and seventy-five troops of horse each sixty strong, (Warburton). These forces were collecting at Northampton, and the Earl of Essex had been appointed to command.

Elsewhere the prospects of the Royalists appeared equally gloomy. The Marquis of Hertford had raised a force for the king in Somersetshire, but the Earl of Bedford soon appeared with a much superior force for the Parliament, drove Hertford out of Somerset into Dorset, and besieged him in Sherborne Castle with a force of 7000 foot, eight troops of horse, and four cannon, (Clarendon's *History of the Great Rebellion*, vol. ii.) Goring, it is true, held Portsmouth for the king, but Sir William Walker, with an army collected near London, marched down and besieged that most important port. A few days after the raising of the standard, Goring surrendered Portsmouth without resistance and on ignominious terms.

Only in the north were Charles' prospects somewhat brighter. There the powerful and popular Earl of Newcastle represented the Royal cause. He had secured the greater part of Northumberland, Durham, and Yorkshire, and was busily raising forces at Newcastle. His great opponents. Lord Fairfax and his son Sir Thomas, were then comparatively weak.

But strong as the land forces of the Parliament appeared when compared with its opponents, of far greater weight, and of far more lasting importance, was the fact that the fleet, under the Earl of Warwick, was entirely devoted to its cause, and with the fleet went all the more important military ports. (The captains of five ships demurred when Warwick declared for the Parliament, but they were easily overawed.—Rushworth's *Historical Collections*, vol. iv.)

Few responded to Charles' call to rally to his standard. His cause was as yet almost universally unpopular. He, therefore, determined to make fresh overtures for peace. On the 26th August, Lord Southampton and Sir John Culpepper were sent to London to ask both Houses that commissioners should be appointed to treat. They returned with the answer that Parliament would not consent to treat till the Royal standard was taken down. On the 5th September, Charles again sent more definite proposals, to form the basis of a treaty, which were entrusted to Lords Spencer and Falkland. These proposals were that both sides should mutually withdraw the accusations of treason brought against the other, and that the Royal Standard should then be taken down.

The reply of the Houses was most ill-considered and ill-worded. They refused to treat until Charles had withdrawn his protection from all persons who had been, or should hereafter be, proclaimed delinquents, in order that future generations might be warned of the heinous nature of such offences, and that the great charges to which the State had been put should be borne by those who had been the cause of them. (Gardiner's *History of the Great Civil War*, vol. i.; Warburton, vol. i.)

The effect of these answers on the country at large was excellent for the king. He had posed in the negotiations as the peacemaker, the Parliament as the aggressor. Whatever may have been his faults, it was the Parliament who had maliciously refused to listen to proposals for a treaty by which all things might have been decently settled. Recruits flocked to his standard. Thousands of country gentlemen who had hitherto hung back through dislike of his unconstitutional acts, now gave scope to their natural feelings of loyalty, and hastened to raise men and money for his service.

Thus, the Civil War opened with forces far more evenly balanced than could have been supposed possible a few weeks before. How were these forces raised, armed, and equipped? how were they formed for battle? what tactics did they employ? To understand the war aright, to follow intelligently the movements of the armies and their action in battle, to appreciate the designs of the generals, and their skill in carrying them out, some knowledge on these points is necessary. The next chapter is, therefore, devoted to a sketch of the constitution, drill, and tactics of the armies engaged in this war, avoiding technicalities as far as possible, so as to make the picture clear even to those unacquainted with any but the most ordinary military terms.

Military organisation of England before the Civil War

The well-known German military historian and critic, Fritz Hoenig, in his work *Oliver Cromwell*, states that:

The military forces of England consisted in those days of the standing army, the militia, and the fleet. All three bodies rested on special laws, which, accepted by king and parliament, formed part of the Constitution.

In opposition to the foreign author all English writers agree that the standing army was not legally recognised in England till after the Revolution in 1688, when the principles relating to the government of the army were laid down in the Bill of Rights and Act of Settlement. (Clode's *Military Forces of the Crown*, vol. i.)

Liability to serve in the "trained bands," as the militia was called, was universal. Since the days of the early Plantagenet kings every freeman between the ages of fifteen and sixty had been liable to be called under arms for the defence of the country. He might be called out either to assist in putting down riot or insurrection, or in case of invasion to resist the king's foreign enemies; but in the former case he could only be called on to serve within his county. (The earliest Act appears to have been passed in 1285. Clode, vol. i.) The duty of defending the realm lay with the king.

This was acknowledged by St. John, who defended Hampden in the famous ship money case in 1637. (Clode, i.). With the king alone lay the power of calling out the trained bands and directing the measures to be taken for defence. And if an invasion occurred, the enemy's forces were actually within the realm, and a state of war existed, the ordinary law lapsed; the king could then establish such a code as he should think the emergency required, and could therefore undoubtedly press men for service in the royal army as well as in the trained bands.

By an Act of Edward VI. the military forces could be called out by a "Commission of Array," granted by the king to the lieutenants of the counties. But this Act was allowed to expire at the end of Elizabeth's reign, though afterwards acted on by Charles I. (Clode, i.)

Although men could not be legally pressed as soldiers on shore, except in the case of invasion by a foreign enemy, the duty of defending British ships at sea devolved also on the king. In those days, the high seas were by no means safe. Pirates abounded, to say nothing of privateers and buccaneers; even the regular warships of the European states often stopped and plundered merchant vessels belonging to nations with which their sovereigns were at peace.

Therefore, it behoved the king always to keep an armed navy afloat to protect the flag at sea; and he was legally empowered to press men as sailors for that service. (Clode, i.) But the sailors of those days were not as now considered as combatants, therefore it appeared but a slight stretch of prerogative, and might even be considered a necessity, to press men as soldiers to fight the ships. It was illegal to press soldiers to fight *beyond* the seas, but once on board there was no difficulty in getting them to land and fight in foreign countries. (Clode, i.)

Under such pretences and subterfuges, therefore, it was customary to press men for service on those expeditions which the Stuart kings sent out from time to time. On the return of the expedition to Spain in the latter part of 1625, Charles ventured a step further, and directed that the troops should not be disbanded but employed as he should direct. (Clode, i.) In those days, there were no barracks for soldiers, therefore it was necessary to billet them on the householders.

This soon became an intolerable nuisance, especially as the soldiers were ill paid and lived for the most part at free quarters. Moreover, the king used the hardships inflicted by billeting to coerce refractory subjects. Should a town refuse to subscribe to a loan, or otherwise make itself obnoxious to the Crown, a party of soldiers was sent to be billeted upon it. As the discipline in an army must be kept up by sterner laws than those which suffice for a civilian population, commissions were issued to certain persons to proceed by martial law, in cases in which soldiers were involved, in the districts where they were billeted. (Clode, i.) As these powers were used not only for the punishment of soldiers, but also of civilians associated with them, (Clode, i.), another very serious grievance was caused by the retention of an army in peace.

When, therefore, Parliament was assembled in 1628, one of the most important measures passed was the Petition of Rights. In this it was declared that as during the time of peace the civil magistrate had cognisance of all offences by whoever committed, these Commissions of Martial Law, against any person whatsoever, were wholly and directly contrary to the laws and statutes of the realm. (Clode, i.) It was also declared that the billeting of soldiers on the people was against the laws and customs of this realm. For as a previous petition said, "every freeman hath, and of right ought to have, a full and absolute property in his goods and estate." (Clode, i.) The army was disbanded in this year.

As martial law and billeting were essential to keeping up an army in peace as well as in war, it was evident that the retention of a standing army or the levying of soldiers in time of peace was illegal. So, when Charles granted Commissions of Array for raising an army in 1639, sought to legalise his proceedings by declaring the men were levied to protect the realm against invasion by the Scots. But having levied them, he could not pay or clothe them by legal means, as he had not called a Parliament and obtained a subsidy. His own revenues were not sufficient for the purpose. One of the illegal taxes which caused great discontent was called Coat and Conduct Money. Each county was assessed to find the money for the recruiting and clothing of a certain number of men, one shilling as bringing money to the recruiter for each man, and fourteen shillings for the recruit's coat. (Clode, i.)

In 1640, Parliament having been summoned, subsidies were granted for the subsistence of the army. Both these armies of 1639 and 1640 were governed by martial law, and as an actual state of war existed, there appears to have been no demur to its execution.

As the dispute between the king and Parliament became accentuated, each side endeavoured to obtain the power over the militia. The king claimed to exercise it through the lieutenants of the counties, but the Parliament objected that as the Act of Edward VI.'s reign had been allowed to expire the older Acts returned to force, and by these "the military forces were arrayed and mustered under commissions from the Crown directed to two or more persons of honour, reputation, and estate in each particular county," (Clode, i.), and the Houses proceeded to lay before the king the names of persons in each county to whom they proposed entrusting the power of militia. But these the king refused to accept. The Houses then passed in June, 1642, the "Ordinance for the Militia," (Clode, i.) by which they professed to take the power over it into their own hands.

Another Act of this Parliament, 16 Car. i. c. 2), declares that impressment by the Crown is illegal, but authorises Justices of the Peace by order of Parliament to impress all men not under eighteen or above sixty years for the war, with certain exemptions. (Clode, i.) The men impressed under this Act were nominally levied as reinforcements for the army in Ireland, but were really employed against the king.

Thus, at the outbreak of the Civil War both sides were endeavouring to obtain legal right to levy troops, but in fact neither side could justly claim to possess such a right. The king and Parliament are so closely connected in the government by the English Constitution, that it was impossible for either to legally raise and maintain troops without the consent of the other. For even if the king retained, as he asserted, the power to levy the trained bands by the lieutenants of counties for the preservation of internal peace, he had no power to tax the people for their maintenance when embodied; and he certainly had no right to recruit his own army by impressment. On the other hand, the Parliament's "Ordinance of Militia," having never received royal assent, could not be legally placed on the statute-book.

Yet such is the veneration of the English people for the law, that wherever one side could show what appeared to be legal authority for levying troops, such levies were submitted to without much demur. But the trained bands when thus called out would only perform such duties as they believed themselves bound by law to do. The difficulties of the commanders on both sides were much increased by this disposition on the part of a great portion of their forces, which will be best shown by an example. The campaign of Sir Ralph Hopton in Cornwall at the outbreak of the war illustrates these points admirably, and as it was simple, and lay apart from the campaigns of the main armies, it will be very briefly discussed here.

When the Marquis of Hertford was driven out of Somerset, Sir Ralph Hopton repaired to Cornwall, where he concerted measures for raising forces for the king, and occupied Pendennis Castle. The Parliamentary party had meanwhile overrun Devonshire and possessed themselves of all the principal towns. Two of their members. Sir Richard Buller and Sir Alexander Carew, proceeded to Cornwall during quarter sessions and brought an indictment against Hopton for disturbing the peace. Hopton appeared in person and produced his commission from the king, issued through the Marquis of Hertford, as lieutenant-general of the horse in the western army.

The grand jury recognised the validity of the commission, and at the instigation of Hopton drew an indictment against Buller and Carew for an unlawful assembly at Launceston, where they had collected forces for the Parliament. The sheriff was also directed to call out the *"posse comitatus"* and disperse the unlawful assembly. The Cornish trained bands, recognizing the lawful authority of the sheriff, readily obeyed, and in a few days Hopton found himself at the head of 3000 well-armed foot. He advanced on Launceston, whereupon Buller and Carew retreated to Plymouth. But when he wished to follow up the fugitives, the Cornish trained bands refused to do so, alleging that as their sheriff had no authority outside his own county, they could not be called on to serve outside it. They were then dismissed.

These events occurred in October and November, 1642. Hopton then proceeded to raise forces for the king by voluntary enlistment.

The gentry of the county were mostly Royalists, who assisted him in raising, arming, and maintaining the men. Having no regular source of revenue, "the money that was raised for the maintenance and payment of that army was entirely on the reputation, credit, and interest of particular men." (Clarendon, vol. ii.) In this manner some 1500 soldiers, well-armed and disciplined, were soon raised. At first ammunition was much wanted, but soon this defect was made good by Captain Cartaret, who had been controller of the Royal Navy. Leaving his home in Jersey, he proceeded to France, where he purchased ammunition, partly on his own credit, partly with money remitted to him from Cornwall, and sent it over for the use of the Cornish forces.

About this time, Lord Mohun, who had hitherto taken no active part in affairs, proceeded to Brentford, where the king was, declared he had been sent by Sir R. Hopton to obtain the kings orders, and succeeded in getting the latter to associate him in the command of the Cornish forces with Hopton, Berkley, and Ashburnham, who were respectively lieutenant-general of the horse, commissary-general, and major-general of the foot. This characteristic action of Charles gave considerable offence to the other commanders, who had received their commissions from Hertford, and who felt that Mohun had done nothing to deserve the honour.

Meanwhile, Ruthven, the Parliamentary Governor of Plymouth, had collected considerable forces, and early in January' crossed the Tamar, six miles above Saltash. He was followed two or three days later by the Earl of Stamford with reinforcements of horse and foot. Hopton, whose forces were very inferior, fell back on Bodmin. Again, the trained bands were called out, and again they responded readily to the call to fight on Cornish soil. Ruthven advanced to Liskeard, and Hopton, having mustered the trained bands, moved to meet him. Ruthven, without waiting for Stamford, drew out of Liskeard, and formed up on Braddock Down.

Although the position was a strong one, Hopton, recognising the importance of fighting before Stamford's arrival, attacked Ruthven on January 19th. The numbers were somewhat in favour of the Parliament's forces, but the Cornishmen attacked them with such vigour that they were completely routed, and lost 1250 prisoners and all their cannon. Ruthven retreated in haste to Saltash, which he rapidly fortified, and anchored a ship so that she could command the approaches with two guns. Stamford at the same time fell back on Tavistock, in Devonshire.

The Royalist troops now divided; Berkley and Ashburnham leading the voluntarily enlisted troops across the Tamar in pursuit of Stamford, whilst Hopton and Mohun proceeded with the trained bands to Saltash. A vigorous attack drove Ruthven out of the latter place in spite of his barricades. Cornwall being again free of the enemy, the trained bands again disbanded. Berkley and Ashburnham overran Devon, driving Stamford back into Exeter, but they afterwards fell back to Tavistock, and then recrossed into Cornwall. During the early spring a sort of local truce appears to have been agreed on. (Account taken from Clarendon's *History of the Rebellion,* vol. ii. Gardiner vol. i.)

It will be seen from this short campaign how readily the Cornish trained bands responded to the call of what they believed to be lawful authority, how positively they refused to follow their leaders into what they considered unlawful enterprises, and how important therefore it was for each side, at the beginning of the war, to make it appear that the law was with them. It also shows the sacrifices that the Royalist gentry were willing to undergo for the Royalist cause, and the weakness with which Charles granted commissions for the higher ranks of the army; thereby multiplying commanding officers, and creating confusion and friction.

But indeed these sacrifices and this weakness held to one another the relation of cause to effect. The Houses of Parliament, having in their power London and all the principal ports, the navy, and the richest counties and inland towns, held control over the trade of the country and the principal sources of revenue. Consequently Charles' financial resources were never sufficient to pay his troops, and throughout the war he depended to a large degree on the voluntary contributions of the nobles and gentry. Many a regiment in his army was raised and maintained entirely at the cost of some rich noble or great landowner; others contributed largely with plate and money.

It was difficult to refuse high rank and command to a man who was ruining himself in the royal cause, or whose disaffection would mean the loss of hundreds of pikes or sabres. In return for their devotion the king had nothing to give but honours or rank, so honours and rank had to be distributed with a free hand. But the confusion and jealousies which the multiplication of officers of high rank gave rise to, did the king's cause incalculable harm.

The Parliament, on the other hand, although voluntary contributions were at first resorted to, raised its revenues in a more regular way. Taxes on imports and exports were collected as usual. Towns and counties were assessed to pay fixed sums weekly or monthly, and though at first there was difficulty in collecting these assessments, afterwards money came in with tolerable regularity. The revenues of the king's estates, which lay mostly in counties where the Parliament was supreme, were seized, as were the estates of the Royalist nobility wherever possible. These were either entirely forfeited or the owners were compelled to pay heavy fines to recover possession.

By these means the Houses obtained sufficient money to raise, equip, and pay their troops with tolerable regularity, except just at first, and thus retained their authority over officers and men. They also from the first instituted the excellent rule that the grant of commissions and the promotion of officers lay in the hands of the general-in-chief, by whom they were invariably issued and regulated. Thus, the officers and soldiers looked to their general for promotion and reward, and to the Parliament for their pay. and maintenance, so that a proper discipline was more easily upheld.

It should be remembered that the times of the Tudor and early Stuart kings had been times of peace for the gentry and peasantry of England. In the middle of the sixteenth century war with Scotland had broken out once or twice, but the Battle of Pinkie, the last important action fought between the two nations, occurred in 1547, some ninety-five years before the outbreak of the Civil War. The great struggle with Spain during Elizabeth's reign had been a struggle at sea. The army she had collected at Tilbury had never been called on to strike a blow. Armed insurrections had now and again broken out, but all had been easily suppressed.

The expeditions which had been sent from time to time against an enemy's territory had never entailed large armies. With internal peace had come prosperity, but prosperity of a sort that had not produced effeminacy among the lower orders. The courtiers of Charles I.'s day were luxurious, extravagant, and inordinately fond of dress, but the country gentlemen lived healthy out-of-door lives. The peasantry were better off and better fed than any in Europe. Fond of rough sports, especially of wrestling, their limbs were strong and supple.

Therefore, the material for soldiers was excellent. The large degree of liberty they enjoyed raised them morally above the level of the lower orders on the Continent. The spirit of the nation was high. Their fleets had broken the pride of Spain, swept the sea of her treasure ships, and captured her galleons in her own ports. No foreign nation had dared put foot on English soil in return. Many English gentlemen had crossed the seas to support the Protestant cause under Gustavus and the Prince of Orange. With them had gone servants and retainers, who were ever welcome in Protestant ranks.

Gustavus, whose so-called Swedish Army was really cosmopolitan, had whole regiments of English and Scots in his service, which he valued perhaps more than those of any other nationality, except his own Swedes. Orrery says, in his *Art of War*, that the English foot would rally again and again when broken, which men of few other nationalities would do. Thus, at the beginning of the Civil War, officers and men were of splendid raw material, but for the most part unaccustomed to the discipline and hardships of war, ill-trained in the use of arms or in drill, with a sprinkling, especially in the higher ranks, of veterans trained in the wars of Europe.

The constitution of the armies bore its fruit in the conduct of the war. Eager to fight, enthusiastic for their cause, disliking the restraints of discipline, the English soldiers could ill brook the wary generalship, the marches and counter-marches, the manoeuvring, leaguers, and fortified camps, which those of the Continent delighted in. The latter, for the most part, were professionals who attached themselves to one side or the other because the pay or the prospects of plunder were good. Though they fought bravely in battle, they had no wish to risk their lives oftener than they could help. They had no sympathy with the inhabitants of the countries through which they marched, and they wanted to live by their profession. Therefore, the longer the war lasted the better for them, the better chance of plunder and promotion. They liked living at free quarters, and loved a siege because of the spoils when the place fell.

The English soldier, in the early campaigns of the Civil War at any rate, was not a soldier by choice. He fought because he believed no other solution of his quarrel with the other side possible. He longed for peace and to lay aside his arms, and therefore desired a decisive battle to settle the quarrel. The author of the *Memoirs of a Cavalier* says:

> I believe, I may challenge all the historians in Europe to tell me of any war in the world where in the space of four years there were so many pitched battles, sieges, fights, and skirmishes, as in this war; we never encamped or entrenched, never fortified the avenues to our ports, or lay fenced with rivers and defiles; here were no leaguers in the field, as at the story of Nuremberg, neither had our soldiers any tents, or what they call heavy baggage.

Twas the general maxim of this war—Where is the enemy? Let us go and fight them. Or, on the other hand, if the enemy was coming, what was to be done? Why what should be done! draw out into the fields and fight them.

✶✶✶✶✶✶

Memoirs of a Cavalier.—This work was published during the eighteenth century, and is supposed to contain the personal narrative of an ancestor of the editor's, who had been an officer in the king's army as well as in that of Gustavus Adolphus. It is discredited by Gardiner and others; but, genuine or not, it was written by someone with considerable military knowledge and acquaintance with the incidents of the Civil War. Many of its military criticisms are, like the one quoted above, extremely shrewd and to the point.

✶✶✶✶✶✶

At first it was universally believed that one battle would settle the question. Both sides underrated the power of endurance of the other. As battle after battle proved indecisive, and campaign followed campaign, the spirit of the professional element became stronger and stronger, until it culminated in Cromwell's famous new model army, perhaps the best organised and disciplined the world had seen since Caesar's. But the enthusiasm for the cause, and the dislike of delay and unnecessary manoeuvring survived, and, animated by this spirit and guided by the genius of Cromwell, this army became the swiftest and most invincible engine of war in Europe. Cromwell was himself the personification of the genius of the Puritan soldiery. Eager for the battle, fierce in the charge, cool in the *mêlée*, unsparing in the pursuit, but merciful when victory was complete, these were characteristics common to leader and men.

✶✶✶✶✶✶

The sack of Drogheda and the slaughter of the prisoners taken there, and in a few other cases in Ireland, are exceptions to Cromwell's usually merciful treatment of prisoners, and of the inhabitants of fortresses taken by him. The cruel fate of the Scotch prisoners taken at Dunbar was no fault of his or of his army. At the sack of Basing House, taken by storm, many Royalists were killed in the fighting, but it does not appear that those who surrendered were ill-treated. Many were burnt trying to hide in the cellars.

✶✶✶✶✶✶

In this army, the spirit of modern war was perhaps, for the first time, awakened. Tactics rapidly improved, the enemy's force in the field, not this or that town or strip of country, came to be recognised as the true objective of a campaign.

Let us look for a moment at the dress, arms, and drill of the soldier of the day, that we may get a clearer idea of those dim old battle scenes. Ward's *Animadversions of Warre; or, a Militarie Magazine*, published in 1639, gives us a good idea of the equipment, drill, &c., of the English soldier at the outbreak of the Civil War. It was apparently written for the benefit of the officers of the trained bands, and is a dull old book, relieved by many unintentionally comic passages, from which a good deal of information can be gleaned. In the first place, we learn that the trained bands, horse and foot, assembled once a month under their "noble" captains for training.

Their discipline and drill, when thus assembled, was most deficient; excuses, delays in attendance, inattention at drill, and drunkenness, abounded. The arms were ill kept, and often unserviceable. The foot were mustered in companies, the horse in troops. The foot companies were nominally 200 strong and divided into four divisions, two of pikes and two of muskets. The pikes were sixteen to eighteen feet long, and the pikemen should have worn back and breast-pieces over their buff coats, but they very seldom had them. Steel helmets or pots were generally worn. The musketeers carried no defensive armour except the pot. Their clumsy muskets were provided with rests, and were for the most part matchlocks.

Flint locks, called "firelocks" or "snaphaunces," had been lately invented and were just coming into use. The powder was carried in powder-horns for priming, but the charges were made up and carried in bandoliers; bullets were carried loose in haversack or pocket. Both pikemen and musketeers carried swords. The men of each company wore a doublet of their captain's colours; knee-breeches, stockings, and shoes, completed their attire. The musketeers often carried "Swedish feathers," which were short stakes some four feet long, with an iron point at each end. If threatened by the enemy's horse, they stuck these stakes in the ground, sloping upwards, and fired from behind them.

The drill was most complicated, and no wonder that the men, exercised in a dilatory fashion once a month, were not proficient. In the manual exercise given by Ward for the musket, there are no less than fifty-six words of command. Some of these sound very quaint nowadays, such as "Blow the ashes from your cole," and "Cast off your loose cornes." The manual for the pikes was much simpler, and the words of command resemble those of the manual exercise of today.

The companies were drawn up ten deep, after the model of the army of the Prince of Orange, whereas Gustavus Adolphus only placed them six deep. In military parlance, this may be expressed by saying there were ten or six men in a file, a file being a number of men standing one behind the other, whilst a rank is a number of men standing side by side. The men in each rank were not drawn up touching each other shoulder to shoulder, but there was a distance between the files as well as between the ranks.

These distances were "close order" 1½ft., "order" 3 ft., "open order" 6 ft., "double distance" 12 ft. In battle the men stood generally at order both in rank and file, that is 3 ft. between the files and between the ranks. The two divisions of pikes formed the centre, with a division of muskets on each flank. Thus, a company was formed on parade as in the following figure:

• denote pikes.   o denote musketeers.

The drill consisted of what we should now call "squad drill," and consisted of facing, filing, countermarching, wheeling, and "doubling." This last consisted in doubling the number of men in each rank, by forming two ranks into one, either by bringing the men of one rank into the intervals of another, or by prolonging one rank by another. In the same way files could be doubled, the alternate files being doubled by the other. Thus, the length, depth, or density of a company could be altered at pleasure. There are no less than thirty ways laid down of doubling either ranks or files.

The first rank consisted of picked men called "file leaders," the next best men were placed in the last rank and were called "bringers up." Each company had its flag borne in front of the pikes, with the captain's device or coat of arms on it. When two or more companies were embodied in a regiment or brigade they lost their identity, the divisions of pikes being all drawn up in the centre, and the musketeers on the flanks. The drill was exactly the same as for a company.

When within musket shot of the enemy the musketeers began to fire. This was done either halted or advancing. The front rank moved out a little in front of the pikes, fired a volley, wheeled or filed off right and left, and formed up in rear, the second rank taking their place in front, firing in their turn, and so on. By the time all the ranks had fired, the first rank had reloaded and regained its proper place. If done on the move the pikes advanced slowly, the leading ranks of the musketeers being always level with, or a little in advance of, the front rank of pikemen. The same order was observed in retiring, the ranks of musketeers facing about in turn to fire. Or in firing to a flank the outer file faced to right or left, fired, and formed up inside the other files nearest to the pikes.

The Horse were divided into Cuirassiers, Harquebusiers, Carbineers, and Dragoons. The first were heavy cavalry, the next two light, and the last simply mounted infantry. (When the dragoons dismounted to fight, one man held the horses of ten others). The cuirassier was armed *cap-à-pie* with long straight sword or tuck and a brace of pistols eighteen inches long in the barrel, in holsters. The light cavalryman carried a pot, back and breast-pieces and gorget, a tuck, and harquebus or carbine. The latter was carried, when not in use, by a swivel attached to a broad leather belt over the shoulder. The dragoons carried musket and short sword like the infantry.

Ward says that some of them even carried pikes, but I can find no mention of such in accounts of the battles of the Civil War. The lance had gone out of fashion; why, it is not easy to understand, except that the cavalry placed much reliance in their firearms. Orrery, (*Art of War*), and Turner, writing later, (Sir J. Turner's *Pallas Armata*, published in 1671), both state that many great soldiers, Henry IV., of France, for one, regretted its disappearance, and placed great value on the few lancers that remained. Only with the Scots does it still appear to have existed in Western Europe, frequent mention of its use in their army being found during the Civil War. (Turner, who was a Scotsman, says the lance was not used in England, Scotland, France, Germany, Denmark, &c.)

The art of training horses in the riding-school had at this time reached great perfection among the richer classes, and the animal's education was nearly as elaborate as that of a modern circus horse, as anyone may see by a glance at the Earl of Newcastle's book, *A General System of Horsemanship*. Ward gives elaborate directions as to training the troop horse. A fallow field was substituted for the riding-school, and the horse was taught his paces, to stop and start quickly, to turn, rein back, passage, and rear up, at his rider's will.

Some of the instructions are quaint, and the following, if quoted alone, as it is by Captain Fortescue, in his excellent history of the 17th Lancers, would lead one to imagine that the process of training was brutal:

> More over, if your horse be wresty, so as he cannot be put forwards; then let one take a cat tyed by the tayle to a long pole, and when he goes backwards thrust the cat towards him, where she may claw him, and forget not to threaten your horse with a terrible Noyse:—or otherwise take a hedgehog and tye him streight by one of his feete to the inside of the horse's tayle, so that he may squeake and pricke him.

But, in reality, this is the only instruction which savours of brutality; while, on the other hand, the instructions for the position of the bridle hand might be considered with profit by many a riding master of the present day.

The horse were drawn up six deep; there were generally 120 men in a troop. At close order, they rode knee to knee; at open order six feet (accounted a horse's length) between ranks and files. The drill was very similar to that of the foot. They trusted in the fight still a great deal too much to their fire-arms, though Gustavus Adolphus had taught his cavalry to fire their pistols or carbines whilst advancing, and then, without reloading, to fall in with their swords. Their movements were slow and generally directed at the enemy's flank. Ward says:

> In a pitcht battell he (the captain) must seldome or never seeke to charge the enemie in the front . . . . the best and safest place to charge the enemie upon is the flanks and reare. (If the enemy's horse charged first, he was not to rush forward to meet him, but to advance slowly), untill the enemy be within 100 paces of you, and then fall into your careire, by this meanes your horse will be in breath and good order wheras the enemie will be to seeke.

As a matter of fact, the cavalry of that day often stood to receive a charge, firing their carbines or pistols. Another manoeuvre, given by Ward, to be used if charged by cuirassiers, was to open the troop from the centre, allow the enemy to pass through, and as he did so, face the files inwards and charge him in the flank. Captain Rudd, in his supplement to Elton's *Compleat Body of the Art Military*, published in 1663, thus describes the action of the cuirassier:

> He is commonly to give the charge upon a trot and seldome gallopeth, but upon a pursuit. Having spent both his pistols and having no opportunity to load again he must then betake himself to *the last refuge his sword*.

Such was the role of cavalry at that day, according to the military pedants. The great cavalry commanders, Gustavus, Rupert, Cromwell, knew better.

The breast-pieces of the horse-soldier were to be musket-proof, the back-pieces pistol-proof. Under their armour the men wore buff coats. For the most part they wore no armour below the thigh, but breeches and long boots, the tops of which were generally turned down below the knee, but could be pulled up over it. Long leather gauntlets covered the hand and arm up to the elbow. The sword had a basket hilt, and the spurs were heavy and curved. Their horses were probably small but strong. Ward says that for cuirassiers and harquebusiers they should be at least fifteen hands. They were probably underbred according to our ideas, as but few Barbs or Arabs had been imported then.

Newcastle says that many breeds of English horses were well fitted for military purposes. The wood-cuts in his book and other contemporary pictures show them as heavily-topped horses but deficient in bone, and cow-hocked, with high crests, thick manes and tails, and singularly ill-shaped heads. Charles I.'s horse in Van Dyke's famous picture in the National Gallery, is a good example. The saddles had high pommels and cantles, and the reins were lined with chains to prevent their being cut. Apparently, when formed into regiments, the troops were kept together and not mixed up as the foot companies were, but the authorities are not very clear.

Precedence seems to have carried great weight in these days. Ward, Elton, and Turner all devote pages as to the order in which companies or troops should stand on parade. When all the pikes of the companies of a regiment were massed for a parade or battle, they occupied, relatively to each other, the same position as the companies did on first forming up. The same held good with the musketeers. The colour of each company was carried in front of its pikes.

As to the artillery, it was so cumbersome and inefficient that it is surprising so much trouble was taken in bringing it into the field.

There were, however, recognised calibres for the different natures of gun, each of which had a name. Ward gives sixteen different natures on a table which shows the dimensions and weight of each piece and its projectile. It begins with the "canon," which weighed 8000 lbs. and fired a 64-pounder shot, and terminates with the "base," which weighed 200 lbs. and fired a 4-lb. ball. A similar table, given in the supplement to Elton's book, (*Compleat Body of the Art Military*), agrees very closely with it. The carriages and equipment were very cumbrous. Some of the heavier weapons required twenty-four horses to drag them.

In the field the artillery, together with the ammunition waggons, both for infantry and artillery, formed what was called the "train," or "artillery train," (to distinguish it from the baggage-train). This was under a superior officer, called by Ward the Master of the Ordnance. Turner calls him the General of Artillery. Under him was a lieutenant, and the lower ranks were called, "Master Gunners," "Under Canonires," "Waggon Master," "Furriers," (equivalent to our quartermaster-serjeant), and "Clerks." The soldiers were, as now, termed gunners, and were looked on as specialists. A considerable number of artificers of all sorts were attached to the train.

Gustavus Adolphus, who was always seeking to supplement his cavalry divisions by troops who, by their fire, could throw the enemy into confusion, and thus prepare the way for the charge of his own horse, hit upon the expedient of making guns of light metal tubes strengthened with leathern jackets. These were very mobile, could keep up with the cavalry divisions, and were, in fact, the origin of the modern horse artillery. They were a good deal used in the English Civil Wars, but along with them were much heavier pieces. The most efficient of these appear to have been the culverines and demiculverines, which were long pieces shooting 20 lb. and 12 lb. shots, and, according to Ward, the distance they could carry "at utmost random" was 2100 yards. They could fire about ten times in an hour, (*Pallas Armata*), so they had time for four or five rounds at an advancing enemy before he came to push of pike, even if he did not halt.

All writers insist on the necessity of marching on as broad a front as possible, and keeping well closed up. If marching along a road, as many files as it would admit—say five—led off from the right or left of the leading company, followed by the next five, and so on. On the march, each company appears to have kept together. The men marched with the files at "Order" (three feet apart), and the ranks at "Open order" (six feet from one rank to the next).

In a mixed force, the cavalry led the column and brought up the rear. The train was generally towards the centre, or rear of the column. Its heavy, clumsy vehicles often caused great delay on the bad roads of the day.

★★★★★★

The artillery train in the Prince of Orange's army consisted of eight half-cannon, six quarter-cannon, sixteen field-pieces, and 134 waggons. The bridge and ammunition train consisted of another 134 waggons. These were quite apart from the baggage train.—Elton.

★★★★★★

Advanced guards and rear-guards were formed by a regiment or so of horse supported by one of foot, followed by a company of pioneers and a few field guns.

When drawn up for battle, the foot were generally formed in three lines, called respectively the "vanguard," "battle," and "rear-guard"; the horse, somewhat similarly arranged, formed the flanks. Sometimes divisions of musketeers were inserted between the troops or regiments of horse. Gustavus Adolphus adopted this system for the same purpose as he employed his "leathern" guns, and he selected his most active men for this duty. Intervals were kept between the regiments or *tertias* (as brigades were then called), so that if the "vanguard" were discomforted, it could retire through the intervals of the "battle" and re-form. The rear-guard, which corresponded to our modern reserve, was generally considerably weaker than the other two lines. Those who are curious in such matters will find a number of forms of battle given at the end of Ward's *Militarie Magazine*. In these the three lines of infantry are often hedged by a column on each flank to protect against attacks from the sides.

The cannon were generally dispersed along the front in groups of two to six each. But there were instances of their being used in large batteries.

Such were the formations and tactics in vogue in the armies at the outbreak of the Civil War. As the war progressed they considerably improved. The formations became broader and shallower. The old, dense, unwieldy masses were given up, and the troops fought in smaller, handier bodies. This is shown by the various works on the art of war. Ward's book, published in 1639, forms the basis of the sketch given above. In the Duke of Albemarle's *Observations upon Military and*

Political Affairs, written when he, as Colonel Monk, was a prisoner in the Tower in 1646, we find the infantry formed only six deep, and when firing he recommends the musketeers being drawn out to the front only three deep, and firing volleys.

******

Colonel Monk was originally in the king's service, was taken at Nantwich in 1644, and sent to the Tower. In 1647, he obtained employment under Cromwell.

******

The first rank kneeling, and the second standing, fire a volley; then the second also kneels, and the third fires a volley. To receive a cavalry charge the musketeers form two ranks round the pikemen, kneel, and fire under the pikes. The cavalry are formed only three deep. A troop or regiment is formed in sub-divisions of ten to twenty files each, with twenty yards between the sub-divisions. When within fifty paces of the enemy the flank sub-divisions advance at a trot, and then charge; when these have mingled with the enemy, the centre sub-divisions charge. But when infantry is placed in the intervals between the regiments of horse, the latter are not to charge until the enemy's horse are disordered by infantry fire.

Lieut.-Col. Elton's, (he was one of Cromwell's officers), *Compleat Body of the Art Military* was published in 1663, but probably written earlier. It was written for the Honourable Artillery Company, and is a work of much pedantry. Many pages are devoted to the "honour and dignity," not only of each officer according to rank and precedence, but also of each soldier as he stands in rank and file. The facings, doublings, &c., are numerous and wonderful, but there is a good deal of sense in the book too.

At the end the author acknowledges that most of these gymnastics are superfluous, and gives the manner of exercising a company as practised in the army, which is simple, and contains only forty-two words of command. By this time, the fire-arm was gaining favour rapidly owing to the introduction of the flint-lock, and the musketeers now form two-thirds and the pikes only one-third of the company. The regiment is no longer formed into a mass of pikes with two wings of musketeers; but if of six companies, it is formed into two masses called "grand divisions"; if of ten or more companies, into three grand divisions. (This term was employed up till quite recently to express a front of two companies.—Ed.) The foot of an army is divided into three *tertias*, each consisting of from two to six regiments, drawn up in three lines: vanguard, battle, and rear-guard.

In Sir J. Turner's *Pallas Armata*, published in 1671, the tactics have become still more modern. Turner was a dry, shrewd, Scotch soldier of fortune, said by Carlyle to have been the original of Scott's *Dougal Dalgetty*. He recommends the foot to be drawn up in five ranks. Fewer than this will not do, he says, because the musketeers cannot load quick enough to keep up a continuous fire when firing by ranks, and volleys of two or three ranks should be kept for decisive moments. Though still devoting much space to precedence and to the evolutions of facing, counter-marching, doubling, &c., he remarks:

> It is my private opinion that there be many superfluous words in the exercise.

A company was now only 100 or 120 strong. Armies were generally drawn up for battle in two lines only, the "Battel" and the "Reserves." Turner gives the proportion of waggons for a company which were allowed in the different foreign armies. According to his calculations, a Swedish army of 5000 horse and 9000 foot dragged along with them no less than 1796 waggons. These were in addition to those of the artillery train. He calculates that an army of 15,000 foot and 3000 horse, ten demi-cannon and twenty field-pieces, occupies over nine miles without intervals between regiments or brigades. And this on a road which allows the foot to march ten and the horse five abreast.

Lastly, Lord Orrery's *Treatise of the Art of War* (1677) shows how the experience of the civil wars continued to bear fruit in the continual improvement in tactics for years after the last shot had been fired. Owing to the increased rapidity of fire, acquired by the introduction of the flint-lock, Orrery recommends that the foot should be drawn up in four ranks instead of six. The horse should, he thinks, be drawn up in two instead of three ranks. The right cavalry spirit pervades his remarks on that arm:

> He (the general) ought never to think upon, much less order his army in a plain field to receive the charge, but still to meet the enemy in giving it.

Again, in speaking of a charge, he says:

> When the squadrons advance to charge, the troopers' horses and their own knees are as close as they can well endure; . . . the close uniting of the rank, which is so necessary to make the charge effectual.

The pace is also better "while I advanced at a *round trot* with my cavalry, and charged that of my enemies." His squadrons are not to have more than forty files. He is also the first who recommends cartridges for the muskets with the bullets attached, partly because of greater rapidity in loading, and partly to prevent a careless soldier loading his musket without a patch or paper round the bullet. Often, instead of ramming home, such a one would simply tap the butt of the musket to shake the bullet down, with the consequence that it very frequently rolled out before the piece was fired.

The art of fortification was held in great esteem in those days, and many and intricate are the rules given in the books of the period for designing bastions, ravelins, horn-works, counter-guards, &c.; for siege works, and for lines of circumvallation and countervallation.

All the above-quoted authors advise great caution in giving or accepting battle, preferring a cautious war of manoeuvre to the decisive effect of battle. The Continental generals were much addicted to "leaguers," or fortified camps, in which they would maintain themselves for months, hoping to tire or starve out their enemy.

Discipline was maintained and the "justice of war" administered according to articles of war in much the same fashion as today, (1899). Officers punished inferiors either by their own authority, or assembled in "courts of war." The judge advocate, or judge-marshal, the provost-marshal-general, and the regimental provost had much the same duties and functions as now. Officers and non-commissioned officers were allowed to strike their subordinates with the flat of their swords or sticks for certain offences, such as disobedience of orders, insubordinate language, &c.

The names and duties of the various ranks were much the same as now; the principal exception being that the serjeant-major was the same as the major of a regiment, and the two terms were used indifferently. The rank of this officer was the same as that of the major of today, but his duties were those of the adjutant. In Turner's days, the adjutant was beginning to appear. There were certain individuals called "gentlemen of companies" who have now disappeared. They appear to have received better pay than the privates, were excused guard duties, but took the most dangerous posts, both as sentinels and in the ranks, when close to the enemy.

Officers were armed with sword and *bâton,* but often carried half-pikes on service. Sergeants carried halberts.

Before closing this chapter, the meanings of a couple of terms not now used will be given, as they occur in *Cromwell's Letters* and other quotations. A "forlorn" of horse or foot means those troops which were thrown out towards the enemy on the march or before a battle. "Commanded" troops were those detached from their companies or troops to perform particular duties, such as musketeers to line a hedge, or to support a body of horse.

Battle of Edgehill

Although recruits began to come in rapidly to Charles at Nottingham, so that by the beginning of September his forces had risen to some 10,000 men, (Gardiner, vol. 1), he was still very inferior in numbers to Essex, whose army was gathering not far off at Northampton. The inhabitants, too, of the neighbouring counties favoured the cause of the Parliament for the most part. Both armies were raw, and a good deal of plundering and other symptoms of indiscipline occurred on both sides. Charles, therefore, determined to remove further west, where his cause was popular, and where he could organise his army in greater security. On the 13th September, therefore, he left Nottingham for Derby. On the 17th he reached Stafford, and on the 20th, Shrewsbury. Here he found himself amidst a friendly population and in a town, which being astride of the Severn, offered many advantages for defence, and secured the communications with Wales and the English counties on the west bank of the river.

He had, as he advanced, disarmed the trained bands in the districts unfavourable to his cause, and thus supplied himself with one of his principal requirements, at the expense of his enemy. The Parliament possessed the arsenals, the fleet, and principal ports. Charles, therefore, found it very difficult to manufacture or import arms, and at the outset, at any rate, this proved one of his chief difficulties.

On the 9th September Essex left London to assume the command of the army and arrived at Northampton the next day. It was high time that a responsible officer took command, for in this army, no less than in the king's, the soldiers were giving themselves over to plunder, ransacking churches, and plundering the houses of the Royalist gentry, in which they were often assisted by the country folk. Both the king and Essex honestly endeavoured to restrain their men, but the troops were raw, unaccustomed to discipline, and not easy to manage.

Cromwell, who had received a commission as captain from Essex, joined the army, whilst assembling at Northampton, with his troop, now called the 67th. It differed from most in the army, having been raised from among the yeomen and small farmers of Cambridgeshire. The troopers were apparently all personally known to their captain, and had been selected by him as earnest, devout, God-fearing men. Together with the troops of Sir Philip Stapleton, Captain Draper, Serjeant-Major Gunter, Lord Brooke, Captain Sheffield, and Captain Temple, they formed the "Lord General's Regiment," (Fiennes to his father. *King's Pamphlets*), a sure sign that they were considered amongst the best soldiers in the army. Some authors describe Cromwell's troop as dragoons, but probably they were harquebusiers or light cavalry.

Essex found himself at the head of 20,000 men, and on the 19th he left Northampton and moved west to seek the king. On the 23rd he was advancing towards Worcester, and had reached a point somewhat east or north-east of Evesham, with an advanced guard under Colonel Fiennes at Pershore.

At the first signs of an appeal to arms being likely, the University of Oxford had energetically taken the king's side. The undergraduates mustered themselves into companies, and the authorities raised money. On the 28th August Sir John Byron arrived with a troop of horse to encourage the Royalists to further activity. But Town was, as usual, in opposition to Gown, and when, early in September, Byron heard of the approach of Parliamentary forces under Lord Say, he thought it prudent to decamp. He left on the 10th, taking with him a company of scholars and as much money as he had been able to collect. (Gardiner vol. 1.) Charles, fearing he would be cut off, sent Rupert with a party of horse, to Worcester to secure that town and protect Byron's convoy.

Meanwhile, Lord Say entered Oxford without resistance. On the 22nd September, Byron reached Worcester and found Rupert, and the next day (23rd) he resumed his march on Shrewsbury. Fiennes, hearing reports of the movement of Royalist troops in Worcester, moved forward with the horse of the Parliamentary advanced guard, under Colonel Sandys, to reconnoitre. Rupert, having seen the convoy safely through Worcester, moved out south of the town with the same object. Fiennes appears to have crossed the Severn, for he met Rupert somewhere near Powick Bridge, which crosses the Teame west of the former river. Of the skirmish that ensued no two accounts agree. It appears that Rupert caught sight of the Parliamentary troopers crossing a bridge into so narrow lane, and rapidly drawing up his own men on a common, charged them as they were deploying on quitting the lane.

★★★★★★

The account given by Warburton, and generally followed by

modern writers, describes Rupert in his shirt sleeves, rushing wildly on the enemy, followed by his men at a mad gallop. Here is how Fiennes describes one of the charges: "But as soon as Lewis Dive's troope had discharged upon us, we let them come up very neere that their horses' noses almost touched those of our first rank before ours gave fire, and then they gave fire, and very well (to my thinking) with their carbines, after fell in with their swords pell mell into the midst of their enemies."

★★★★★★

At any rate, his victory was complete. Sandys' troopers fled in utter rout, leaving their colonel and a large proportion of their officers and comrades dead on the field or prisoners in the hands of the enemy. On through Pershore they galloped, where 100 of Essex's body-guard caught the panic and joined in the flight, and never stopped till they reached the headquarters of the army.

The physical results of this skirmish were small. Essex advanced next day (24th) with his army, and Rupert fell back without further fighting towards Shrewsbury; Essex then occupied Worcester. But the moral results were considerable. The Parliamentary horse had been considerably the more numerous, but had been badly beaten, and thoroughly frightened. The prestige of Rupert and his gallant cavaliers had risen prodigiously. Cromwell as yet had not seen blood drawn, but he looked at the raw, undisciplined horsemen, now disheartened by defeat, and shook his head. His unerring military genius saw at once the cause of failure and its remedy. He said to Hampden:

> Your troops, are most of them old, decayed servingmen and tapsters, and such kind of fellows; and their troops are gentlemen's sons and persons of quality. Do you think that the spirits of such base and mean fellows will ever be able to encounter gentlemen that have honour, and courage, and resolution in them? ... You must get men of a spirit ... that is likely to go on as far as gentlemen will go, or else you will be beaten still. (The date of this conversation, so often quoted, is uncertain; probably it took place soon after the skirmish of Powick Bridge).

Hampden agreed with him, but did not know whence such men were to be got. Cromwell knew, and in those sixty or seventy men which formed his troop, he had already a nucleus of such men, to be expanded in course of time by his diligence, wisdom, and energy, into a whole army.

Meanwhile the king's army at Shrewsbury was rapidly increasing in numbers and efficiency. Clarendon, (vol. ii.), says that in three weeks from his arrival there it amounted to 6000 foot, 2000 horse, and 800 dragoons, with train and artillery, all in excellent order. As far as courage, physique (both of man and horse), arms, equipment, and skill in horsemanship go, the cavalry was the finest that had been seen since the days of chivalry. Many troops were composed entirely of gentlemen, others of their servants. In the king's royal troop of guards rode none but nobles and gentlemen of the highest birth and fortune.

Prince Rupert commanded the horse. But twenty-three years old, he had already seen service on the Continent. Strong and handsome, a fine horseman, daring to a fault, the nephew of the king, the son of the beautiful and unfortunate Princess Elizabeth, he seemed endowed with all the qualities necessary for the leader of his highborn, reckless troopers. The Earl of Lindsay, a veteran of the Dutch wars, commanded in chief under the king. Under him Sir Jacob Astley, one of the stoutest soldiers that ever fought, was major-general of the foot, which was divided into three brigades under Sir Nicolas Byron, Colonel H. Wentworth, and Colonel R. Fielding. Sir Arthur Aston commanded the dragoons, (Clarendon, ii.).

One of the great advantages of the position at Shrewsbury was that it covered the approaches to Chester and the ports on the Mersey, by which communication was maintained with Dublin. This was of great importance to Charles, as the army in Ireland was believed to be loyal, and he hoped to obtain assistance thence, especially if a truce could be patched up with the Irish rebels. But by the beginning of October the king felt himself strong enough to adopt a bolder action than the passive guarding of his communications. By moving on Worcester, Essex had uncovered the direct road to London.

The capital was not then fortified, the king had many sympathizers in the City, and once there, at the head of a powerful army, his prestige would be so greatly increased, and his position so favourable, that doubtless he would be able to make what terms he liked with the refractory Houses. Essex was certainly nearer London, but if he marched to intercept the king, the latter would give him battle, and if he hesitated, then London could be occupied, probably without a blow. On the 12th October, therefore, Charles quitted Shrewsbury and marched to Bridgenorth, thence by Wolverhampton and Birmingham to Killingworth, (Clarendon, vol. ii.; probably Kenilworth is intended), which he reached on the 19th.

It was not till this day that Essex moved. When he took command at Northampton his army was more numerous and better equipped than the king's. Cromwell in his place would have pressed Charles' retreat on Shrewsbury and offered him battle under its walls, or stormed the town. Not so Essex, who had all the cautious prudence of the Continental soldier of fortune. Preferring a war of manoeuvre, his choice of Worcester was a good one. His object was to prevent the king advancing either against London, or down the west bank of the Severn against Gloucester and Bristol. Posted at Worcester, astride of the river, a short march in the right direction would bring him on to the king's line of march in either case. But to make proper use of such a position, good information and prompt decision was required.

In both these respects Essex was deficient. His scouting was badly performed, and he knew little of the king's movements. When he heard of Charles' first march on Bridgenorth, he was still undecided. It seemed to point more to a movement on Bristol than London. Therefore, he still remained at Worcester. But Parliament was thoroughly alive to the danger. Post after post was despatched to Essex bearing positive orders to him to intercept and fight the king. On the 16th, 8000 men of the trained bands were called out in London, (Gardiner, vol. i.), and on the 21st an additional army of 16,000 men was voted for its protection. (Gardiner, vol. i.). At last Essex discovered the true direction of the king's march, and, on the 19th hastened after him, marching that day to Stratford.

Meanwhile in Charles' army things were not going quite as they should. The troops were doubtless high mettled and loyal, but discipline was sadly lacking. Worse still, the principal offenders were officers of the highest rank, who should have set an example to the others. In a weak moment, Charles had acceded to Rupert's request that he should receive no orders but from the king himself, and the prince refused to accept others. Lindsay thus found himself in an anomalous position, and unity of command was lost. Clarendon, (vol. ii.), says:

> When the whole army marched together, there was quickly discovered an unhappy jealousy and division between the principal officers.

Rupert neglected to keep touch with Essex's army.

> So that the two armies, though they were but twenty miles asunder when they first set forth, and both marched the same way, gave not the least disquiet in ten days' march to each oth-

er, and in truth as it appeared afterwards, neither army knew where the other was.—Clarendon, vol. ii.

Thus, on the 22nd October Charles reached Edgcot and quartered his army in villages round about, intending to halt there with the greater part of his forces the next day, whilst he sent out a strong detachment to summons Banbury. About midnight Rupert came to him with the intelligence that Essex, with the main body of his army, had arrived at Keinton, about nine miles off on the other side of Edgehill, and lay quartered in the town and neighbouring villages. A hurried council of war was summoned, at which it was determined that a further movement on London would look like a retreat before Essex, and that therefore it was necessary to fight.

******

Warburton says the council of war took place earlier in the evening, and that the king ordered the preparations for the battle at Rupert's request. (*Rupert and the Cavaliers*, vol. ii.)

******

It was obviously desirable to forestall Essex on the strong position of Edgehill. Rupert, therefore, occupied it the first thing in the morning with such cavalry as he could collect, whilst the rest of the troops were roused in their quarters and ordered to retrace their steps and assemble on the hill. If Rupert had been remiss in his scouting, Bedford, who commanded the Parliamentary horse, had been far more so. When Essex arrived at Keinton he had no idea of the close proximity of his enemy, and for ease of supply quartered his men, especially his horse, widely among the neighbouring villages.

The next morning, as he was about to resume his march, he found Rupert's troopers on the hill over which he would have to pass, and learnt the true facts of the case. It was then too late to seize the advantage of the hill, although his quarters had been nearer to it than the king's. He therefore selected a position between Keinton and Edgehill, and gave orders for the assembling of his forces. (Clarendon, vol. ii.)

Slowly the different regiments of horse and foot drew in to the rendezvous from their widely-scattered quarters, and were marshalled into line of battle. The foot, as usual, formed the centre, the horse the wings. Sir J. Ramsay commanded the horse on the left. On the right, some thickets and briars protected the flank, and only three regiments of horse were disposed here. These were the Lord-General's regiment, Sir William Balfour's, and Lord Fielding's. The two former seemed to have formed a brigade under Balfour. It is not clear whether any infantry were placed among the regiments of horse. On the right wing this was probably the case, the cavalry being drawn up in rear of the foot. Sir Richard Bulstrode, who was with one of Rupert's regiments, thus describes the Parliamentary order of battle:

> The enemy had all the morning to draw up their army, in a great plain field, which they did to their best advantage, by putting several bodies of foot with retrenchments and cannon before them, and all their foot were lined with horse behind them, with intervals betwixt each body for their horse to enter, if need required, and upon their right wing were some briars covered with dragoons, and a little behind on their left wing was the town of Keinton, which supplied them with provisions, and where their baggage and carriages were.—Bulstrode's *Memoirs and Reflections on the Reigns of Charles I and II.*

The retrenchments, if any, must have been slight. A hedge in front of the line was occupied by musketeers.

The means of sending orders appear to have been deficient in Essex's army. Keightly, who commanded a troop, says in a letter to his brother:

> I was quartered five miles from the place and heard not anything of it, until one of the clock in the afternoon.—*King's Pamphlets.*

Other troops were in a like plight and continued to arrive during the evening. Want of draught horses had rendered it necessary to leave some of the train behind during the hasty march from Worcester, and Hampden had been left with two regiments of foot and a few horse to bring them on. On the night of the 22nd he had been a march behind the main army, and orders were now sent him to press on as quickly as possible.

Meanwhile the king's army had been assembling on the hill, but it was past noon before the troops had all arrived. They then began to descend to the plain, the horse leading, the foot and cannon following. The descent was so steep that the gun-teams had to be unhooked. (Bulstrode). No attempt was made by Essex to molest the Royalists in the confusion caused by the steep, broken ground. His own army was too raw to render manoeuvring on the field of battle advisable. The king's forces therefore arrived safely at the bottom of the hill and leisurely formed their order of battle.

Lindsay had desired to be excused from commanding when his orders were disputed by his subordinates, and took his post at the head of the King's own regiment of foot-guards, of which he was colonel. (Gardiner, vol. i.; Warburton says Lindsay commanded a Lincoln regiment, (vol. ii.) The Earl of Forth reluctantly took the command. Sir Jacob Astley commanded the foot in the centre, which was divided into three brigades. Rupert led the horse on the right wing, his squadrons being apparently more numerous than those on the left under Wilmot, because the ground on his side was more favourable for cavalry. A reserve of horse, which included the king's body-guard, remained with Charles. The troops were formed after the Swedish fashion, the foot six deep, the horse three. The foot were apparently formed in two lines, but this is not clear. After forming his horse, Rupert rode down the ranks:

> Giving positive orders to the horse to march as close as was possible, keeping their ranks with sword in hand, to receive the enemy's shot without firing either carbin or pistol till we broke in amongst the enemy, and then to make use of our firearms as need should require, which order was punctually observed.— Bulstrode.

About 2 p.m. the Royal Army being drawn up, some dragoons were pushed forward and drove Essex's musketeers from the hedge. The whole army then advanced, the cannon on either side opening as the enemy came within range. Rupert moved forward at an increased pace, preparatory to charging. As he did so, a regiment under Sir Faithful Fortescue moved out of Ramsay's ranks, and, firing their pistols into the ground, joined Rupert's horsemen. The movement was at first misunderstood, and a few men were killed in the confusion, but the error was soon rectified.

This regiment had been enlisted for service in Ireland, and then compelled by the Parliament to march with Essex against the king. They thus took the first opportunity of deserting to the Royal Army. Then Rupert charged. As was his custom, his first line was far stronger than his second, if, indeed, he had any. Moreover, there appears to have been no attempt to keep any of the regiments back, so the whole force broke into the gallop together, and came swinging down on Ramsay's horsemen without checking to fire. The latter, outflanked by the broad front on which Rupert had formed his men, disconcerted

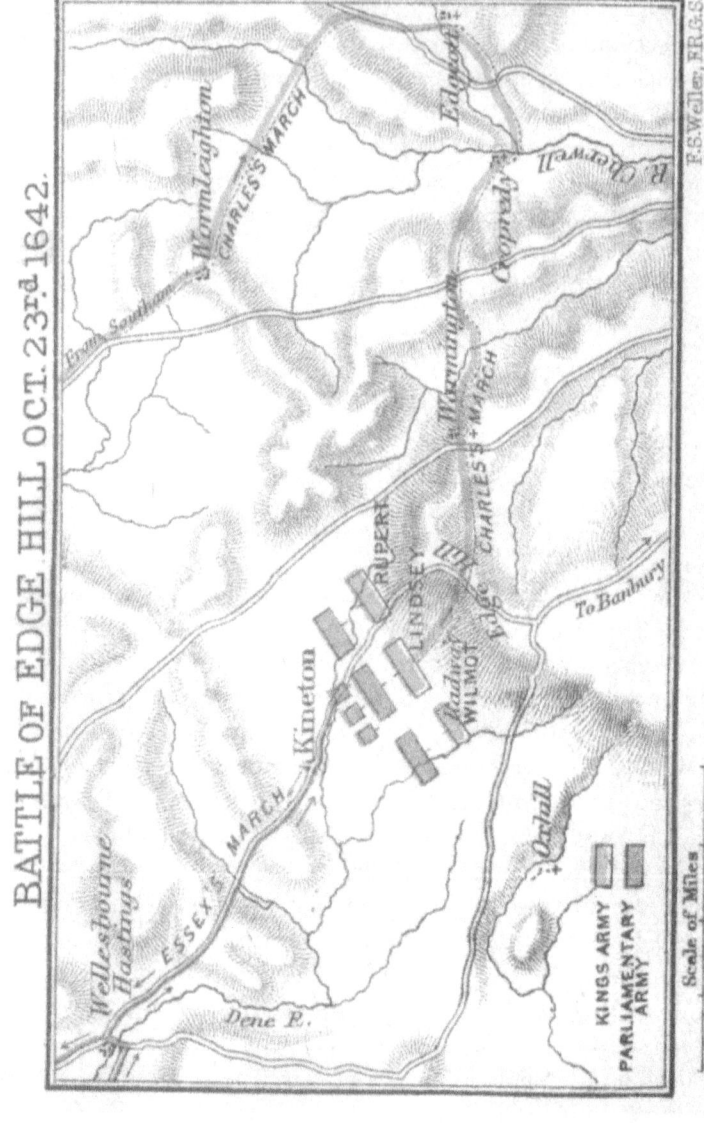

by the desertion of Fortescue's regiment and the unusual rapidity of the charge, and dispirited by the memories of Powick Bridge, never awaited the shock, but turned and fled. They rode through and dispersed the nearest infantry regiments of their own side, and galloped wildly off the field.

At this moment some troops of horse, John Fiennes', Keightly's, and one commanded by another Cromwell, (probably Oliver's son, also named Oliver), among them, who had been quartered far off and had been late in receiving orders, were approaching the field. In vain their officers drew these troops up across the path of the runaways and attempted to rally them. The only result was that most of their own men caught the panic and galloped off with the rest, (*King's Pamphlets*). Through Keinton they fled, Rupert's horsemen in hot pursuit. Some of these latter stopped in the town to plunder the baggage, others followed the fugitives till they met Hampden's two regiments escorting the train which had been left behind. A volley or two checked the pursuit, but Ramsay's regiments were utterly dispersed, and Rupert's, though victorious, but one degree less so.

Not only had the right wing of the Royalist horse charged in one mass, and then scattered entirely in pursuit, but the reserves with the king, believing the victory assured, had spurred forward and joined in the chase. The left wing, under Wilmot, had also advanced, but either on account of the difficulties of the ground, or the dispositions of the Parliamentary forces on this side, it appears to have encountered only Lord Fielding's regiment. This Wilmot routed, and then, as on the right wing, his men dispersed in pursuit.

Consequently, when the opposing foot in the centre joined flight, the only horse left on the field were Balfour's two regiments. These promptly availed themselves of the opportunity, and charging the Royal infantry on the left flank, whilst they were hotly engaged with Essex's infantry in front, broke their left and centre and rolled them back on their right, (*King's Pamphlets*). In the centre of the line fought the king's red regiment, or foot-guards, led by the Earl of Lindsay. In their midst, borne by Sir R. Verney, floated the Royal standard. Closing round it the men fought desperately, and repulsed repeated charges of the Parliamentary horse and foot. At last their ranks were broken and they were cut down almost to a man. Lindsay and Verney were both killed, and many other officers of distinction. The Royal standard was taken, though it was recaptured later by a Captain Smith, by stratagem.

✶✶✶✶✶✶

The standard was given to Essex's secretary. Smith, plucking an orange scarf, which distinguished the Roundheads that day, from a dead man, rode unrecognised in the confusion up to the secretary, and telling him that a civilian could not properly guard the trophy, took it from him and rode off.

✶✶✶✶✶✶

The right of the king's foot stood firm, and then retired in good order towards Edgehill. By this time, Rupert's horsemen had begun to reassemble. Charles urged them to charge, but they could not be induced to do so:

> The officers pretending that their soldiers were so dispersed that there were not ten of any troop together, and the soldiers, that their horses were so tired that they could not charge.—Clarendon, vol. ii.

However, their appearance in support of the undefeated foot of the right wing checked the advance of Essex's forces, and thus, as night fell, the armies were still facing each other; the Roundheads being in possession of most of the field of battle. During the night, the king drew back to the top of Edgehill, Essex remaining on the field, where Hampden joined him.

The next day (24th), both armies retained their relative position, but no encounter took place. The fact was that the losses had been severe, some 6000 altogether, and the raw levies on both sides were too much demoralised to render a renewal of the engagement possible. Essex had lost nearly all his horse, whilst the king's foot had suffered very severely, whole regiments having been cut to pieces. As to the numbers engaged on both sides, no accurate figures can be given. Warburton estimates the king's as 12,000, and Essex's 16,000 strong; Gardiner gives them as the king's 14,000, and Essex's 10,000. Neither of them explain how they arrive at their figures.

In the evening, Essex drew back to Keinton and quartered his men there that night. The next morning, he retreated further to Warwick, Rupert engaging his rear-guard and capturing some baggage waggons. On this day, or the 25th, the king resumed his march; but he was in no condition to advance upon London. The trained bands of the capital were numerous, zealous in the cause of the Parliament, and, as after events proved, of good fighting material. Street fighting and attacks on barricades require infantry, and the king's foot had been broken and disorganised at Edgehill. His powerful cavalry would avail him little in such work. It was, therefore, necessary to recruit and reorganise the foot. Charles, therefore, turned aside to Oxford, which he entered on the 29th, Lord Say leaving on his approach. (On the way, Banbury had surrendered to him on the 27th). Here the army was reorganised, the Earl of Forth being given the command under the king.

Rupert now pushed his foraging parties into Buckinghamshire and Berkshire. On one of these expeditions he encountered on the 1st November a party of Balfour's horse and was beaten. It is not known whether Cromwell was present. The skirmish was quite unimportant, and the Roundheads outnumbered their opponents, but it showed that Rupert was not quite invincible. (Warburton, vol. ii.; also, *King's Pamphlets*). A few days after he was repulsed in an attempt to surprise Windsor, and, on the 7th November, in an attack on Kingston.

On the 3rd November Charles quitted Oxford, and on the 4th entered Reading. Here negotiations for peace were proposed by the Parliament, and the commissioners to treat with the king were agreed on, after he had rejected some of the names at first submitted. Meanwhile Essex had reached London, marching by Northampton, Woburn, and St. Albans. On the 11th Charles moved to Colnbrook, and the negotiations were proceeding favourably, although no cessation of arms had been agreed to, when, on the 12th, Rupert attacked a Parliamentary outpost which held the bridge at Brentford. This he carried after very severe fighting, in which the regiments of Holies and Brookes were nearly cut to pieces.

This act of Rupert's broke off the negotiations. The Parliament considered it as a breach of truce. Essex was sitting in the House of Lords when the news arrived. He immediately hurried out to Turnham Green with such troops as he had at hand, and the trained bands were ordered to rendezvous at the same place. All night long they were pouring out of London. (Rushworth, vol. v.) Whatever might be his political leanings, no one wished to see Rupert and his undisciplined troopers plundering the city.

Thus, when Charles arrived on the morning of the 13th to support Rupert, he found Essex ready to meet him with far superior forces. 24,000 men were drawn up to oppose him on Turnham Green, whilst 3000 more secured the bridge over the Thames on the king's right rear at Kingston, (Gardiner, vol. i.) All day long the armies faced each other; Ramsay and the professional soldiers, or "soldiers of fortune," as they were called, advised remaining on the defensive, though others

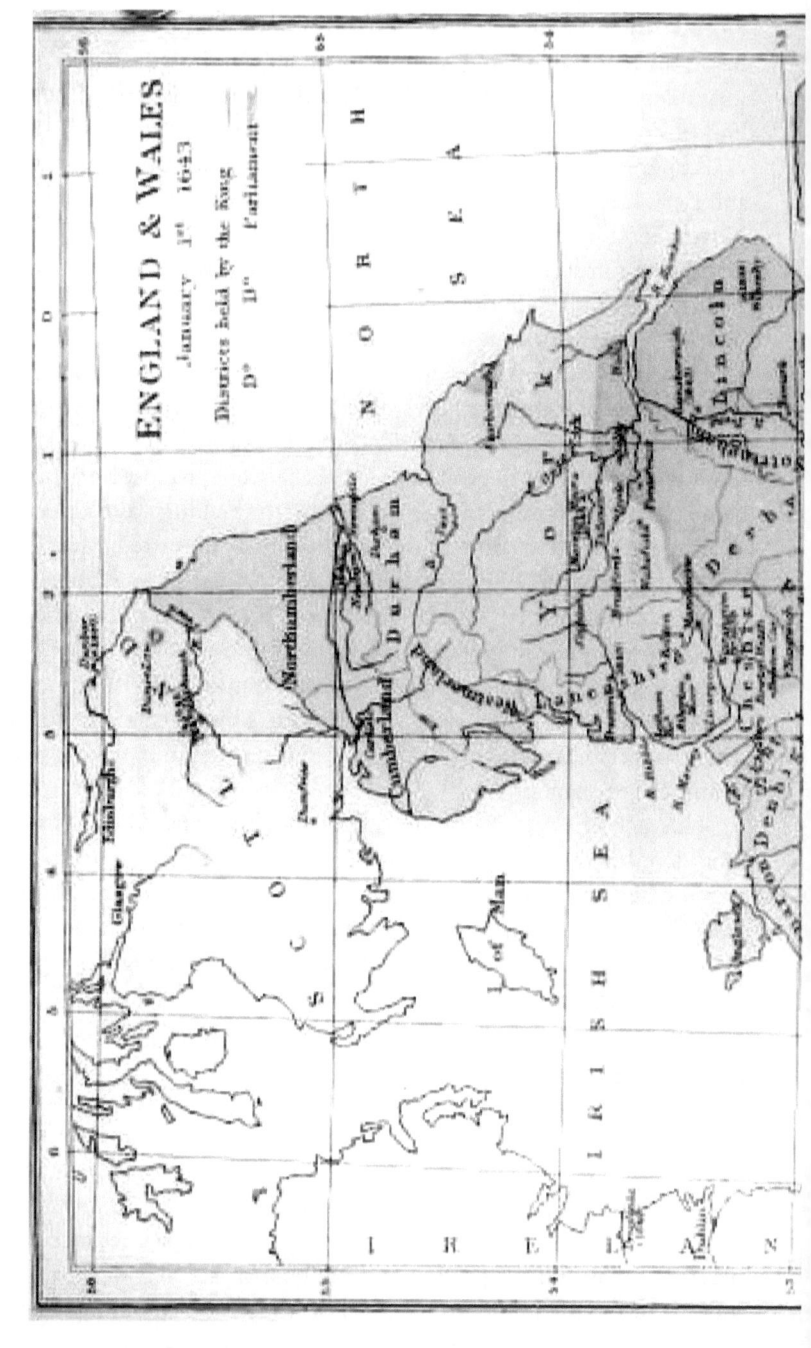

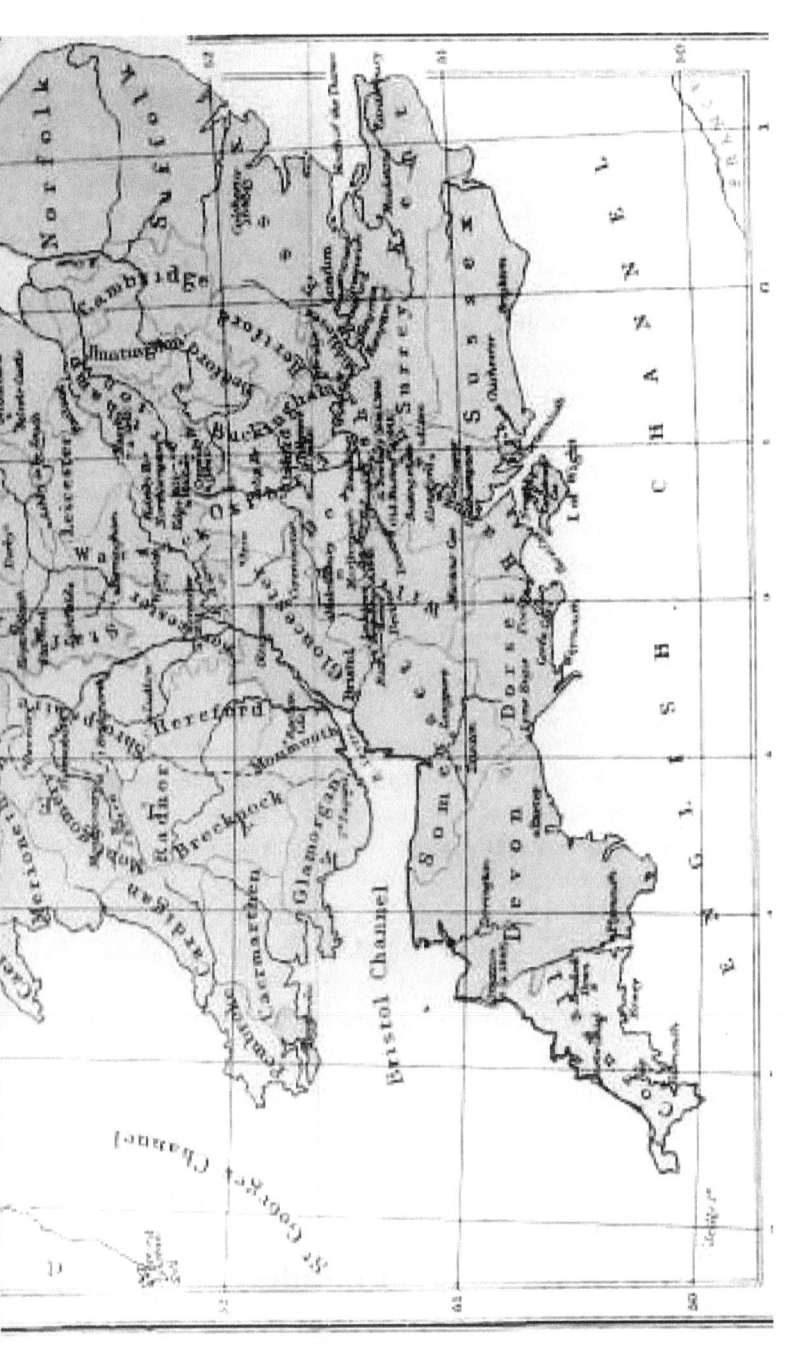

strongly urged Essex to attack the king on one or both flanks. (Rushworth, vol. v.) Essex, listening to the former, and perhaps distrusting his newly-raised forces, being also weak in cavalry, not only refrained from all offensive movements, but gave the king every chance of retreating unmolested, by withdrawing the detachment from Kingston and ordering it to rejoin his army by London Bridge.

Accordingly, Charles fell back on the 14th to Oatlands and Kingston, whilst Essex contented himself with constructing a bridge between Putney and Fulham. On the 19th the king withdrew to Reading, and on the 29th he went into winter quarters at Oxford, placing garrisons in Reading, Wallingford, Banbury, and Brill. The horse occupied Abingdon. (Gardiner, vol. i.; Clarendon, vol. ii.) On the 5th December Marlborough was stormed and plundered; and about this time Worcester was abandoned by the garrison Essex had left there. The main Parliamentary army remained in and about London.

Such was the opening campaign between the main armies of the Civil War, a campaign fought by raw, untried troops, yet illustrating the tactics of the day and the individual qualities both of the armies and of the generals who led them. It shows the king's army a gallant, ill-disciplined, disconnected force; the Parliament's better under control, but still ill-trained, and with a very inferior cavalry. It shows the king weak, vacillating, utterly unable to enforce discipline or quell the jealousies of his ill-chosen generals; Essex slow, cautious, wanting military insight and the power of seizing the fleeting opportunities of war; Rupert restless, insubordinate, impetuous, quick in seizing the advantage of the moment, but spoiling all from want of control over himself and over his troops.

Edgehill was a fair trial of strength; a decisive battle would have placed the control of the nation in the hands of the victors, but neither side was capable of winning a decisive victory. Under such leaders, with numbers fairly equal, battles must be undecisive, the war must linger on.

But fighting in the ranks of the Parliamentary forces was a great military genius, one of those who instinctively understand the requirements of the moment, and are prompt and untiring in fulfilling them. Where the Parliament's Army failed, most was in the cavalry. Cromwell saw this at a glance, and determined to supply the want.

Origin of the Ironsides

After Edgehill, we lose sight of Cromwell for some weeks, but in the winter, we find him back again in Cambridgeshire and the neighbouring counties. It was high time that some zealous, energetic servant of the Parliament should proceed to those parts, to direct the measures to be taken for opposing the further progress of the northern Royalist Army. It has been seen how Charles, when he quitted Yorkshire, had entrusted the command of his forces in the northern counties to the Earl of Newcastle. The earl was then in the town of Newcastle, where, in addition to troops, he raised a considerable revenue for the king by export duties on coal.

A better choice could not have been made; indeed, it would have been hardly possible to select another commander. Possessed of great riches and commanding influence, brave and devoted to the king, highly skilled in horsemanship and manly exercises, with some experience in war, it was Newcastle whom the stout Yorkshire squires and Northumberland yeomen naturally regarded as their leader. But he was luxurious and artistic in his tastes, disliked hardship and drudgery, and lacked the dogged, obstinate perseverance through good and ill fortune which is so necessary in a great commander.

To advise him in military matters, and to relieve him of the care of technical details, he called to his side General King, an experienced Scotch soldier. In order, more readily to combine the forces and resources of the northern counties, he, in November, 1642, formed an Association of Northumberland, Cumberland, Westmoreland, and Durham. (Rushworth, vol. v.) This was the first of those many associations of counties made on both sides, of which the Eastern Association for the Parliament became by far the most famous and important.

The Earl of Cumberland held York for the king with a considerable garrison, and attempted to levy forces under a commission of array. In this he was strenuously opposed by Lord Fairfax and his son, Sir Thomas, men of spotless integrity, who carried great weight in the south of Yorkshire, especially in Leeds, Bradford, and what were called the clothing towns. By their exertions, a force was raised for the Parliament, part of which was sent into the north of the county under the younger Hotham. These levies were not only raw and ill-disciplined, but many of them but half-hearted in the cause.

There was no connection between the different contingents, York separated those of the north from those of the south. The commanders had no experience of war, and were disinclined to obey orders, their object being for the most part simply to protect their own districts from pillage. A strong party was in favour of neutrality, and articles, declaring the county would remain neutral during the struggle, were actually drawn up and signed by many of the leading men on both sides. It is even said that Lord Fairfax signed them. But the Parliamentary leaders at Westminster informed their adherents that such an agreement could not be made by them, and would be most injurious to the cause. They declared that they would consider those that were not with them as against them, and directed Hotham to seize all delinquents. (Clarendon, vol. ii.)

On the 1st December, the earl quitted Newcastle with 3000 foot and 600 horse, and a few days later encountered Hotham ready to dispute the passage of the Tees at "Piercebrig," (old spelling for Pierse Bridge, five or six miles above Darlington). In the skirmish that ensued, Hotham was beaten, (Rushworth, v.), and 1000 of the Richmond and Cleveland men, under Sir Edmund Loftus and Sir Henry Anderson, dispersed to their homes. Only 130 foot and a troop of horse joined Fairfax at Tadcaster. Sir Hugh Chomeley (or Cholmondelay), whom Fairfax first ordered to join Hotham and afterwards to come to Tadcaster, neglected both orders, and went with 700 men to Scarborough. Newcastle now entered York, and his forces, combined with Cumberland's, amounted to 6000 foot and 2000 horse and dragoons.

Fairfax disposed his twenty-one companies of foot and eight troops of horse and dragoons at Wetherby and Tadcaster, on the River Wharfe, with outposts at Selby and Cawood Castle. On hearing of the enemy's advance from York, he concentrated at Tadcaster. He was attacked by Newcastle on the 6th December, but repulsed him and defended the town till nightfall. His men, though greatly outnumbered, "behaved themselves with great resolution, far beyond expectation." Having expended all his ammunition, he fell back to Cawood and Selby, thus approaching Lincolnshire, but getting farther from the clothing towns. He therefore sent his son. Sir Thomas, with five companies and two troops to secure Leeds, but the enemy was too strong, and the younger Fairfax had to fall back on Selby. (Lord Fairfax to Committee of Safety, 10th December, 1642. "Fairfax Correspondence.")

Afterwards, on the 7th January, he succeeded in getting into Bradford at the head of a small party of horse, (Gardiner, vol. i.)

Newcastle occupied the castle at Pontefract with a detachment, and threw a garrison into the very important fortress of Newark on the Trent, in Nottinghamshire. Another detachment of his army, under Sir William Saville, occupied Leeds and Wakefield, but was repulsed by Sir T. Fairfax at Bradford, Hotham having joined the latter with three troops of dragoons, Saville evacuated the towns he had entered, but later reoccupied Leeds. Skirmishes occurred at Wetherby and Tadcaster, and on the 27th January Sir Thomas drove Saville out of Leeds. (Gardiner, vol. i. *Fairfax Correspondence*).

Thus, at the end of January, 1643 (1642 old style), Newcastle, securely based on the north-eastern counties, had reached the south of Yorkshire with a formidable force. If he advanced to join the king at Oxford, or if the two principal Royalist armies advanced simultaneously towards London, there was nothing immediately in his path that could seriously retard him. For though the counties of Leicester, Derby, Nottingham, Rutland, Northampton, Buckingham, and Huntingdon were nominally associated together to support the Parliamentary cause, yet the Royalists in these counties were so strong that they neutralised the forces of the Association. In particular, Newark and Ashby-de-la-Zouch, fortified by Colonel Hastings, formed centres whence cavalry raids were perpetually directed against the lands and property of the Roundheads.

Nor could Newcastle's advance be threatened in flank from the west. In this quarter, the Parliamentary leader, Sir William Brereton, had gained a small success at Nantwich, and in Lancashire the large towns had mostly declared for the Parliament, in spite of the influence of the loyal and powerful Earl of Derby. But Lord Byron had collected a considerable force for the king at Chester, principally from North Wales, and the Parliamentary troops were absorbed in opposing him.

But in the east other conditions prevailed. On the 20th December, the counties of Essex, Suffolk, Norfolk, Hertfordshire, and Cambridgeshire had been formed into the Eastern Association. The eastern and northern frontiers of this Association were secured by the sea, on which the Parliament was supreme. Its southern boundary rested on London and the Thames, beyond which the county of Kent was in the power of the Parliament, if not altogether devoted to its cause. On the west, the counties of the Midland Association formed a buffer between it and the enemy.

Many of the gentry were Royalists, but the yeomen and lower classes were Puritans or Presbyterians almost to a man, and devoted to the cause of political and religious liberty. Above all, in one of the members of its Committee the Eastern Association possessed a man of immense power of will, and a soldier and organiser of the first order. Cromwell, although not nominally the chief, was from the commencement the leading spirit in the Association.

When Cromwell returned to Cambridge after the Edgehill campaign, he found confusion everywhere. Besides a considerable number of Royalists who were ready to rise at a favourable opportunity, many of the gentry and others were neutral. Their chief wish was simply to save their property from exactions or plunder. Both classes refused to subscribe to loan or assessment, or contribute in any way to the necessities of Parliament.

Danger threatened from the north, and immediate steps were necessary to repel it. To overawe the Royalists, suppress opposition, enforce the collection of taxes and assessments, and guard the approaches to the Association, a strong mounted force was required, which could be moved rapidly to any threatened point. But it was in cavalry that the Parliamentary forces were most deficient, and therefore Cromwell, who was promoted to the rank of colonel about this time, proceeded to raise a regiment of horse. His unerring military insight taught him that the true action of cavalry in battle should be the shock of man and horse, the momentum of a close-knit mass, moving rapidly without check against the enemy. He, therefore, discarded the harquebus with which his troop had been armed at Edgehill, and equipped his men as cuirassiers, whose offensive weapons were swords and pistols.

Later on, in the summer of 1643, certain zealous young men and maids of Huntingdon had raised a company of foot at their own expense, and Cromwell writes to them:

> I approve of the business, only I desire to advise you that your foot company may be turned into a troop of horse, which indeed will (by God's blessing), far more advantage the cause than two or three companies of foot, especially if your men be honest, godly men .... therefore, my advice is, that you would employ your twelve score pounds to buy pistols and saddles, and I will provide four score horses .... Pray raise honest, godly men, and I will have them of my regiment.—Letter dated 2nd August, 1643, in *Fairfax Correspondence*, Carlyle, vol. i.

Huntingdon had by this time become one of the counties of the Eastern Association.

The men were all carefully chosen; no tapsters or such base and mean fellows were allowed to ride in Cromwell's regiment. They were nearly all yeomen and men of that class, accustomed from boyhood to the saddle, to exposure and fatigue, and knowing every lane and path in the country. Stern, fanatic Puritans, nearly all of them, who carried their Bibles in the same holsters as their pistols. The discipline was very severe. An old newspaper says:

> As for Colonel Cromwell, he hath 2000 brave men well disciplined. No man swears but he pays his twelve pence; if he be drunk, he is set in the stocks or worse. If one calls the other 'Roundhead,' (apparently, a term of abuse at the outset of the war), he is cashiered, insomuch that the counties where they come leap for joy of them, and come in and join with them. How happy it were if all the forces were thus disciplined.—*Special Passages*, 16th May, in *Cromwelliana*.

The officers were chosen with great care. No one had a keener knowledge of men than Cromwell; no general was ever better served by his officers. Among those in his regiment at this time were many who rose to distinction and high rank later.

No doubt this famous regiment was not brought all at once to the perfection it afterwards attained. A certain amount of weeding out was at first necessary. Horses and men required to be trained and diligently exercised; and to render all this more difficult the men were no sooner raised than they were of necessity constantly employed on detached duties where they would be away from their colonel's eye. Yet in spite of these disadvantages the work must, under Cromwell's indefatigable guidance, have gone rapidly on, for in September, 1643, he writes to Oliver St. John:

> I have a lovely company; you would respect them, did you know them. No 'Anabaptists,' they are honest, sober Christians; they expect to be used as men.

******

Letter above dated 11th of September, 1643. Carlyle, vol. i. According to the Squire Papers, one Bose, a Dutchman, was drill instructor in Cromwell's regiment. Squire himself was his auditor, an official who seems to have combined the duties of paymaster and quarter-master. Carlyle, vol. ii.

******

The troopers in this regiment were apparently all voluntarily enlisted. A few months later, in September, 1643, the Parliament pressed men freely in the Eastern Association, but Cromwell always preferred volunteers. His officers were not all gentlemen by birth. He looked rather to personal merit and zeal for the cause than to birth and fortune in selecting them. Here are his own words on the subject, written in September, 1643, just after his victory at Gainsborough, when Newcastle, in spite of that check, was pressing on strongly towards the Association.

> I beseech you be careful what Captains of Horse you choose, what men be mounted: a few honest men are better than numbers. Some time they must have for exercise. If you choose godly, honest men to be Captains of Horse, honest men will follow them, and they will be careful to mount such.
>
> The king is exceeding strong in the West. If you be able to foil a force at the first coming of it, you will have reputation; and that is of great advantage in our affairs. God hath given it to our handful, let us endeavour to keep it. I had rather have a plain russet-coated captain that knows what he fights for, and loves what he knows, than that which you call a gentleman, and is nothing else. I honour a gentleman that is so indeed.—Carlyle, vol. i.

The officers and men thus enrolled required arms, food, clothing, and pay. The principal difficulty which Cromwell shared, in common with Fairfax and most of the leaders on both sides, was want of money. It was difficult to get the local authorities to raise and forward their share of the financial burden of the war. Thus in writing to the Mayor of Colchester on the 23rd March, on behalf of Captain Dodsworth, an officer in command of a Colchester company, Cromwell writes:

> He hath diligently attended the service, and much improved his men in their exercise; but he hath been unhappy beyond others in not receiving any pay for himself, and what he had for his soldiers is out long ago. He hath by his prudence, what with fair and winning carriage, what with money borrowed, kept them together. He is able to do so no longer; they will presently disband if a course be not taken.—Carlyle, vol. i. See also similar letter about Captain Nelson to Deputy-Lieutenants of Norfolk, in App.

Cromwell appears to have shared, or let it appear that he shared, the common delusion that the war would not last long, for he ends his letter thus—

"One month's pay may prove all your trouble."

Again, in writing to this same Mayor of Colchester on the 29th May, 1643, he says:

> I beseech you hasten the supply to us; forget not money! I press not hard, though I do so need, that, I assure you, the foot and dragooners are ready to mutiny. Lay not too much upon the back of a poor gentleman, who desires, without much noise, to lay down his life, and bleed the last drop to serve the cause and you. I ask not money for myself; if that were my end and hope, *viz.* the pay of my place, I would not open my mouth at this time. I desire to deny myself, but others will not be satisfied. I beseech you hasten supplies.—Carlyle, vol. i.

Parliament, no doubt, did what it could. Money was voted for the assistance of the different Associations, even collected and sent down. But it did not always reach its proper destination. Read the letter to St. John already quoted. In it Cromwell says:

> Of all men I should not trouble you with money matters did not the heavy necessities my Troops are in press upon me beyond measure. I am neglected exceedingly! ... If I took pleasure to write to the House in bitterness I have occasion. Of, (this word inserted by Carlyle), the £3000 allotted me I cannot get the Norfolk part nor the Hertfordshire; it was given before I had it. I have minded your service to forgetfulness of my own soldiers' necessities.
>
> I desire not to seek myself. I have little money of my own to help my soldiers. My estate is little. I tell you the business of Ireland and England hath had of me, in money, between eleven and twelve hundred pounds; therefore, my private can do little to help the public. You have had my money: I hope in God I desire to venture my skin. So, do mine. Lay weight upon their patience; but break it not. Think of that which may be a real help. I believe £5000 is due.—Letter dated 11th of September. Carlyle states that the figures £5000 have been erased in the original. Carlyle, vol. i.

The assessments were raised by Instructions issued by Parliament to the lords lieutenant, deputy-lieutenants, mayors, and other local authorities to raise so much money in the county or Association, proportioning the amount among the various towns, villages, and districts as might seem just. But, as has been seen in the case of Colchester, these authorities were often remiss in collecting the money, or devoted it to other objects.

Fairfax was in the same plight. In his report to the Committee of Safety, dated the 20th December, he describes his difficulties for want of money. Hitherto his army had been supported by loans and contributions from the clothing towns, but, on Saville's advance, that source of supply had been cut off. He objected strongly to free billeting. After stating he has no future means of subsistence, he adds, "unless I give my soldiers free quarter upon the country, a cure in my conception as dangerous as the disease." (*Fairfax Correspondence*). But Parliament had sometimes to resort to this means of subsisting the army. Thus Lenthall, the Speaker, writing to Fairfax on the 23rd December, says:

> The House hath appointed £20,000, for the payment of your army.... They likewise approve of your lordship's billeting your soldiers on the country (upon the case of extreme necessity), and have engaged the public faith of the kingdom for the repayment thereof, as by the enclosed order under the clerk's hand.—*Fairfax Correspondence*.

Thus, by one means or another, by assessments, by voluntary loans and contributions, by fines and penalties on Malignants, as Royalists who had taken an active part against the Parliament were called, and, as a very last resort, by free quarters, these great Parliamentary leaders succeeded in raising means to subsist their forces, and to pay the men sufficiently to keep them from disbanding. But the pay ran greatly into arrear, and these arrears, as will hereafter be seen, became the cause of the great quarrel between the House and the army, which broke out at the termination of the first Civil War.

In Cromwell's and Fairfax's forces promiscuous plunder was unknown. But Malignants were obliged to pay heavy penalties, when their estates came within reach of the Roundhead troopers. The money so obtained went to the general purse, and was levied on fixed principles according to the value of the estate. There appears to have been a sort of appeal from the Committee of the County or local authority who assessed the fine. Thus, we find Barnard, who had once been a fellow Justice with Cromwell for Huntingdon, but was now a Royalist, appealing to the Earl of Manchester, as chief of the Eastern Association, from a "contribution" which he had been adjudged to pay by the Committee of Huntingdon. (See Cromwell's Letter, Carlyle, vol. i.)

Thus, the fines, though severe, were levied and collected with due form, and in an impartial manner. But plate and horses were often seized for the support or use of the troops by the officer on the spot, and all arms were removed from the houses of Royalists when found. By an Ordinance passed in March, 1643, Parliament also made provision for maimed soldiers, and for the widows and children of those killed on service. The local authorities of the town or parish to which the man belonged were bound, on the production of a certificate from the colonel under whom he had served, to afford such relief as might be reasonable to himself or his widow or orphans. They were authorized to lay a special rate on the inhabitants for this purpose.

Under these conditions, Cromwell raised and organised the troops of the Association, and by the time that Newcastle's advance began to threaten its frontier, he had a considerable force on foot. The Committee of the Association sat at Cambridge, an important town, the seat of a rich University, whose funds had by Cromwell's precautions been diverted to the use of the Parliament. It also, from its position on the edge of the Fens, formed the best base for the defence of the Association against attack from the north. It was, therefore, determined to fortify it.

Thus, by the end of January, the general situation was somewhat as follows: The king lay with the bulk of his army at Oxford, with outposts in Reading, Banbury, Marlborough, and elsewhere. Opposite him, Essex's army occupied Windsor and its neighbourhood. Newcastle, with considerable forces, was in South Yorkshire, with only some feeble levies in his immediate front, but with the hostile Eastern Association on the flank of his line of march, either towards London or Oxford. The campaign already described in Chapter I. had put the affairs of the Royalists on a good footing in Cornwall and Devon.

The king's prospects showed a great improvement on those with which he opened the war. If he now called Newcastle southward, whilst he marched with his own army to meet him, their united forces might have fallen upon Essex and at least driven him back into London. But there were reasons which made Charles hesitate to assume such vigorous strategy. Negotiations were being carried on with Parliament, and there was some hope that the basis for a treaty might be arrived at. He knew that if he advanced negotiations would be immediately broken off. Besides this he was badly in want of money and arms, and the queen, who had procured a supply on the Continent, was ready to embark for England.

Charles held no port in the south of England, and the approach to

Chester through the narrow Irish Seas, dominated by the Parliamentary fleet, was too hazardous to be attempted by the queen's convoy, even under the protection of Dutch men-of-war. Therefore, her destination was some port on the north-east coast, and it was necessary that Newcastle should remain to cover her landing.

Some such considerations probably induced the king to delay any advance towards London. Essex, however, had some inkling of the danger. Writing to Sir T. Fairfax, who was clamouring for support, on the 31st January, he says:—

> I have already written to the Lord Grey and into Lincolnshire to march into your county and to join with you, that while fear possesseth the enemy you may fall upon them at York, or wheresoever they now quarter.

Fairfax had just recovered Leeds and Wakefield from Saville, and Essex evidently thought a combined advance might check the danger from the north. Lord Grey was either Lord Grey of Groby, who commanded the Leicestershire levies, or Lord Grey of Wark, who then nominally commanded those of the Eastern Association. Nothing came of this order, and it must be urged in excuse for the inactivity of the leaders that the local troops they commanded were exceedingly unwilling to leave their own counties.

On the 22nd February, the queen landed at Bridlington Bay under the escort of Van Tromp and some Dutch men-of-war. Captain Batten arrived with an inferior force of Parliamentary ships as the landing was being carried out, and immediately opened fire. He was, however, compelled by Van Tromp to desist, and the queen, who had taken shelter in a ditch, was able to get safely to York with her convoy.

Whilst the main armies on both sides remained inactive, enterprises were undertaken by subordinate commanders, and conducted often with great spirit but without any combination on a proper strategical plan, which alone would render the results of permanent value. Thus, Lord Capel, having collected the Royalist forces of the western midlands, advanced about the end of February towards Cambridge. On the alarm being given, the militia of the Eastern Counties was called out. The men readily answered to the summons, and soon a considerable force was under arms, estimated in the newspapers, &c., of the day, variously at from 12,000 to 30,000. The Parliament also sent down ammunition and cannon, and Capel retired without attempting anything.

As in the case of the militia in Cornwall, as soon as the enemy withdrew, the trained bands disbanded, and only the regular regiments, which Cromwell had raised, remained under arms. These were now employed in suppressing the Royalists within the Association, who, encouraged by Capel's approach, had risen in places against the authority of the Committee. A party of horse was sent to Norwich, where the Mayor and some other Royalists were arrested without difficulty. Here news was received on the 13th March of a more serious rising at Lowestoff, where the Royalists had secured the town.

> The colonel (Cromwell) advised no man might enter in or out the gates (of Norwich) that night. And the next morning, between five and six, with his five troops, with Captain Fountain's, Captain Rich's, and eighty of our Norwich volunteers, he marched towards Lowestoff, where he was to meet with the Yarmouth volunteers, who brought four or five pieces of ordnance. The town had blocked themselves up, all except where they had placed their ordnance, which were three pieces, before which a chain was drawn to keep off the horse.
>
> The colonel summoned the town, and demanded, if they would deliver up their strangers, the town, and the army? promising them then favour, if so; if not, none. They yielded to deliver their strangers but not the rest. Whereupon our Norwich dragoons crept under the chain before-mentioned, and came within pistol-shot of their ordnance, proffering to fire upon their cannonier, who fled; so, they gained the two pieces of ordnance and broke the chain, and they and the horse entered the town without more resistance.—Letter of Mr. John Corey to Sir John Potts, printed in Carlyle, vol. i.

A number of prisoners were taken, and a good store of pistols and saddles.

> This is the best piece of service that hath been done a long time, for both counties will now be freed of their fears of the Malignants.—So, says an old newspaper, (*Perfect Diurnal*, 18th March, in *Cromwelliana*).

The distance from Norwich to Lowestoff is over twenty miles, which is probably the reason Cromwell took no foot with him to attack a barricaded town.

Cromwell stayed only two nights at Lowestoff and then returned to Cambridge. On the 20th, he started for Lynn to suppress a Royalist rising there, but on the 23rd, he appears to have received orders from Essex to join him.

> To advance with what force we can to put an end, if it may be, to this work.—Cromwell to the Mayor of Colchester. Carlyle, vol. i.

Nothing came of this proposed combination, although Cromwell, about this time, advanced to Peterborough and Nottingham, perhaps with a view of assisting the Midland Counties' forces. He was, however, soon back in Cambridge. Great efforts were made to complete the fortifications of this town, and a quaint old letter from the Committee to the inhabitants of Fen Drayton soliciting their contributions is printed by Carlyle, (vol. i.) It was to be read to them after divine service on Sunday.

Meanwhile in the south, whilst Charles lay at Oxford, Rupert made an attempt to clear the country westward and to seize the very important port of Bristol. On the 2nd February, he took Cirencester, and on the 7th March, he appeared before Bristol with 4000 horse and 2000 foot. He hoped, with the assistance of some Royalist merchants within, to surprise the gates, but Colonel Fiennes, the Parliamentary governor, discovered the plot, and hanged Yeoman and Bourchier, two of the ringleaders. Rupert then fell back to Oxford, and afterwards employed his horse in raiding the country towards Aylesbury.

Scarcely had Rupert returned from the west, when Sir William Waller crossed his track on a similar and more successful expedition. This energetic Parliamentary officer had during December cleared the Royalists out of Farnham, Winchester, Arundel, Chichester, and most of their posts in Surrey, Sussex, and Hampshire, with the exception of Basing House. He now marched through Dorset and Wilts to Bristol, where he arrived on the 15th March. Turning northward, he surprised Malmesbury on the 21st. Then crossing the Severn at Framlet Ferry below Gloucester, he defeated the Royalist Lord Herbert, at the head of his Welsh levies at Highnam.

Still advancing he occupied in rapid succession Newnham, Ross, Monmouth, and Chepstow. Here he heard that Prince Maurice was following him with superior forces; so, sending his infantry and baggage across the left bank of the Severn at Auste, he retraced his steps up the right bank with his cavalry. He met Maurice at Little Dean, but throwing his dragoons into the village he held the prince in play whilst he manoeuvred his cavalry round and got away to Gloucester. Massey, the Parliamentary governor of Gloucester, took Tewkesbury shortly afterwards.

Further north the town of Lichfield had been the centre of some severe fighting. Taken by the Royalists in February, it had been retaken by Sir John Gell with the Derbyshire troops on the 4th March. Brereton had occupied Middlewich, when the Royalists from Stafford and the Earl of Northampton from Banbury made a combined effort to regain lost ground. They met Gell and Brereton on Salt Heath, (also called Hopton Heath, near Stafford), on the 19th March, and a severe, but indecisive engagement took place, in which Northampton was killed. Thus, in desultory fighting and predatory raids, the winter campaign was carried on, a system of war which inflicts the greatest injury to the country with the least strategical advantage.

Even Waller's expedition, much as it had added to his prestige, had gained little material advantage to the Parliament. The towns he so easily captured were re-occupied by the Royalists directly he had passed, Cromwell alone understood that it was necessary to solidify his position in the eastern counties and thoroughly organise his troops, before any real success could be obtained from expeditions beyond.

With the arrival of the queen's convoy, however, Charles felt himself strong enough to adopt a bolder strategy. The negotiations with the Parliament were abandoned, and preparations for a spring campaign, on a combined plan, begun.

Cromwell's activity in the Eastern Association

From the outset of the war the strength of the Parliamentary party lay in London and the eastern counties, whilst the west and the north were for the most part loyal to the king. There were many exceptions to this general rule; the Parliament, for instance, had considerable forces on foot in Devonshire; in Lancashire, the principal towns had actively espoused its cause, whilst all the chief ports, with the exception of Chester and those north of the Humber, were held by its garrisons. It should be remembered that a great proportion of the people were neutral, or at any rate preferred peace and the safety of their person, and property to their interest in either party. These readily submitted to whichever side was the most powerful in their locality, and the more violent partisans of the other side were soon either reduced to submission, or moved off to some other county where their own party was uppermost. But between the strongholds of the two parties lay a belt of debatable land in which neither side could attain a decided superiority. In this was included the counties of Dorset, Wilts, Berks, Buckingham, Northampton, Warwick, and Stafford.

The king's first object, after the landing of the queen in Yorkshire, would naturally be to obtain from the convoy she brought with her the arms and money necessary to put his army at Oxford on an efficient footing. On the 1st April, therefore, Rupert was sent northward to clear the communications with Newcastle's army. On the 3rd he entered Birmingham, after some severe street fighting, in which the Earl of Denbigh was killed, and sacked the place. On the 10th he reached Lichfield, where he besieged the Cathedral Close, which had been fortified by the Parliamentary forces. Repulsed in several assaults, he allowed the garrison to march away with bag and baggage on the 21st. Before he could advance further he was recalled to assist the king in resisting Essex.

The Parliament had reinforced their commander-in-chief to 16,000 foot and 3000 horse, (Warburton, vol. ii.), 5000 of whom came from the Eastern Association with Lord Grey of Wark, (Gardiner, vol. i.) Under an able, energetic commander, such a force would have sufficed to finish the war. But Essex was slow and cautious to the extreme. Hampden urged him to pass by Reading and attack Oxford at once. Had he done so, Charles would have marched north to join Newcastle, (Clarendon, vol. ii.) But he would not, and marched on the 15th April towards Reading. Here he opened a formal siege, though the defences were weak and ammunition scarce. Sir Arthur Aston, the governor, was soon wounded by a falling tile, and Colonel Fielding, his successor, had already opened a treaty for the surrender of the place when the king and Rupert made on the 24th April an unsuccessful attempt to relieve it from Caversham.

On the next day the treaty was signed, and the garrison marched out on the 27th with the honours of war. Nothing could induce Essex to advance further. His troops were certainly raw levies, but nothing demoralizes young soldiers so much as inaction or the tedious operations of a siege. His army wasted away rapidly by sickness and desertions, whilst the Cavaliers recovered their confidence and reorganised their forces. On the 13th May a convoy of arms and ammunition, part of that which the queen had brought with her, reached Woodstock in safety.

The news from the west was also most reassuring for the Royalists. On the 25th April Chudleigh, in command of the Parliamentary forces, had defeated Sir R. Hopton at Stourton Down. But he was superseded by Lord Stamford, who divided his forces, sending his cavalry into the heart of Cornwall, about Bodmin, to prevent the Royalists levying fresh troops, whilst with the foot he took up a position on a high down in the north-eastern corner of the county before Stratton, (called ever since Stamford Hill). Hopton immediately advanced from Launceston, though much inferior in numbers. Availing himself of the intimate knowledge of the country possessed by his officers, he attacked Stamford with four columns on the 16th May and utterly routed him, capturing all his cannon. Chudleigh, who was taken, joined the Royalist party. Hopton then overran all Devonshire, with the exception of the fortified towns.

The Parliament was thoroughly alarmed. Not only were its armies unsuccessful in the field, but a very serious Royalist conspiracy, headed by the poet Waller, was discovered in London itself. Nevertheless, the Commons refused even to listen to a proposal from the king to treat, and committed his messenger to the Tower. The members of both Houses then took an oath not to lay down their arms "so long as the Papists, now in open war against the Parliament, shall by force of arms be protected from the justice thereof;" also to "assist the forces raised and continued by both Houses of Parliament against the forces raised by the king without their consent." (Clarendon, vol. ii.) This oath appears to have afterwards been subscribed to by the army.

To meet the impending danger in the south, Waller was ordered to collect all the forces he could raise in Gloucestershire and march into Somerset to oppose Hopton's further advance. The king, on his side, determined to reinforce Hopton; and having now a general of proved ability and energy in command of his western army, he, with his usual fatuity, immediately determined to supersede him, and sent the Marquis of Hertford to command over his head. Prince Maurice was given the command of the cavalry in this army.

Meanwhile, Cromwell, who had not accompanied Lord Grey of Wark when he joined Essex, was about the beginning of April at Cambridge or, as Carlyle thinks, at Huntingdon, with "six or seven troops of horse, such as I hope will fight," (Cromwell to J. Burgoyne, Carlyle, vol. i.), when news arrived that Lord Camden, with a party of horse, was at Stamford plundering the country and threatening the Association. This Lord Camden was a Rutlandshire nobleman, whose house had been taken by Lord Grey on the 20th February, but who was now at the head of a numerous and ill-disciplined party of horse.

On the 10th April Cromwell wrote a letter to Sir John Burgoyne, chief of the Committee of Bedfordshire, asking for the assistance of some dragoons, if they could be spared, "to help in this great exigence." The Camdeners passed on to Croyland, which they took, and thence made a raid on Spalding on the 25th March, from whence they carried off some of the Puritan divines and other leading men of that sect. The trained bands of Spalding and the neighbourhood, however, flew to arms and drove them back to Croyland on the 13th April, where they besieged them in a desultory manner. The Cavaliers placed their prisoners bound on the walls, so that the besiegers were afraid to fire. Cromwell, however, moved up on the 25th April to assist the Spalding men, and the place soon fell on the 28th, (Vicars' *Jehovah Jireh*; *King's Pamphlets*). He was still in great straits for money, and according to the *Mercurius Aulicus* (a Royalist newspaper) he about this time demanded a contribution of £6000 from Cambridge University. It was refused, whereupon he seized all the cash found with the college bursars and sequestered the University rents.

Having now consolidated his power in the Eastern Association, Cromwell devoted his energies to form a combination of his own forces with those of Leicestershire, Derbyshire, and Lincolnshire, commanded by Lord Grey, Sir John Gell, and Hotham respectively. It was evident that the most effectual way of protecting these counties lay in joining with Fairfax to resist Newcastle.

But of the three leaders Gell was the only one who could appreciate and assist in such a project. Grey was no general. He thought only of preserving his county and his father's house from inroads of the enemy. He was afraid that if he quitted Leicestershire, Hastings from Ashley would devastate his lands in his absence. Hotham was a traitor who was already intriguing with the Royalists, and his men were ill-disciplined and subsisted on plunder. We find, therefore, from Cromwell's letter to the Committee of Lincoln, dated the 3rd May, that Grey had already failed to join him at an appointed rendezvous at Stamford, although he and Sir John Gell had received orders from Essex to do so.

******

Carlyle, vol. i. In this letter Cromwell says, "Believe it, it were better, in my poor opinion, Leicester were not, than that there should not be found an immediate taking of the field by our forces to accomplish the common ends."

******

Cromwell's first object was to capture Newark, and stamp out the nest of Cavaliers which, from that fortress as a base, harried the greater part of Lincolnshire. This done, the combined forces could advance to Fairfax's assistance with their communications secure, and with this important fortress on the Trent as an advanced base.

In his letter to the Committee of Lincoln, Cromwell mentions that:

> I have offered him (Grey) now another place of meeting; to come to which, I suppose, he will not deny me, and that to be tomorrow.

But this meeting also either failed, or nothing came of the junction of forces, for we hear no more about it. It is very difficult to trace Cromwell's movements about this time (the end of April and beginning of May). The old newspapers and Vicars, who are the principal contemporary authorities for this part of his career, mention him as sometimes in Lincolnshire, sometimes in Nottinghamshire, sometimes in Huntingdon, now as combined with Willoughby, now with Grey, and then again with Hotham. His forces are variously estimated at from 1800 to 7000 men. (newspaper extracts in *Cromwelliana*). It seems probable that at the head of his now fine body of horse, he first stamped out any sparks of Malignancy in Huntingdonshire before proceeding to the help of the Spalding troops at Croyland; and that after his success there he passed on into Nottinghamshire and Lincolnshire.

On his way to Croyland he also visited Peterborough, where his men are said to have defaced the Cathedral, (extract from *Mercurius Aulicus*, dated the 28th April, in *Cromwelliana*), and about the same date the *Continuation of certain Special and Remarkable Passages* reports a skirmish at Ancaster, in which Cromwell was not engaged, and in which the Roundheads were defeated. On his appearing later, the Cavaliers drew off to Newark. The same newspaper of the 10th May reports that Grey and Gell defeated Hastings in a skirmish near Loughborough. This would free them of fears of an interruption from him should they move north to join Cromwell in Lincolnshire, and a rendezvous at Grantham was about this time arranged. The *Special Passages* of the 9th to the 16th May says, after describing Cromwell's movements in Lincolnshire:

> It were to be wished that he and the Lord Grey and Sir John Gell had joined together to have withstood the convoy that

came from Newark (probably that sent by the queen, which reached Woodstock on the 13th May), with the ammunition, but whether their power were sufficient is a question yet, it being not attempted.—*Cromwelliana*

Some attempt on Newark appears to have been made, for the same newspaper of the 9th to the 16th May, after reporting the action at Grantham, says:

> Now all the Lincolnshire forces are joined with Colonel Cromwell, God grant they may manage the business they go about better than it was at Newark in their former action.

✶✶✶✶✶✶

This may refer to the repulse of an attack on Newark, to which Clarendon makes allusion, vol. ii., which apparently took place much earlier, whilst Cromwell was in the Eastern Association.

✶✶✶✶✶✶

Cromwell, always ready and eager for a decisive blow at Newark, moved to the rendezvous at Grantham about the 12th May, but few, if any, of the other troops had arrived. The *Special Passages* says:

> Colonel Cromwell came last week to Grantham where he was to have met the forces of Lord Willoughby, Master Hotham, and others, but the town not being of receipt, they met not, which occasioned those of Newark to go forth with twenty-two troops, thinking to surprise them before they were united, and fell upon the troop of Captain Wray and a Dutchman's troop, and forced them out of their quarters, but Colonel Cromwell, having thereby the alarm, advanced against them and routed them.

Here is Cromwell's own account of this skirmish, the first in which the men of his newly-raised regiment met the Cavalier horse in a fair fight. (Neither address or date are given in the *Perfect Diurnal, &c.*, in which the letter was printed, the action occurred on the 13th May):—

> Sir,
> God hath given us this evening a glorious victory over our enemies. They were, as we are informed, one-and-twenty colours of horse troops, and three or four of dragoons.
> It was late in the evening when we drew out; they came and faced us within two miles of the town. So soon as we had the alarm we drew out our forces, consisting of about twelve

troops, whereof some of them so poor and broken that you shall seldom see worse; with this handful it pleased God to cast the scale. For after we had stood a little above musket-shot, the one body from the other, and the dragoons had fired on both sides for the space of half an hour or more, they not advancing towards us, we agreed to charge them.

And, advancing the body after many shots on both sides, we came on with our troops a pretty round trot; they standing firm to receive us, and our men charging fiercely upon them, by God's providence they were immediately routed, and ran all away, and we had the execution of them two or three miles. I believe some of our soldiers did kill two or three men a-piece in the pursuit, but what the number of dead is we are not certain. We took forty-five prisoners, besides divers of their horse and arms, and rescued many prisoners whom they had lately taken of ours, and we took four or five of their colours.

Of this action, Gardiner (vol. i.) says:

The whole fortune of the Civil War was in that nameless skirmish.

Nor is this an exaggeration. True it is that the Cavaliers were led by neither Rupert nor Goring, and that their tactics were diametrically opposite to those of their famous cavalry leaders. Their commander, whoever he was, committed the fatal mistake, which Rupert, with all his faults, never committed, of *waiting to receive an attack*. And Cromwell gave him time to take the initiative. The opposing squadrons had stood facing each other "a little above musket-shot for the space of half an hour or more." Cromwell was still unaccustomed to the battlefield. He required experience to teach him, as all men do; but with him, experience once gained was never thrown away.

It may well be that the result of this action taught him the supreme value of the *initiative* in a cavalry combat, that is of the superior readiness to engage which compels the adversary to conform his movements to yours, to assume the defensive instead of the offensive. At any rate, he never hesitated again, but was invariably the first to charge. The moral advantages gained by Cromwell in this action were immense. For the first time the Parliamentary horse had fairly routed a superior force of Cavaliers.

After the action, Hotham joined Cromwell with the Lincolnshire forces, and there now seemed a good prospect of forming a junction with the Leicester and Derbyshire troops and combining for an attack on Newark. Accordingly, Cromwell and Hotham marched to Nottingham, where, by the 25th May, they were joined by Lord Grey and Sir John Cell.

Meanwhile, Lord Fairfax was hard pressed at Leeds. Reports reached London on the 20th April of a successful sally from that town, which resulted in driving back the Royalists and taking a number of prisoners. (Vicars' *Jehovah Jireh*). At this time, Sir Thomas Fairfax was at Bradford, and communications were still open with Nottingham and Derbyshire, by Barnsley, Rotherham, and Sheffield, as well as with Lancashire on the west. (Sir T. Fairfax to Lord Fairfax, 20th April, *Fairfax Correspondence*). But the Royalists were already at Pontefract and Wakefield, and a little later Newcastle took Rotherham and Sheffield, thus cutting Fairfax off from the Midland and Eastern Associations. Money and provisions were very scarce, and Fairfax's position was becoming very precarious.

On the 20th May he directed 1000 foot and 500 horse, taken from the garrisons of Leeds, Bradford, Halifax, and Howley House, to rendezvous at the last-named place, under the command of his son. Leaving Howley at midnight, they arrived before Wakefield at 4 a.m. on the morning of the 21st, The Royalists in the town numbered 3000 foot and seven troops of horse, but Fairfax's foot carried the barricades at the entrances with a rush, and his horse, dashing through the streets, routed the Royalist horse as they were forming on the market-place. The foot then threw down their arms or fled, 1500 were taken prisoners and considerable booty. But Sir Thomas found himself too weak to hold the town and fell back again. Among the prisoners was General Goring, who had joined Newcastle with the queen. (Vicars' *Jehovah Jireh*. Letter from Lord Fairfax to Parliament in Rushworth, vol. v.)

In reporting this brilliant little victory to the Houses, Fairfax points out the straits to which, in spite of it, he is reduced, and begs that Cromwell may be at once sent to his assistance. The latter was keen enough to respond to Fairfax's appeal. Writing on the 28th to the mayor, &c., of Colchester, he says:—

> I thought it my duty once more to write unto you for more strength to be speedily sent unto us for this great service. I suppose you hear of the great defeat given by my Lord Fairfax to the Newcastle forces at Wakefield. It was a great mercy of God to us. And had it not been bestowed upon us at this very pre-

sent, my Lord Fairfax had not known how to have subsisted. We assure you, should the force we have miscarry, expect nothing but a speedy march of the enemy up unto you. Why you should not strengthen us to make us subsist, judge you the danger of the neglect, and how inconvenient this improvidence, or un-thrift, may be to you.

I shall never write but according to my judgment. I tell you again it concerns you exceedingly to be persuaded by me. My Lord Newcastle is near six thousand foot and above sixty troops of horse; my Lord Fairfax is about three thousand foot and nine troops of horse; and we have about twenty-four troops of horse and dragooners. The enemy draws more to the Lord Fairfax, our motion and yours must be exceeding speedy, or else it will do you no good at all.

******

Carlyle, vol. i. Carlyle inserts Lincolnshire as the place where the letter was written, but by comparing newspaper reports, &c., Nottingham seems more probable. The rest of the letter has been quoted earlier.

******

But military motion, to be exceeding speedy, must be directed by a single head. Here no unity of direction existed. Grey, Gell, Hotham, and Cromwell all exercised independent commands, and drew their supplies from different sources. Cromwell might be eager to push on; the others were not so. The Royalist forces at Sheffield and Newark threatened both Derbyshire and Leicester. Grey and Gell were probably anxious above all things to preserve their counties from foraying parties of Royalist horse. Hotham, always insubordinate, was already meditating treachery. As early as the 27th January Sir Thomas Fairfax, in writing to his father, had reported of Hotham:

> No order will be observed by him but what he please.—Sir T. Fairfax to Lord Fairfax *Fairfax Correspondence*, vol. i.

He now contemplated deserting to the queen. No wonder, then, that the counsel of those who wished to stay prevailed over Cromwell's wishes. Alone he was not sufficient to break through the forces now interposing at Sheffield and Rotherham between him and the Fairfaxes. Besides, his own opinion appears to have been that a joint attack with the forces of Derbyshire, Leicestershire, and the Eastern Association on Newark was the best and surest way of relieving the pressure on Fairfax at Leeds, (*Cromwelliana*; *Perf. Diur*, the 26th May), and Essex had ordered Grey and Gell to join him for that purpose.

Accordingly, the four commanding officers and Mr. Herbert signed, at Nottingham, on the 2nd June, a joint report to Fairfax, in which they explain their reasons for not advancing directly to his assistance. They said they had got ready to march when they received "certain information" that Newcastle had weakened his forces near Leeds by sending "a good strength of horse and foot" to Newark, and that the troops which remained were so distracted, that he was in no condition to press Fairfax. On the other hand, a force of forty troops of horse and dragoons had been seen only four miles from Nottingham, and were "still within six or seven miles, hovering up and down the country." Until it was known what this party intended, they considered it better to remain at Nottingham, especially as, if they entered Yorkshire, they would soon eat up the scanty stock of provisions left there. But if Fairfax still required them to advance, they would obey. (Fairfax Correspondence, vol. i.)

Fairfax promptly replied with an order to advance:

> I do, notwithstanding all the objections and difficulties therein represented, desire that, as you tender the public safety, you draw down this day with all the forces you have, and join with me to suppress this Popish Army here, which else, whatsoever report gives it out to you, is of power, without God's miraculous deliverance, to destroy our force, and so by degrees to ruin the kingdom.

But Hotham, who was intriguing with the queen, had made combined action impossible. He insulted Cromwell, and turned two guns against the troopers of the Eastern Association. On a quarrel with Grey about forage, he suggested that their respective forces should fight it out. Essex sent Sir J. Meldrum to take command of all the forces at Nottingham. He arrested Hotham, but the latter escaped to Lincoln, where he corresponded with the queen for the surrender of that place and Hull to the Royalists. The queen had meanwhile reached Newark with a large convoy on the 16th June.

Hotham now joined his father. Sir John, at Hull. But the citizens were on the alert. On the evening of June 27th, the commander of the Parliament's ship *Hercules*, which lay in the roads, sent a communication to the mayor, who immediately collected a force of citizens, and, assisted by 100 seamen, secured all the guards. He arrested the younger Hotham; but the father, hearing this in time, escaped on foot to one of the gates where the guard had not been changed. He here obtained the horse of a man who was entering from the country, and galloped off.

Just then the mayor's party arrived, and fired a cannon after him without effect. He tried to cross at one or two ferries over the Hull; but the tide being unfavourable, pushed on for Beverley. Here, however, the news of his intended treachery had preceded him; and he was seized by the officer in command of the outpost there, and sent back a prisoner to Hull. (Vicars' *Jehovah Jireh*; Rushworth, vol. v.) Both father and son, after each had vainly endeavoured to save his own life by accusing the other, were eventually executed.

Meanwhile, though Meldrum had been sent down to assume command of the forces under the different commanders at Nottingham, nothing in the shape of combined action was attempted. On the contrary, when it was known the queen had reached Newark, the forces again separated. Gell went to Derby, Grey to Leicester, whilst Cromwell remained at Nottingham. (In some of the newspapers Cromwell is said to have gone to Leicester with Grey, Meldrum remaining at Nottingham); and on the 23rd June repulsed an attack of Cavaliers from Newark with loss.

The result of this dispersion was disastrous for the Parliament's cause. Fairfax was exposed to the full weight of Newcastle's attack, whilst no one of the other commanders was sufficiently strong to effectually oppose the queen. In a letter to the king dated the 27th June, (in Rushworth, vol. v), she describes her situation very clearly. She is only waiting, she says, two more days, hoping for a happy result from the Hothams' treachery, and thus to be able to secure Lincoln and Hull before moving south. She intends taking with her 3000 foot, thirty troops of horse and dragoons, six cannon, two mortars, and a large convoy under command of Harry "Girmin" (Jermyn).

She intends moving by Wirton and Ashby, the enemy lying principally at Leicester and Derby, with 1000 men at Nottingham. She will leave 2000 foot and twenty troops under Charles Cavendish for the garrison of Newark and other places in Lincolnshire. The Hothams were arrested before they could betray Hull. The attempt on Lincoln was made, as had been arranged, on the 2nd July, but failed; so, the queen marched up the Trent without further delay. Passing through the Parliamentary garrisons apparently without opposition, for no mention is made of any engagement, she made her way to Ashby-de-la-Zouch, which Colonel Hastings held for the king; and leaving this, she took Burton on the way to Lichfield, where she would find another Royalist garrison. On the 11th July, (Rushworth, vol. v.), she met Rupert at Stratford-upon-Avon. He had been sent with a party of horse to strengthen her escort, and on the 13th she met the king himself at Edgehill, and thus got safely to Oxford.

Meanwhile Newcastle had turned against Fairfax. On the 22nd he took Howley House, and then moved on Bradford. Fairfax collected what troops he could, and encountered Newcastle on the 30th June at Adwalton Moor. The former mustered some 4000 soldiers and a number of apprentices and peasants, armed with clubs and scythes. The latter commanded 10,000 well-armed troops. At the first charge the younger Fairfax drove back the Royalist foot till he was checked by a stand of pikes. Newcastle's horse then charged him in flank and rear, and the raw Parliamentary levies broke and fled. (Rushworth, vol. v.; Gardiner, vol. i.)

The Fairfaxes escaped to Bradford, and thence to Leeds. Here they heard of Hotham's treachery, and that there was no one in Hull to take command as governor. They therefore determined to break through to Hull. The elder succeeded in making his way thither by Selby, whilst his son checked the pursuit by engaging the Royalist horse. He was driven back on Leeds; but a day or two later succeeded, by dint of hard fighting and hard riding, in breaking out by the south bank of the Aire, and in cutting his way through by Crowl and Barton, in Lincolnshire, to join his father in Hull. In the fighting near Bradford his wife was taken prisoner and all his baggage captured; but the lady was sent to Hull with a courteous message from Newcastle.

The clothing towns could no longer hold out; and Leeds, Halifax, Bradford, and the neighbouring villages were abandoned by the Parliament's troops, and occupied by Newcastle's. They had been of great importance to Fairfax: not only were they devoted to the cause, and furnished him to the utmost of their means with recruits, supplies, and money, but from their position they covered the communications with the populous county of Lancashire, where the Parliamentary party had been making good way.

The district immediately round Hull was now the only foothold that remained to the Fairfaxes in Yorkshire. The town itself was strongly fortified, the surrounding country could to a large extent be inundated, and above all, the place could be supplied and relieved by sea. Its capture, therefore, was not likely to prove an easy task for the

Royalists. Newcastle appears to have lingered somewhat unnecessarily in the Leeds district, and then to have turned south-west towards Lincolnshire.

Thus, the Parliamentary leaders in this theatre of war had frittered away the spring in disjointed efforts, with the result that Newcastle had driven them out of Southern Yorkshire, and the Queen had passed reinforcements, money, and ammunition through their separated forces to the King at Oxford. That the result had not been still more disastrous must be attributed more to Newcastle's dilatory movements than to any skill in generalship displayed by his opponents. Want of combination had been the cause of their failure. Together the forces of Gray, Gell, Cromwell, and Hotham must have amounted to at least 6000 or 7000 men in the field, after providing for the necessary garrisons. Fairfax disposed of 4000 more.

Combined they would have formed a force well able to cope with Newcastle, and even to assume the offensive against him. The one redeeming feature of the campaign had been the conduct of the troops. Pitted, through bad generalship, against superior numbers, both Fairfax's and Cromwell's men had proved themselves capable of routing their foes. Their discipline in garrison and quarters had been excellent. In both Fairfax and Cromwell, the Parliament had men of first-rate ability as soldiers. Both had done their best, both understood and did their utmost to rectify the cause of failure. But the one was only in local command, and the other was still nominally a local subordinate. The failure lay in the higher authorities.

The Parliamentary leaders had selected Essex as their commander-in-chief; and it must be said, to their credit, that they supported him fully. When the first great battle had resulted in a fierce and equal fight, the effects of which were advantageous to the king, instead of in an easy victory, as the Parliament had expected, Essex had not been blamed. On the contrary, a vote of thanks had been granted him, and he had been well received on his return to Westminster. His authority had always been upheld. He granted all commissions and appointments in the army. Even when the Houses desired to place a certain man in a certain post the appointment was made through him.

He had therefore all the outward authority of a commander-in-chief, and a strong man would have made himself one in reality. But Essex, though honest and upright, was lethargic and weak. Though he always served the Parliament faithfully, his heart had never wholly been in the war. On more than one occasion he showed himself in favour of peace. An experienced soldier and a nobleman of great position and influence, perhaps the Parliament could hardly have passed him over, in the first instance, when all the generals were untried. But the appointment had very bad results.

Trained to war under Prince Maurice of Orange he was a soldier of the old school—slow and cautious, accustomed to dealing with armies of professional soldiers. He did not understand or appreciate the raw enthusiastic levies whom he was now called on to command, and who, like those of France in the next century, were changing the art of war. Their eagerness for battle and impatience of delay, their want of drill and technical knowledge, were alike strange to him. He could neither guide the one or supplement the other. The local levies, commanded by fellow-townsmen or by the country gentlemen, required to be taught that local interests were best defended by combined action on the broad principles of strategy.

Essex had neither the talent or industry to infuse such a spirit into his subordinates. His orders were therefore neglected, because they appeared to be in conflict with local interests. Thus, all his orders and directions to Grey, Hotham, Gell, and Cromwell to join with Fairfax for combined action, failed to bring about any appreciable result. Newcastle, with a very correct appreciation of the position of affairs, had taken the first opportunity of placing a numerous garrison, well furnished with cavalry, in the strong and important fortress of Newark. From thence Lincolnshire and the Midland and Eastern Associations were threatened with inroads of pillaging parties, which kept their forces from uniting with those in South Yorkshire.

His own authority was paramount amongst the Royalists of the north; and thus by combination he was enabled to baffle and defeat the disconnected efforts of the Parliamentary leaders, even though amongst these were Cromwell and Fairfax, both of whom possessed military talents of a far higher standard than his. We shall see how very soon afterwards similar causes re-acted in favour of the Parliamentary leaders against Newcastle, and how Hull proved as much a bar to his progress as Newark had been to theirs.

Battle of Gainsborough

Before following the campaign in Lincolnshire and Yorkshire further, it will be as well to take a glance at the progress of the war elsewhere. For it is impossible to appreciate the motives which governed the conduct of the opposing leaders, or the importance of this or that action, without understanding the strategical position generally in the country.

After remaining inactive for some six weeks at Reading, Essex at last made a movement towards Oxford. Crossing the Thames and moving north, he arrived about the middle of June at Thame, fifteen miles east of Oxford. He was comparatively weak in cavalry, and the more powerful Royalist horse had raided freely in Buckinghamshire. His men were a good deal demoralized by inaction, and the outpost and guard duties were badly performed. For the sake of facilitating the subsistence of the army the troops were a good deal scattered in quarters.

A Colonel Urry, or Hurry, a Scotch officer, deserted Essex's army about this time and joined Rupert in Oxford. Hearing that Essex was expecting a convoy of money, Rupert, on the afternoon of the 17th June, left Oxford, and guided by Hurry, who knew exactly where the Parliamentary troops lay, he slipped in the night through their quarters. He was accompanied by 700 foot and 1000 horse, and during the night surprised one or two regiments in their beds, capturing a good many prisoners, but failed to find the convoy. Returning by a detour on the morning of the 18th he descried Essex's cavalry in pursuit just as his horse were entering a narrow lane.

Fearing to be caught at a disadvantage, Rupert sent his foot on to secure Chiselhampton Bridge, over the Thame, and, recalling his horse from the lane, formed up on an open piece of ground called Chalgrove Field. The Parliamentary horse, pursuing too eagerly, came on in disorder, and Rupert charging completely routed them with considerable loss. Hampden was among those mortally wounded, and he died on the 24th. His death was a great blow to those who still hoped an honourable peace might be concluded. Though so keen for the cause that he rode on this occasion a volunteer with the horse, being properly a colonel of foot, yet his unselfish patriotism made him most earnest in his desire to finish the war, whilst his unsullied integrity rendered him one whom both sides could implicitly trust. After the fight, Rupert did not pursue far, but, wheeling about, crossed over Chiselhampton Bridge and reached Oxford with his prisoners and booty.

Towards the end of June Essex, finding his men slipping away through disease and desertion, fell back to Aylesbury and St. Albans.

******

Like Fairfax, Cromwell, and the other generals, Essex was in straits for money, and his men were mutinous for pay. The Parliament did the best they could to supply the deficiency.

✶✶✶✶✶✶

At least on one occasion Hurry again passed through the Parliamentary quarters, and plundered the country in rear right up to the walls of the capital. In July Rupert advanced into Buckinghamshire with one or two regiments of horse. Essex drew out to oppose him, but Rupert, turning north-west, proceeded to meet the queen at Stratford. Murmurs against Essex now arose in Parliament and the City. Men said that his army was no protection against the raids of the Royalist horse. He offered to resign his command, but his offer was refused.

A desultory movement towards Brickhill and Stoney Stratford formed the sum of Essex's efforts for some months; whilst the Royalists, encouraged by his inactivity, broke out in Kent, but were soon suppressed by Colonel Brown.

Reinforcements joined the Royalists under Hopton at Chard in the beginning of June, and Hertford assumed command. Hopton not only refrained from showing annoyance at his supersession, but repressed the murmurs of his subordinates. The combined forces amounted to 7000 men, with a good train. The Cornish foot under Hopton were admirable—as good as any raised for either side during the war—their fighting powers and discipline alike excellent. The horse under Maurice were ill-disciplined plunderers. However brave personally, they, like all troops whose discipline is lax, wanted cohesion to render them formidable in the field.

Waller at this time was at Bath. He had made strenuous endeavours to augment his small army from Bristol and the neighbouring garrisons, and he had also received reinforcements of horse from London. (Clarendon, vol. ii. says, "Waller had been in London and set out from there with his army." But in this he is not confirmed by other writers).

Amongst these was Hazlerigg's regiment of cuirassiers, who, from their complete armour, obtained the nickname of Lobsters. (At least we hear nothing of them before this time, though Hazlerigg had been with Waller all the spring). Clarendon says they were the first cuirassiers that appeared in the war, but in this he must be mistaken. There had been regiments so armed on the Parliament's side since the beginning. Ludlow, who had ridden as a volunteer in the Life-Guard troop of Stapylton's regiment at Edgehill, describes, in his *Memoirs*, his difficulty in remounting after having been knocked off his horse, owing to his heavy armour. And all writers agree that Cromwell's regiment in the Eastern Association from the first wore defensive armour. (It is possible that Hazlerigg's men were more completely armed; Cromwell's only wore back and breast-pieces).

Waller then was at Bath, with an outpost of horse under Colonel Popham at Wells. His forces were about equal to Hertford's, and he, too, was now strong in horse. Hertford's army left Chard early in June and advanced towards Waller. Taunton, Bridgewater, and Dunster Castle fell in rapid succession to the Royalists. On the 12th June, their advanced guard, under Lord Carnarvon, came into collision with Popham's troopers before Wells. After a smart skirmish, the latter were driven back in confusion through Wells and Chewton, losing many prisoners and all their baggage.

Waller thereupon marched out of Bath with a considerable force, rallied Popham's fugitives, and drove Carnarvon in turn back on Prince Maurice who arrived in support. After another sharp action, both sides retired—Waller on Bath, Maurice on Wells. For a fortnight after this ensued one of those wars of manoeuvre and skirmish so dear to the professional soldier of that day. Neither side would fight except with advantage of the ground. Hopton had shown them that a vigorous attack would overcome a passive defence, even when the ground and the odds were greatly in favour of the latter.

But the moral of the fight at Stamford Hill had been neglected, or misread, and Hopton, though present, was now only a subordinate. Waller knew that time would be in his favour. He rested on Bath, a town well supplied, and he could afford to wait. But with Hertford the question of supply was difficult. The country around was not over friendly, and his troops would soon have to disperse in order to subsist. Besides, his object was to drive Waller out of the west and clear the country of the rebels.

Passing round to the south of Bath he reached Marshfield, on the Oxford Road, five miles from Bath, on the 3rd July. Two more days were lost in manoeuvring. On the 5th, Waller's army was drawn up on the brow of Lansdown Hill, across the Oxford Road, his foot and cannon in breastworks on the brow, his musketeers in two woods which ran down the slopes and flanked the road at some distance. He then sent some parties of horse to annoy the enemy.

Hertford drew out of Marshfield and formed up his army opposite Waller's, but considered the position too strong to attack. He, therefore, fell back again to Marshfield, but, as he did so, Hazlerigg, with his own regiment and the rest of the Parliamentary horse, fell upon the Royalist rear-guard, which was composed of Maurice's cavalry. Clarendon says of the Lobsters that they were:

> The first that made any impression upon the king's horse, who being unarm'd were not able to bear the shock of them, besides that they were secure from hurts of the sword, which were almost the only weapons the other were furnished with.

He says that on this occasion they did great execution, striking terror into the king's horse, who could not be brought to charge as before. (Clarendon, vol. ii.) The latter were consequently driven in confusion back on the foot. These, however, turned about, and steadily facing Hazlerigg's troopers, checked them. The horse then rallying behind the foot, the whole Royalist army re-formed, and again advanced towards Lansdown, the Parliamentary horse falling back before them.

The Cornish foot, tired of these perpetual counter-marches, were clamouring to be led against the cannon. An attempt of the Royalist horse to reach the brow only resulted in their more complete discomfiture, and then Hopton was allowed to attack with the foot. Pushing his musketeers into the woods to clear them of the enemy, he led his gallant Cornish pikemen up the hill against the breastworks, and after sharp fighting at push of pike carried them, and captured several of the cannon. Waller's troops fell back in good order, under cover of his powerful cavalry, to a stone wall a little way back.

Night separated the combatants before anything further was effected, and, during it. Waller fell back on Bath. The Royalists had paid dearly for their success. Sir Bevil Grenvile, the darling of the Cornishmen, was killed in the fight for the breastwork, and many of the best officers were wounded. The Royalist horse were so shattered that out of 2000 but 600 remained with the army at the end of the day. (Clarendon, vol. ii.) The next morning another great blow befell the Royalists. Hopton was viewing the field when a passing powder-cart blew up; he was knocked down and was so badly injured and burnt that for some days he could neither stir nor see. Hertford now fell back to Marshfield and sent to Oxford asking for fresh cavalry and a supply of ammunition. The Earl of Crawford was thereupon ordered to his assistance with 500 horse and an ammunition train.

Hertford, although he had gained a tactical success at Lansdown, did not consider himself strong enough to cope with Waller, being now so inferior in horse. He, therefore, fell back on the 7th towards Oxford, and reached Chippenham; Waller followed. On the 8th, Hertford offered battle on ground favourable to infantry, but Waller' refused. On the 9th, Hertford fell back to Devizes, Waller following and pressed his rear-guard smartly.

******

It is not very clear why Devizes was the next stage. The old road to Oxford, whence reinforcements would come, ran through Marlborough.

******

From Devizes to near Oxford the ground is open and favourable to cavalry; Hertford, therefore, determined to push on with his horse whilst the foot was left in Devizes, which, though an open town, was surrounded by enclosures and favourable for infantry. Waller then invested it.

Marlborough and Mohun were left in the town with Hopton, still unable to move. Ammunition was very scarce, and matches for the firelocks had to be improvised from bed cords. The streets were barricaded; but the garrison was so small, compared with the size of the place, that the men were exhausted with continual duty. Waller surprised Crawford's convoy, and captured all the ammunition and one or two troops of horse. He now felt sure of his prey, and sent a trumpet into the town to suggest conditions of surrender. The tired Royalists obtained a few hours' rest by pretending to consider the conditions. The negotiations had not been broken off many hours before Waller learnt that Wilmot with a large body of horse was approaching from Oxford.

Through bad scouting on the part of his own troopers, he did not learn this till Wilmot was only two or three miles off. Hastily drawing his forces off the town and forming them for battle, he advanced to meet the fresh enemy. In the advance, the horse got too far ahead of the foot and out of hand. The Lobsters endeavoured to charge uphill on Roundway Down, but were defeated by Sir J. Byron's regiment, and then Wilmot swooped down on the Parliamentary line, charging their horse "from division to division as they were ranged," and routed them. Some pieces of artillery were captured and turned against Waller's troops. At the same time the Cornish foot from Devizes appeared on the scene, and both they and Wilmot's horse charged the Parliamentary infantry, who then broke and fled. Waller, himself, with a small following, escaped to Bristol. This battle occurred on the 13th of July. On the same day, the queen met the king at Edgehill.

******

These battles are very interesting and are given in considerable detail by Clarendon, vol. ii., and, I think, with fairness. They, and the accompanying skirmishes, are well worth the study of cavalry officers.

******

All this time Essex remained inactive in Buckinghamshire. He made no attempt to interrupt the queen's march to Oxford, which crossed his front within two days' march of it, or to prevent reinforcements being sent to Hopton by pressure on Oxford. Waller reproached him bitterly. Essex retorted by saying that Waller had allowed himself to be beaten by an inferior force. The quarrel between them became embittered.

The king's cause had never appeared so flourishing as now. Both in north and west it had been victorious. The garrison of Bath had been withdrawn to Bristol to replace some of those troops which had been sent thence to reinforce Waller. There remained, therefore, only Bristol and Gloucester to complete the king's possession of the rich and important basin of the Severn. The armies of the west and of Oxford had been united, and were now, thanks to the Queen's exertions, well provided with arms and ammunition. Newcastle's army had swept Yorkshire clear of the rebels, with the exception of the Fairfaxes, shut up in Hull. The Parliament's forces in the eastern and midland counties appeared disconnected and inactive. Essex's troops were demoralized through inaction and sickness, and mutinous for want of pay.

Gardiner asserts (vol. i.) that the king's general design in 1642 and 1643 was to push his northern army through the Eastern Association to the Thames in Essex, Hopton's western army through Hampshire to the Thames in Kent, whilst he himself advanced directly from Oxford, thus investing London on all sides. Such a plan, if really entertained, was a very bad one, as it would force the Parliamentary armies to concentrate, whilst his own would be out of touch of each other and exposed singly to the combined attack of the enemy. London was too strong to be taken by assault, whilst the fleet would keep the river open for supplies. At any rate, there would at the present juncture be time to attempt Bristol before Newcastle was sufficiently advanced to co-operate towards London, and Bristol was of immense importance to the king. Rupert was therefore directed to attempt its capture.

Picking up Hopton's forces at Bath, the prince arrived before the town on the 23rd July, with fourteen weak regiments of foot, a strong body of horse, and an artillery train. Waller had gone, and Colonel Fiennes commanded the garrison. The defences consisted of an outer line no less than five miles long, formed by a low parapet and shallow ditch, and, inside this, the old walls of the town itself. The garrison was only 1800 strong, 300 of which were horse. On the 26th the outer line was carried, and the next day the governor surrendered. Thus, with a loss of some 500 men, the Royalists acquired an excellent port and a large quantity of guns, ammunition, and stores.

Had Charles now kept his forces together, and, cooperating vigorously with Newcastle, advanced on London, he might have achieved success. But the indiscipline of his army ever marred his best opportunities. Rupert and Hertford now quarrelled over the nomination of a governor for Bristol; and Charles, too weak to repress the disputes, again divided his forces. The western army, under Carnarvon, Maurice, and Hopton, was sent into Wilts and Dorset; whilst himself, with Rupert, Hertford, and the Oxford troops, turned against Gloucester, which he hoped to capture easily.

Gloucester, though of secondary importance to Bristol, commanded the most direct road to South Wales. Charles appeared before it with 8000 men on the 10th August. Massey, the governor, was an energetic soldier. The garrison was some 1400 strong; the works extensive. Massey burnt the suburbs and abandoned some of the outworks to concentrate the defence.

Meanwhile, the Parliament had been taking measures to counteract Fairfax's and Waller's defeats. Since the Catholic insurrection, a Scotch force had been operating in Ulster, under Monro, to assist the English Army, under the Earl of Ormond, in repressing the rebellion. During the summer of 1643 Charles had been negotiating with the Catholics for a cessation of hostilities, in order to free the English troops for service in England against the Parliament. Early in June Monro discovered, by intercepted letters, that there was a plot on foot either to bribe him to bring his forces also over to the king's assistance, or, if he refused, to crush him with the aid of the Catholics.

In any case, Irish Catholics were to be joined to the English Army brought back into England. The letters were published by the Scotch Government, and copies sent to London, where they were also published. The greatest indignation was aroused. A Convention of Estates had been summoned in Scotland, and when it met, military assistance to the Parliament of England was voted. (Gardiner, vol. i.)

After the defeats of Adwalton Moor, (modern spelling; formerly Atherton Moor.—Ed), and Roundway Down, the English Parliament sent commissioners to Scotland to ask for the loan of 11,000 men. The Scots proposed that a Solemn League and Covenant should be entered into by the adherents of both Parliaments for the "Reformation and Defence of Religion," &c. This was accepted at Westminster, and eventually a treaty was entered into, in which it was stipulated that the Covenant should be taken throughout the kingdom; that a committee of Scots should be joined to the "close" committee at Westminster for carrying on the war; and that no treaty should be made with the king except with the joint consent of the Parliaments of both countries. (Clarendon, vol. ii.)

But before these arrangements had been settled, the Scots had begun to raise their army, which had been disbanded in 1640, and it was well known that they intended to assist the English Parliament. As early as the 24th July the London newspapers noted the expected advance of the Scots. Considerable delay however, was necessary to raise and organise the new army.

Meanwhile, Parliament had not neglected other means of providing for its immediate defence. Ordinances were rapidly issued for levying men and money. The greatest deficiency was in cavalry. In July, an ordinance was issued directing that on the 1st August the trained bands of horse of the Eastern Association should rendezvous at Cambridge—those of Bedford, Herts, Bucks, and Northamptonshire at Bedford; those of Middlesex, Kent, and Essex at Tothill Fields. (*King's Pamphlets*). The London trained bands of foot were to be assembled under the command of Waller, and Essex's own army was to be largely recruited. In order to ensure more combination among the forces of the eastern counties, Leicestershire, Northampton, &c., the Earl of Manchester was sent to command them all.

Another ordinance detailed a fresh assessment to be laid on each county and important town in the hands of the Parliament, and the names of the committees for each, and on the 10th August a fresh act was passed directing the impressment of soldiers for the Parliament's armies. (*King's Pamphlets*).

Great exertions had been made to complete the fortifications of London, and they were now about finished. The citizens of all classes had worked at them with their own hands. Lithgow, the Scotch tailor and adventurer, in his *Present Surveigh of London and England's State*, (Somers' Tracts, Charles I.), written about the last days of June, 1643, says:

> The daily musters and showes of all sorts of Londoners here were wondrous commendable in marching to the fields and outworks (as merchants, silk men, macers, shopkeepers, &c.), with great alacritie, carrying on their shoulders yron mattocks and wooden shovels; with rearing drummes, flying colours, and girded swords, most companies being also interlarded with ladies, women, and girles, two and two, carrying baskets to advance the labour, where divers wrought till they fell sick of their pains. All the trades and whole inhabitants (the insey courts excepted—*excellent example of phonetic spelling, i.e. Inns of Court.*—Ed.) within the citie liberties, suburbs, and circumjacent dependencies went, day about, to all quarters, for the erection of their forts and trenches,, and this has continued these foure months past.

He walked round the entrenchments—a perimeter of eighteen miles. He first went to Wapping, where:

> I found a seven-angled fort erected of turffe, sand, watles, and earthern worke (as all the rest are composed of the like), having nine port holes and as many cannons, and near the top round about pallosaded with sharpwooden stakes fixt in the bulwarks right out and a foot distant from one another, which are defensive for sudden scalets, and single ditched below, with a *court du guard* within.

From Wapping the trench ran by Whitechapel, Mile End Green, Shoreditch, Kingsland, Finsbury Fields, Tollington, Holborn Fields, Marylebone, Hyde Park Corner to Tothill Fields, where it rested on a fort on the river. It was continued on the other side by Nine Elms, Vauxhall, St. George's Fields, Southwark, to Redcliff, where another fort on the river, opposite to Wapping, was under construction. The trench formed a continuous curtain, flanked and supported by forts at intervals. "All the forts about are blank and blank in sight of other." There were fourteen forts north and five south of the Thames, besides half-moons, "rampires," and other small works. Inside these works "the city hath many *courts du guard* with new barrocaded ports, and they strongly girded with great chaines of yron, and all the opening passages at street ends, for the fields and road-wayes, are in like manner made defensive, and strictly watched."

The same existed in the towns of Southwark and Westminster. The garrison consisted of six old and six new regiments of trained bands, each 1000 strong, and fourteen troops of horse.

Thus, fortified and garrisoned, London was secure against any force Charles could bring against it. The trained bands soon proved at Newbury that they could fight well, and the spirit of the inhabitants must have been excellent. The river, Lithgow says, was full of ships, and the only scarcity was of coal. Parliament contemplated raising the curious rate of £1 for every chaldron of coal used, on an average, by each house during the year; and with the money so raised it was proposed to equip ships to force the Tyne and bring back coals. Soon afterwards an ordinance was issued for cutting and stacking wood for fuel.

To go back to Lincolnshire, it is difficult to understand why Meldrum allowed the queen to pass unmolested through Nottinghamshire to Ashby-de-la-Zouch. By collecting the available forces of all the counties under his command, he could apparently have got some 5000 or 6000 men together. The queen had only 3000 foot and thirty troops of horse, according to her own statement. Yet the *Parliamentary Scout*, of the 20th July, (*King's Pamphlets*), says:

> Her Majesty brought with her so great a power that Sir John Meldrum thought not good to encounter her.

Cromwell must have chafed under his enforced inaction. Indeed, some of the old newspapers mention a skirmish of his horse with the queen's, near Ashby-de-la-Zouch. Meldrum apparently received an order from Essex to join him at Stony Stratford about the 18th July, an order which he found it impossible to comply with. Newcastle was still lingering in southern Yorkshire; but about that date some 1000 Cavaliers from Newark appeared before Peterborough, and summoned the place to surrender. Colonel Palgrave, who defended it, refused, and Cromwell, coming up from Nottingham, attacked the Cavaliers, and beat them back to Stamford with loss. Here they threw themselves into Wothrop House and began to fortify it, but the next day Cromwell attacked them with six or seven troops of horse and a few foot, and drove them out.

They then took refuge in Burleigh House, a strongly built manor with a high park wall. Finding himself unable to attack without means of battering the wall, Cromwell withdrew a short distance on the Stamford Road. Heavy rain prevented any further operations taking place until the 23rd, when Colonels Palgrave and Hobart joined him, and raised his forces to 3000 or 4000 men, and twelve or fourteen cannon. On the 24th, Cromwell attacked the house, and, after nine or ten hours' fighting, the garrison surrendered on quarter for life. About 400 foot and 150 horse were taken. A large party of armed peasants had approached with a view of relieving the Cavaliers, but were easily beaten near Stamford. (*A true relation of Colonel Cromwell's proceedings against the Cavaliers*, and Newspapers. *King's Pamphlets*).

Hardly had Burleigh House been taken, when Cromwell got news which made him hasten northward. Lord Willoughby, of Parham, who, since the defection of Hotham, had himself taken command at Lincoln, had on the 20th surprised Gainsborough by a night attack, and taken it. The governor, the Earl of Kingston, defended his own house for a day, but then had to surrender. He was put into a boat to send down to Hull, but a fort, garrisoned by Cavaliers on the river, opened fire on it, and Kingston was killed by a shot fired by his friends. In his house, Willoughby captured a considerable sum of money and plate, and in the town many prisoners were taken, and some 200 Parliamentary soldiers, who had been captured by the Royalists, were released and armed with weapons taken from the Cavaliers. (Newspapers. King's Pamphlets). Willoughby was not left a day to enjoy his success in peace. Gainsborough was very important strategically, commanding, as it did, a bridge over the Trent. Newcastle and the Cavaliers from Newark and Belvoir hastened to retake it, and Willoughby was scarcely in the town before he found himself besieged.

Cromwell, therefore, hurried forward to his relief. Leaving his foot at Stamford on the 26th, he reached Grantham that evening, where he met Meldrum with 300 horse and dragoons from Nottingham. The next day they marched to North Searle, where they met some Lincoln horse, and at two o'clock on the morning of the 28th July, they marched for Gainsborough. About a mile and a half from the town they met the advanced guard of Cavendish's force, which had been sent to invest the place, but had drawn off to oppose them. The action that ensued shall be told in Cromwell's own words. Meldrum being the senior officer present, the command must nominally have rested with him, but Cromwell appears to have exercised it throughout the day, and the victory is attributed by all writers to him. Three reports, signed by him, of this battle, are extant; one a letter by him to the Committee of the Association sitting at Cambridge, (Carlyle, vol. i. there is an introductory paragraph omitted here), another to Sir John ———, (Carlyle, v. guesses that the surname which has been erased should be Wraye), and the third, a joint report, signed by him and two others, to Speaker Lenthall. (Carlyle, vol. i.) The three agree closely, and the first, which is the shortest, is given here:—

> It hath pleased the Lord to give your servant and soldiers a notable victory now at Gainsborough. I marched, after the taking of Burleigh House upon Wednesday, to Grantham, where I met about 300 horse and dragooners of Nottingham. With these, by agreement, we met the Lincolneers at North Searle, (now spelt North Scarle), which is about ten miles from Gainsborough, upon Thursday in the evening, where we tarried until two of the clock in the morning, and then with our whole body advanced towards Gainsborough. (Which amounted, according to the letter to Sir John Wraye, to nineteen or twenty troops of horse, and three or four of dragoons).
>
> About a mile and a half from the town we met a forlorn hope of the enemy of near 100 horse. Our dragooners laboured to beat them back; but not alighting off their horses, the enemy charged them, and made them retire unto their main body. We advanced, and came to the bottom of a steep hill; we could not well get up but by some tracks, (in the joint report this hill is called a coney warren), which our men assaying to do, the body of the enemy endeavoured to hinder, wherein we prevailed, and got the top of the hill. This was done by the Lincolneers, who had the vanguard.
>
> When we all recovered the top of the hill, we saw a great body of the enemy's horse facing us, at about a musket-shot or less distance, and a good reserve of a full regiment of horse behind it. We endeavoured to put our men into as good order as we could. The enemy in the meantime advanced towards us, to take us at disadvantage; but, in such order as we were, we charged their great body. I having the right wing, we came up horse to horse, where we disputed it with our swords and pistols a pretty time, all keeping close order, so that one could not break the other. At last, they a little shrinking, our men perceiving it, pressed in upon them, and immediately routed this whole body, some flying on one side and others on the other of the enemy's reserve; and our men pursuing them had chase and execution about five or six miles.
>
> I perceiving this body, which was the reserve, standing still

unbroken, kept back my major (Whalley) from the chase; and with my own troop and the other of my regiment, in all being three troops, we got into a body. In this reserve stood General Cavendish, who one while faced me, another while faced four of the Lincoln troops, (these Lincoln troops were yet unbroken according to the letter to Sir John Wraye), which was all of ours that stood upon the place, the rest being engaged in the chase. At last General Cavendish charged the Lincolneers, and routed them. Immediately I fell on his rear with my three troops, which did so astonish him, that he did give over the chase, and would fain have delivered himself from me. But I pressing on forced (Carlyle inserts the word "them" here), down a hill, having good execution of them; and, below the hill, drove the general with some of his soldiers into a quagmire, where my captain-lieutenant slew him with a thrust under his short ribs. The rest of the body was wholly routed, not one man staying on the place.

After the defeat, which was so total, we relieved the town with such powder and provision as we brought with us. We had notice that there were six troops of horse and 300 foot on the other side of the town, about a mile off us. We desired some foot of my Lord Willoughby's, about 400, and, with our horse and these foot, marched towards them; when we came towards the place where their horse stood, we went back with my troops to follow two or three troops of the enemy's, who retired into a small village at the bottom of the hill. When we recovered the hill, we saw in the bottom, about a quarter of a mile from us, a regiment of foot; after that, another; after that, the Marquis of Newcastle's own regiment, consisting in all of about fifty foot colours, and a great body of horse, which, indeed, was Newcastle's army, which, coming so unexpectedly, put us to new consultations.

My Lord Willoughby and I being in the town, agreed to call off our foot. I went to bring them off, but before I returned, divers of the foot were engaged, the enemy advancing with his whole body. Our foot retreated in disorder, and with some loss got the town, where now they are. Our horse also came off with some trouble, being wearied with the long fight and their horses tired, yet faced the enemy's fresh horse, and by several removes got off without the loss of one man, the enemy following the rear with a great body.

The rest of the letter urges the Committee to send 2000 foot to the relief of the town.

With regard to this last retreat of the horse in the face of a superior enemy, the other report is more explicit. It says:

> Colonel Cromwell was sent to command the foot to retire and to draw off the horse. By the time he came to them, the enemy was marching up the hill. The foot did retire disorderly into the town, which was not much above a quarter of a mile from them; upon whom the enemy's horse did some small execution. The horse did also retire in some disorder, about half a mile, until they came to the end of a field where a passage was; where by the endeavour of Colonel Cromwell, Major Whalley, and Captain Ayscoghe, a body was drawn up. With these we faced the enemy, stayed their pursuit, and opposed them with about four troops of Colonel Cromwell's and four Lincoln troops; the enemy's body in the meantime increasing very much from the army.
>
> But such was the goodness of God, giving courage and valour to our men and officers, that whilst Major Whalley and Captain Ayscoghe, sometimes the one with four troops, faced the enemy, sometimes the other, to the exceeding glory of God be it spoken, and the great honour of those two gentlemen, they with this handful faced the enemy so, and dared them to their teeth in at the least eight or nine several removes, the enemy following at their heels; and they, though their horses were exceedingly tired, retreating in order, near carbine shot of the enemy, who thus followed them, firing upon them; Colonel Cromwell gathering up the main body and facing them behind those two lesser bodies, that in despite of the enemy we brought off our horse in this order, without the loss of two men.

These two narratives, in spite of the absence of full stops and the confused construction of the sentences, describe the battle clearly enough. No circumstances could have better displayed Cromwell's genius as a cavalry leader. No problem is more difficult to solve than how to attack an enemy drawn up ready for the encounter, with squadrons disordered by broken ground; unless it is how to withdraw them, when tired out, in face of a fresh and superior foe. Yet both these problems Cromwell solved with success in the course of a couple of hours. His squadrons displayed a flexibility and steadiness quite marvellous, when the clumsy drill of the day is considered.

In all the wonderful and complex evolutions described in the old military works, quoted in Chapter 2, there is not a single example given of how to form line from column. Yet here we find Cromwell's troopers, after straggling up through the steep slopes of the rabbit warren, formed up and charging before the Royalists, only some 200 yards away, can take advantage of their confusion. Defeat in such a position meant absolute ruin, for the broken squadrons could never have rallied had they been flung back over the crest among the rabbit-holes. Both the temerity and skill of the attack are admirable. Admirable, too, is the conduct of the retreat during the afternoon—the steady falling back by alternate squadrons, always slipping away from the enemy, yet never giving him a favourable opportunity to charge.

The Roundhead troopers showed a great superiority to the Cavaliers in manoeuvring, the inevitable result of more careful drill and more exact discipline. Had the Royalists been able to form their order of battle before Cromwell's troopers had slipped out of their reach, they must have ridden over men and horses exhausted by severe fighting and a prolonged pursuit.

Sir T. Fairfax Joins Cromwell

The defeat of Cavendish's horse had given Cromwell the opportunity of passing a small quantity of ammunition and provisions into Gainsborough, but he was in no condition to oppose, with his horse alone, the advance of Newcastle's whole army, which amounted to 6000 or 8000 men. He therefore fell back, after the actions of the 29th July, to Lincoln, and thence to Stamford, where, it will be remembered, he had left his foot on his advance to relieve Gainsborough.

Meanwhile, Newcastle had lost no time in investing Gainsborough and in planting his cannon against the place. Although Lord Fairfax, from Hull, had sent 200 foot and some five or six cannon by water into the town a few days before the arrival of Newcastle, and though Cromwell had thrown a few supplies into it, it was not in a condition to sustain a prolonged siege. The population was, for the most part, Royalist. When Newcastle's cannon opened, the town caught fire, and Willoughby found great difficulty in stopping the conflagration and keeping order in the place. He therefore accepted terms to surrender the town with its artillery, and to march out with arms, baggage, &c. (Willoughby's report to the House, *Cromwelliana*). On the 31st July he retreated to Lincoln, but not considering himself strong enough to hold so exposed a position, he fell back a day or two afterwards to Boston.

Newcastle was now on the frontier of the Eastern Association. He had received the king's order to press on towards the Thames without waiting to besiege Hull. But with an army constituted as his this was impossible. The Fairfaxes were acting with their usual energy. They had collected 700 horse, occupied Beverley, and raided through the eastern Riding. On one occasion, they defeated a party of horse at Stamford Bridge, near York. The Yorkshire Royalists were clamouring to be led back into their own county. The day he arrived before Gloucester, Charles received Newcastle's reply to his order, he wrote:

> The gentlemen of the country, who had the best regiments and were among the best officers, utterly refused to march, except Hull were first taken; and that he had not strength enough to march and leave Hull securely blocked up.—Clarendon, vol. ii.

Neither in the west did the Royalists display combination or vigour. Maurice, after taking Dorchester, Weymouth, and Poole, turned back west again and besieged Exeter, whilst Carnarvon rejoined the king, who was detained before Gloucester. Massey by frequent sallies delayed the besiegers' works, and even swept the cattle they had collected into the fortress.

Meanwhile, the Parliamentary leaders were exerting themselves to recover lost ground. They directed Essex to relieve Gloucester, gave Waller the command of a fresh army raised in London, and sent Manchester to Cambridge with 4000 men. *(Mercurius Civicus,* 16th August, *King's Pamphlets).*

Whilst Newcastle threatened the Eastern Association, Cromwell strained every nerve to repel him. On the 31st the latter was at Huntingdon, having left his forces at Stamford; and on this day, he wrote the account of the actions near Gainsborough, quoted in the last chapter. The Houses highly appreciated the morale effect of the victory over Cavendish's horse, coming as it did in the midst of reverses elsewhere. They directed that 2000 more men be sent to Cromwell out of the Eastern Association, each with a month's pay in his pocket; and that £3000 out of the assessments on those counties be paid him for his troops. (*Cromwelliana, Perf. Diur.* 4th August).

Meanwhile, he was stirring up the county committees to do their utmost. On the 6th August, he wrote to the committee of the Association at Cambridge:

> You see by this enclosed how sadly your affairs stand. Its no longer disputing, but out instantly all you can. Raise all your bands; send them to Huntingdon; get up what volunteers you can; hasten your horses. Send these letters to Norfolk, Suffolk, and Essex without delay. I beseech you spare not, but be expeditious and industrious! Almost all our foot have quitted Stamford; there is nothing to interrupt an enemy but our horse, that is considerable! You must act lively; do it without distraction; neglect no means.—Carlyle, vol. i. On the 2nd he had written the letter to the young men and maids of Huntingdon, quoted in Chapter 4.

The enclosed referred to was a letter from Willoughby at Boston, in which he informs Cromwell that his force had been falling away rapidly from desertion since the surrender of Gainsborough, and that he was now very weak. Cromwell saw the danger of the Royalists getting possession of the low marshy country near the Wash, where his horse could not act, and whence it would be very difficult to dislodge them again. On the 8th he went to Peterborough, having been a few days before at Cambridge interviewing the committee. On this day he again writes to them explaining the position in more detail:—

> Finding our foot much lessened at Stamford, and having a great train and many carriages, I held it not safe to continue there, but presently, after my return from you, I ordered the foot to quit that place and march into Holland, (low country southwest of the Wash), which they did on Monday last. I was the rather induced to do so because of the letter I received from my Lord Willoughby, a copy whereof I sent you. I am now at Peterborough, whither I came this afternoon.
> I was no sooner come but Lieutenant-Colonel Wood sent me word from Spalding that the enemy was marching with twelve flying colours of horse and foot within a mile of Swinstead, so that I hope it was a good providence of God that our foot were at Spalding; it much concerns your association and the kingdom that so strong a place as Holland is, be not possessed by them. If you have any foot ready to march, send them away to us with all speed. I fear lest the enemy should press in upon our foot; he being thus far advanced towards you, I hold it very fit that you should hasten your horse at Huntingdon and what

you can speedily raise at Cambridge unto me.

I dare not go into Holland with my horse, lest the enemy should advance with his whole body of horse this way into your association, (*i.e.* more to the west, *via* Peterborough), but am ready endeavouring to get my Lord Gray's and the Northamptonshire horse to me, that so, if we be able, we may fight the enemy, or retreat unto you with our whole strength. I beseech you hasten your leavers, what you can, especially those of the foot; quicken all our friends with new letters upon this occasion, which I believe you will find to be a true alarm. The particulars I hope to be able to inform you speedily of more punctually, having sent in all haste to Colonel Wood for that purpose.

The money I brought with me is so poor a pittance when it comes to be distributed amongst all my troops that, considering their necessity, it will not half clothe them, they were so far behind; if we have not more money speedily they will be exceedingly discouraged. I am sorry you put me to write thus often, it makes it seem a needless importunity in me; whereas, in truth, it is a constant neglect of those that should provide for us. Gentlemen, make them able to live and subsist that are willing to spend their blood for you. I say no more, but rest, &c.—*Fairfax Correspondence*, Civil Wars, vol. i.

The month of August must have been a most anxious one for Cromwell. Newcastle lingered about Newark, Grantham, and Lincoln, unwilling or unable to persuade his troops to advance. At last, about the middle of the month, he moved up the Trent, appeared before Nottingham, and summoned the town. Being refused admittance, he lay before it four days. Then the activity of the Fairfaxes at Beverley and Hull made itself felt, and Newcastle gave way to the entreaties of his Yorkshire officers. Probably he was not difficult to persuade, but preferred his independent command in the north to a fusion with the king's Oxford army. An advance, too, was certain to be hotly contested.

Manchester had reached the neighbourhood of Cambridge with reinforcements; and though the gathering of the harvest had delayed the assembling of the local trained bands, Cromwell had succeeded in collecting a considerable force in Holland and about Peterborough. The Royalists had tasted the quality of his horse at Grantham and Gainsborough, and knew that wherever he opposed them hot fighting must be expected. Besides, rumours of the advance of a Scotch army into England were already prevalent. It was well known that the negotiations between the English and Scotch parliaments were progressing favourably.

About the 20th August, therefore, Newcastle broke up his camp before Nottingham and retreated on York, leaving, as before, a strong party of horse with the garrison at Newark. (See old newspapers in the *King's Pamphlets*, for Newcastle's movements during August). Remaining but a few days in York, about the first week in September he advanced on Hull, driving Sir Thomas Fairfax out of Beverley.

On arriving before Hull, he commenced a regular siege of the place, which had a garrison of some 1200 foot and 400 horse. (*Short Memorial*, T. Fairfax). The town could not be properly invested, as the Parliament held command of the sea, and thus kept open the communication to the port by river. Reinforcements, supplies, and ammunition could therefore be sent in, and the Fairfaxes were soldiers who would avail themselves of every advantage. They commenced by cutting the sluices and flooding the ground where Newcastle was commencing his batteries. The latter was obliged to approach by the banks and devise means of draining off the water. In return, he cut off the water supply of the town. (According to Rushworth, Newcastle commenced the siege on the 3rd September).

One effect of Newcastle's advance south of the Humber had been a revival of unrest and excitement among the Royalists of the Associated Counties. Lynn, a port on the south-eastern corner of the Wash, became particularly unquiet, and on the 1st September the mayor definitely declared for the king. Manchester, accompanied by Cromwell and Hobart, immediately marched thither. On arriving, they found the place secure against assault, and were obliged to construct batteries against it. Though too late to obtain Newcastle's direct assistance, the Royalists in Lynn might hope to detain Manchester's army, and prevent its going to the assistance of Fairfax. Cromwell constructed his batteries at Old Lynn, and commenced battering the town fortifications from that side.

But in a day or two he was sent with the horse to Spalding, to guard the siege against attacks from Newark; this was about the second week in September. (Cromwell was very hard up for money. It was at this time he wrote the letter to St. John, already quoted). He very soon pushed up into the north of the county with part of his force. Fairfax had no use for his horse, which now amounted to some twenty-five troops, in Hull. He desired, therefore, to send them across into Lincolnshire to join Cromwell, who consequently moved towards the Humber to meet them.

Some of the latter's forces were at Barton on the 18th September, nearly opposite Hull, (*A True Relation from Hull*, by T. May, dated the 19th September, *King's Pamphlets),* to meete with our Horse which are going over to them at every tyde, as many as can goe in the boates. There goes 21 Troops, and 4 Troops stay in the Town." The enemy had burnt all the larger boats, so small ones had to be used, carrying only four or five troopers at a time. On the 22nd September Cromwell went himself into Hull to concert measures with the Fairfaxes, and remained a day or two there. Willoughby also came in on the 23rd, but left again that day. (See *Court Informer* of the 2nd to the 9th October, *King's Pamphlets;* Rushworth says Cromwell went to Hull on the 26th).

Apparently, the method of ferrying the horses across in small boats proved too slow. The enemy had tried to establish a fort commanding the Humber below Hull, but it was demolished by a sally of the garrison. The horse were then shipped at Hull in sea-going vessels, and landed at Saltfleet, on the Lincolnshire side of the mouth of the Humber. (*Court Informer* 25th September to 2nd October; *True Informer* 30th September to 7th October, in *King's Pamphlets; Cromwelliana;* Rushworth, vol. v.)

On the 26th September Sir Thomas Fairfax went in command. He joined Cromwell and Willoughby, and together their forces amounted to some 2000 or 3000 horse. These were not of uniform quality. Cromwell's own regiment and Willoughby's Lincolnshire horse were excellent, soldiers proved at Gainsborough, but the newer levies from the Eastern Association were indifferent; they were probably pressed men. In his letter to St. John of the 11th September, he says, (Carlyle, vol. i. previously quoted in chap. 4):

> Many of my Lord of Manchester's Troops are come to me: very bad and mutinous, not to be confided in.

They had apparently been raised without a proper organisation for their maintenance and discipline, for Cromwell adds in a postscript:

> There is no care taken how to maintain that Force of Horse and Foot raised and a-raising for my Lord of Manchester. He hath net one able to put on. The Force will fall if some help not. Weak counsels and weak actings undo all; all will be lost, if God help not.

Again, writing on the 28th September, he says to Sir W. Spring and Mr. Barrow, members of one of the County Committees:

> I protest unto you many of those men which are of your country's choosing under Captain Johnson are so far from serving you, that, were it not that I have honest troops to master them—although they be well paid, yet they are so mutinous that I may justly fear they would cut my throat.—Carlyle, vol. i.

Fairfax's men were also probably for the most part new levies.

A strong party of horse from Newark had attempted to interfere with the landing of Fairfax's troops, but had fallen back on Cromwell's approach. The united Parliamentary horse then moved southward towards Lord Manchester and the foot at Lynn. Here is Cromwell's own account of the retreat, given in the above-quoted letter of the 28th September:—

> It hath pleased God to bring off Sir Thomas Fairfax his horse over the river from Hull, being about one and twenty troops of horse and dragoons. The Lincolnshire horse, (*i.e.* Royalist horse from Newark and elsewhere), laboured to hinder this work, being about thirty-four colours of horse and dragoons; we marched up to their landing-place, and the Lincolnshire Horse retreated.
>
> After they were come over we all marched towards Holland, and when we came to our last quarter upon the edge of Holland, the enemy quartered within four miles of us, and kept the field all night with his whole body; his intendment, as we conceive, was to fight us; or hoping to interpose betwixt us and our retreat; having received to his thirty-four colours of horse, twenty fresh troops, ten companies of dragoons and about a thousand foot, being General King's own regiment.
>
> With these he attempted our guards and our quarters; and if God had not been merciful, had ruined us before we had known of it, the five troops we set to keep the watch failing much of their duty. But we got to horse, and retreated in good order, with the safety of all our horse of the Association, not losing four of them that I hear of, and we got five of theirs. And for this we are exceedingly bound to the goodness of God, who brought our troops off with so little loss.

It was not advisable to fight the Royalists in Lincolnshire until

Manchester brought up the foot. Their horse were superior in numbers, and supported by a good regiment of foot. Many of the Parliamentary horse were, as has been seen, of indifferent quality, and mutinous. Their conduct during the skirmish with the outposts had showed that they were not reliable. Their leaders would not be justified in engaging them in a fight against odds. Manchester had taken Lynn on the 16th September, but was still in that neighbourhood settling the garrison and quieting the country. The country gentlemen, many of whom were Royalists, had become restless on Newcastle's advance into Lincolnshire. The impressment of men as soldiers was unpopular, the burden of the war pressed heavily on all classes, and there was much discontent.

The murmurs of the disaffected became louder and more openly expressed. One Captain Margery, a man apparently of low extraction, was raising a troop of horse in the Association. He was accused of requisitioning horses without authority, and of taking them, not only from known malignants, but also from men against whom no opposition to Parliament had been proved. One of the Committees supported the accusers and censured Margery. Cromwell, in his letter of the 28th September, takes his part. Margery was indeed a man after his own heart. If he had, perhaps, once or twice made a mistake and taken a horse unjustly, better so than that the Parliament's cause should suffer for want of horses.' Any individual beast could be returned, or its owner compensated, but Margery's zeal should be commended instead of censured. He wishes that all such men "accounted troublesome to the country" be sent to him, where they will do good service, he says:

> Gentlemen, it may be it provokes some spirits to see such plain men made Captains of Horse. It had been well that men of honour and birth had entered into these employments; but why do they not appear? Who would have hindered them? But seeing it was necessary the work must go on, better plain men than none;—but best to have men patient of wants, faithful and conscientious in their employment.

The best way to prevent discontent from breaking out into open opposition was to render all hope of outside assistance impossible. This could be most easily effected by clearing Lincolnshire of the Royalist forces, which, based upon Newark, raided in all directions and kept that county and Nottinghamshire in a state of unrest. Manchester, therefore, having settled affairs at Lynn, marched through the fens to Boston about the beginning of October. At the same time, he sent a reinforcement of 500 foot under Sir John Meldrum to Hull, apparently by sea. At Boston Cromwell, Willoughby, and Sir T. Fairfax joined him, and he was now at the head of a considerable and well-appointed force.

Immediately to the north of Boston and about twelve miles off lay the castle and town of Bullingbrooke (or Bolingbroke). The castle was a stronghold of the Royalists, who were also fortifying Wainfleet, with a view apparently of completing a line of fortified posts from the Trent to the sea, running from Newark through Lincoln, Bullingbrooke, and Wainfleet, and thus preventing Manchester's advance to the relief of Hull. It was determined to seize Bullingbrooke, break up this line, and clear Lincolnshire of Royalists.

Accordingly, on the 9th October, Manchester advanced with the foot to Bullingbrooke, occupied the town, and summoned the castle. The governor, however, refused to surrender, and Manchester thereupon made preparations for a siege. His headquarters were fixed at Kirkby, a village about a mile off, the foot being quartered there, at Stickford, and other villages close by. Ten companies under Sir Miles Hubbard occupied Bullingbrooke town, where the enemy had fortified and garrisoned the church, as well as the castle outside. On Manchester's approach, he had abandoned Wainfleet. The horse were pushed some eight or ten miles out on the Lincoln side, to protect the siege against attacks from that place and Newark.

Their headquarters were at Horncastle, with outposts as far as Edlington, three miles beyond, and the regiments were quartered in various villages about, with orders to assemble at Horncastle in case of alarm. Fairfax commanded that night. Cromwell and Willoughby were at Kirkby with Manchester. It was anticipated that the Royalists would try to interrupt Manchester's advance, and the horse had been worked hard for the last few days at scouting and outpost duties.

On the 10th the outpost at Edlington reported the advance of the enemy. Fairfax sent out a reconnoitring party, which discovered nothing. Manchester himself rode to Horncastle, and on obtaining further information gave orders in the afternoon that the horse should be assembled there. In truth, Sir John Henderson, the governor of Newark, was advancing with a strong force of horse and dragoons from Lincoln. The Parliamentary troops lay scattered in their billets in villages, some of which were a good way off, and time was required to collect them. As they were assembling at the end of Horncastle nearest Bullingbrooke, the Royalist horse entered it at the other from Lincoln. Some skirmishing ensued in the streets, and the troops of Captains Moody and Player, who had been on outpost in the Lincoln direction, were cut off. They, however, charged the enemy with such determination that they cut their way through two bodies of the Royalists with little loss. Captain Johnson's troop also, in drawing into the rendezvous, fell in with a party of the enemy, but being at first mistaken for Royalists, they not only got through, but carried off twelve prisoners.

Lord Manchester, finding that many troops were still absent, gave orders towards evening to fall back to Kirkby and Bullingbrooke Hill, Henderson appears to have made no attempt to interfere with the retreat, and during the night the whole of the Parliamentary horse were safely assembled.

The next morning, the 11th, news was received that Henderson was advancing, and Manchester drew up his whole force on Bullingbrooke Hill to receive him. Three troops were sent to Stickney, three or four more to Tattershal, to prevent parties of the enemy cutting in between the army and its base at Boston. (These detachments were posted during the night of the 10th and 11th. It is not clear whether they rejoined before the fight. See *A True Relation*, &c.)

By twelve o'clock the rest of the horse were drawn up on the hill. They were formed into three lines—Cromwell led the van, formed of his own and Manchester's regiments and some other troops; Fairfax commanded the main body, which consisted of his own Yorkshire horse; the rear was apparently under Sir Miles Hubbard. The foot were not yet ready, but as the enemy had not appeared, the horse were ordered to advance. It is said that Cromwell "was no way satisfied that we should fight, our horse being extremely wearied with hard duty two or three dayes together."

Five troops were drawn out to form the "forlorn hope," under Quartermaster-General Vermuden, and the advance began—the Puritan troopers singing a psalm as they rode down the hill. After they had advanced a mile, the forlorn hope first descried the enemy. Regiment after regiment appeared in turn, until in a few minutes Henderson's whole force, 74 colours of horse and 21 of dragoons, appeared advancing in good order. They, too, were formed in three lines—Sir William Saville led the van, Sir W. Withrington the main body, behind that again rode the reserve. Though the Parliamentary squadrons were fewer than the Royalist, their *cadres* were stronger, so the actual numbers were about equal. The old report says:

> We had not many more than halfe so many colours of horse and dragooners, but I beleeve we had as many men, besides our foot.
>
> On a fair plain, between two gently rising hillocks near the hamlet of Winceby, the two forces met. Both threw out their dragoons, who dismounted and opened fire. The horse on either side checked to close up and order their ranks, but not for long. In a few minutes, Cromwell's and Manchester's cuirassiers were seen advancing.

✦✦✦✦✦✦

The account given in the *Fairfax Correspondence*, vol. i., apparently not signed, says that "the armies faced one another about one hour," but this does not agree with others. Vicars and the *True Relation* say Colonel Cromwell fell with brave resolution upon the enemy immediately after their dragoons had given him the first volley.

✦✦✦✦✦✦

On they came—a solid wall of steel and iron, the troopers pressing knee to knee. Right out in front rode Cromwell himself. Henderson's dragoons greeted them with a volley as they trotted steadily forward; and so nimble were these musketeers that, as the heavy mass rushed at the charge on Saville's buff-clad Cavaliers, they let fly a second volley at them at half pistol-shot. Cromwell's charger pitched forward, shot dead, and rolled over his rider; and as the latter endeavoured to extricate himself the *mêlée* joined over his head. A Cavalier knocked him down as he rose, only to be himself cut down by a Puritan trooper. One of his men then brought Cromwell "a poor horse," and flinging himself into the saddle he again joined in the fight. Saville's men had not been able to stand a moment against the shock of those heavy, steel-clad warriors; and pursuers and pursued had together dashed into the midst of Withrington's ranks as he moved forward to support his van.

For a moment, a desperate hand-to-hand fight ensued; and then Fairfax's Yorkshire men, who had pressed on eagerly in Cromwell's support, crashed into Withrington's flank and drove his shattered squadrons into and through their reserve. Before the Parliamentary rear-guard could arrive on the scene, the whole Royalist force was flying in utter rout. The Roundheads pursued fiercely, killing their enemies with the sword, driving them into bogs and rivers, where they were smothered or drowned. In a quarter of an hour the battle was over. The Royalist dragoons, unable to remount in time, were taken or killed to a man. The Parliamentary foot were not up soon enough to see anything of the fight. The pursuit was pressed beyond Horncastle, some five miles or more in all. The Parliamentary reports claim that some 300 of the enemy were killed, between 100 and 200 drowned, and 700 or 800 taken, with eighteen colours.

Withrington himself admits the losses were heavy, not many killed, he thinks, but 800 utterly dispersed. He attributes his defeat to the superiority of the Roundhead cavalry. "Their horse are very good and extraordinarily armed," he says. The Parliament are said to have lost only twenty killed, but a great many wounded. In those days, far more men were killed during the pursuit than in the battle, and this always holds good of hand-to-hand fights.

******

The account of this fight has been collated from Vicars, quoted by Carlyle, vol. i.; *A True Relation* in *King's Pamphlets*, the account in the *Fairfax Correspondence*, vol. i.; T. Fairfax's *Short Memorial*; Rushworth, vol. v.

******

At Winceby none of those difficulties arose which necessitated such tactical skill in handling the troops in the two fights near Gainsborough. It was a fair fight between two equally-matched opponents on favourable ground. The Roundheads proved themselves conclusively the superior. Cromwell's promptitude in the attack and the steady discipline of his well-drilled troopers proved irresistible. There is no mention of a dispute with sword and pistol before the Royalists gave way, as at Gainsborough. The well-ordered charge of the heavy Roundhead cavalry broke, by sheer weight of man and horse, through the looser ranks of their lighter armed opponents. Withrington himself says that Saville's troopers broke at once. Fairfax's well-timed flank attack completed the victory. The action is a lesson in cavalry leading for all times.

That night Manchester occupied Horncastle with his foot. On the very same day Lord Fairfax and Meldrum had sallied out from Hull and made a determined assault on Newcastle's siege works. They succeeded in entering the trenches at the first rush, but were beaten back with loss. Reinforced from the town, they again stormed the batteries, and this time drew off several guns, spiked others, and destroyed the platforms and magazines. Hotly pressed by the Royalists in their retreat, they succeeded in getting back safely into the town after severe fighting close under the walls. Among the trophies, they carried back was one of the two great French cannon called the "Queen's Pocket Pistols." The next morning, they found that Newcastle had raised the siege during the night. Exposed without proper shelter in marshy fields and flooded trenches, constantly annoyed by the garrison, numbers of his men had fallen victims to disease. Numbers had also deserted. The defeat at Winceby and the successful sally completed their demoralisation.

Winter was approaching; the town as far from capture as ever. Without the command of the river, it was impossible to prevent the Parliament from relieving it whenever it chose. Manchester's army was now free to advance, in a few days it might be between Hull and York. The Scots were preparing to advance into England. A Parliamentary force had been sent by sea to Berwick, had seized and garrisoned the town, and thus opened the gate for the Scots. Newcastle, therefore, wisely determined to fall back, and accordingly in the night of the 11th—12th he withdrew his guns, broke up his works, and retreated leisurely to York.

Manchester, in reporting the capture of Lynn and his junction with Cromwell, Willoughby, and Fairfax at Boston, to Parliament about the 6th October, had stated that his design was to press Newcastle in rear, whilst the latter was engaged with the Scots in front. (*Cromwelliana. Perfect Diurnal* of the 9th October). But the Scots were not yet ready, and the time for combined action had not yet arrived. Manchester's forces were therefore employed in suppressing such Royalist parties as were still in the field in Lincolnshire, Leicestershire, Derbyshire, and the neighbouring counties, and in besieging such towns and castles as were held for the king. A lull, therefore, occurred in this theatre of war for some weeks.

Meanwhile, important events had taken place in the south and west during the months of September and October. Essex, who had been lying about Kingston, was reinforced on the 22nd August by four regiments of London trained bands and auxiliaries. He then mustered some 8000 infantry, but was weak in horse, and marched to Aylesbury, where some of the Eastern Association horse joined him. Proceeding thence by Bicester, Brackley, Chipping Norton, and Stow, he drove back the Royalist horse, which, under Rupert and Wilmot, had been sent to attack him on the Cotswolds, and on the 4th September reached the edge of the plateau where it falls steeply into the valley of the Severn,

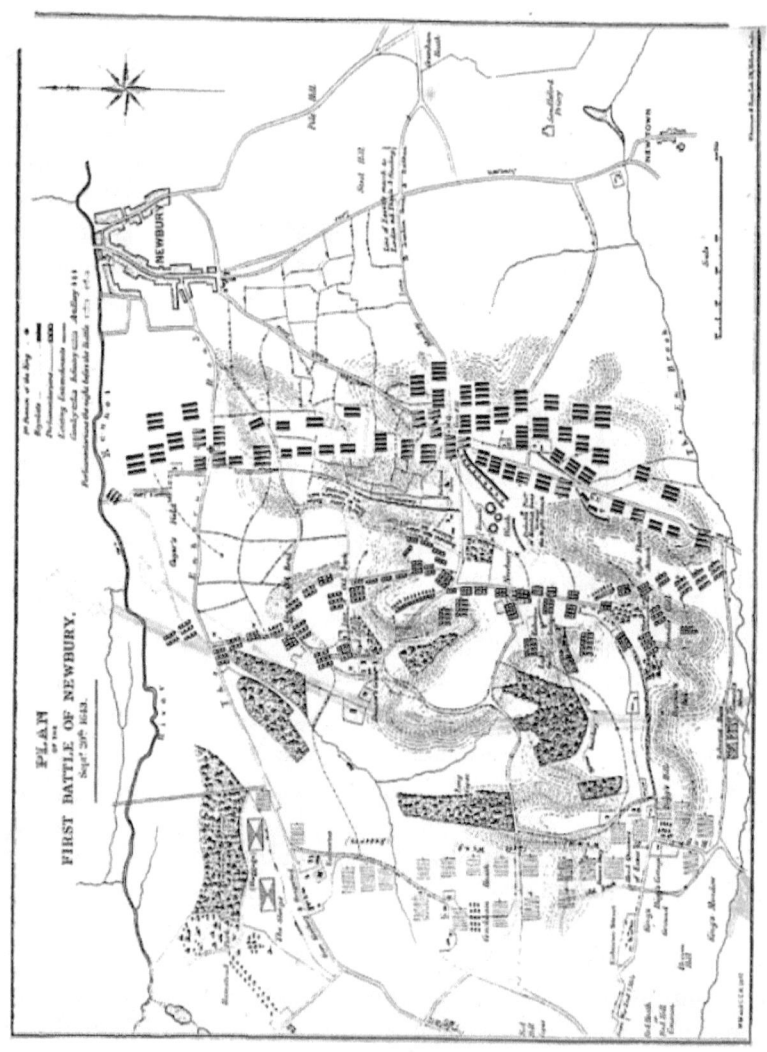

near Prestbury. That night his watch-fires were seen in Gloucester, where the garrison had but one barrel of powder left.

The next day, Charles broke up the siege and marched across Essex's communications to Sudeley Castle. Essex moved on to Gloucester and relieved the town with ammunition and supplies. Then wishing to return to London, he, by way of a feint, marched to Tewkesbury on the 10th, which drew the king on to Evesham, but countermarching rapidly in the night of the 13th he surprised two Royalist regiments of horse at Cirencester early in the morning of the 15th, killing or taking them all.

The king, finding himself out-manoeuvred, followed rapidly, and Rupert with the horse overtook Essex at Aldbourn Chase on the 18th. His march being thus delayed, the latter on starting from Hungerford the next day, found Charles already in front of him near Newbury. The king was in position between the Kennet and the Embrook, which flows into it from the south-west, and here, on the 20th, Essex attacked him, and, after severe fighting, which lasted all day, broke through towards Reading. Reaching this town, he withdrew the garrison and retreated to London. Waller, who lay at Windsor, made no effort throughout the campaign to support him. At Newbury, the king lost two of his ablest soldiers, Lords Falkland and Carnarvon.

In the west, Exeter had surrendered to Prince Maurice on the 4th September, and Dartmouth a few days later. In Ireland, Lord Ormond had patched up a truce with the rebels, and Charles could now withdraw the army thence to England for use against the Parliament.

Cromwell in the Midlands

Hitherto both sides had displayed a lamentable lack of military skill. The nation had long enjoyed the blessings of peace, and its leaders knew little of the art of war. But the strategy of the Parliament had been far the worse of the two. The king had, at any rate; shown some energy in consolidating his position in the west, and in clearing out the Parliamentary garrisons, even if he had undertaken no vigorous forward movement. This was all the more necessary for him, as organised as his army was, it was almost impossible to induce the levies raised on Commissions of Array to move far from their homes when threatened by the proximity of a hostile garrison.

On their side the Parliamentary leaders had done absolutely nothing calculated to ensure permanent success. Possessed of far greater and more easily available resources, they made no attempt to employ them in an attack on the positions vital to the King. Pym, whose political energy and strength raised him far above his fellows in the House, was no soldier. His military advisers were incompetent. Essex, slow, inert, and perhaps only half-hearted in the cause, was a palpable failure.

Waller, more energetic and vigorous, could design nothing better than an isolated expedition which could have but little effect on the general course of the war. Both had received a military training on the continent, but the strategy of the professional soldiers of the day, under whom they had served, was always rather to avoid defeat than to gain a victory, to prolong a war than to finish it. Both possessed some tactical skill, neither could initiate a combined and vigorous strategy.

Under such conditions the war languished. Sir Jacob Astley occupied Reading with 3000 foot and 500 horse. Rupert and Essex conducted a few desultory manoeuvres in the Midlands. Waller attempted the siege of Basing House, but his London regiments deserted him.

Both king and Parliament looked for help from outside. The troops from Ireland were already on their way to reinforce the Royal army. Late in October 500 men were landed at Minehead and Bristol, others disembarked at Chester. The treaty between the Parliament and the Scots was now complete, and the army assembling near Edinburgh would soon be ready to march. But the Scots had been careful that their assistance should only be given on sound business conditions. They required £100,000 before their army crossed the border, and a subsidy of £30,000 a month whilst it was employed in England. On these terms, they agreed to keep a force of 21,000 men in the field. The Parliament resorted to a forced loan to raise the necessary funds. Meanwhile recruiting went on busily in London and the Eastern Counties, men being freely impressed for the service.

After Winceby Manchester took Lincoln, and his horse under Cromwell were employed in clearing that county of Royalists. Later, when Rupert in October advanced into Bedfordshire, Cromwell was sent to Huntingdon to oppose him. But Essex detached Skippon from his own army to relieve Manchester's troops on this side. Skippon drove Sir Lewis Dyves out of Newport Pagnel, and Rupert's advance was stopped. The horse of the Eastern Association were then employed in investing Newark. Newcastle, however, again advanced from York, driving back Sir Thomas Fairfax, who had penetrated into South Yorkshire and attempted to recover the clothing towns.

Newcastle's troops occupied the line of the Trent and the Parliamentary horse fell back. A good deal of skirmishing ensued, the London newspapers reporting two reverses to the Leicestershire horse. General King, Newcastle's lieutenant, who was about this time created Lord Eythin, besieged Derby, whilst, on the other side. Lord Fairfax from Hull took Burton and Axholme, and Meldrum carried Gainsborough by assault on the 20th December.

Meanwhile Pym died on the 8th December. Had his death occurred earlier, the war might have ended in a compromise. But Parliament had now gone too far for negotiation. The "root and branch" party were in the ascendant in the Commons, led by Sir Harry Vane and Cromwell, who during this lull in the war was more than once in his seat in the House. The arrival of the Irish contingent also exasperated the king's opponents, and even caused much dissatisfaction among his adherents. Though the troops brought over were Protestants, it was firmly believed that Charles was about to employ Irish Catholics in England. There is no doubt that he endeavoured to obtain 10,000 men from the Catholic leaders, but failed to come to terms with them. At any rate the withdrawal of the English garrison from Ireland left the Protestants there at the mercy of the Irish. Only Monro's Scots remained in Ulster, and these the Parliament took into its pay.

Nor were the troops brought over at all satisfied with their new employment. Their Protestantism had been accentuated by their struggle with the Catholic rebels, and they were by no means pleased at finding themselves allied to Catholic noblemen and a Catholic queen. On the 18th November, 2500 of these troops were landed at Mostyn, near Chester. In conjunction with the local Royalists they took Hawarden and Beeston Castles, and defeated a Parliamentary force at Middlewich. Byron then joined them with a contingent from Oxford, and laid siege to Nantwich.

Sir T. Fairfax was ordered to relieve the town, and marching from Lincolnshire, through Leicestershire with 2300 horse and dragoons, he joined some local foot in South Lancashire, and appeared before the town on the 25th January. A swollen stream separated Byron's horse from the foot, and Fairfax routed the latter before the former could get across; 1500 prisoners were taken, including the famous Colonel George Monk, and of these 800 took the covenant and entered the Parliament's service.

A little before this Newcastle had been repulsed in an attack on Northampton, and he then hurried northwards to meet the Scots who were now advancing. Leaving Dunbar in deep snow, Leven moved southward with 10,000 men. His passage through the difficult defile at Cockburn's-path was covered by a detachment the Parliament had thrown into Berwick by sea. The Scots crossed the border on the 19th January, 1644. Their progress was slow, their troops being raw, provisions short, and the roads bad. (See Sir J. Turner's *Memoirs*). It was on the 5th February before their advanced troops, having avoided the Royalist fortress of Alnwick, reached the Tyne at Corbridge. Here they were checked by Sir Marmaduke Langdale with Newcastle's advanced-guard. Eythin held Newcastle with a strong garrison, whilst the marquis lay with the rest of his army about Sunderland. Leven, who depended on the sea for the transport of his artillery and train, moved to Tynemouth, where he awaited a second detachment which was following him.

When Newcastle quitted the Trent to move north, Manchester made no attempt to follow him, or to take advantage of his retreat. Indeed, both he and Cromwell appear to have been employed on political duty in Parliament a good deal at this time. Newcastle had left a good garrison and a strong body of horse in Newark, under Sir R. Byron, and the Association horse was principally employed in observing them. On one occasion when Cromwell was in London three of the best troops of his own regiment, those commanded by Desborough, Eyres, and Bethell, were surprised in their beds near Sleaford by a party of Newark horse. Six score men and nearly all the horses were taken. An old newspaper says:

> Their loss is much lamented because they were all godly men, (Certain Information, of the 19th February, *King's Pamphlets*).

This is perhaps the only occasion on which any party of this famous regiment was caught napping. Some idea seems to have been entertained at this time of a combined attack by Essex and Manchester on the king at Oxford, and as a first step there followed a movement of part of the Association horse into Bedfordshire and Huntingdon. Early in February a force of 5000 foot and 2000 horse was assembled, partly from Derbyshire, and partly from the Association, under Sir John Meldrum, for the siege of Newark, which was then opened in due form.

About this time, Gloucester was very short of ammunition, and the Parliament had prepared a convoy for its relief. This convoy had been for some time at Warwick, beyond which point it had been found impossible to bring it in safety. Cromwell, who was with the horse in Bedfordshire, was ordered to try and get it through. (*Scottish Dove*, of the 23rd February, *King's Pamphlets*). He however found the Royalists too strongly posted on the road he must follow, so gave up the attempt. He then turned towards Buckingham, and appeared before Hilsden House, some four miles south of the town, where a party of Cavaliers from Oxford had fortified themselves and were harrying the country.

Having no cannon, he carried the place by assault on the 4th March, capturing Sir Charles Denton, Colonel Smith, and 160 men; forty men were killed in the action. Then pressing forward, he reached Banbury, drove the Royalists out of the town into the citadel, but having no means of effecting a breach, he had to withdraw, after driving off a herd of cattle from under the walls of Oxford. (*Mercurius Britannicus*, of the 11th March, *Cromwelliana*). He then placed a garrison of 700 local troops from Bedford and Northampton in Buckingham, which was a very important place, in view of the contemplated advance towards Oxford. The garrison was afterwards reinforced by 1000 regulars from the Eastern Association. Cromwell then returned to Bedford.

The troops of the Association had by this time been placed on a properly organised footing. They were to amount to 14,000 men, (this in addition to the local trained bands), and each county was assessed to contribute a fixed sum weekly to their support—Essex £1687 10s., Suffolk £1875, and so on, the total amounting to £8395. Manchester commanded as the General, Cromwell was Lieutenant-General of the horse, Crawford Major-General of the foot. Crawford was a Scotch soldier of considerable experience, a bigoted Presbyterian, and a staunch advocate of Church discipline and of Church interference in affairs of State.

Such tenets Cromwell detested; indeed, the narrow Presbyterian doctrine was as hateful to him as episcopacy. He and Crawford soon disagreed. On the 10th March he was at Cambridge, where he found a Lieut.-Colonel Packer, whom Crawford had reported to Manchester as an Anabaptist, and therefore unworthy of a commission. Cromwell, as second in command, sent him back to his duty, with the following characteristic letter to Crawford, (Carlyle, vol. i.):—

Sir,—The complaints you have preferred to my Lord against your lieutenant-colonel, both by Mr. Lee and your own letters, have occasioned his stay here—my Lord being employed, in

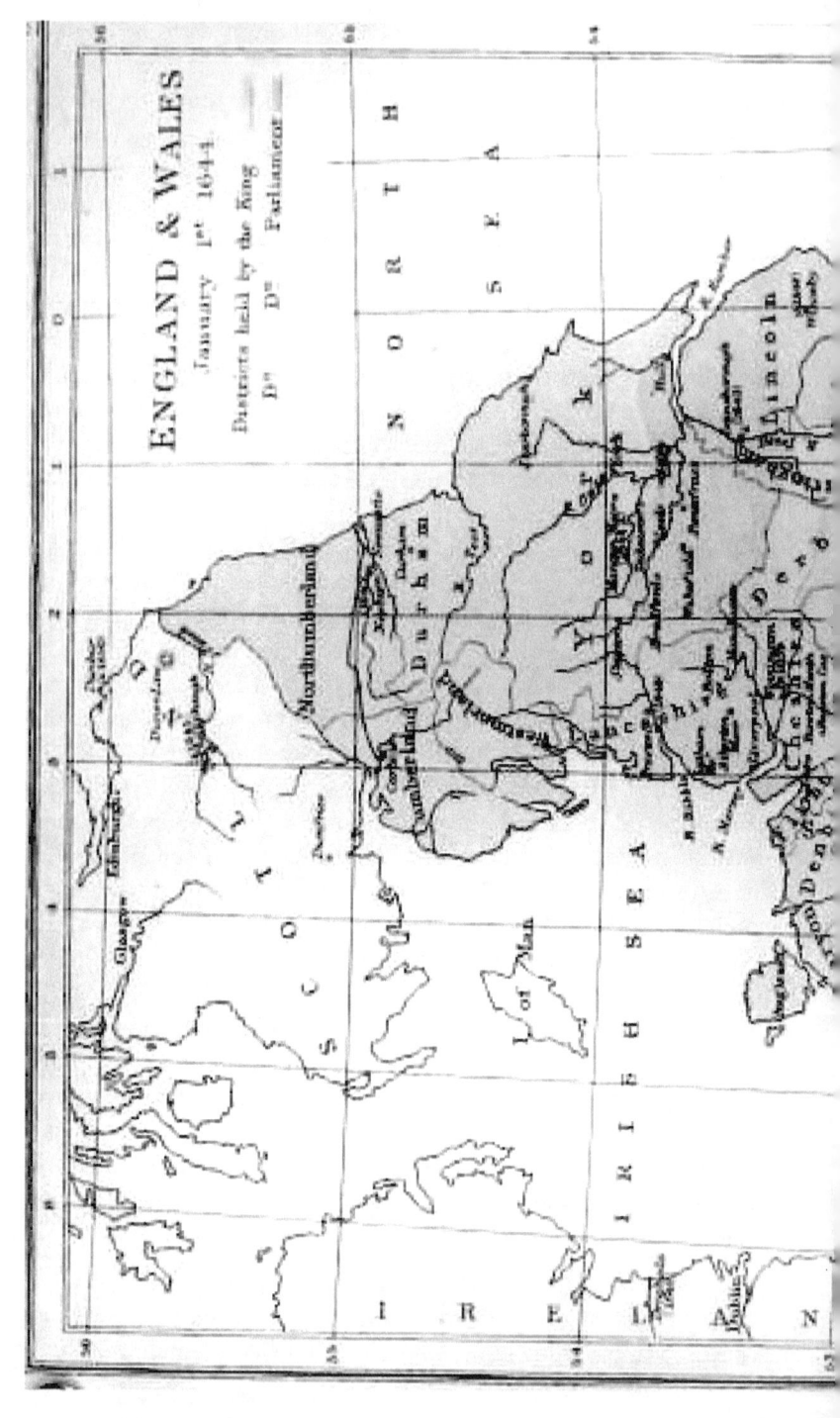

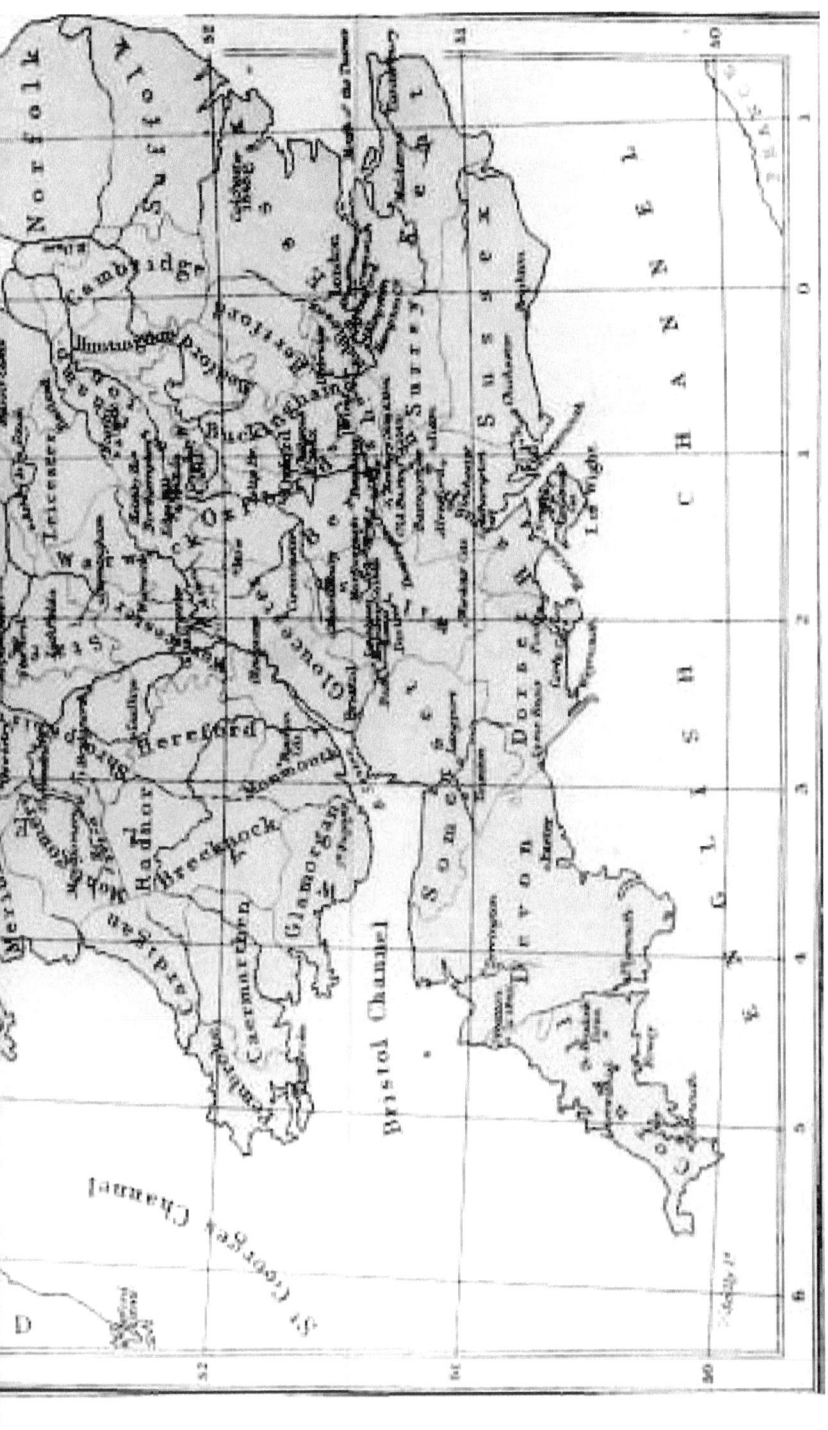

regard of many occasions which are upon him, that he hath not been at leisure to hear him make his defence; which in pure justice, ought to be granted him or any other man before a judgment be passed upon him.

During his abode here, and absence from you, he hath acquainted me what a grief it is to him to be absent from his charge, especially now the regiment is called forth to action; and therefore, asking of me my opinion, I advised him speedily to repair to you. Surely, you are not well advised thus to turn off one so faithful to the cause, and so able to serve you as this man is. Give me leave to tell you, I cannot be of your judgment, if a man notorious for wickedness, for oaths, for drinking, hath as great a share in your affection as one who fears an oath, who fears to sin, that this doth commend your election of men to serve as fit instruments in this work!

Ay, but the man is an Anabaptist. Are you sure of that? Admit he be, shall that render him incapable to serve the public? He is indiscreet! It may be so, in some things; we have all human infirmities. I tell you if you had none but such indiscreet men about you, and would be pleased to use them kindly, you would find as good a fence to you as any you have yet chosen.

Sir, the State, in choosing men to serve it, takes no notice of their opinions; if they be willing faithfully to serve it,—that satisfies. I advised you formerly to bear with men of different minds from yourself; if you had done it when I advised you to it, I think you would not have had so many stumbling-blocks in your way. It may be you judge otherwise; but I tell you my mind. I desire you would receive this man into your favour and good opinion.

I believe if he follow my counsel, he will deserve no other but respect of you. Take heed of being sharp, or too easily sharpened by others, against those to whom you can object but little, but that they square not with you in every opinion concerning matters of religion. If there be any other offence to be charged upon him—that must, in a judicial way, receive determination. I know you will not think it fit my Lord should discharge an officer of the field but in a regulate way. I question whether you or I have any precedent for that.

I have not further to trouble you, but rest

   Your humble servant,

Oliver Cromwell.

Hitherto Manchester, himself no soldier, had listened chiefly to Cromwell's advice on military matters, but since the appointment of Crawford to be his major-general he had, unfortunately for himself, begun to pay more attention to the counsels of the latter. Baillie, the Scotch divine and Commissioner to the English Parliament, writing later, says:

> The Earl of Manchester, a sweet, meek man, did formerly permit Lieutenant-General Cromwell to guide all the army at his pleasure: the man Cromwell is a very wise and active head, universally well-beloved as religious and stout; but a known Independent or favourer of sects. But now our countryman, Crawford, has got a great hand with Manchester, stands high with all that are against sects.— Baillie, ii., dated 16th September, 1644, quoted by Carlyle, vol. i.

The importance of Newark, with its bridge across the Trent, was of such proved importance to the king, that he determined to make a vigorous effort to break up the siege. The task was entrusted to Rupert, who was then at Chester. Marching thence on the 13th March, with the regiments of Tillyer and Broughton lately arrived from Ireland, and some horse, he passed through Bridgenorth and Wolverhampton, picking up any detachments from the Royalist garrisons that could be spared. On the 20th he was joined by two parties of horse under Major-General Porter and Lord Loughborough, at Bingham.

Early on the morning of the 21st, he arrived before Newark, which is built principally on an island, formed by two branches of the Trent. Charging down from Beacon Hill, he dispersed Meldrum's horse, and, when his own foot arrived, drove the besiegers into their works, where they found themselves shut in between Rupert's force and the garrison of the town. The next morning Meldrum capitulated, being allowed to march off with his arms, but surrendering all his artillery and train. (See H.R.H. Prince Rupert's *Raising of the Siege*, &c., *King's Pamphlets;* Rushworth, vol. v.)

This dashing stroke of Rupert's struck such a panic in the neighbouring Parliamentary garrisons, that those of Lincoln, Gainsborough, Crowland, and Sleaford abandoned their posts forthwith. Cromwell and Manchester from Cambridge, Denbigh from Coventry, Gell from Derby, and even Sir Thomas Fairfax from Lancashire, were directed against Rupert; but the latter, having achieved his purpose, retired to

Shrewsbury, and the Parliamentary generals resumed their interrupted operations. It was April, however, before Manchester commenced to move towards his junction with Essex. On the 12th he reached Oundle.

In the south, the campaign of 1644 opened with an important action. In November, 1643, Hopton, reinforced by some troops from Ireland, advanced to Winchester, which Lord Ogle held for the king. He thus again found himself opposed to Waller, who lay at Farnham. The two commanders had apparently been intimate friends before the war broke out, and sometimes corresponded during it. The following extract of a letter from Waller to Hopton shows the detestation with which this civil strife was regarded by many of those who took a most active part in it:

> That great God who is the searcher of my heart knows with what a sad sense I go on upon this service, and with what a perfect hatred I detest this war without an enemy; but I look upon it as sent from God, and that is enough to silence all passion in me. The God of Heaven in His good time send us the blessing of peace, and in the meantime fit us to receive it! We are both upon the stage, and must act such parts as are assigned us in this tragedy. Let us do it in a way of honour and without personal animosities.

Such were the sentiments of the nobler spirits on both sides—of Waller and Hampden, of Falkland and Hopton. But it needed the fiercer enthusiasm of such as Cromwell to accomplish the longed-for peace by the only way possible—the complete defeat of one or the other party.

Hopton, seizing a moment when Waller was weakened by the desertion of many of his Londoners, penetrated, early in December, into Sussex, and seized Arundel Castle. But Waller, reinforced from London, fell upon Hopton's own regiment which he had left at Alton to observe the Farnham garrison, and killed or captured them all. Hopton, who had hoped to raise a considerable force in Sussex and Kent, immediately fell back to Winchester. Waller then recovered Arundel.

During February, the Earl of Forth joined Hopton with 2000 men from Oxford, which brought his army up to some 5000 infantry and 300 horse. Forth remained with him to give advice, but refused to take command. On the 25th March, Waller, whose strength was about the same as his opponent's, lay at East Meon. Hopton moved to Alresford on the 27th, and Waller to Hinton Ampner on the 28th—a false movement, as it placed Hopton almost on his nearest road to Farnham. The latter, seizing his opportunity, occupied a position on a gently-rising ridge between Cheriton Wood and the Itchen, here an insignificant stream, a mile or two north of Hinton Ampner. Here Waller was obliged to attack him on the 29th, in order to regain his communications.

At first, he was unsuccessful, Hopton, on Forth's advice, standing on the defensive. But the impetuosity of some of the Royalist horse engaged them at disadvantage too far in front of the position; they were roughly handled by Hazlerigg's Lobsters, and Forth counselled a retreat during the night. The horse and train retired to Basing House, the foot to Winchester, and afterwards to Andover. Thither Waller followed them, but had to fall back owing to the discontent of his London regiments, and returned to Farnham, sacking Winchester on his way back. He had certainly gained a tactical success, but little or no strategical advantage accrued.

In the north, a campaign, conducted on the methods approved by the soldier of fortune, was dragging along. On the 28th February, Leven, leaving six regiments of foot and some horse below Newcastle, crossed the Tyne, about Ovington, with the remainder, unopposed, and on the 4th March, drew up his forces opposite Bowden Hill, where the marquess occupied a position. Thus, they faced each other for some days in bitter weather, neither daring to attack. Eventually the Royalists fell back to Durham, unmolested by the Scots, who were short of provisions. On the 23rd March Newcastle again advanced, and again the armies faced each other for some time without fighting. The Royalists once more fell back, and the Scots moved leisurely by Essington to Quarendon Hill. They had, meanwhile, captured a fort at Tynemouth, which had previously, prevented Parliamentary ships entering the Tyne.

Had these two commanders been left to themselves, the war might have dragged on indefinitely. But the Parliament had ordered Lord Fairfax to assist the Scots. He therefore sent his son directions to join him for an advance northward. Sir Thomas, after his success at Nantwich, had taken several minor Royalist garrisons in Cheshire. Then crossing the Mersey, he joined the Lancashire forces and drove the Royalists into Lathom House, where he besieged them. His forces were unpaid and mutinous; many deserted. He seems to have lacked Cromwell's genius for organisation and for enforcing discipline. The defence was vigorously conducted by the famous Countess of Derby, and little progress had been made with the siege, when, in compliance with his father's orders, he handed over its conduct to Colonel Rigby, and marched off with 2000 Yorkshire horse.

Newcastle had left Colonel Bellasis in command of a force to garrison York and oppose Fairfax at Hull, and Lambert, who now commanded a small Parliamentary force at Bradford. Hearing of Fairfax's advance, Bellasis concentrated 3000 men at Selby. On the 10th April Lord Fairfax crossed the Ouse ten miles lower down, joined his son, and the next day drove Bellasis out of Selby, capturing him, all his artillery, and 1000 prisoners.

The effect of this action on Newcastle was instantaneous. He quitted Durham on the 13th April, and reached York on the 19th, closely followed by the Scots. Here he mustered 5000 horse and 6000 foot. The horse he sent under Goring southward to attempt a junction with Rupert. To the king he wrote reiterating his entreaties for assistance. Ever since the arrival of the Scots in England he had pointed out that Charles' first effort should be to crush them in order to free his northern army for the contemplated advance southward. The only step Charles had taken towards counteracting the Scotch invasion was to send Montrose to the north with a commission as his Captain-General in Scotland, and with directions to raise an army which would act in Leven's rear; whilst Hamilton, who had believed himself influential enough to restrain the Scotch Committee of Estates, was imprisoned in Pendennis Castle.

Meanwhile, Leven and Fairfax joined forces at Tadcaster on the 20th April, and immediately advanced on York. That city, situated at the junction of the Ouse and the Foss, was favourably placed for defence. Its works were extensive and in good repair, the garrison strong. Therefore, though their united forces mustered 16,000 foot and 4000 horse, (*Short Memorial*; *Mercurius Civicus* May 2nd), the allies found themselves unable to invest the place closely on all sides. Leven occupied Bishopsthorpe and Middlethorpe on the west bank of the Ouse, and Fairfax, Fulford, and Heshington on the east bank. The north side was merely watched by horse till the arrival of reinforcements. (Slingsby's *Memoir*).

Marston Moor

The result of the war during the early spring of 1644 had been, on the whole, unfavourable to the king. The Battle of Cheriton had put an end to his designs on Sussex and Kent; that of Selby had compelled Newcastle to relinquish all action in the field and shut himself up in York. On the other hand, the brilliant relief of Newark by Rupert had proved that the royal armies were capable of great deeds when properly handled, whilst the dissolution of Waller's army, so shortly after his victory, had shown that a large part of the apparently formidable numbers arrayed against the king were not to be relied on for continuous military effort.

Both parties now took earnest counsel how the war might best be carried on. Proposals for a treaty, which had been made during the winter, through foreign envoys and others, had failed as soon as made. Neither side would abate a jot of the fundamental principles for which they were contending, though there was a tendency on the king's part to concede some minor points. Rupert was summoned to Oxford, and on the 26th April a council of war was held, the debates of which extended over several days. Charles' attempt to obtain the services of 10,000 native Irish had failed. In face of the violent opposition of his English Protestant adherents, the concessions of freedom of religion and an independent Parliament in Ireland could not be seriously considered. But on no other terms would the Catholic leaders grant the men.

The council of war determined that the principal effort must be made in the north, with a view of relieving the Marquess of Newcastle, and, if possible, of beating the Scots. To Rupert this task was assigned, and he received orders to collect all the troops he could in Shropshire, Cheshire, and Wales, march into Lancashire, relieve Lathom House, reinforce his troops from Derby's Royalist tenantry, and then march into Yorkshire. Meanwhile, the king would remain about Oxford and prevent Essex and Waller from interrupting Rupert's march, or from overwhelming Maurice, who, tired of investing Plymouth, was now besieging Lyme, in Dorsetshire. Oxford was, by now, surrounded by a ring of fortified towns and posts, such as Bannbury, Abingdon, Marlborough, Farringdon House, and from its salient position formed an admirable base, which threatened an enemy's flank should he attempt to pass it either on the north or south.

It was evident that the crisis of the campaign would occur near York, and every effort should have been directed towards making Rupert as strong as possible. But Maurice, who was wasting his forces in the siege of an unimportant harbour, demanded reinforcements, and in a weak moment Charles granted them.

The Parliament, on its side, had not yet learned that concentration of effort is the base of all sound strategy. Essex was ordered to attack Oxford, Waller to relieve Lyme, where the famous Colonel (afterwards Admiral) Blake was conducting a gallant defence. Both these generals were to be reinforced to about 10,000 men.

Meanwhile, Manchester's movement towards his junction with Essex at Aylesbury had been arrested by the news that a force of Cavalier horse was approaching the Eastern Association. These were Goring, with Newcastle's horse, who had avoided Sir T. Fairfax and reached Newark, plundering everywhere they went. In the last week in April, Manchester was at Stamford, whence he sent forward Cromwell with his horse, who cleared Lincolnshire of marauding parties of Newark Cavaliers and drove them across the Trent, where they joined Goring at Mansfield.

Manchester himself marched to Lincoln, which was still held by the Royalists, and where he arrived on the 3rd May. Cromwell posted his horse so as to cover the siege from any interruption from Goring, and so well did he make his dispositions that, hearing on the 5th that Goring had crossed the Trent, his troopers were assembled and drawn up in little over an hour from the news being received. Goring, finding the outposts on the alert, fell back again. That night Lincoln Castle was stormed with the aid of scaling ladders; Sir Francis Fane, 100 officers and gentlemen, and 800 soldiers being taken. (Goode's *True Relation*, &c.; *King's Pamphlets*).

Manchester next threw a bridge of boats over the Trent at Gainsborough, and Cromwell crossed with 3000 horse, whilst two regiments of foot held the bridge. Goring would appear to have had at least as many troopers as Cromwell, but the latter drove him up the Trent towards Newark, and heading him off at Mascomb Bridge, forced him to swim the river in order to escape.

Cromwell then returned to Bawtree and Tuxford, where David Leslie joined him with a strong party of Scotch horse and placed himself under his command. Goring crossed from Newark into Leicestershire, where he commenced plundering the country up and down. The allied generals, however, refused to allow their horse to follow him, being convinced by this time that Rupert intended to relieve York. They therefore kept their horse at hand in south Yorkshire.

Goring is reported to have got plunder worth £40,000, (*Weekly Intelligence*, 28th May; *Parliamentary Scout*, 30th May; *King's Pamphlets*), and great discontent was caused in London. The following extract from the *Parliamentary Scout* of the 23rd May, (*King's Pamphlets*), is worth quoting, as showing the reputation Cromwell had already won as a cavalry leader:

> Why the powers in Leicestershire are permitted to do such spoil, and not resisted at all by my Lord of Manchester . . . especially in regard we have been several times confirmed that a party of horse and dragoons have been designed against them under the command of Lieutenant-General Cromwell, and that he hath been gone upon the design six or seven days, and is none of the slow men in business he is put upon.

Manchester had now been ordered to join Leven and Fairfax before York, but though urged by both these commanders to come as quickly as possible, he still lingered in Lincolnshire. Ever fearful lest the associated counties, by whom his troops were raised and paid, should be attacked, he was not soldier enough to understand that the best defence of a frontier is to carry the war into the enemy's territory. It was not till the 24th May that he reached Gainsborough and crossed the Trent.

Cromwell and Leslie were then in the Doncaster district with nearly 7000 horse. They then moved on to Sheffield and Rotherham, whilst Manchester, advancing slowly behind this powerful cavalry screen, marched by Axholme, Thorn, and Selby, and reached York on the 3rd June. Here he took up the line of investment on the northwest of the town, his headquarters being at Clifton, and drove his approaches towards Bootham-bar, whilst Fairfax's trenches faced Walmgate-bar. Cromwell by the 1st June had disposed the horse along the line from Wakefield on the Calder, to Knaresborough on the Nidd, watching for Rupert's approach.

On the 6th June Newcastle burnt the suburbs and retreated within the walls of York. Provisions and supplies were plentiful, but neither he nor Sir Thomas Glenham, the governor, had any money. On the 17th, Crawford, who was conducting Manchester's attack, lodged a mine and blew down a tower on the walls. His stormers, some 500 men, rushed over the breach and entered the town; but as he had not acquainted either of the other generals with his intention, his party was unsupported, no attacks were made elsewhere, and he was driven out again with the loss of half his men.

Rupert had returned to Shrewsbury from Oxford on the 5th May. Leaving again with all the forces he could raise on the 16th, he first captured the Parliamentary post of Newport, a few miles to the east. Then, turning northward, he forced the passage of the Mersey at Stockport on the 25th May, relieved Lathom House, drove Rigby into Bolton, and stormed that place after desperate fighting on the 28th. Then marching to Liverpool, important as a small but convenient port for Ireland, he compelled the Parliamentary garrison to take themselves and their artillery on board ship, and sacked the town. He then marched for Yorkshire, by Blackburn and Clithero, being joined in Lancashire by Goring, who had made his way through the local Parliamentary forces in the midlands.

About this time, Rupert received an often-quoted letter from the king, very ambiguously worded, directing him, if possible, to relieve York, and then, if Newcastle and he felt themselves strong enough, to attack the Scots; but if not, to at once march south and join the king. This letter was dated Tickenhall, the 14th June, so that Rupert must have already been on his way towards York when he received it. He crossed the rugged moorland between Clithero and Skipton, and soon came in contact with Cromwell's outposts. The latter's scoutmaster—Watson—wrote to Manchester as follows:—

My Lord,
Our intelligence from divers places agreeing that the enemy's horse and foot did advance this day towards Otley, and quarter there and the towns thereabouts this night, hath occasioned us to draw all our horse of both nations into a body upon the moor close by Long Marston, within five miles of York, where now we are, expecting what further orders we shall receive from your lordship and the other generals.
My Lord, I humbly offer this, that exact orders might be sent to my Lord Fairfax's troops that are in general parts of this country to march up either to us or you, that they may not by their absence be made useless. The Lieutenant-General commanded me to send this express to your lordship, being in expectation to hear your lordship's further resolutions.
My Lord, I am,
Your lordship's most humble servant,
Leon Watson.
Long Marston this 30th June, 1644. Between one and two o'clock in the morning. The enemy's whole body is about 15,000.—*Fairfax Correspondence*, vol.

On receipt of this intelligence the three generals before York determined to temporarily raise the siege and meet Rupert. If Sir Thomas Fairfax's numbers are correct, Leven and his father had mustered 16,000 foot and 4000 horse about six weeks before, and Manchester had brought a reinforcement of 6000 foot and 3000 horse. (*Short Memorial*). The total force at the disposal of the three generals would therefore be 29,000 men; but a considerable deduction must be made, on account of losses in action and from sickness, &c., in calculating the numbers that could now be put into the field. On the other side, Newcastle had 6000 men at his disposal, besides Rupert's field army of 15,000.

It is therefore evident that the Parliamentary forces were not strong enough to maintain the investment of York and at the same time meet Rupert with sufficient numbers to give them the probability of victory. The generals were therefore right in raising the siege and concentrating all their forces against Rupert. If he were beaten, York must soon fall, whereas the experience of Newark had taught them the danger of being caught between a relieving army and a garrison. But their proper action was to seek out Rupert, attack and defeat him before he could obtain assistance from York. This required a rapid, well-planned march and a determined attack. No one of the three generals was capable of such intrepid action, even had he been the sole commander. When acting together, their inactivity was accentuated.

On the 30th June Rupert reached Knaresborough; and on the 1st July the generals marched to Hessay and Marston, some six or seven miles from York. On this morning, Rupert sent his horse forward, towards York, whether by the right or left bank of the Nidd is not certain—probably the former. About half-way they came in view of the Parliamentary army drawn up on Marston Moor, facing west. The generals had received intelligence of Rupert's advance, and hoped to bar his way. Rupert deployed his cavalry and made a demonstration as if about to attack. He had, however, already ordered his foot and guns to march on Boroughbridge, where they crossed the Ure and the Swale above the point where they join to form the Ouse.

As soon as they were safely across he withdrew his horse from before the enemy and followed. Then, marching down the east bank of the Ouse, he seized the bridge at Poppleton, which the besiegers had constructed to maintain the communications between the Scots and Manchester's army during the siege, and which had now been left slenderly guarded.

Thus Rupert, by his own rapid and skilful movements and the inertness of the generals opposed to him, had, without firing a shot, raised the siege of York, reached the town, and, by possession of the bridges over the Ouse, had gained the option of fighting or not, as he chose. Nor was he the man to neglect the prosecution of his advantages. Leaving his army outside the town, he rode that evening (the 1st July), with a force of cavalry, into York, where he discussed with Newcastle and Eythin the next steps to be taken.

******

Gardiner, basing his opinion on a passage in the Slingsby *Memoirs*, says Rupert never entered York, but sent an order to Newcastle to join him next day, and that the discussion took place on the road the next morning.

******

The two latter, as usual, wished to avoid a battle. The three Parliamentary generals did not agree well, and would probably part; reinforcements might be received from Northumberland; the garrison had been hard pressed, and required rest and refreshment. Rupert, however, urged that this was the time to strike. The generals had been out-manoeuvred and disheartened; delay would probably allow them to call up stronger reinforcements than the Royalists could hope for; Denbigh could be brought from Leicestershire; the Scotch forces from before Newcastle; a victory now would decide the war; finally, he declared he had the king's positive orders to fight.'

******

Rupert referred to the king's letter of the 14th June. If it did not actually order him to fight, it certainly intimated that the relief of York without the defeat of the Scots would be useless.

******

Then Newcastle gave way, and it was decided that a combined advance against the Roundheads should be made the next day.

On the other hand, the Parliamentary generals found themselves out-manoeuvred. At the council of war which was held to consider the position, the idea that Rupert would move out to fight does not seem to have been entertained. It was thought he would seek to break into the East Riding and thence into the Eastern Association. It was therefore determined to fall back by Tadcaster on Cawood and Selby, where the possession of the bridges over the Ouse would enable the generals to oppose him directly, or fall on his flank should he attempt to move south. It is remarkable that the over-cautious Leven appeared to be under no apprehension lest Rupert should make a sudden march northward and fall upon the Scots before Newcastle, whilst the combined army was watching for him to the south of York.

At any rate, Leven consented to accompany Manchester and Fairfax on their march to Tadcaster. All this points to the conclusion that the three generals considered Rupert's forces to be considerably inferior to theirs, whatever they may have said afterwards. Accordingly, early in the morning of the 2nd July, the combined army commenced its march southward, the Scots leading. Cromwell and Fairfax, with 3000 horse and dragoons, brought up the rear.

Meanwhile, Rupert was bringing his army over from the left to the right bank of the Ouse, by the bridge at Poppleton. This must have been partly done during the evening of the 1st and in the night, as it would take a long time to move 15,000 men across a single bridge. About 9 a.m. Rupert's advanced guard of 5000 horse and dragoons appeared on Marston Moor, which the Parliamentary foot had just quitted. The baggage train was just filing off, and the rear-guard was still on the ridge to the east of Long Marston.

The Cavaliers pressed after the rear of the carriages, but were prevented doing anything serious by the attitude of the Parliamentary horse under Cromwell and Sir Thomas Fairfax. Immediately messengers were despatched to the generals to inform them that Rupert was advancing to the west of the Ouse, apparently seeking battle, and that his advanced guard was so close that it would be impossible to withdraw the train without fighting. On receipt of this intelligence, orders were issued without hesitation to the army to counter-march and offer Rupert the battle he desired. The head of the column had by this time arrived within two miles of Tadcaster, four or five miles from Marston.

Both sides now began to form their lines of battle. The moor reached to where the road from Tockwith to Marston runs. South of this the ground sloped gently upwards to a low ridge, and was cultivated. Separating the fields from the moor ran a ditch, somewhere about the site of the present road. It was deep and lined with hedges near Long Marston, whilst towards Tockwith it disappeared, or at any rate became an insignificant obstacle. The Royalists, arriving first, drew up on the moor immediately beyond the ditch. The very full account given in the *Mercurius Britannicus* of the 8th July, (*Cromwelliana*), states that the Royalists had four brigades in the ditch. Gardiner, rely ing on other contemporary evidence, states that Rupert drew his men up a little back from the ditch, and was blamed by Eythin for doing so. It would, however, be the proper position for troops who relied principally on "shock" tactics, as they could charge the enemy as he clambered with broken ranks out of the ditch.

The Parliamentary generals formed their regiments as they arrived in the cornfields in succession from the right, resting that flank on the village of Long Marston. Both sides attempted to prolong their flanks towards Tockwith as much as possible, and desultory fighting occurred when some of Cromwell's dragoons beat back the attempt of a Royalist regiment to establish itself on the left flank of the Parliamentary Army. When its line was completed, the latter extended for about one and a half miles, from Marston to Tockwith. Both armies assumed the usual formation, with the infantry in the centre and the cavalry on both flanks.

Of the formation of the Parliamentary army we have very full information from the *Mercurius Britannicus* and other old newspapers. The extreme right rested on the village of Long Marston. The horse on this flank was commanded by Sir Thomas Fairfax. Under him were all his own horse and three Scottish regiments, the Earl of Dalhousie's, the Earl of Eglington's, and Lord Balgony's; in all, some eighty troops. The right wing of the foot was commanded by Lord Fairfax, who had under him all his own Yorkshire foot in the first line, and two brigades of Scots in reserve. In the centre stood four regiments of Scots, the Earl of Lindsay's, Lord Maitland's, the Earl of Cassilis', and Kelhead's. On their left were the foot of the Eastern Association, in two brigades, under Crawford. The reserve to the centre consisted of six Scotch regiments, those of the Earls of Buckleigh, Lowdon, and Dunfermline, Lord Cowper, General Hamilton, and one Edinburgh regiment.

Another brigade of the Eastern Association stood in reserve to Crawford's brigades. The horse of the left wing was commanded by Cromwell, and consisted of the regiments of the Eastern Association in the first line, with three regiments of Scotch horse under David Leslie in reserve; in all, seventy troops. Leven himself was with the infantry of the centre, where Lumsden commanded the reserves. On the extreme left were placed the Scotch dragoons under Frizell.

Much less detailed information is available concerning the Royalist army. That Goring's horse were on the left, whilst those of Rupert's own army, including the troops from Ireland, were on the right, and the foot of both Rupert's and Newcastle's armies formed the centre, is about all that can be affirmed as certain.

✶✶✶✶✶✶

The plan and text in Warburton's account of the battle, vol. ii., are most unreliable. He places the ditch on the wrong flank, puts infantry officers in command of horse, and makes other blunders.

✶✶✶✶✶✶

Authorities contradict each other as to the position of Rupert and the other superior officers. Some say Rupert commanded the horse on the right, and others on the left wing. The balance, both of evidence and probability, points to the former. The newspaper reports and those written within a few days of the battle all place him there. It is most improbable that he should have taken the immediate command of the Yorkshire horse out of the hands of Goring, who would have highly resented such supercession, whilst he left his own troopers to be led on by a comparatively inferior officer, such as Byron. Apart, then, from such anecdotes as that told by Gardiner, that he asked where Cromwell was, and deliberately placed himself in opposition to him, it is most probable that he commanded in person the right wing of horse. (Had he wished to oppose Cromwell personally, the latter's *cuirassiers* must have been easily distinguishable).

Goring commanded the horse of the left wing, and Newcastle the foot. Under him, Tillyer probably commanded the foot of Rupert's army, and Eythin that of Newcastle's.

As to the numbers engaged on both sides there is a good deal of uncertainty. Deducting 4000 men for losses by sickness and battle during the siege from the Parliamentary total of 29,000, there would remain 25,000 fit for duty on the 2nd July, which agrees with the numbers given in the Parliamentary accounts. Of these some 8000 or 9000 were horse.

As to Rupert's army, the Parliamentary accounts make it of about the same strength as their own. This is probably an exaggeration. Watson, as we have seen, estimated it when approaching Knaresborough as 15,000, and though, in writing his account after the battle, he raises the figures to 20,000, it is evident that in the first report it was of the utmost importance to give the three generals the most accurate information possible, whilst, when writing an account of the battle afterwards, he would be tempted to exaggerate in order to enhance merit of the victory.

Assuming, then, that the relieving army mustered 15,000 men, all accounts agree that Newcastle had 6000 foot with him in York. Slingsby says that when he went out to join Rupert he only left three regiments—Colonel Bellasis', Sir T. Glenham's, and Slingsby's—in York, say 1000 men. Deduct another 1000 for sick and losses during siege. Newcastle may thus have joined Rupert with 4000 men. (Warburton, vol. ii. says only 2500). The total of the Royalist Army was therefore probably some 19,000 men. Cromwell puts it at 20,000. (Fairfax says the Royalists were "about 23,000 or 24,000 men, we something more." *Short Memorial*). The horse were probably as strong as the Parliaments—some 8000 or 9000 men. The Royalists had twenty-five pieces of ordnance.

By two o'clock the bulk of the forces on both sides had arrived on the field, but it was not till three or four that the opposing forces had completed their formations. The cannon opened on either side, but their fire had little effect. Young Walton, Cromwell's nephew, was one of the few struck. About five o'clock the useless cannonade ceased, and an ominous silence reigned on the field. It must have been an impressive sight. Forty-five thousand men stood facing one another, silent and motionless, breathlessly awaiting the signal for battle.

The day was changeable. Drenching showers swept over the wild moor, and rattled on the tall rye-stalks where the Roundheads stood, soaking the buff coats, and draggling the gay plumes of the Cavaliers, sprinkling the armour of Cromwell's Ironsides with red spots of rust. Then the sun would burst through the clouds, his rays glittering on raindrop and pike-head, on morion and breastplate, warming the bright hues of the horsemen's scarves, or of the colours fluttering above the ranks. Then the horses would toss their heads and shake the wet out of their manes, only to droop their crests and cower as the next squall swept down upon them.

Lower and lower dropped the sun, longer and longer grew the shadows. Still the dense masses faced each other motionless, still the leaders on either side anxiously scanned the enemy, seeking to find a weak point or sign of wavering in his array. The ditch between the armies deterred either side from advancing. On the Parliamentary right where Fairfax's horse stood, the ground was broken by hedgerows and furze bushes, and a narrow lane led across the ditch, here at its broadest. Both lane and ditch were lined with thick hedges, and Goring had placed musketeers in the intervals between his horse, and in the hedges, to command the approach from the lane with their fire.

Away towards the Royalist right, their foot, closing in towards their centre, had left a gap between themselves and Rupert's horse, opposite the left of Crawford's brigades. Rupert and Newcastle met and discussed the situation. It was seven o'clock, too late to begin the action. The Roundheads were short of provisions, there was no water but that in puddles on their side, the wells near Marston had already been drunk dry. It would be better to rest and refresh their men, and attack the fasting enemy in the morning. Newcastle turned off to his coach to sup and sleep. Rupert to his, to solace his impatient temper with a pipe. Probably an order was passed through the ranks that the men might eat their suppers.

But there were quick eager eyes watching every movement in the Royalist Army from the corn-fields on the gentle slopes yonder. Scarcely had Rupert lit his pipe, when the well-known Puritan war-cry, the drawling chant of some old psalm tune, struck his ear. He looked round—the whole Puritan Army was advancing! Down off the Cow Warrant past Bilton Breame came Cromwell's steel-clad horsemen. Three hundred picked men of his own regiment led by himself formed the forlorn hope. On his right Crawford's infantry were pressing forward at the run, and further to their right the Scots and Lord Fairfax's infantry were pushing through the hedgerows towards the ditch.

Down by Long Marston village Sir Thomas Fairfax's horse were crowding into the narrow lane which led across the ditch or picking their way through the furze bushes on the extreme flank. The roar of cannon, the ring of musketry, the loud cries, the chanted psalms, and the tramp of man and horse confused the ear. A moment before all had been stillness and silence, now all was movement and noise. Swinging himself into the saddle, Rupert galloped down to lead on his men and stop the rush of Cromwell's troopers. It is said he led his own regiment in the van.

But the Puritan forlorn crossed the ditch in unbroken order, and crashed into the Royalist ranks. Unable to sustain the weight of the heavily-armoured close-knit mass, Rupert's regiment gave way. The Cavalier second line came to its support and restored the fight, and pressing on the flanks of Cromwell's chosen troopers, succeeded even in driving them somewhat back. But they were in turn supported, and a furious fight ensued. Walton says:

We stood at swords point a pretty while, hacking at one another.

Then David Leslie with his reserve of Scotch horse pushing into the gap between the Cavalier horse and foot, fell upon Rupert's flank, and at last, Cromwell's squadrons "brake through them, scattering them like a little dust." (Watson's *Narrative, King's Pamphlets*).

✶✶✶✶✶✶

In *A Full Relation,* &c., it is stated that Leslie's horse fell first on the Royal foot, and after defeating two or three regiments charged the flank of Rupert's horse; but the account as given in the text seems the most probable one.

✶✶✶✶✶✶

Slingsby says:

They fly along by Wilstrop wood-side as fast and as thick as could be.

Sending his leading troops on to press the pursuit, Cromwell re-formed the remainder ready for use elsewhere. In the centre the battle was raging furiously. Crawford's brigades, running on level with Cromwell's horsemen, crossed the ditch, and their left wing, pouring into the gap between the Royal horse and foot, swung round to the right and fell on Tillyer's flank, driving back the regiments on that side. This success enabled the Scots of the centre to cross the ditch. But then the forward movement was checked. Away on the Parliamentary right Fairfax's troopers had dashed down the lane and through the furze bushes in some disorder.

As they approached the Royalist line, the fire from the musketeers behind the hedges and between the squadrons added to their disorder. Debouching on to the moor, they attempted to re-form, but being charged by Goring's horsemen, they were flung back in great confusion. Without giving them a moment's respite Goring pressed furiously on, and drove them back to and through the reserve of Scots. In a few minutes, Fairfax's horsemen were scattered in hopeless rout. Galloping wildly back, they trampled the Yorkshire foot under their horses' hoofs. The panic spread; the men threw away their arms and ran. Sir Thomas, plucking the white symbol out of his helmet, with a few followers broke through the Royalist horse and joined Cromwell on the left.

✶✶✶✶✶✶

The Parliamentary forces on this day wore something white, a ribbon, a knot, or even a piece of paper in their head-dress, as a distinguishing badge.

✶✶✶✶✶✶

A troop of Balgony's Scotch lancers did the same. Eglington's horsemen preserved their ranks, but lost heavily. Excepting these, the whole Parliamentary right wing, horse and foot, were streaming across the fields in the wildest flight. After them spurred Goring in hot pursuit.

Sir Charles Lucas, who commanded part of the Royalist horse of this left wing, kept his men back when Goring galloped off in pursuit. Wheeling to the right, he flung himself on the flank of the Scotch foot, now across the ditch, and hotly engaged with the Royalist foot. The Scotchmen fought gallantly, but lost heavily. Twice were the Cavaliers repulsed, but at a heavy price. Whole regiments disappeared or became mixed with others. Lumsden, seeing the danger, hurried up his reserves to support Lindsay's and Maitland's regiments, who were making a gallant stand. A third charge was repulsed, and Lucas himself dismounted, wounded, and taken prisoner. But no foot could much longer withstand these repeated attacks in front and flank. Unless help came soon they must be crushed.

Cromwell, as soon as he had rallied his own and Leslie's squadrons, wheeled to his right, as Lucas had done on the other flank, and fell on the right and rear of the Royalist foot, hotly engaged with Crawford's brigades. Conspicuous amongst the Royalists stood Newcastle's own Northumbrian regiment. These men had sworn to dye their white coats red in the blood of their foes. Attacked by horse and foot, in front, flank, and rear, they refused to fly or yield; and, like the king's regiment at Edgehill, died where they stood in their ranks. Only forty of them escaped.

Sweeping down the line, Cromwell's troopers rode over and dispersed one Royalist regiment after another. Suddenly, through the deepening twilight, their leader perceived the Royal horse charging the flanks of the Scots and pursuing the Yorkshire foot over the ridge beyond. He thus became aware for the first time that the Parliamentary right wing had been routed. Ever cool in the hottest fight, with his well-disciplined squadrons always well in hand, Cromwell called his men off and re-formed them in line of battle; re-formed them on the same ground and facing the same way as Goring's horse had stood before the battle commenced. Crawford formed up his Eastern Association foot on Cromwell's right. When all was ready the signal to charge was given.

Lucas' and Porter's men were reeling back from their last charge on the Scots, Goring's horsemen were returning from the chase, when

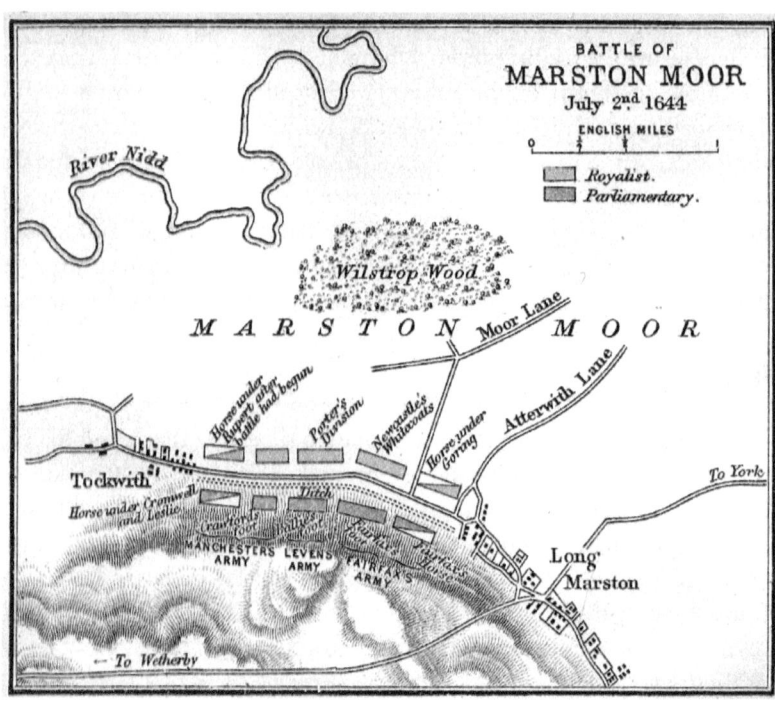

they found the dreaded Ironsides drawn up across their path. In vain they tried to rally. Hampered now, as Fairfax had been before, by hedgerows and bushes, they were, like him, caught before they could re-form. Cromwell's heavy compact masses burst through their scattered squadrons. In a few minutes the Cavaliers were urging their tired horses more vigorously in flight than they had just before in pursuit.

The remaining foot were soon dispersed. Darkness—it was now ten o'clock—stopped the pursuit, but the victory was already complete. Lucas, Porter, and Tillyer were prisoners, with 1500 officers and men. All the Royalist cannon, 130 barrels of powder, and 10,000 arms remained in the hands of the victors.

******

A great many colours were taken and sent to London; such of them as "could be got from the soldiers, who esteem it a great glory to divide them in pieces and wear them."—*A Full Relation, &c. King's Pamphlets.*

******

But the battle had been dearly purchased, and the result hung long in the balance. If Rupert and Newcastle were fugitives, so also were Leven, Manchester, and the elder Fairfax. To Cromwell's nerve and insight, and to the wonderful discipline he had taught the army of the Association, must the victory be ascribed. When Rupert met him on this day the fate of the battle, the fate of the war, hung on that one charge. The victor in the charge won the battle, and the battle was the turning point of the war. As to the numbers killed, but little certain is to be learnt. They must have amounted to thousands. The Parliamentary newspapers pretend they lost only 300 men. This is hardly possible, considering how completely their right wing had been routed and how close and far the pursuit had been followed.

At York, the confusion that evening was great. The guards refused to allow any but members of the garrison to enter the gates. Outside surged a panic-struck host of horse and foot, unable to enter the town or cross the river. At last Rupert succeeded in restoring order. The next morning he rode out at the head of 6000 demoralised troopers, whilst Newcastle and Eythin, fearing the ridicule of the court more than the arms of their enemies, fled to Hamburgh. Sir Thomas Glenham was left to defend York, or make the best terms he could.

The 3rd July was spent by the Parliamentary generals in rallying their shattered right wing and gathering the spoils. The three principal generals had all shared in the rout of the right of the line, and did not return to the army till this day. Cromwell and Sir Thomas Fairfax were both wounded slightly in face and neck. It was therefore not till the 4th that the army was in a condition to follow up the success. On this day, the leaguer before York was resumed, and Cromwell, with his own, the Scotch, and 1000 of Fairfax's horse, 7000 in all, was sent in pursuit of Rupert. But the latter had got too much start, and marching by Buroughbridge towards Westmoreland, was joined on the 4th or 5th by 2000 horse and foot under Clavering and Montrose.

The country proving unfavourable to cavalry, Cromwell found himself unable to press Rupert's retreat, and therefore returned to York. The *Parliamentary Scout*, of the 19th July, says:

"Colonel Cromwell, finding the passages strait, and musketers lining the hedges, thought it not fit to advance any further after the prince, but is returned to Yorke, with his horse not worne to skin and bone, but only breathed a little."

Rupert then passed through Westmoreland, southwards into Lancashire. Meldrum and Brereton, who appear to have been in the West Riding on the borders of Lancashire, were ordered to attempt to intercept him. But he was too strong to be meddled with by them. Denbigh, who about July had been at Manchester, was now as far south as Nantwich.

On the 15th July, a fortnight after the battle, Sir Thomas Glenham surrendered York on good conditions, being allowed to march out with the garrison. They were committed to the escort of the horse of Manchester's army, who disgraced themselves by breaking the conditions and plundering and insulting the Royalist soldiers. It is satisfactory to learn that these excesses were not committed by Cromwell's own men, as Slingsby, who was one of the officers of the garrison, expressly states that on reaching Knaresborough they were handed over to Whalley, who then commanded Cromwell's regiment, and who treated them civilly.

It has already been seen that Cromwell himself had to complain bitterly of the want of discipline in the later raised horse of the Association. The three generals were much concerned on hearing of this behaviour of the men, and issued an order for the punishment of the offenders and recovery of the plunder, but little of the booty was ever got back. The garrison marched into Lancashire, and Glenham went to Carlisle, where later on he conducted a gallant defence against the Scots.

York having been now surrendered, the object for which the three armies of Leven, Fairfax, and Manchester had originally combined was now attained. The question naturally arose—what to do next? The council of war decided that the armies should again divide—the Scots going north to reduce Newcastle and other garrisons in Northumberland, Cumberland, and Durham; Fairfax to garrison York and clear Yorkshire of the Royalist fortresses; Manchester to return to the Eastern Association, to secure the districts, whence his army was raised, from incursions of the Royalists, and possibly to besiege Newark.

When the characters of the three generals are considered, this impotent conclusion is hardly to be wondered at. Leven and Lord Fairfax were soldiers of the old methodical school; Manchester no soldier at all. Here was a great victory at last—the first decisive one the Parliament had won during the war. The whole north of England was at their feet. When Rupert turned south into Lancashire, Goring, with a few horse, went into Cumberland. Beyond these there were no Royalist forces in the field.

A few important towns, such as Newcastle and Carlisle, and many country houses and small places, still, it is true, held Royalist garrisons, but, removed from all chance of relief, they could not long hold out against the attacks of detachments well equipped for siege work. Yet the whole of the Scotch and Parliamentary forces were to be monopolised in this comparatively unimportant work. The beaten army was not to be pursued; Rupert was to have time to recruit his shattered forces in Wales and elsewhere; no attempt was to be made to follow up the success in the north by combining with Essex against the king's own army in the south.

The Committee of Both Kingdoms was wiser than its generals. Manchester had marched to Tadcaster on the 20th July; and at Ferry Bridge, on the 22nd, he received a letter from the committee, directing him to move at once into Lancashire and attack Rupert wherever he could be found. Manchester, instead of obeying, requested his brother generals to meet him and discuss the situation. Accordingly, on the 30th July, a meeting was held at Ferry Bridge, at which it was decided that the information received by the committee was inexact; that Rupert had already passed over the Mersey into Cheshire, where, with Wales so close at hand, it would be useless to pursue him, and that some of his foot under Montrose and of his horse under Goring had gone north into Cumberland and Westmoreland. They therefore adhered to their original decision to divide.

Writing from Blyth on the 1st August, Manchester informs the committee of this decision and of his own intention to refresh and recruit his army about Lincoln. He complains much that his men are neither paid nor clothed, and that consequently there are many sick. Also, that a levy, recently made in the Eastern Association, had been diverted from his army, to whom they properly belonged, to that of Essex. (Quarrel of Manchester and Cromwell; Bruce).

Another cause lay at the bottom of the inactivity of the three generals. This was alarm at the increasing power of the Independents. All three were Presbyterians and members of the nobility. The Independents, with Cromwell at their head, spurned at the narrow doctrine and strict church discipline of the Presbyterians, and esteemed a man for what he was worth himself, not for what he acquired by birth or fortune. In religion and in politics they were diametrically opposed to a dogmatic faith and a hereditary aristocracy.

When the news of the victory reached London, the Presbyterians of both countries did their utmost to decry Cromwell's share of the victory and to exaggerate that of the Scots. But in spite of their attempts to garble the accounts, it was patent to everyone that, however well the Scots may have fought in the centre, the whole merit of the victory lay with the horse commanded by Cromwell and with the foot of the Eastern Association, that is, with those forces where the "Sectaries" mustered strongest.

Later, Crawford, who, though he commanded the foot of the Association, was a strict Scotch Presbyterian, condensed the jealousy of the parties into a personal attack on Cromwell, who he asserted had, after receiving a slight scratch in the face, left the field and relegated the leading of his men to David Leslie. (*Quarrel of Manchester and Cromwell*; Crawford's report). But in spite of all the endeavours of the Presbyterians, the true story asserted itself, and the prestige of the Independent or Sectarian party in the army grew apace. Jealousy of this party and natural indolence and ignorance of military art, combined to induce Manchester to retain his army idle, when the affairs of the Parliament were assuming a very critical aspect in the south. How critical the situation became must now be briefly disclosed.

Royalists march to Oxford

In the spring, Parliament had ordered Essex from Beaconsfield and Waller from Farnham to advance simultaneously on Oxford. If they found the king still there, they were to besiege the place; if he had gone northward to join Rupert, Essex was to pursue him, whilst Waller was to operate against Maurice in the west.

Charles, whose object was to contain his two opponents without allowing himself to be shut into Oxford, first concentrated his forces by withdrawing the garrison of Reading and destroying its fortifications. He then waited till the two Parliamentary generals had arrived before Oxford, and had nearly completed the investment, they having occupied Abingdon, which had been abandoned without his orders, and was never afterwards recovered. He then slipped away between the two on the night of the 3rd June, and reached Burford. Thence he marched by Evesham to Worcester, breaking the bridges behind him. Essex now sent Waller to pursue him, and himself turned against Maurice, who was still before Lyme.

Waller, moving leisurely, was at Evesham on the 12th, when the king marched out of Worcester to Bewdley, as if he were about to join Rupert. This brought Waller forward in a hurry to Broomsgrove, but Charles, putting his infantry into boats, dropped again to Worcester. Thence he marched rapidly back to Oxford, where he picked up his train, which he had left there, and moved on by Buckingham towards the Eastern Association. Waller finding the king had not gone north, at first thought he would cross into Wales, and marched down the Severn to Tewkesbury, but then getting better information, moved across the Cotswolds to Banbury. On the 29th June both armies were in the vicinity of that town, marching up the Cherwell on either bank in sight of one another.

Waller noticing a gap in the king's order of march, tried to cut in between his divisions at Copredy Bridge, but was repulsed with loss. Then, as usual, his London trained-bands clamoured to be led home, and many deserted. Waller was forced to take the rest back by Towcester, which he reached on the 2nd July. Writing thence to the Committee of Both Kingdoms, he gave expression to an opinion concerning citizen soldiers on which Cromwell had ever acted, and which afterwards formed the main argument for the reorganisation of the army:

> My Lords, I write these particulars to let you know that an army composed of these men will never go through with your service, and till you have an army merely your own, that you may command, it is in a manner impossible to do anything of importance.

With such men as he could induce to remain with him Waller

returned towards London.

The king, having disposed of Waller, now turned after Essex, who had reached Dorchester on the 13th June, whereupon Maurice raised the siege of Lyme. Essex then moved to Weymouth, and, after some rest there, resumed his march westward, driving Maurice into Exeter. Passing on, he compelled Grenvile to raise the siege of Plymouth, and then, forcing the passage of the Tamar at Tavistock on the 27th July, he drove him down the Cornish peninsula, and reached Bodmin on the 29th. Here he found himself among a hostile population, short of provisions, and heard that the king was following him. He then wrote to the Committee of Both Kingdoms, urging them to send assistance. They sent Middleton to follow the king with Waller's horse, and to press his rear; but too late.

The king reached Exeter on the 26th July, and Maurice's forces joined his at Crediton. On the 3rd August he was at Liskeard, Essex being at Lostwithiel, a few miles south of Bodmin. He then joined hands with Grenvile, and the two armies hemmed the Roundheads in. They next seized a fort commanding the little port of Fowey, by which Essex obtained access to the sea, and by continual skirmishes so drove his forces back, that presently he had no provisions or forage left. Seeing there was no hope of extricating his army, Essex ordered Balfour to try and break out with the horse, handed over the command to Skippon, and escaped to Plymouth in a small boat.

Balfour slipped through the Royalist forces, thanks to a dark night and to the fact that Goring, who commanded the outposts, was drunk, and reached Plymouth with little loss. Skippon surrendered all his arms, ammunition, camp, &c., to the king, his soldiers being marched under escort to Plymouth and handed over to the Parliamentary governor there. They were plundered by the Royalists on the way.

Thus, the king had every cause to be satisfied with his campaign in the south. By cleverly seizing the opportunities offered him by the blunders of his adversaries, without much loss, without even risking a pitched battle, he had disposed of two Parliamentary armies, each equal to his own. He had weakened his own force to strengthen Rupert's, and had the latter been equally successful, the Parliament must have submitted to his terms. And Rupert had almost won a brilliant success. On that long July evening, at Marston Moor, the three generals who opposed him were spurring in headlong flight before his victorious left wing. One successful charge on his right and the day was won, and here he himself led on his own ever victorious squadrons.

But against those close-knit ranks of steel-clad warriors sweeping down through the rye, the gallant Cavaliers dashed themselves in vain. Inspired by the sternest fanaticism, and bound together by the strictest discipline, Cromwell's Ironsides were indeed invincible. The ceaseless toil, the ceaseless exhortation of two years, had here their reward. On that one charge hung the fate of the campaign, the fate of the Parliament, and Cromwell had turned the tide of war. During the summer the Parliament was making strenuous efforts to recover from the defeats in the south. On the 12th July an ordinance was voted, calling out fresh levies for *permanent service*.

But Manchester, who was at the head of the best organised army in England, loitered about Lincolnshire. True, a few towns and fortified posts, Tickhill Castle, Sheffield, Bolsover, and Alfreton, fell to detachments sent against them, but Newark, the great stronghold of the Royalists in these parts, was not even besieged. His army was sufficient to prosecute this siege, and yet spare a strong detachment for service elsewhere. Again, and again the Committee of Both Kingdoms urged him to march in pursuit of Rupert, but again and again he adduced some excuse for not complying.

Now it was sickness amongst his men, now want of money and clothing, now he had called a council of war among his officers, and they were unanimously against the project. This, however, Cromwell afterwards denied, and, when examined by a Committee of the Commons, declared that Manchester never summoned a council of war, and when urged by himself and others to do something, and at least besiege Newark, always put them off on one pretext or another.

At last the committee heard, about the end of August, that Rupert was marching south to meet the king. On the 28th August, they wrote pressing orders to Manchester to march towards Abingdon, sending his horse on ahead, and these orders were repeated still more urgently on the 1st September, and again on the 2nd. Very deliberately Manchester prepared to comply.

Cromwell was all this time chafing under his forced inaction. Here is a letter to Colonel Walton, dated Sleaford, the 5th or 6th September:

> We do with grief of heart resent the sad condition of our Army in the West, and of affairs there. That business has our hearts with it; and truly had we wings, we would fly thither. So soon as ever my Lord and the foot set me loose, there shall be in me no want to hasten what I can to that service.

For indeed all other considerations are to be laid aside, and to give place to it, as being of far more importance. I hope this Kingdom shall see that, in the midst of our necessities, we shall serve them without disputes. We hope to forget our wants, which are exceeding great and ill cared for; and desire to refer the many slanders heaped upon us by false tongues to God, who will, in due time, make it appear to the world that we study the glory of God, and the honour and liberty of the Parliament. For which we unanimously fight, without seeking our own interests.

Indeed, we never find our men so cheerful as when there is work to do. I trust you will always hear so of them. The Lord is our strength, and in Him is all our hope. Pray for us. Present my love to my friends. I beg their prayers. The Lord still bless you. We have some amongst us much slow in action: if we could all intend our own ends less, and our ease too, our business in this Army would go on wheels for expedition. Because some of us are enemies to rapine, and other wickednesses, we are said to be factious, to seek to maintain our opinions in religion by force, which we detest and abhor. I profess, I could never satisfy myself of the justness of this War, but from the authority of the Parliament to maintain itself in its rights: and in this Cause, I hope to approve myself an honest man, and single-hearted.

Pardon me that I am thus troublesome. I write but seldom, it gives me a little ease to pour my mind, in the midst of calumnies, into the bosom of a friend.—Carlyle, vol. i.

Indeed, the dispute which had arisen between Cromwell on the one side, and Manchester and Crawford on the other, had now risen to such a height that all three repaired to London in order that the House might decide in the matter. Here they were reconciled for a while and returned to their commands. Manchester had accused Cromwell of insubordination and threatening that he and all his colonels of horse would resign if Crawford were not removed, but these charges do not appear to have been proved.

Manchester, who had heard the news of the Lostwithiel surrender on the 8th September, moved towards the Thames valley, and on the 22nd September, was at Watford. He had sent Cromwell forward with 2000 horse to cover the siege of Banbury by Colonel Fiennes, and to watch Rupert who was reported to be at Evesham. But having got so far, Manchester, always loath to quit the Association, began to hang back. A broken bridge at Maidenhead was his excuse this time, but he betrayed the true reason of his reluctance to advance, by writing to the committee:

> Your Lordships know what my humble opinion was, I am still of the same minde, that if the kinge be upon his march, in that condition that I see these armys in, you doe expose us to scome if not to ruine—but my Lords when my sense is delivered I shall obey as farre as in me lies. (A reservation he never acted on).

The committee now ordered him to leave 1500 horse to cover the siege of Banbury, and send the rest of his cavalry to reinforce Waller, who had joined Middleton in the west, to oppose the king. Manchester said he would comply, but sent Fleetwood with 500 troopers back into the Association to guard it against incursions from Newark. Cromwell, however, reported that Sir T. Glenham with most of the horse in Newark—twenty-one troops—had left for Ashby-de-la-Zouch with the intention of joining Rupert. The committee, therefore, on the 28th September, directed Manchester to recall Fleetwood, and added:

> We again desire your Lordship to use all possible expedition in your march westward, and to send your horse before your foot.

But all in vain. Manchester, on one pretext or another, neglected to comply with these reiterated orders; on the 30th the bulk of his squadrons were between Newbury and Basing.

Although Manchester was urging that it was unsafe to advance, the king at the end of September was still nearly 100 miles away. Retracing his steps after his success at Lostwithiel, he made an unsuccessful assault on the Plymouth forts on the 10th September, and then got as far as Chard, pushing back Middleton, who fell back to Shaftesbury, where Waller joined him. The king's army now only mustered some 5500 foot, and 4000 horse, many of the Cornish militia having returned to their homes, and a large detachment having been left under Grenvile to invest Plymouth. Manchester's forces alone were equal to Charles', and the committee, tired of his pusillanimous strategy and neglect of their orders, wrote again on the 2nd October:

> Having taken into consideration how prejudicial delays have always proved to the public service, and how necessary it is

that your Lordship should advance speedily westward, we have thought fit again to renew our desire to your Lordship to send your horse and foot according to our former orders, which we hope you will do with that expedition that we shall not need to iterate it again to your Lordship.

But these orders, although repeated on the 7th and 8th, and backed by a vote of the House, which directed that Manchester should observe the orders of the Committee, produced no more effect than the former ones. He remained about Reading, and even allowed the Royalist Colonel Gage to pass provisions and ammunition from Oxford into Basing House under his nose on the 11th October.

Essex had come round by sea to Portsmouth, whither his disarmed foot had followed him. They were now being re-armed and re-organised. On the 11th October, the Committee directed the armies of Essex and Manchester to rendezvous towards the west and unite to oppose the king. Finding that neither general would obey orders, they put the chief command into the hands of a Council of War, to which they added two civilian representatives of their own, Johnston of Warriston, and Crewe. Essex and Manchester agreed to unite at Basingstoke, which again was not to the westward, as the Committee had directed.

Manchester reached the rendezvous about the 17th October. Most of his horse was now with Waller, and the squadrons which had been covering the siege of Banbury had rejoined him; with these apparently was Cromwell. On the 18th October, Essex with some 6000 foot and a new train was at Alresford. Balfour, with the horse which escaped from Lostwithiel, had previously joined Waller.

The king left Chard on the 30th September. The next day he met Rupert, who had left some 2000 horse under Sir M. Langdale in Monmouthshire. Instead of joining the main Royalist army with every man he could raise, Rupert went off again to make a diversion towards Gloucester. (Sir E. Walker; Clarendon, vol. ii. pt. ii.). Charles advanced slowly, sending out detachments, and dropping garrisons on the way. On the 15th October, he reached Salisbury—Waller having retired to Andover. On the 18th the king, advancing rapidly without his train, drove Waller out of Andover, and forced him to retire hastily to Basingstoke. On the 21st Essex also joined Manchester at the same place, whilst the king on that day reached Kingsclere.

Reinforcements from London also reached the Parliamentary generals, who were now at least twice as strong as the king. But they could no longer interpose between him and Oxford, or force him to fight against his will. He marched on the 22nd to Newbury, the siege of Donnington Castle being raised at his approach, and sent the Earl of Northampton with a party of horse to Banbury, where he compelled Fiennes to relinquish the siege.

The Parliamentary Council of War now determined if possible to fight the king. Essex was sick and Manchester became president. The army marched by Aldermaston Park and Bucklebury Heath, and on the afternoon of the 25th quartered in some villages a little to the east of Newbury, and north of the Kennet. The king was still near Newbury, and on the 26th a reconnaissance in force was made of his position. His outposts were driven in, and he was found to be occupying the eastern slopes of Speen Hill, between the Lambourne brook and the Kennet, which unite just to the east of Newbury. His right rested on that town, his left was protected by Donnington Castle, which is on high ground on the north bank of the Lambourne. The road to Oxford crossed this brook immediately in his front, and the passage was secured by a strongly-built manor called Shaw, or Dolman's House, which was garrisoned and prepared for defence.

As the position could not be attacked on either flank, and the front was very strong, the Parliamentary council of war determined to divide their forces and attack the king in front and rear at the same time. The latter had some 10,000 men, whilst their own forces amounted to at least 19,000, so that the risk of splitting them for a time was not too great. That night the troops of Essex and Waller, with part of Manchester's horse under Cromwell, marched off, and, making a considerable circuit northwards to avoid Donnington Castle, crossed the Lambourne higher up the next morning. The movement was a ticklish one, as the position of the castle offered the king a favourable opportunity for attacking them in flank on the march without risk to himself. Probably with a view of diverting his attention, Manchester, early in the morning, made a feint attack with some 400 musketeers, who, pressing on too far, got roughly handled.

The king, however, got early news of the turning movement from the garrison of Donnington. Hitherto he had thought his position too strong to attack, or he would not have lingered at the risk of being cut off from Oxford. He now made no attempt to interfere with the flank march, but directed Maurice to entrench the crest of Speen Hill and to prepare for an attack from this side.

It was three o'clock in the afternoon of the 27th before Skippon and Waller had drawn up their forces to the west of the king's position, and sent them forward to attack the field-works which Prince Maurice had thrown up on the hill. Cromwell's horse formed the left wing, Balfour's the right, the foot formed the centre. The ground was much intersected with hedges and unfavourable for cavalry; and besides, on Cromwell's side, it was under the fire of the guns of Donnington. A narrow lane led up to the position, which was swept by some guns planted on the top of the hill. The Parliamentary foot pressed steadily up, in spite of a heavy fire from the guns and earthworks.

A sharp fight occurred at the top, but finally Maurice's foot were driven out of their entrenchment, down into and through Speen village, halfway down the slope. The guns were taken, Essex's veterans recognising with a shout the very ones they had lost at Fowey. Beyond the village, the king's reserves restored the fight and checked the advance. Now was the time that Manchester should have been pressing the king vigorously from the east, thus preventing the latter's reserves from moving to Maurice's assistance. But Manchester refused to budge. The battle had now been raging for more than an hour; Crawford and his other officers urged him to attack, but still he refused to give the command.

Between Skippon and Maurice a stubborn fight continued. At last night fell, and in consequence the Parliamentary commanders on the west stopped the attack when but one fence separated them from the open ground over which their powerful cavalry could have acted. It was this moment, in the short dusk of an autumn evening, that Manchester chose for a feeble attack on Shaw House, which was repulsed with some loss. The action had been principally confined to the foot in both armies, and the losses were not very great. Balfour's leading squadrons did, indeed, succeed in penetrating to the open ground, near Newbury, and driving back some Royalist horse. But a charge of Sir John Causfield with the queen's regiment compelled them in turn to retire. On the other flank the gallant Earl of Cleveland, in attempting to charge the Parliamentary foot, was wounded and taken prisoner.

******

Clarendon and Walker say that Cleveland was taken through his horse falling during a successful charge of Cavaliers, under Goring, against the horse of the Parliamentary left, which would be those of Waller or Cromwell.

★★★★★★

After nightfall Charles called a council of war, at which it was decided that if the army remained where it was, it might probably be surrounded, and that it would be better to move off at once. Accordingly, at ten o'clock, the royal forces silently left the field, moving across Manchester's front. Their cannon and train were left at Donnington, and then, gaining the Oxford road, they marched for Wallingford, where they intended to cross the Thames. They would thus reach Oxford by the left bank, as the garrison of Abingdon blocked the way on the right.

Seldom, indeed, had a battle been worse managed. The original plan of the Parliamentary leaders had given the king the opportunity of compensating for his inferior forces by attacking his enemy in detail. But when Charles' inaction had given them the opportunity for which they sought, of crushing him between their two wings, Manchester's delay in attacking had allowed the opportunity to slip away. Finally, the royal army had, on a bright night, been allowed to march away without molestation. Such military incapacity, after the experience of two years of war, seems impossible; and Cromwell afterwards roundly declared that Manchester had deliberately allowed the king to escape, as he did not wish to see him reduced to extremities. The subsequent proceedings only confirmed his suspicions.

On leaving the field, the king, with an escort of 300 men, rode to Bath with the intention of hurrying on Rupert's reinforcements. He arrived on the evening of the 28th, and met the prince. The rest of the army, under Goring, Hopton, and Maurice, reached Wallingford during the morning of the 28th, their retreat having been quite unmolested by the enemy. Here they crossed the Thames, and were disposed in quarters in and round Oxford.

The Parliamentary horse, under Waller, Cromwell, and Balfour, did not start in pursuit of the king till the morning of the 28th. And for this delay it would appear that Cromwell was in part to blame, as his horse had fought on the 27th on the flank nearest Donnington, that is, nearest the king's line of retreat. He was therefore most favourably situated for the pursuit. It is true that, in the darkness the horse could have effected little, especially in that intersected country and that the castle covered the principal road along which the retreating forces marched.

The foot regiments, by which the pursuit should have been properly undertaken during the night, were exhausted by the long march of the previous twenty-four hours and by the severe fighting—except those under Manchester's immediate command at Shaw. But though the unmolested retreat of the king's army was therefore principally due to Manchester's inactivity, it would seem that Cromwell, whose horse had not been very seriously engaged during the battle, should have kept touch of the retreating enemy during the night, and made arrangements for the earliest and most rapid pursuit possible in the morning.

As it was, when the horse reached Blewbury, at the foot of the downs which separate the valleys of the Kennet and Thames, some six miles from Wallingford, it was found that the king's forces were already across the Thames. As the bridge at Wallingford was held by the Royalists, the only road open to the Parliamentary horse by which to continue the pursuit was that to Abingdon and across the river there. This was a shorter road than that the king's army had taken, and it might thus have been intercepted before reaching Oxford. But this movement would have brought the cavalry into a country very unfavourable to that arm, intersected by many streams, and within the girdle of fortified posts by which Oxford was surrounded. It was therefore considered unadvisable to continue the pursuit without the assistance of the foot.

Leaving their troopers quartered in Blewbury and the neighbouring villages. Waller, Cromwell, and Hazlerigg hastened back to the army at Newbury. Here, according to Cromwell's narrative, they urged on Manchester the advisability of advancing at once with the whole army, crossing the Isis above (west of) Oxford, and driving the Royalists out of their quarters at Witney, Burford, and Woodstock. By this movement, they would also interpose between Oxford and Rupert at Bath and Gerard at Evesham.

Such a bold movement was not within Manchester's capacity, though it would probably have succeeded with an energetic commander, as the fortress of Abingdon would have protected the line of retreat. Failing his consent, the cavalry leaders urged that two or three thousand foot should be at once sent to join the horse and assist them in the difficult country in which the latter would find themselves if they followed the Royalists. This also the earl refused. He contented himself with summoning Donnington Castle, the governor of which (Colonel Boys) had been knighted by the king for his previous gallant defence.' Finding his summons disregarded, Manchester directed an assault on the 30th, which, badly planned and feebly carried out, was repulsed.

At last, on the 2nd November, Manchester was induced to advance towards Oxford. But his movements were slow and reluctant. That night he only reached Compton, and the next day Harwel, thus taking two days to cover less distance than the king's army had marched in one night. Arrived there, he would advance no further, and he called a council of war at which the majority of the officers appear to have considered, that owing to the bad condition of the roads, the late season, and the fatigues the army had already undergone, it would be unadvisable to advance further.

✶✶✶✶✶✶

The evidence on this point is contradictory. Cromwell in his narrative says, "All were against drawing back to Newbury that I know or heard save his Lordship only. *Quarrel of Manchester and Cromwell*.

✶✶✶✶✶✶

On the contrary, they thought the army should retire to Newbury. It could remain concentrated there until the king's forces dispersed to winter quarters. Manchester then sent off the civil commissioners, Warriston and Crewe, to report to this effect to the Houses, who, through the Committee of Both Kingdoms, withdrew an order just issued to Manchester to advance, and informed him he might withdraw his foot to Newbury and make the best use he could of his horse and dragoons.

Meanwhile Cromwell and his party had been urging Manchester to cross the Thames to Dorchester, and thus prevent the king marching to the relief of Donnington and Basing, through Wallingford, or down the north bank to threaten London. At least, they urged, if it was not considered advisable to advance any further, let a good position be prepared on the ground they now occupied to cover the siege.

But Manchester was obdurate, and without even awaiting the return of the commissioners with the sanction of the Houses, he ordered the army to rendezvous on the 6th at Compton and thence marched back to Newbury. According to Cromwell's narrative, the next day he again spoke to Manchester, pointing out that in the position they then occupied about Newbury, they could obtain no information as to the king's movements beyond the river. If they waited for certain information of his drawing over in strength at Wallingford, he could be at Donnington before the Parliamentary leaders could collect their horse from the villages in which they must be quartered for forage and shelter.

If, on the contrary, the latter ordered out their horse at every sign of an advance on the king's part, he could by continual feints weary out their horses in useless concentrations, and then seize a moment when they had just been dispersed to cross in earnest. Manchester replied that if he wished it, the horse should be quartered in advance of Donnington, but the foot must remain at Newbury, he having orders from the Houses to that effect.

******

Manchester's own account of this transaction was that he *ordered* Cromwell to draw his horse together to a rendezvous, but that the latter replied by asking whether he intended to flay his horses, "for if I called them to a rendezvous I might have their skins but no service from 'em." Rushworth, vol. vi.

******

Cromwell, however, considered that such an arrangement would not improve matters, as the horse must still be widely quartered, and could not therefore assemble in time to dispute the king's advance unless supported by foot. Consequently, the whole army fell back and quartered near Newbury, the horse being scattered in villages on both banks of the Kennet for ease of supply.

Charles, having joined Rupert at Bath, nominated him to the command-in-chief in place of Brentford, who had been wounded. They again reached Oxford on the 1st November with reinforcements from the west, and now determined to recover the artillery which had been left in Donnington during the retreat from Newbury, and if possible to relieve Basing House. On the 7th November, they marched to Wallingford with 5000 horse and 6000 foot. On the 8th they reached Ilsley, and Donnington on the 9th, at noon. Manchester, having no outposts in that direction, had not learnt the movement in time to oppose it. (See Skippon's report in Rushworth, vol. vi.)

That afternoon the Royal Army crossed the Lambourne by fords near the castle, and drew up in a large field between Speen and Newbury. Here they found Manchester's foot lying behind breastworks which stretched from Newbury to Shaw House. But few of his horse were with him under Balfour; the rest, under Cromwell, could be seen drawing to a rendezvous on Newbury Wash, the other side of the Kennet.

A charge of the Royalist horse drove Balfour behind the foot, but it was stopped at the breastwork, and no further fighting happened.

Towards evening the king drew back to Donnington, Rupert sending a challenge to Manchester to attack the rear-guard. As the Royal forces drew off, Cromwell's horse began to arrive, but no fighting took place.

The next morning the king drew his artillery and as much of the ammunition as he could carry out of the castle, and then drew up his army on a heath about a mile to the north of it.

******

Sir E. Walker, whose narrative was written within a few months of these events makes no mention of this halt on the heath. He merely says that the retreat was carried out in good order. (*Historical Discourses*)

******

The Parliamentary horse started in pursuit, but finding the king strongly posted, the generals held a council of war as to whether they should attack. Cromwell argued vehemently in favour of immediate and vigorous action, most of the others considered it imprudent to fight. One argument employed, some say by Manchester, others by Sir A. Hazlerigg, was to the effect that Charles, though beaten again and again, would still be King of England, whereas if he beat the Parliament's army but once, its cause would collapse, and they would all be hanged. To this Cromwell replied, that if this were so, they should never have entered into the contest at all. Meanwhile the king withdrew unmolested in good order.

That evening, Manchester, Waller, and Balfour signed a report to the Committee of Both Kingdoms in which they state that it was impossible for them to prevent the Royal Army relieving Donnington, because if they had drawn up:

> ..... between the castle and the king, the king had wheeled about and possessed the town (*i.e.* Newbury). Then the weather and want would have driven us to a retreat. The king would not only have his train, but the town as a quarter, and Basing relieved.

Further, as to not attacking him on the 10th they say:

> But considering his many advantages of ground and the weather falling bad, following might break our army, *(i.e.* the army might be ruined in the pursuit), the officers of the foot complaining of the lessening of their foot, and many hundreds of our, horses be already dead, and the living very weak, and many

of the troopers run from their colours. And being assured that upon our quitting Newbury the enemy would forthwith take it, we thought it fittest to return to Newbury, where we are now watching the king's motions, and waiting your Lordships' further orders.

It hardly required a soldier to point out that if the king had endeavoured to slip past a Parliamentary army posted between Wallingford and Donnington, he would have exposed his forces on the march to an attack in flank and rear. The excuses for refusing an engagement on the 10th were such as were always available in an army which lived more or less from hand to mouth, and in which desertion was always more or less rife. The opinion of the committee on the action of their generals is best expressed in their own words.

> We have received your letters concerning the relief of Donnington Castle by the enemy, and are very sorry that they met not with that opposition that was expected from an army that God had blessed lately with so happy a victory against them. So long as the enemy continues in the field, we cannot advise that you should go to your winter quarters, but are very desirous that keeping your forces together you will use your best endeavours to recover the advantage the enemy hath lately gained in relieving Donnington.... And because the enemy probably doth intend the relief of Basing, we recommend it to your special care to prevent that design, which, not prevented, would exceedingly encourage the enemy, and be very prejudicial to public affairs.—*The Quarrel between the Earl of Manchester and Oliver Cromwell.*

Essex, himself a most cautious and inert commander, was dissatisfied with a report Skippon, his second in command, sent him. In this the latter had tried to throw on Cromwell's choice of a rendezvous for the horse south of the Kennet all the blame for the inaction of the Parliamentary commanders on the 9th. He asserted that in consequence the horse had not arrived on the field in time to take part in the action or attack the enemy during his retreat. As to the movements on the 10th he said:

> This day the king's army marched leisurely and soldierlike from the further sides of the Castle, whither they retreated last night Wantage way; 'tis said to have drawn us out of our strengths,

and that he might the rather thereby have had advantage (we being necessitated to march somewhat about to come at him because of the castle) to have got into Newbury behind us, and so to have had the freer way to Basing, or to have forced us to fight with him upon great disadvantage, he having the liberty to chose his own ground; whereupon it was resolved we should march back to Newbury, where all our foot forces lie miserably pestered.—Rushworth vol. vi.

To cover the siege of Basing was thus the task still remaining for Manchester before sending his army into winter quarters. He had express directions from the committee to that effect, and had himself excused his remissness in not fighting the king by his desire to avoid the risk of allowing the place to be relieved. On the 10th the king had retired to Lambourne, where he had remained on the 11th, and on the 12th he marched to Marlborough. Here it was determined to attempt the relief of Basing with a party of 1000 horse under Colonel Gage, who had previously succeeded in a similar attempt. Each horseman was to carry on his saddle a sack of corn or other provision.

On the 17th the king's army marched to Hungerford, from whence Basing might be reached in one day. Should Gage's party succeed in reaching it, the sacks of provisions were to be thrown down and the return to the army commenced immediately. On the 19th the Royal forces which had been reinforced by 500 horse from the West, were drawn out to a rendezvous near Hungerford. Thence 1000 men were despatched under Colonel Lisle with provisions for Donnington, and with orders to bring away the rest of the train. Gage's party, also started for Basing. (Sir E. Walker, *Hist. Discourses*).

Meanwhile, rumours of the king's intention to relieve Basing had reached Manchester at Newbury. On the 17th November, the day on which Charles advanced to Hungerford, he marched towards Kingsclere, where he would be in a better position to intercept any parties sent from Marlborough across the downs direct to Basing, or to fight the king should he advance in strength. But, hearing on the march of the Royalist movement on Hungerford, he changed his destination to Aldermaston. He alleged that he would here be nearer Basing and cover the siege more effectually.

The next day, the 18th, he moved as far as Mortimer's Heath. Further than that in the direction of Basing he refused to go, in spite of the protestations of Cromwell and others, who urged the importance of preventing the relief of the place. On the contrary, the siege was this day raised, and on the 19th the army fell back to Reading, Manchester declaring that the privations the soldiers were enduring in the field induced them to desert in hundreds, and that it was absolutely necessary that he should retire on his magazines. Thus, when Gage appeared before Basing on the 19th, he found the enemy gone, and nothing to prevent the house being provisioned.

After this both armies went into winter quarters,—the king's forces at Oxford, Marlborough, Newbury, Basing, &c.,—and the Parliament's at Reading, Henley, Farnham, &c.

Cromwell's charge against Manchester

Manchester's mismanagement of the campaign had been so complete, his disregard of the orders of the Houses and of the Committee of Both Kingdoms so glaring, that Parliament could no longer pass over his conduct in silence. The indecisive termination of the campaign had encouraged those who still believed a compromise possible to re-open negotiations between king and Parliament, and a Committee to carry proposals to that effect to Charles had already been appointed by the House.

But there were those who with Cromwell believed that no lasting peace could be arrived at, except after the complete defeat of one side or the other. These were convinced that if the cause of the Parliament were to triumph, a complete regeneration of its armies was necessary. The first step was to get rid of those commanders whose incompetence or inertness had hitherto prevented all decisive action.

On the 13th November, that is before the siege of Basing had been raised, the Commons had ordered:

> That the Members of this House that are of the Committee of Both Kingdoms do tomorrow give an account to this House concerning the carriage of the business at the relieving of Donnington Castle, near Newbury, by the king's forces.—*Quarrel between Manchester and Cromwell*. The quotations in the following pages are from the same tract, except where otherwise noted.

On the next day Hazlerigg, who had been sent expressly for this purpose by Manchester, made a relation to the House of the whole affair. The House, however, does not appear to have been satisfied, for on the 22nd, after the raising of the siege of Basing, it was ordered:

> That the Members of this House that are of the Committee of Both Kingdoms do tomorrow give an account to this House of the whole carriage and motions of the armies, both near Donnington Castle, Newbury, Basing-house, and of the present posture of them.

And again, on the 23rd it was ordered:

> That Sir William Waller and Lieutenant-General Cromwell do on Monday morning next declare unto the House their whole knowledge and information of the particular proceedings of the armies since their conjunction.

Accordingly, on the 25th November, Cromwell made his statement to the House. It amounted to a direct charge against Manchester of causing unnecessary delays, of neglecting the instructions received by him from the committee and the House, of a half-hearted prosecution of the Parliamentary cause, and of a desire to save the king from being reduced to extremities.

******

> It is curious that Whitelocke, referring apparently to the same speech, says that it "seemed, but cautiously enough, to lay more blame on the Lord General's (*i.e.* Essex's) army than upon any other."

******

A brief summary of his speech has been recorded by Rushworth, and a document entitled *An Account of the effect and substance of my Narrative made to this House for soe much thereof as concerned the Earl of Manchester*, has been brought to light, and published by the Camden Society in the tract, *The Quarrel between the Earl of Manchester and Oliver Cromwell*. This document is apparently a reduction to writing by Cromwell himself of his speech to the House. It is a most able and soldierlike criticism of Manchester's whole proceedings, from the reduction of York to the raising of the siege of Basing.

It is difficult to believe in reading it that the author was a man who till two years before had made no study of military affairs. Every strategical or tactical error is clearly pointed out, and the action which a zealous, energetic commander should have taken tersely described. Yet it appears that, with the exception of a few unimportant intercalations, it is entirely in Cromwell's own words. It has been argued that such clearness and terseness are foreign to his style, and that there is an absence of those scriptural allusions with which his speeches and writings were generally interlarded. But those who have studied his *military* reports must allow that they are always terse and to the point, and that scriptural phrases occupy a very small portion of them. Indeed, they differ much from his letters on religious matters or affairs of state.

The document commences by Cromwell's declaration that he believed Manchester's "backwardness to all action" did not arise from "dulness or indisposedness to engagement," but from a desire to have the war ended by accommodation on certain terms, to obtain which it might be disadvantageous to reduce the king too low. After asserting generally that Manchester avoided every action which might have brought on an engagement, constantly declined to avail himself of advantages which offered themselves, and deliberately neglected to obey the commands of the Houses and the Committee, Cromwell proceeded to give instances. He pointed to the earl's inaction at Doncaster and Lincoln after the capture of York, and declared that though pressed to attack the fortresses of Newark, Belvoir, &c., he persistently refused to do so on one pretext or another.

Then having been ordered by the Committee to march into Cheshire, he used the presence of these fortresses, which he had refused to reduce, as an impediment to such a march. When, however, Rupert had quitted Cheshire, Manchester had insisted on sending a party of horse in that direction, and then used their absence as an excuse for not attacking the fortresses. He also quartered his forces in those parts of the Association which were already secure, leaving large tracts of land open to the forays of the enemy. By neglecting to reduce the enemy's posts, he was obliged, when he at last marched south, to leave behind a far larger force to secure the Association than would otherwise have been necessary.

These errors had often been pointed out to the earl by his officers, but he had neglected their advice, and only called his Council of War once. Though he received orders to march south at the end of August, it was the 13th September before he reached St. Albans, and when pressed by his officers to hasten his march, he had threatened to hang them. At St. Albans, he had remained eight or nine days, and then marched slowly to Reading, where he stayed till the 16th October. Then he advanced south to Basingstoke instead of west to join with Waller, in spite of direct orders to do so from the Committee, and of the entreaties of Sir William Waller.

Cromwell points out that there was nothing to prevent Manchester from marching westward to succour Waller, instead of loitering at St. Albans and Reading, and that Essex's forces and the City regiments could then have joined them at Salisbury. In that case, the king could not have crossed the Avon, the sieges of Donnington, Basing, and Banbury would have been covered, and those places taken. But as it was, when Waller fell back and joined Manchester at Basingstoke, the latter had ordered a retreat on Odiham, although the king was still at Andover, and his own reinforcements within seven miles.

This retreat had only been prevented by Waller's and Hazlerigg's persuasion. Then after the junction of all the forces at Basingstoke, Manchester, having 19,000 men against the king's 10,000 at Kingsclere, had, by a roundabout march of four days to Newbury, given the king an opportunity to retreat unmolested to Oxford, had the latter cared to do so; and by advancing from the east he had conceded to the Royalists at Newbury the advantage of a castle on their left flank and a stream in their front, over which the passages had been secured. This necessitated the danger and delay of dividing the forces and making a long flank march with one part, which might have been avoided by an attack from the south. (Cromwell does not point out how, in that case, he would have crossed the Kennet, the passages of which, it may be presumed, the king would then have held).

As to the Battle of Newbury, the arrangement arrived at by the Council of War on the 26th October was that Manchester should attack Shaw House immediately he saw or heard the battle begin on the Speen side. Yet, although the opening guns were fired at 2 p.m. on the 27th, although he could see the Royalists driven from hedge to hedge down Speen Hill, and although his own officers implored him to attack, he refused to move till half an hour after sunset, when the attack on the Speen side had been stopped by the coming darkness; and then he attacked on the side on which the house was most strongly fortified.

Cromwell then described Manchester's supineness throughout the fortnight after the battle, and how he rejected every proposal to take advantage of the success already gained to prevent Rupert and Gerard from joining the king's army, and to cover the sieges of Donnington and Basing. He points out that though the king had concentrated all his available forces about Oxford by the 1st November, he did not start for the relief of Donnington till the 7th, when Manchester, by drawing back to Newbury, had left the way open.

Cromwell declared that when the earl had been urged to advance

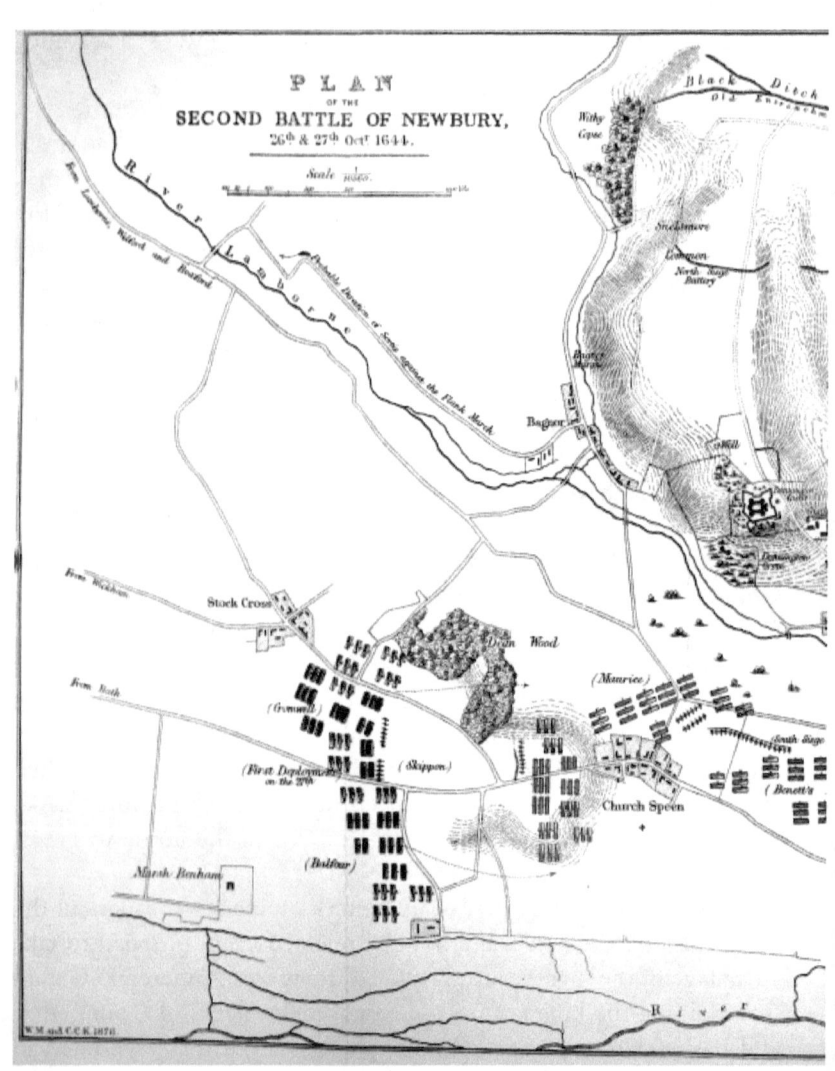

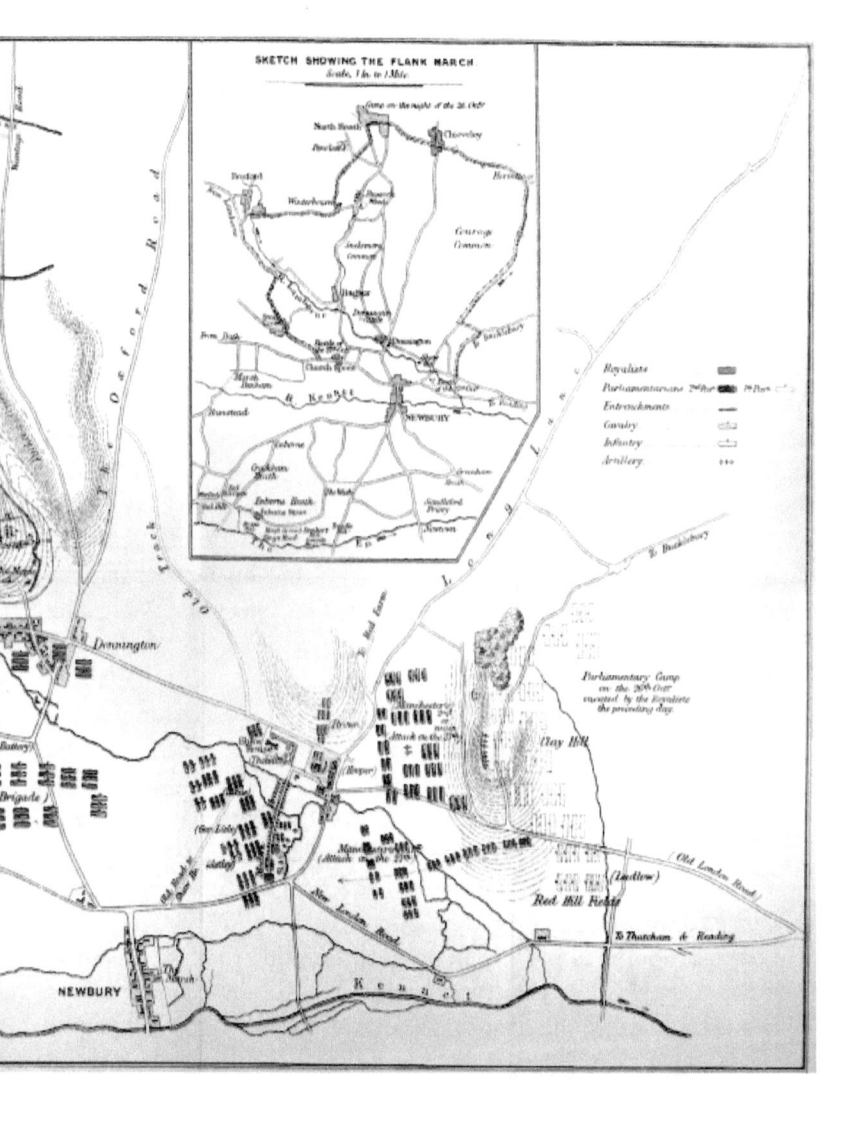

from Harwell, or to take up a position about there, he had refused, on the plea that he could not move until Warriston and Crewe returned with the directions of the House; yet he ordered and commenced the retreat on Newbury before they got back. Further, that on his retreat from Compton he sent all the provisions, which had come by water for the army, to the garrison of Abingdon, thereby himself occasioning that scarcity at Newbury which he afterwards urged as his principal reason for giving up the siege of Basing and retiring to Reading.

Cromwell then points out how impossible it was, from a position to the south of Donnington and near Newbury, to subsist the horse in quarters and yet collect them sufficiently soon to intercept the king before he reached the castle. And that when this had been impressed upon Manchester he still refused to allow the foot to support the horse in a more advanced position, without which the latter could not safely be drawn forward. On the 8th the king advanced from Wallingford about two o'clock. (Whether a.m. or p.m. is not stated, but from Manchester's narrative, evidently p.m.)

Information of this was brought about five o'clock by a fugitive, and the horse ordered to rendezvous at Redhill, near Shaw. But owing to the faulty dispositions it was found impossible to draw them together in time to prevent the king relieving the castle, and that then it had been arranged to attack him during his retreat, and the rendezvous for the horse had been altered to Newbury Wash. The horse, Cromwell affirms, did reach the rendezvous that night, and many urged their drawing out to meet the king, who had unexpectedly passed the night at Ilsley, six miles from the castle, and might still be intercepted. But so much time was consumed in debate that the opportunity was lost.

After the withdrawal of the king back to Donnington on the evening of the 9th, it was arranged, said Cromwell, that the horse should start in pursuit at 3 a.m., and delay his retreat till the foot, which were to start at daybreak, came up. The horse discovered the king's forces at daybreak, not retreating, but in position on Winterbourne Heath. It was then only by the greatest importunity that Cromwell and others succeeded in getting the foot drawn out of quarters and marched to the Heath by 11 a.m. Arrived there, and having no further excuses to urge, the king's army being still on the ground, Manchester "plainly declared himself against fighting," and, whilst the Royalists withdrew, contented himself with viewing their forces, and discussing the situation. Then at a Council of War which was held on the ground the earl opposed fighting so vehemently that it was determined to allow the king to retire unmolested, and to fall back to Newbury.

The king having retired to Marlborough, awaiting an opportunity to relieve Basing, Manchester stirred up the soldiers to clamour for return to the Association, his agents informing them that they would receive no pay till they got there.

Although, when it was a question of advancing beyond Donnington, Manchester had harped upon the importance of Newbury as covering the siege of Basing, yet when the king was at Marlborough, watching for an opportunity to relieve that place, the earl became very anxious to quit Newbury. And at last, on hearing of the advance of a force by another road towards Basing, he did quit it with the whole army, under pretence of intercepting the relieving party at Kingsclere. But instead of marching to the latter place, he moved to Aldermaston, informing his officers that he was going to Basing to immediately cover the siege, but in reality, his aim was to approach Reading. When the proximity of this town induced many men to slip thither without leave, he used the pretext thus created, to avoid going to Basing, and finally withdrew all the troops to Reading.

Such was the charge made by Cromwell against Manchester in the House. A drastic criticism truly, mercilessly exposing all the faults committed by the earl in the conduct of the campaign, and attributing them, not to oversights or incapacity, but to a deliberate attempt to avoid inflicting a defeat on the king. Whitelocke says that the narrative gave great satisfaction to the Commons, by whom the whole business was referred for inquiry and report to a Committee of the House, of which Mr. Zouch Tate was president.

Manchester replied by assuring the House of Lords that he was ready to give an account of his conduct during the campaign; which he was permitted to do on the 28th November. The Lords also referred the matter to a committee, and directed Manchester to reduce his narrative to writing, which he accordingly did, and presented it to the House on the 2nd December. He divided it into two parts, in the first of which he endeavoured to rebut the charges made by Cromwell, and in the second, he in turn formulated charges against the latter of using disrespectful language concerning the House of Lords, and of opposing by every means in his power, both the establishment of a Presbyterian Church, and the alliance with the Scots.

In the first part, Manchester asserted to begin with, that:

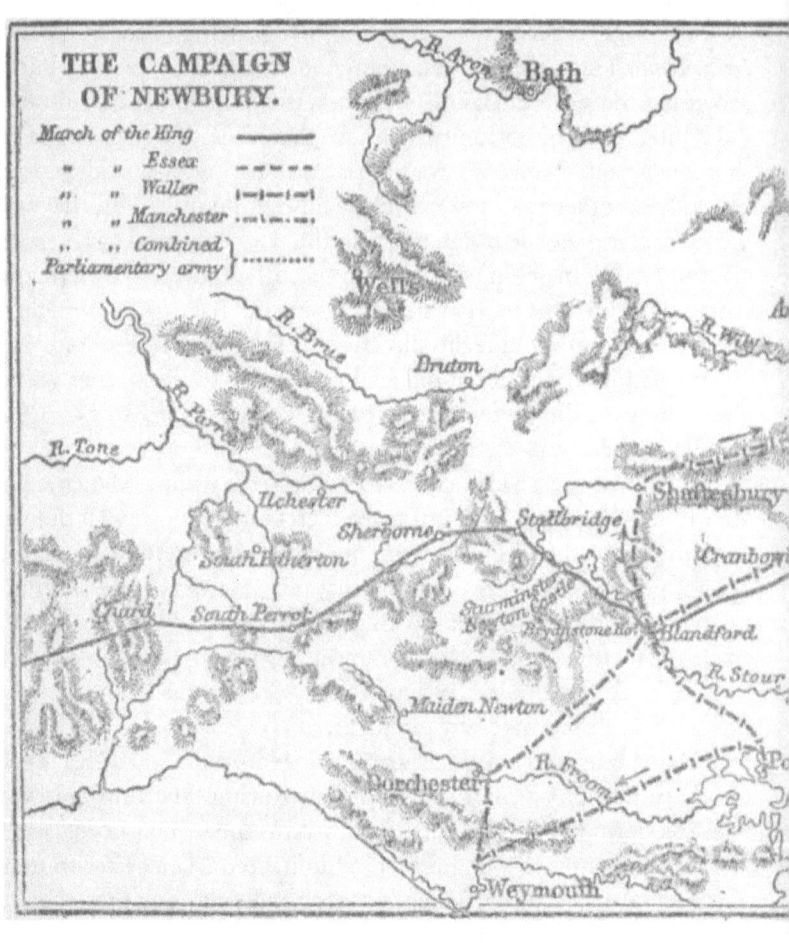

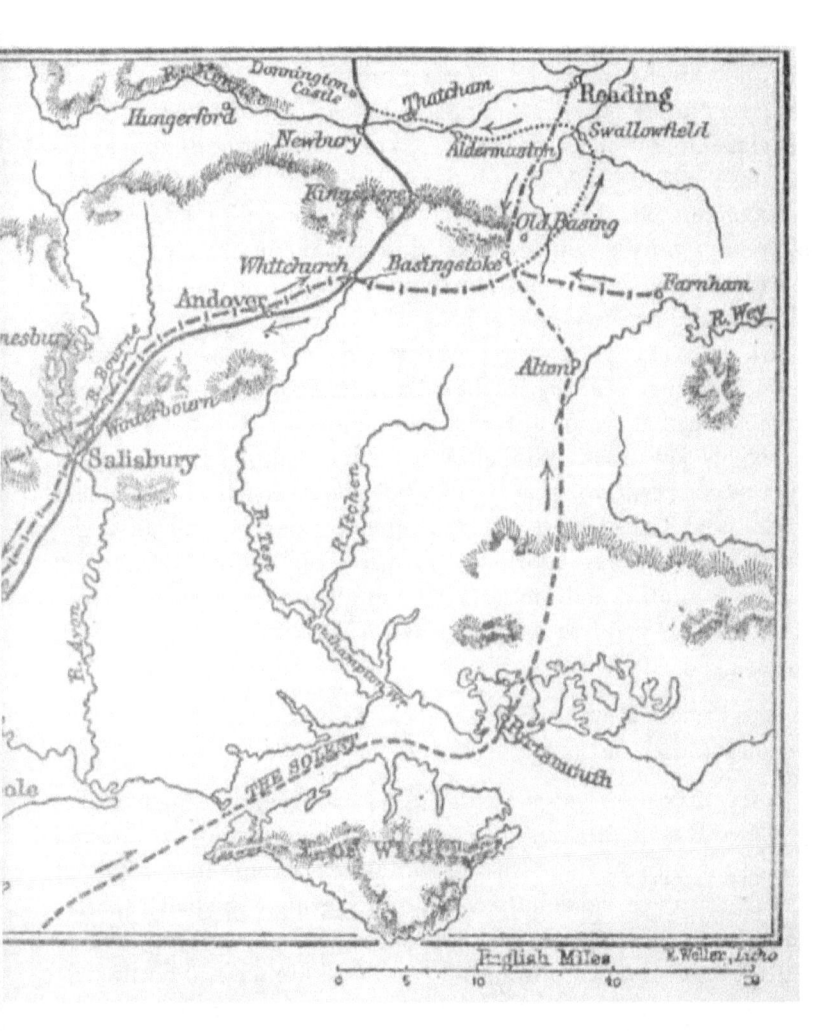

From the time I came to join my Lord General's army I never did anything without joint consent of those that were the best experienced and chiefest commanders in all the armies.

Then as to the Battle of Newbury, he had punctually carried out the arrangement agreed on, but "where those horses were which Lieutenant-General Cromwell commanded, I have yet had no certain account." Afterwards, when information was received that the king was intending to relieve Donnington, he had consulted with Major-General Skippon, and both had agreed to draw their horse into a rendezvous the next day. Balfour had complied, but Cromwell had asked in discontent whether "I intended to flay my horse, for if I called them to a rendezvous I might have their skins but no service for them." As he had persisted in his opposition to the arrangement, Manchester had told him to do as he pleased.

On the evening of the 8th it was arranged that all the horse should be on Newbury Wash by six the next morning, yet, when the king's horse charged at two in the afternoon, Cromwell had not sent over any of his squadrons, although Manchester "had desired that all of them might be drawn over on that side the river where the present service was." The horse did not reach the field of action till late in the evening. On the next morning, when the king's forces were found marching in an orderly retreat, the commanders agreed it was not safe to engage at present, principally on reasons adduced by Sir A. Hazlerigg—

> And there was not one present that delivered his opinion for fighting with the king at that time.

A few days afterwards, when it was believed that the king intended to relieve Basing, the horse of each of the three armies was directed to take the outpost duties in rotation. When it came to the turn of Cromwell's horse, he demurred, but on receiving Manchester's direct order the duty was performed. The subsequent movements were all settled by the Council of War, and Cromwell himself had borne witness to that fact. For on one occasion when some letters had been received from London, blaming Manchester and others for acting without consulting the Council of War, Cromwell had exclaimed:

> My Lord, I hold him for a villain and a knave that would do any man ill offices, but there was nothing done but what was justifiable, and by the joint consent of the Council of War. (The

words here quoted are from Crawford's narrative, *Quarrel between Manchester and Cromwell*).

As to the charges against him of dilatoriness and supineness in Lincolnshire, Manchester said Cromwell, himself could bear witness, that as soon as he received the orders of the committee to march to the west, he had given the latter instructions to go on at once with twenty troops of horse, informing him that he would himself follow with the foot. It was Cromwell who made difficulties, urging the necessities of his men, which Manchester overcame. "Some discontents then in my army was the cause of retarding that service." By this Manchester evidently referred to the disputes between Cromwell and Crawford, the Independents and the Presbyterians.

The House of Lords professed themselves satisfied with Manchester's narrative, and at a conference with the Commons placed both it and the personal charges against Cromwell in the hands of the Lower House. The latter appointed a Committee to inquire into the matters raised, which eventually found that the charges, as preferred, constituted a breach of privilege.

Meanwhile, Tate's Committee continued to take evidence, notes of which will be found in the *Quarrel between Manchester and Cromwell*. Gardiner dilates more fully on it, and gives extracts from the dispositions of the witnesses which have lately come to light. The weight of the evidence is strongly in favour of Cromwell's version; and indeed, the whole spirit of the charges made by him against Manchester is amply proved by the latter's own correspondence with the Committee of Both Kingdoms. On the other hand, except for two rancorous and disjointed narratives prepared by Crawford and another opponent of Cromwell, no evidence which could support a charge of delay or fractiousness against the latter appears to have been given.

The only point which denotes backwardness on his part and which he does not appear to have cleared up, is the retention of his horse inactive on Newbury Wash all day on the 9th November. By his own narrative his squadrons were assembled by 6 a.m., yet none of his troops arrived to support the foot engaged north of Newbury till late in the evening. He must, from his place, have seen the king's forces march down to oppose the Parliamentary foot. Be the reason what it was, it cannot have arisen from a disinclination to fight.

The charges made against Cromwell as to his hostility towards the establishment of a Presbyterian Church, further incensed the Scots and the stricter Presbyterians against him. They gained over Essex to their side, and a conference was held at his house, at which the two Scotch Commissioners were present, when some means of getting rid of Cromwell were discussed. Whitelocke and Maynard, two lawyers in the Commons, were sent for, and a very graphic account of what followed is given by the former. They were asked the meaning of the word "incendiary" in English law, and whether Cromwell could not be proceeded against as an incendiary between the two nations.

The lawyers replied that, considering the loss of dignity which would accrue to persons in the position of the commissioners if they made such a charge and failed to prove it, and considering the very conclusive proofs which would be required before a man of Cromwell's great and increasing influence in the Commons could be convicted of such a charge, they strongly advised the Lord General and his associates not to proceed in the matter. Their advice was taken, and the matter dropped.

Cromwell, on the other hand, had no wish to attack Manchester personally. His object all along had been to reorganise the army under capable commanders. As a first step, he had attempted to convince the Commons and the public of the mismanagement of the war under the present leaders, and with the present organisation. This he had fully and publicly done in his charge against Manchester. The next step was to substitute a better organisation and more competent commanders. If this could be done without distinguishing between individuals, so much the better. No man was ever more proof against personal vindictiveness than Cromwell. Already schemes for the attainment of the aims he had in view had been submitted to the House.

As early as the 19th November, that is before Cromwell gave his account of the campaign, it had been resolved—

> That it be referred to the Committee of Both Kingdoms to consider the state and condition of all the armies and forces under the command of the Parliament, and to put them into such a posture as may make them most useful and advantageous to the kingdom.

And again, on the 23rd:

> Ordered—that it be referred to the Committee of Both Kingdoms ... upon the consideration of the present state and condition of the armies, as now disposed and commanded, to consider of a frame or model of the whole militia, and present it to

the House, as may put the forces into such a posture as may be most advantageous for the service of the public.

Ever since the victory of Marston Moor, Cromwell's influence in the House and country had been steadily rising. Since Pym's death the more ardent reformers both of state and religion looked more and more to the party with which he was associated to carry out their views. Sir Harry Vane represented this party for the most part in the House, Cromwell's military duties preventing his frequent attendance. Now, however, when the army was in winter quarters near London, and whilst the peace negotiations suspended hostilities to a great degree, he took the opportunity of being continually in his seat. How long the scheme, which he and his colleagues adopted for the ousting of the present commanders from the army, had been considered by them is uncertain.

On the 9th December, Rushworth says:

> The Commons having long debated the sad Condition of the Kingdom, unless the Treaty of Peace take effect or the war be successfully prosecuted, resolved into a Grand Committee; wherein after long Silence every one looking who should begin—Cromwell himself stood up and spoke to this effect:—

> 'It is now a time to speak or forever hold the tongue. The important occasion now is no less than to save a nation, out of a bleeding, nay, almost dying condition: which the long continuance of this war hath already brought it into; so that without a more speedy, vigorous, and effectual prosecution of the war—casting off all lingering proceedings like those of soldiers-of-fortune beyond the sea to spin out a war,—we shall make the kingdom weary of us, and hate the name of a Parliament.

> 'For what do the enemy say? Nay, what do many say that were friends at the beginning of the Parliament? Even this—that the members of both Houses have got great places and commands and the sword into their hands; and, what by interest in Parliament, what by power in the army, will perpetually continue themselves in grandeur, and not permit the war speedily to end, lest their own power should determine with it. This I speak here to our own faces, is but what others do utter abroad behind our backs. I am far from reflecting on any. I know the worth of those commanders, members of both Houses, who are yet in power: but if I may speak my conscience without

reflection upon any, I do conceive if the army be not put into another method, and the war more vigorously prosecuted, the people can bear the war no longer, and will enforce you to a dishonourable peace.

'But this I would recommend to your prudence—not to insist upon any complaint or oversight of any commander-in-chief upon any occasion whatsoever; for, as I must acknowledge myself guilty of oversights, so I know they can rarely be avoided in military matters. Therefore, waving a strict inquiry into the cause of these things let us apply ourselves to the remedy, which is most necessary. And I hope we have such true English hearts, and zealous affections towards the general weal of our Mother Country, as no Members of either House will scruple to deny themselves, and their own private interests, for the public good; nor count it to be a dishonour done to them, whatever the Parliament shall resolve upon in this weighty matter.'—Carlyle's *Cromwell*, People's Ed. i.

Truly a remarkable speech—remarkable for its patriotism and its political perspicuity. Most remarkable to the military reader in that it expounds, perhaps for the first time, the spirit of modern war. Cromwell saw that the method of war adopted by the continental generals commanding armies of mercenaries was inapplicable to a civil struggle, in which the soldiers in the ranks were citizens on whose labour in their trades the welfare of the nation depended. A mercenary army was so costly to the prince who maintained it, that its defeat was not to be risked except when unavoidable.

Besides, the mercenary lived by war, and therefore wished to prolong it. But when the whole manhood of the nation became involved in the struggle, it was of the highest importance to its welfare that the speediest possible decision should be arrived at. Prompt, vigorous action and a commander willing to undertake great risks for the sake of speedy and decisive victory were in the highest degree desirable.

Cromwell was the first to understand the essential differences in the two methods of war. He wished to adopt the one appropriate to the exigencies of the case, to strike promptly and decisively. But the difficulties before him were enormous, the task such as only a great genius could perform. When a continental nation now goes to war, its leaders find its manhood so trained and organised that they can expend its whole strength in rapid and decisive blows. But Cromwell found the forces of the Parliament keen indeed for the triumph of its cause, but dispersed, ill led, and disorganised. He had to organise and strike almost simultaneously; organise effectually and strike decisively.

Cromwell knew well that even the greatest soldiers of history had often made mistakes; that amidst all the accidents and uncertainties of war this must ever be so. Napoleon said:

> He is the greatest general who makes fewest mistakes.

Cromwell said:

> For as I must acknowledge myself guilty of oversights, so I know they can rarely be avoided in military affairs.

But in the best organised army mistakes in carrying out orders, and miscalculations as to its powers, will be fewest. A capable commander recovers quicker from his own mistakes, and avails himself more promptly of his enemy's, than a slow, incapable one. Therefore, it was of overwhelming importance to reorganise the army whilst the lull in the war lasted, and to substitute commanders in touch with the spirit of the rank and file, for the slow methodical generals, who had blundered through the previous campaigns without attaining any decisive result.

The Commons caught quickly the spirit and drift of Cromwell's speech, and Zouch Tate, the President of the Committee which was inquiring into the charges against Manchester, moved,—

> That no member of either House of Parliament shall, during this war, enjoy or execute any office or command Military or Civil, and that an Ordinance be brought in accordingly.— Whitelocke

And after a long debate the motion was carried. No time was lost in introducing the ordinance, which was reported to the House on 11th December. The spirit of reform thus imparted to the Commons spread rapidly to the public, and on 12th December a petition was presented to the House in the name of the well-affected citizens of London, taking notice of the care the House took of the Commonwealth and the city, and expressing their Resolution to assist them to the utmost in prosecuting their vote of 9th December.

This ordinance, well known as the "Self-denying Ordinance," did not pass through the House without considerable opposition. Whitelocke was one of those who spoke against it, and he gives his speech in full in his *Memorials*. The Presbyterians of the Scotch party foresaw that it would place the command of the army in the hands of the Independents, and though they based their opposition to the measure on the plea of inexpediency—there is little doubt the loss of power to their party was its true motive. But Cromwell with the Independents and the less bigoted Presbyterians who sided with him were too strong for their opponents, and on 19th December the measure passed the Commons.

On the 21st it was introduced into the Lords. Here, however, the opposition was likely to prove much more formidable. The few Lords who still attended at their House in Westminster were all of the Presbyterian party. Few in numbers and with no leader of genius, their influence in Parliament was rapidly declining. The Lower House was beginning to treat them with scant respect. Only by their hold on the army could they enforce any attention to their views. The Earls of Essex, Manchester, and Denbigh, held the chief commands. Deprive them of these and the last hold on political influence would slip from the grasp of the Upper House.

No attempt was made even to debate the Self-denying Ordinance till the 30th December. It was then referred to a Committee who reported against it, and although the Commons offered reasons in its support, and on the 13th January, went up in a body to the Lords with a message to importune them to pass it, the Upper House, on further debate, finally rejected the measure. (Whitelocke; Gardiner, vol. ii.)

This method of ridding the army of incompetent commanders having failed, the majority in the Commons proceeded to work for the same end by a different method. It has been seen that the Committee of Both Kingdoms had been ordered to report on the reorganisation of the army. Of this committee, Cromwell was a member. As a result of their deliberations they recommended that the regular forces should consist of 6000 horse divided into ten regiments, 1000 dragoons organised in independent companies, and 14,000 foot divided into regiments each of ten companies, of 120 men each. One or two of the regiments were given a greater strength.

To support these 21,000 men with their horses, baggage, train, &c., a sum of £44,955 was to be set aside every month from the taxes raised in those counties which were less exposed to inroads from the king's forces, whilst the more exposed counties were to continue supporting the garrisons and local troops necessary to their defence. These proposals had already been debated and passed by the Commons on the 11th January, and they now voted that Sir Thomas Fairfax should be appointed to the supreme command as captain-general, and Skippon to command the foot as major-general. The post of lieutenant-general, or commander of the horse, was left vacant.

Both Fairfax and Skippon fulfilled the conditions of the Self-denying Ordinance, neither being a member of either House. They were both also excellent selections in other ways. Fairfax had shown himself a bold, determined leader, whose spirit never flagged under the most adverse conditions. A man of spotless integrity and winning manners, he was adored by his soldiers, and liked and respected by friend and foe. The son and heir of a peer, he might be expected to sympathize with the Lords and support their influence. Yet he was a personal friend of Cromwell, who had often worked harmoniously with him. No man more likely to propitiate all parties could have been found. Skippon was an honest, experienced soldier of no great talents, but one who understood his business and had done good work for the Parliament. Besides, he was Essex's major-general, and in selecting him for the same post in the reformed army the Commons intended to pay the earl a compliment.

On the 27th January an ordinance embodying the proposals of the Committee of Both Kingdoms for the "new modelling" of the army, and nominating Fairfax and Skippon as captain-general and major-general, was finally passed by the Commons, after several days' debate. On the 28th it was sent up to the Lords, and read for the first time in their House on the 30th. They ultimately sent it back to the Commons with alterations. On the 7th February, the latter agreed to most of the Lords' amendments, and gave reasons for not assenting to others.

Against one they urged that an officer refusing to take the Covenant should not be for ever incapacitated from serving the State as the Lords proposed, but might at any time render himself eligible by taking it. Already the Lower House was beginning to lay less stress on the Covenant, which had always been opposed by Cromwell. It also voted that all officers should be appointed by Fairfax and approved by both Houses: this amendment gave the general far greater power and influence in his army, a most desirable condition in the interests of discipline.

Previously it had been proposed that the officers should be nominated by the Houses. On the 12th February, the Commons requested the Lords to hasten the passing of the Ordinance for the New Model, as the soldiers, in suspense as to what would become of them, were growing mutinous in certain places. On the 13th the Lower House forwarded further reasons in support of the measure, and on the 15th it was agreed between the Houses that officers should take the Covenant on obtaining their commissions. The Ordinance then passed both Houses.

On the 19th February Fairfax was received by the Commons in state, and his commission as general solemnly presented him by the Speaker. He shortly afterwards submitted his list of senior officers to the House, which approved of them on the 28th. The list was then submitted to the Lords, who, however, showed considerable reluctance in proceeding with the matter. On the 6th March the Commons requested them to expedite matters, and on the 10th they returned the list to the Lower House with several alterations. This led to conferences between the two Houses on the 15th and 17th, in which the Commons supported Fairfax's nominations. Finally, on the 18th, the Lords assented to the original list.

Fairfax was now duly commissioned as general, and authorised to appoint his officers with consent of the Houses. But to ensure his being the supreme military authority under the Parliament, it was thought necessary to give him further powers. Accordingly, on the 24th March, an Ordinance was read and passed in the Commons granting him a commission to "execute Martial Jurisdiction to fight with, and slay all such as shall oppose him, and to suppress all forces not raised by Authority of both Houses of Parliament." (Whitelocke). After another conference between the Houses, this measure was also passed by the Lords on the 1st April. Although the commission granted to Fairfax as captain-general had virtually deprived Essex of his command, and though the settlement of the list of officers suspended all others, such as Manchester and Waller, who were not included in it, from employment in the army, the Commons thought fit to bring in another "self-denying ordinance."

This, which was also introduced on the 24th March, differed from the original one on one point. All members of either House were required to resign any commissions they might hold within forty days from the passing of the Ordinance. Nothing was said about their being re-appointed, so that it became possible for Fairfax, with the approval of the Houses, to re-commission any officer who was a member of either House. As the Lords had now no object in disputing the measure, it passed their House also on the 3rd April.

One of the last scenes in the contest between the Houses as to the

New Model for the army was the formal resignation of their commissions by Essex, Manchester, and Denbigh, on the 2nd April. Essex, at a conference of the Houses, presented to the Lords a paper, in which he said:

> That he having been employed for almost three years past, as General of all the Parliament's forces, which charge he had endeavoured to perform with all fidelity and fedulity, yet considering by the Ordinance lately brought up to the House of Peers, that it would be advantageous to the public, he desired to lay down his Commission, and freely to render it into the hands of those from whom he received it, and desired such of his officers who had done faithful service, and were now left out, might have their Arrears, and some others received into favour. (Whitelocke).

Both Houses declared that the giving up their commissions was an acceptable service, and a testimony of the fidelity and care these three lords had of the public, (Whitelocke), and the Commons immediately proceeded to consider their pensions.

The Earl of Warwick surrendered his commission as Lord Admiral on the 9th, and on the 15th a committee of six lords and twelve commoners, of which Warwick and Essex were members, was appointed to manage the business of the Admiralty. Waller soon after also quitted the army. All these aristocratic leaders had deserved well of the Parliament. Whilst most of their social equals and their friends had sided with the king, they had remained faithful to the cause of the Commons.

If Essex and Manchester had proved but indifferent generals, still their influence and social prestige must have been of immense value to the Parliament. Warwick, in addition to being an exceedingly influential nobleman, had proved a very capable Lord Admiral, and Denbigh had done good service in the Midlands. Waller was a good soldier of the old school, and a man of unblemished honour and fidelity to the cause. And yet Cromwell and his party had pushed them aside. The result proves that they were right. The strife had continued so long that it would have been impossible for these lords to have now used their influence in favour of the other side, even had they wished to do so.

On the other hand, there were many signs that it was essential to push the war more vigorously. The country would not endure it much longer. The plunderings and excesses of the soldiers, especially on the king's side, the taxes and assessments, were getting more than men could bear. The price of food was rapidly rising, commerce was dislocated. Armed bands of peasants, called Clubmen, were collecting in many counties, their object being to prevent either side taking plunder or free quarter. Whitelocke speaks of 4000 Clubmen in Dorset and 14,000 in Worcestershire during this March. Sometimes these bands favoured one side, sometimes the other, but they owned allegiance to neither. They were but one sign of the impatience of the country at the continuance of the war.

Cromwell, with his extraordinary political and military insight, had perceived and understood the signs of the times. That he was the originator of the New Model, there can be little doubt. The rancour shown towards him by the Scots and other opponents of the measure proves it. His charge against Manchester was but a preparatory move towards the New Model, to convince the Houses and public of the necessity of the change. Once the Commons were fairly committed to reorganise the army the charges were allowed to drop. They were only taken up again when the Lords threatened to become obstructive.

When the obstruction ceased, the consideration of the charges was dropped. Finally, when the necessary measures had been adopted, nothing further was ever heard about them. It was Cromwell's speech which opened the debate on the Self-denying Ordinance. He was present and very active in the House whilst the Ordinance for the New Model was being pushed through. When that was accomplished, and only the finishing touches remained to be put to the scheme, he was, on the 27th February, called away to his military duties. The occasion was urgent. The horse regiments were becoming mutinous; it required the personal influence of the great cavalry leader to bring them back to their duty.

Cromwell's position was a somewhat peculiar one. As a member of the House of Commons he came under the provisions of the Self-denying Ordinance; but in his military capacity he could not be spared from the Parliamentary army. To enable him to remain with the troops, the period within which he was obliged to resign his command from the date of the passing of the ordinance, *viz.* forty days, was renewed for another forty, by special Act of Parliament, and this was continued from time to time.

Cromwell's Raid Round Oxford

When the main armies went into winter quarters in November,

1644, minor operations were still carried on by both sides. Skirmishes between foraying parties were frequent. These occurred principally in the neighbourhood of garrisons maintained by either side in the counties occupied by the other. The Parliamentary garrison of Abingdon, for instance, was constantly engaged with the Cavaliers from Oxford. Several attempts at surprise were frustrated, notably one undertaken by the Princes Rupert and Maurice on the 10th January, which very nearly succeeded. The energetic Governor, Brown, retaliated by attacks on Royalist outposts, and forays on their sheep and cattle.

The garrison of Newark was, as ever, active in harrying neighbouring Roundhead posts, and plundering the farms and villages. Other engagements arose out of the sieges which were still being prosecuted at Plymouth, Taunton, Weymouth, Scarborough, and elsewhere. In September Lord Byron laid siege to Montgomery Castle, which had lately been acquired by the Parliamentary forces, with near 4000 men. Whereupon Meldrum and Brereton advanced to its relief, and a severe engagement ensued, in which Byron was routed, with the loss of 1000 prisoners. Massey was ever active in the Severn Valley. Meldrum retook Liverpool on the 1st November, and the Fairfaxes, after taking several places in Yorkshire, were engaged about midwinter in the siege of Pontefract.

Goring, in an interval of sobriety, pushed a cavalry raid right up to Farnham on the 9th January and then fell back on Petersfield and Winchester. Afterwards he marched west to Salisbury.

Most of the Parliamentary garrisons occupied seaports, where they could be relieved and provisioned by the fleet. But the important town of Taunton, in the heart of the enemy's country, lay inland, and gave the Houses much concern. It was defended by Colonel Blake, afterwards the famous admiral. There were no regular fortifications, but only field works with shallow ditches and palisades. The defence, however, was most stubborn, and the Parliament, fully aware of the importance of the place, spared no efforts to retain it. It was relieved during December by Colonel Holbourn.

On the 10th February Sir Lewis Dyves surprised one of the forts surrounding Weymouth, which gave him command of the town, and the safety of the port was thereby seriously imperilled. The garrison of Melcombe, on the opposite side, was also hard pressed. Waller was ordered to collect a force from the neighbourhood of London, and march at once to retake the captured fort, and at the same time to push Goring back. But on the 13th he reported to the House from

Farnham, that he found the soldiers mutinous.

In a second letter, he said he should hasten on to Weymouth at any risk, taking with him those who would follow him. But on the 14th the horse broke into open mutiny at Leatherhead. These regiments had served under Essex, and said they:

> We will rather go under any the Lord General should appoint than with Sir William Waller with all the money in England.—Gardiner, vol. ii.

Waller had always been a great favourite with the Londoners, but a rival of Essex, and the soldiers in the latter's army resented this. Apart from personal causes, an insubordinate spirit was becoming dangerously rife in the Parliamentary Army. The uncertainty of their future, owing to the New Model Ordinance, then still under debate, probably unsettled the soldiers. Their pay was largely in arrears, and this was certainly one of the exciting causes. Even in Manchester's forces, hitherto paid with fair regularity, arrears were accumulating. The Eastern Association, finding their soldiers quartered far from their borders, and unable to understand that the best defence is one that keeps the enemy at a distance, felt themselves neglected, and in consequence became dilatory in forwarding the pay. The men began to murmur; but Cromwell's own regiment was conspicuous for its better discipline. Whitelocke writes:

> At the same conference, they (the Commons) offered letters that came from the army, from persons of credit, of the great complaints against some commanders of horse, and of the mutinous and disobedient carriage of the soldiers, refusing to march to relieve Weymouth being in so great distress, and that at the muster, no men appeared so full, and well-armed, and civil, as Colonel Cromwell's horse.

Yet even these did not entirely escape the contagion, judging by his letter dated the 17th March, quoted below.

In this crisis, the House turned to Cromwell, whose personal influence with the soldiers was great. On the 27th February, he was ordered to join Waller and endeavour to persuade the men to return to their duty. His presence seems immediately to have had a good effect, for on the 4th March information was given the House "that the mutinous horse inclined to obedience." Whereupon the Parliament passed an ordinance, "that if they submitted by a day, they should be pardoned and continued in service, otherwise to be proceeded against as traitors." (Whitelocke). On the same day Waller and Cromwell, with 5000 horse and dragoons, started for the west.

Meanwhile Melcombe Regis, on the opposite side of the harbour to Weymouth, had been relieved by sea by Captain Batten, who also landed a number of seamen to assist the garrison. Chapel Fort was retaken, and a determined attack by the Royalists repulsed on the night of the 25th February. The next morning the king's forces left Weymouth and retreated to Dorchester. The first object of Waller's advance was therefore already effected. But another Parliamentary garrison in the west was again in danger. Goring, who had fallen back on Exeter, was collecting troops for the more vigorous siege of Taunton. He called on Berkeley at Exeter, and Grenvile before Plymouth, to send him all the men they could spare.

On the 11th March, he arrived before the place. Blake sent Holbourn and his force out of the town to reduce the number of mouths to be fed. Waller and Cromwell advanced to relieve it if possible, though, being without foot, they could not alone attack an investing force behind entrenchments. The first skirmish with Goring's outposts occurred at Andover, where Lord Piercy was taken. About the 11th March, near Devizes, the Parliamentary forces surprised Colonel Long, who, with 400 horse, was returning to Goring, after conveying Prince Charles to Bristol. Only thirty Royalists escaped, some forty were killed, the rest taken prisoners. Cromwell, writing on the 17th to the Committee of Both Kingdoms, said:

> That since his coming to his regiment the carriage of it hath been very obedient and respectful to him and valiant, a good testimony whereof they gave upon the late service against Long's regiment; and for their late mutinous carriage to the Parliament, they had expressed their hearty sorrow for the same.—*Perfect Diurnal*, March 17th to 24th; *Cromwelliana*.

A few days afterwards Holbourn joined Waller and Cromwell, but about the 21st March they separated, Waller turning north and threatening Bristol and Bath, Cromwell and Holbourn marching to Cerne in Dorsetshire. The reason for this separation is nowhere given, but probably they found Goring now too strong before Taunton to be attacked without the assistance of some foot, and the country so devastated by his horsemen, that they could not subsist if they kept together. Want of provisions shortly forced them to retire without effecting anything further, Cromwell falling back to Ringwood before the end of the month, and Waller by Devizes, where he had a skirmish with the Royalist garrison, to Salisbury. Here Cromwell appears to have joined him, and a fresh advance must have been undertaken, for Cromwell, writing from Salisbury on the 9th April says:

> Upon Sunday last, we marched towards Bruton in Somersetshire, which was General Goring's headquarters; but he would not stand us, but marched away upon our appearance to Wells and Glastonbury.

Then he goes on to say that having but 1600 foot with them they thought it unsafe to risk their horse in such an intersected country. Therefore, they fell back by Shaftesbury to Salisbury. He also mentions that they heard rumours of Prince Rupert's advance to join Goring, and were afraid that he might fall on them front and flank. He also begs that reinforcements may be sent. (Carlyle, vol. i.)

The preliminary negotiations for peace, which were opened when the armies went into winter quarters, had so far succeeded, that the king and Parliament had agreed to appoint commissioners to consider the proposals made by each side, and to attempt to draw up a treaty which would be acceptable to both. The commissioners met for the first time on the 30th January at Uxbridge, but from the very first it was apparent that neither side was prepared to make such concessions as would be accepted by the other. On no one point submitted for consideration did the commissioners agree. The negotiations dragged out until the 22nd February, when the commissioners parted. Both sides then prepared for a fresh attempt at settlement by the sword.

The Parliament, as has been seen, pressed on the scheme for the new modelling or reorganisation of its army. But the mutinous spirit, engendered by the uncertainty of their prospects, which had arisen amongst the soldiers made the position a very critical one during the month of March. Had the king been able to avail himself of this opportunity and to advance in force, it is difficult to give even a guess as to what would have happened. The names of the officers on Fairfax's list were presented to the Commons about the end of February, and passed by the Lords on the 10th March.

Many officers then serving must thus have been aware that they were about to lose their commissions. What would have been their conduct had they been attacked under these conditions, and whilst still at the head of their regiments, by the Royalist forces, it is impossible to conjecture. Many would doubtless have done their duty. Others might have made terms with the king and attempted to take their regiments over to his side; especially as many mistrusted the Independents as much as they did the king, and it was evident that the Independents would, in the New Model, be the preponderating party.

But Charles let the opportunity slip. His generals showed even less discipline under Rupert than they had under Brentford. Rupert himself, though gallant and enterprising, was fitter to conduct a foray than a campaign. He had been the first to set that example of insubordination which his inferiors were now quick enough to follow. His overbearing manner gave offence. He was disliked as a foreigner. He utterly lacked the strength of will and perseverance which, combined with great powers of persuasion and conciliation, could alone have controlled the unruly spirits who now led the king's armies. Disputes and intrigues took the place of obedience and combination.

Prince Maurice had laid down his commission as commander in the west, and Hopton was appointed his successor. Goring schemed to supplant him. Grenvile refused to obey either. Prince Charles was sent to Bristol in the hope that orders emanating from the heir to the throne might be respected by all. Yet though his Council used every endeavour to reconcile the conflicting interests, no improvement ensued. The fortune of war had been unkind to the king in one respect. Most of the men of honour, integrity, and position, such as Falkland and Southampton, whose influence had attracted gentlemen to the king's service and maintained some discipline in his armies, had fallen in battle.

Of such Hopton was about the last survivor. Their places were taken by debauched ruffians like Goring and Grenvile, whose insubordination and orgies were imitated by their inferiors. Wherever their forces went the inhabitants, friends or foes, Royalists or Roundheads, were alike plundered and ill-treated. Every day the Royal cause became more unpopular. Had the king hanged Goring and discharged half his superior officers, his chance of ultimate success would have improved. Instead they were flattered, their preposterous demands treated with attention, and every means tried to conciliate them. Hundreds of the country gentlemen, disgusted by the indiscipline of the army and greatly impoverished by the drain on their resources, caused by the duration of the war, dropped away from the king and compounded with the Parliament as best they could.

Thus, the king's army was in the early spring of 1645 in no condition to take advantage of the opportunity offered. As soon as the New Model had received Parliamentary assent, and the resignation of Essex had given Fairfax a free hand, the latter had hurried down from London to Windsor, where his new army was to rendezvous. Skippon at the same time proceeded to Reading, where the headquarters of Essex's old army lay, to undertake the delicate task of disbanding the old regiments and re-enlisting the men into new. On the 7th April, the garrison, consisting of five regiments of Essex's army and five companies of Lord Roberts', were paraded, and Skippon addressed them.

He told them Parliament had found it necessary to reduce their armies into one, and that therefore the five regiments must be reduced to three; that the officers and men not re-employed would receive a fortnight's pay and debentures for their arrears, and the soldiers who were re-enlisted would receive a fortnight's pay as a bonus, and be re-armed and clothed. He trusted that the orders of Parliament would be carried out without disturbance or discontent. As for himself, he would still adventure his life with them to the last drop of his blood. The soldiers replied with acclamations that they would live and die with Fairfax and Skippon, and serve the Parliament.

The greater part of them were enrolled in the new regiments, but many of the officers returned to civil life. This good example of the Reading regiments proved happily contagious, and the re-organisation of the army proceeded everywhere with far greater ease than had been anticipated. Skippon obtained great and deserved credit for the skill and tact with which he had carried out the first and most critical operation. The result was a proof of Cromwell's extraordinary insight into the characters of men, whether as individuals, or collectively in corporate bodies. From the first he had declared that the fears of those who believed that an attempt to re-organise the army would end in a mutiny were groundless.

On the same day on which he had opened the debate on the "Self-denying Ordinance," he had, in another speech, said:

> I am not of the mind that the calling of the members to sit in Parliament will break or scatter our armies. I can speak this for my own soldiers, that they look not upon me, but upon you, and for you they will fight, and live and die in your cause; and if others be of that mind that they are of, you need not fear them. They do not idolise me, but look upon the cause they fight for. You may lay upon them what commands you please, they will

obey your commands in that cause they fight for. (Carlyle, vol. i.)

In spite of the criticism of Whitelocke and others, who conjured up all sorts of dangers from the removal of so many superior officers at once, he had steadily adhered to his own opinion. And the result had proved he was perfectly right.

Waller's army was disbanded at the same time as Essex's, and the men drafted for the most part into the garrisons of the south, a proportion being enrolled in the regiments of the New Model. Waller himself quietly laid down his commission and resumed his seat in the Commons. Under a genius such as Cromwell he might have risen to greater fame as a subordinate commander, for technically he was a good soldier, and a cautious, prudent general. Though considered by some as a rival to Essex, he never showed the insubordination which disgraced the Royalist generals, or the passive ignoring of orders which rendered Manchester an impossible servant of the State. His faults were the faults of the military system under which he had been trained, and he had not the genius to perceive that the unusual constitution of the armies called into existence in this struggle required modifications in the art of war.

All through April the reconstruction of the regiments was continued. When it was finished, it was found that 8000 men were still wanted to complete the 21,000 which had been fixed by Parliament. These men were obtained by impressment in those counties where the power of the Parliament was undisputed. It must not be supposed that the New Model Army contained all the soldiers under arms for the Parliament. On the contrary, a greater number were absorbed in the garrisons and local troops destined for the defence of certain localities. (Fairfax did not obtain the powers of commander-in-chief over these local forces till 1647). These retained their old organisation.

For instance, the troops which Massey had so successfully commanded in the Severn Valley were left intact. The New Model was the army for the field. Its organisation was based on that of the Eastern Association, which Cromwell had created. The list of officers shows how great his influence had been in their selection. Merit was more considered than birth or interest. Most of them were gentlemen, but a few, such as the well-known Colonel Pride, were of mean extraction. Gardiner, (vol.ii.), says that out of thirty-seven generals and colonels who fought at Naseby only seven were not gentlemen by birth. The pay was to be constant, a most necessary condition in the interests of discipline. That of the officers was much the same as at the present day. A foot soldier received eightpence a day, a horse soldier eighteen pence and had to provide forage for his horse. He received, in addition, sixpence deferred pay, granted on much the same terms as at present.

Almost all the army of the Association was embodied in the New Model, with the greater part of Essex's forces and a less proportion of Waller's and Fairfax's. Thus was created the most formidable army Europe had seen for centuries—formidable not for its numbers, but for its organisation, discipline, and the martial spirit that pervaded it—formidable, most of all, on account of the unrivalled genius that from its formation, either directly or indirectly, controlled its movements and supervised its organisation.

Amongst the king's officers the New Model was held in contempt. They saw the great nobles, the natural leaders of the people, pushed aside. They saw the generals, with whom they had contested so many well-fought fields, withdrawn from their commands in the army. Naturally they believed that the uncompromising ambition of Cromwell and his party had over-leaped itself, that the Parliament's Army, deprived of its leaders, would fail utterly on the field of battle. Charles opened the campaign of 1645 in high hopes. Rushworth gives a statement of the forces on both sides, (*Collections*, vol. v.), together with the territory and garrisons occupied by each.

South of the Mersey and the Trent the king held the western, the Parliament the eastern, half of the country. But the latter also held the important harbours of Pembroke and Plymouth, the inland towns of Taunton and Gloucester, and a few others of less importance, within the king's territory. The north was, with the exception of some towns and castles such as Carlisle, Scarborough, Latham House, and Pontefract, in the hands of the Scots or the Fairfaxes. The frontier between the two parties was indefinite, a good deal of country being held by neither side securely. Basing House gave the king a *point d'appui* within two marches of London, whilst the Parliamentary garrison of Abingdon broke the outer ring of defence to Oxford.

Considerable numbers were absorbed in garrisons on both sides, and in sieges or investments of hostile fortresses. Local troops were also employed to defend localities from hostile raids or to overawe unfriendly neighbours. For service in the field the king had at his disposal the Oxford army, some 11,000 strong, under the Princes Rupert and Maurice, the army of the west under Hopton and Goring, amounting to 10,000 men, some more or less independent bodies of horse attached to the garrisons and elsewhere, and considerable levies under Gerard in Wales. On the other side the Parliament could rely on the New Model Army in the south, the Scotch army, nominally 20,000 strong, in the north, and a few minor bodies, for operations in the field.

Speaking only of the main armies, it is evident that the Scots and New Model army were far superior in numbers to the king's and Goring's. The latter were better placed for combination, but united they did not exceed the New Model. Should the Scots, therefore, come south, it would be difficult, if not impossible, to prevent their junction with Fairfax. The only chance would be to defeat the New Model army before the Scots were within supporting distance.

The original Parliamentary plan of campaign drawn up by the Committee of Both Kingdoms offered just this chance to the king. They decided that Fairfax should march west to the relief of Taunton, whilst the Scots were invited to draw down from the north to attack Rupert and the Royal Army. Such a movement would of itself drive Goring towards the king, and offer the flank of Fairfax's army to their combined attack from Oxford. Besides, would the Scots consent to advance so far south? Scotland, hitherto the secure stronghold of Presbyterianism, was threatened by an unexpected danger—Montrose had begun his wonderful career of victory.

Of all the soldiers who fought on the king's side he only displayed military genius of the first order. He might, under more favourable circumstances, have become an opponent worthy of Cromwell. Sanguine and persevering under the most adverse circumstances, energetic and resourceful, fertile in expedients for avoiding defeat, fierce and rapid in attack, he possessed, like Cromwell, the power of winning the confidence and respect of all who served with him. Like Cromwell, too,, he possessed extraordinary military insight, seeing at a glance the requirements of the moment—a tactician of the first order, never binding himself to rule, but altering his tactics to meet the exigencies of the case. His campaigns can barely be glanced at here; they are worth more careful study.

Soon after Marston Moor he had made his way in disguise through the Lowlands into the Highlands, and there, joining with some Scotch-Irish troops under MacDonald, he had raised the Royal standard. At first the clans responded but feebly, but the defeat of Lord Elcho at Tippermuir on the 1st September, and the capture of Perth,

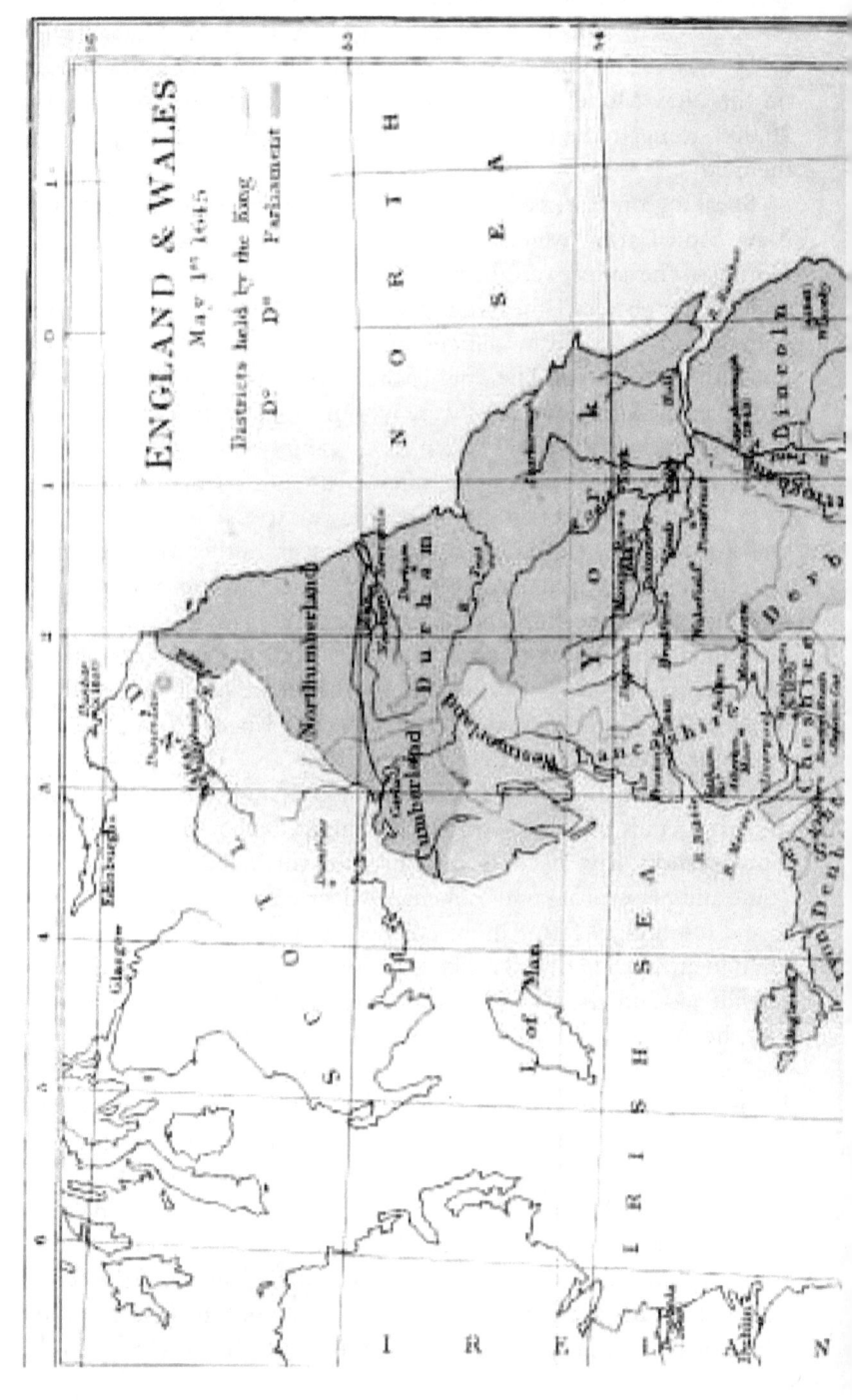

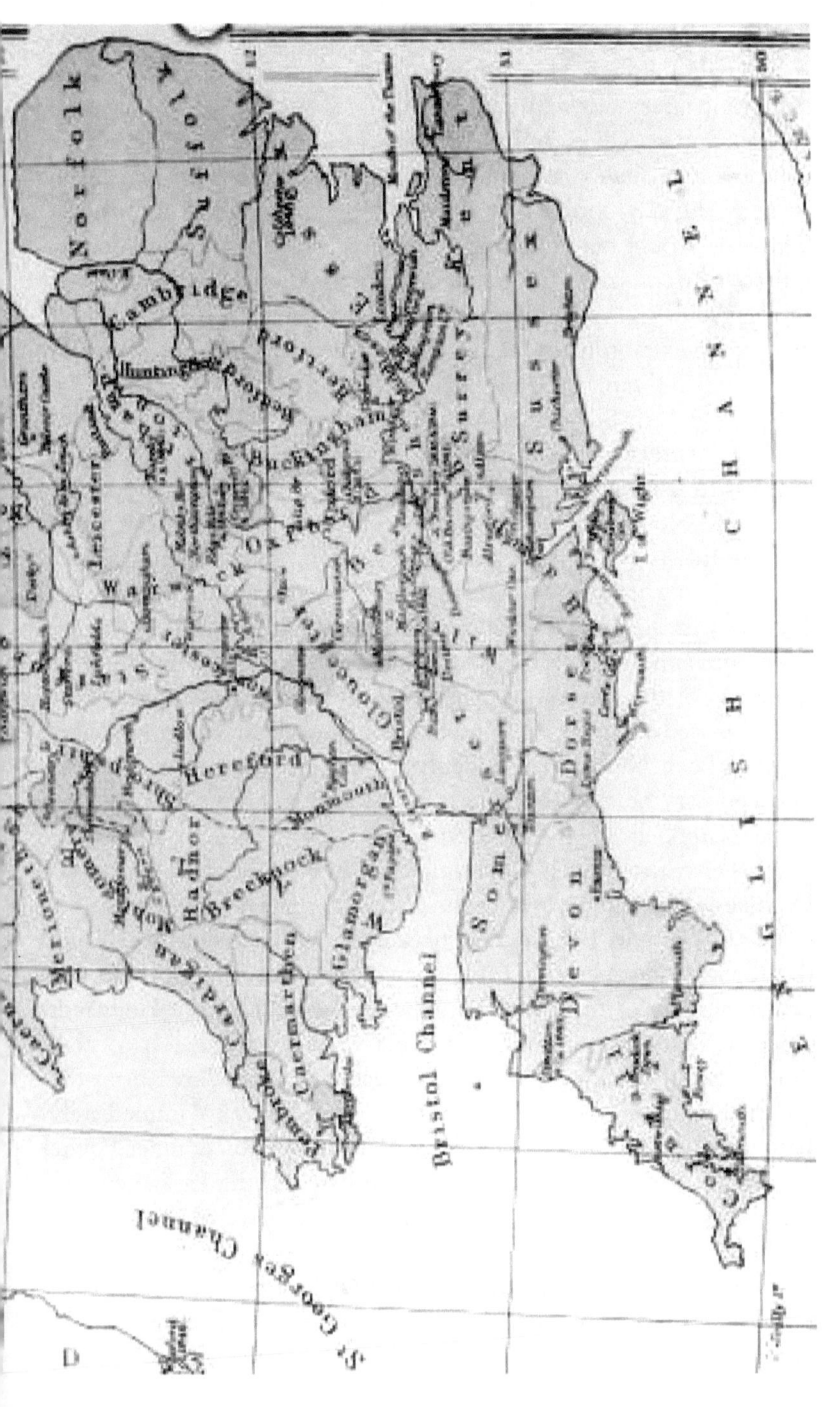

had aroused their sentiments of loyalty to the Crown, as well as their love of fighting and plunder. Henceforward he never lacked a following of wild hillsmen. They came and they went, assembling for battle, dispersing afterwards with their plunder.

Of regular soldiers he had very few, of horsemen but a few score. Of these he made extraordinary use, but his victories were principally won by the claymore. A few small pieces comprised all his artillery. These he would hide in a bog when hard pressed. His clansmen required little commissariat, they brought what they wanted with them, or foraged for it as they went along. The marching powers of such an army were extraordinary. Neither mountains nor rivers, rain nor snow, ever stopped them.

On the 13th September Montrose defeated Balfour of Burleigh outside Aberdeen and sacked the town. The Scotch Parliament, aroused to the danger, sent Argyle to stamp it out. Throughout October and November he followed Montrose through the Highlands with all the power of the Campbells; but to no purpose, and, tired of his unavailing pursuit, he returned to his own country, sending his clansmen to their homes. Suddenly, in midwinter, Montrose and the Camerons appeared over the passes and carried fire and sword through the glens of the Campbells. Argyle hastily summoned his clansmen and advanced to revenge the insult. Montrose fell back over Lochaber towards Loch Ness. Then suddenly turning on his pursuers, on the 2nd February, he routed Argyle at Inverlochy, and crushed the power of the Campbells for a generation.

Hitherto the Scotch Government had thought that Montrose's Highlanders would be overwhelmed by the superior numbers at the disposal of Argyle. But the destruction of the Campbells had swept that belief aside. The Lowlands were now open to Montrose; and to the plunder of the Lowlands almost every clan in the Highlands would send its contingent. Troops were wanted immediately to stem the torrent which might now be expected to pour down from the mountains. Leven was ordered to send some of his troops immediately with experienced officers. He sent a considerable force under Baillie and Hurry, the turncoat, who had once deserted the Parliament for the king just before Chalgrove Field, and again deserted the king for the Scots.

Leven's own army in England was therefore considerably weakened, and it was questionable whether he would feel justified in marching further south. Charles, instead of turning against Fairfax, might attempt to break through northwards and join Montrose. It is said that after the victory of Inverlochy he actually wrote to the latter proposing such a move. Rupert approved and urged him to fall on the Scots before Fairfax was ready with the New Model. Early in March the prince had moved towards Chester with a view of clearing the line of march northwards, and had passed Ludlow, when he was recalled by a rising of Clubmen in Herefordshire and Worcestershire.

He remained in this neighbourhood skirmishing with Massey from Gloucester until the necessary train and artillery for a march were ready, which the king was preparing to send him from Oxford. The Committee of Both Kingdoms, getting information of this, determined to intercept the convoy. Cromwell at this juncture arrived at Windsor on the 21st April in order to lay down his commission and bid Fairfax farewell.

But the latter had received orders from the committee to send a party of horse, and endeavour to intercept the convoy for Rupert. At the same time they specially recommended that Cromwell should be selected for this work. As the forty days' grace allowed by the Self-denying Ordinance had not yet lapsed they made no exception in his favour by doing so. The morning after his arrival these orders were put into his hands, and he immediately ordered a rendezvous at Watlington, some twenty-five miles from Windsor and fifteen from Oxford, of the horse placed at his disposal. These comprised some 1000 men, (*Perfect Diurnal* April 24th, *Cromwelliana*), amongst others his own, now styled Fairfax's, regiment, and some dragoons. What ensued had best be told in his own words. The report is to the Committee of Both Kingdoms and is dated Bletchington the 25th April:—

> So soon as I received your commands I appointed a rendezvous at Watlington. The body being come up (on the 23rd April) I marched to Wheatley Bridge, having sent before to Major-General Browne (Governor of Abingdon), for intelligence, and it being market-day at Oxford, from whence I likewise hoped by some of the market people to gain notice where the enemy was.
>
> Towards night I received certain notice by Major-General Browne, that the carriages were not stirred, that Prince Maurice was not here; and by some Oxford scholars, that there were four carriages and wagons ready in one place, and in another five; all, as I conceived, fit for a march.

I received notice also that the Earl of Northampton's regiment was quartered at Islip; wherefore in the evening I marched that way, hoping to have surprised them, but by the mistake and failing of the forlorn hope, they had an alarm there, and to all their quarters, and so escaped me; by means whereof they had time to draw all together.

✶✶✶✶✶✶

In modern military language, "owing to a mistake on the part of the advanced guard, the enemy's troops got notice of our approach, and assembled out of their billets."

✶✶✶✶✶✶

I kept my body all night at Islip; and in the morning, a party of the Earl of Northampton's regiment, the Lord Wilmot's, and the Queen's, came to make an infall upon me. Sir Thomas Fairfax's Regiment was the first that took the field; the rest drew out with all possible speed. That which is the general's troop charged a whole squadron of the enemy and presently broke it. Our other troops coming seasonably on, the rest of the enemy were presently put into confusion; so that we had the chase of them three or four miles; wherein we killed many, and took near two hundred prisoners, and about four hundred horse. Many of them escaped towards Oxford and Woodstock; divers were drowned; and others got into a strong house in Blechington, belonging to Sir Thomas Cogan; wherein Colonel Windebank kept a garrison with near two hundred men. Whom I presently summoned; and after a long treaty he went out, about twelve at night, with these terms here enclosed; leaving us between two and three hundred muskets, besides horse-arms, and other ammunition, and about three score and eleven horses more. . . . I did much doubt the storming of the house, it being strong and well-manned, and I having few dragoons, and this not my business; and yet we got it.—Carlyle, vol. i.

Colonel Windebank, a young man, had his newly-married wife and some other ladies with him in the house, and it is said that their terror unnerved him. Poor things! they had better have stood what shots Cromwell's few dragoons could have fired at them, for on Windebank's arrival at Oxford, he was tried for yielding up his post without resistance, and shot.

Pushing on thence on the 25th Cromwell made for Witney, where he dispatched Colonel Fiennes after a party of the king's horse, reported to be in the neighbourhood. Fiennes overtook them, and took over 100 horses and forty prisoners, Cromwell himself pushed on for Bampton, driving all the draught horses he could find away with him, to hinder the transport of the king's artillery. He had heard that a party of 300 foot were marching to Farringdon and were only some three hours ahead. He therefore sent forward a "forlorn hope" which succeeded in driving the Royalists into Bampton. On the morning of the 26th, after threats of assault and negotiations, the town was surrendered by Sir William Vaughan, who commanded the party. (Whitelocke calls him Sir H. Vaughan; Cromwell calls him Sir Richard—Carlyle, App. No. 7).

All the officers and men who had escaped in the skirmish the day before were taken. Then crossing to the south bank of the Isis, Cromwell appeared before Farringdon House, which he summoned, but the governor, unlike Windebank, refused to surrender. He then sent off to Abingdon for some foot, but time pressing, and no foot appearing, he attempted, early in the morning of the 27th, to take the house by storm. He was, however, beaten off with the loss of fourteen men. He then fell back to Newbury, whither Fairfax's army had meanwhile advanced.

******

Rushworth's account is somewhat different. He says that Cromwell, "with his own dragoons and the Abingdon foot storms the town, and is repulsed with loss" (*Collections*, vol. v.)

******

The effect of this brilliant cavalry raid on the king's plans is best described in the words of his ever-sanguine Chancellor, Digby. Writing to Rupert on the 29th April he said:

> The late ill accidents here by Cromwell ... have for the present totally disabled the king to move towards your Highness, both by want of a strength to convey him and the train safe to you, and by making it impossible to get draught horses in these parts ... we wanting as yet, though all diligence hath been used, four hundred, though we should leave the four field-pieces behind us. The first difficulty of conveying the king and train safe, I hope, may be removed by Goring's advance with his horse, who is sent for, but how to be supplied with teams unless you can furnish them out of those parts, I cannot imagine. Upon

the whole matter, Sir, I do not think it possible for the king to move towards you, unless you can advance such a body this way as may make us masters of the field, and sweep before you these necessary draught horses, through the counties which you pass.—Printed in a note by Gardiner, vol. ii.

Goring, as this letter mentions, had been ordered to Oxford with his horse, some 2000, and Rupert also hurried thither. On the way to Oxford Goring seized Radcot Bridge over the Isis, whereupon Cromwell, who hurried back on the news of his approach, pushed a party of horse, under Colonel Scroop, across the river lower down to observe his movements. Goring fell upon this party, which included three troops of Cromwell's own regiment, now under Whalley, and defeated them, capturing Major Bethell and several men.

The king's army at Oxford at the beginning of May numbered 6000 horse and 5000 foot, including the troops brought by Rupert and Goring. Fairfax lay at Newbury, and Cromwell with his horse was observing Oxford from the south and east. He was supported by Browne at Abingdon.

Towards the end of April Sir Richard Grenvile had arrived before Taunton and re-opened the siege. He was joined by 1500 foot which had been under Goring's command, but when reconnoitring Colonel Popham's house at Wellington, which held a Parliamentary garrison, he was wounded. The command of the besieging force was then given to Sir John Berkeley, who pressed the siege closely. The commissioners of the four counties of Cornwall, Devon, Somerset, and Dorset, who had been summoned by Prince Charles to meet him at Bridgewater, promised to raise the forces before Taunton to 6000 men exclusive of Goring's foot, and in addition to find 2000 men as guard to the Prince. Taunton was the only Parliamentary garrison then hard pressed.

Its importance was so great that the Committee of Both Kingdoms repeated, on the 28th April, the old mistake of ordering Fairfax and Skippon to march to its relief with 8000 men. (Whitelocke). Cromwell and Browne, with 4000 horse and foot, were to keep touch with the king, observe his movements, and prevent his falling on Fairfax's flank.

Fairfax and Cromwell together were quite a match for the king's forces at Oxford, but the former's march to Taunton required that the latter should remain with the bulk of his forces south of the Isis and Thames in order to meet any advance in that direction. This left the northern road from Oxford open, and offered the king an opportunity of carrying out Rupert's plan of campaign, and falling on the now weakened Scottish force under Leven, before Fairfax could come to its assistance. Perceiving the error, Fairfax protested, but obeyed his orders, and on the 5th May reached Salisbury.

On this day, however, the House learned that Goring and Rupert were at Burford with 7000 men, and that Maurice was on his way to join them with 2000 more, their design being to bring the king and his artillery out of Oxford. They therefore ordered Fairfax to send a detachment of 3000 foot and 1500 horse, under Colonel Weldon, to relieve Taunton, whilst, with the remainder of his forces, he should return, join Cromwell, and attend the king's movements. (Whitelocke).

Meanwhile it had been debated in Oxford whether Charles should throw himself on Fairfax, attempting to separate him from Cromwell, or march north to relieve Chester, and attack the Scots. The majority of the council were in favour of the former course; Rupert and Langdale of the latter. The Royal Army now consisted of 6000 horse and 5000 foot, none too large for either of the plans suggested. But the jealousies and bickerings of the commanders prevented even this small force being kept together. Goring wished for an independent command. Rupert feared lest the former's ready wit would give him a preponderating voice in the council. The two therefore agreed between themselves that Rupert and the king should march north, whilst Goring should take some 3000 men into the south-west, and besiege Taunton, or prevent its relief.

On the 7th May the king left Oxford with his whole army and reached Woodstock that evening. The next day he marched to Stow-on-the-Wold, where a Council of War was held, at which Rupert and Goring succeeded in carrying their suggestions against the older advisers of the king. The next day, therefore. Goring marched off towards Taunton with 3000 of the best horse in the army, and a fresh commission from the King which virtually gave him the command in the west, Prince Charles himself being exhorted to follow his advice. He came too late, however, to prevent the relief of Taunton, for on the 11th Weldon's forces arrived before it and skirmished with the besiegers.

These latter, believing that the whole of Fairfax's army was upon them, drew off in haste and abandoned the siege. On the 12th Weldon entered the town, which had been reduced to extremity. The out-works had been carried, and the defenders driven back to their retrenchments, the town had been burnt in several places, and the ammunition spent. The king, when Goring turned back to Taunton, marched to Evesham, calling on the garrison of Campden House to join him. The house was then burnt by Rupert's orders.

On the 10th May the committee received letters from Cromwell and Browne informing them that the king's army had quitted Oxford, and that the two generals would follow and keep touch with the enemy. It was evidently not the time at which the Parliament could afford to lose its best cavalry general. On the same day Whitelocke reports:

> Both Houses ordered that Lieutenant-General Cromwell should be dispensed with for his personal attendance in the House, and continue his service and command in the army for forty days longer, notwithstanding the Self-denying Ordinance.

Essex's party opposed this as an avowal that the House meant to retain whom they chose in spite of the self-denying pretences, and remove others, but the order was easily passed. On the 12th a similar order was made in the case of Sir William Brereton, Sir T. Middleton, and Sir J. Price, all members of the Commons. Now that the campaign had opened in earnest, it would have been extremely foolish to remove some of the most trusted commanders. On this day (12th May) Fairfax, who had proceeded as far as Blandford before receiving his orders to return, reached Alresford on his way towards Oxford. The king's army was about Evesham, and Cromwell and Browne at Woodstock. Their forces are reported by the old newspapers to be 8000 strong, but this is probably an exaggeration. (*Perfect Diurnal*, 12th May, and *True Information*, 13th to 17th May, *Cromwelliana*).'

The king continued his march through Worcestershire towards Chester by easy stages, taking Hawkesby House on the way. (Sir E. Walker), Cromwell and Browne followed by way of Warwickshire and Birmingham. Fairfax reached Newbury on the 15th May, his first intention being to join Cromwell in pursuit of the king. He therefore marched on the 17th to Blewbury, and thence across the Isis, west of Oxford, to Witney. But on the 17th a debate took place in the House as to the destination of the army, and the decision arrived at was that it should be employed in besieging Oxford. Orders to that effect were sent to Fairfax, and others to Cromwell and Browne, directing them to return and join him.

During the campaign of 1644, the directions of the Committee of Both Kingdoms had shown considerable strategical insight. The campaign had failed, not through mistakes in the orders issued to the generals, but through the neglect and disobedience of these orders by Manchester and Essex. Now, however, the strategical plan was faulty, partly, perhaps, because the House itself appears to have interfered more in the matter, and left it less to the discretion of the Committee of Both Kingdoms. Fairfax and Cromwell knew well that the first aim of their forces should have been the destruction of the king's army in the field, and that the reduction of his fortresses would then become an easier matter.

But, unlike their predecessors in command, they obeyed their orders, though they knew them to be bad. It is an axiom in military affairs that a bad plan energetically carried through is better than a good one prosecuted without vigour. Concentration of effort can only be obtained by the prompt obedience of all subordinate officers, and, therefore, generals in the position of Fairfax and Cromwell are bound to do their utmost to carry out the orders they receive from the Government.

At the same time a civilian government acts wrongly in attempting to dictate a plan of campaign to its generals. It should choose a competent commander and trust him to carry out its views in the manner most suitable to the military conditions. And when once the campaign has been opened, political considerations should, as far as possible, be subordinated to military ones. The Parliament in 1645 was soon to feel the effects of its error.

Fairfax, on the receipt of these fresh orders, turned aside to Newnham, and on the 22nd May opened the siege of Oxford. On the 26th, letters were received by Parliament stating that Cromwell and Browne had joined him at Marston; and about this date Massey from Gloucester captured Evesham, where the king had left but a weak garrison. Thus, all communication had been cut off between the Royal Army in the field and Oxford, On the 20th, Brereton, aware of the king's approach, raised the siege of Chester, and on the 21st crossed the Mersey into Lancashire with a view of joining the Scots.

A day or two later Lord Byron, the governor of Chester, met the Royal Army at Stone, in Staffordshire, and informed the king that Chester was now relieved. He also suggested that Charles should complete the occupation of that part of the country by taking Nantwich, and then continue his march north through Lancashire. However, news came that Fairfax was besieging Oxford, and although that town was known to be in an excellent condition for defence, and well provisioned, its importance was so great, being the seat of the king's government and great depot of the sinews of war, that his council could not resolve to lose all touch of it. It was therefore decided to remain within a few marches of it, and attempt to make a diversion that would bring Fairfax away. The bolder and better plan of rapidly advancing against the Scots was abandoned, and it was determined to turn east, and attack Leicester. This Parliamentary garrison was situated close to the boundaries of the Eastern Association, and its capture would seriously threaten that stronghold of Puritanism. Langdale was therefore despatched at once to surround the town with his northern horse, whilst the king followed with the army through Tutbury.

Directly Parliament learnt of this move of the Royal Army it began to be anxious for the safety of the Association. On the 27th May the committee sent orders to Cromwell, who was governor of the Isle of Ely, to repair thither and organise the defence. On the 29th he was already on his way. Arrived there, he set to work to raise troops, and improve the fortifications, which were in bad condition. In a letter to Fairfax dated Huntingdon, the 4th June, he excused himself for not having previously written, on account of the press of business, (Carlyle, vol. i.), and on the 6th he, with others of the Committee at Cambridge, signed a letter to the Deputy-Lieutenants of Suffolk, urging them to call out the local militia.

The horse and dragoons were to be sent to Newmarket as soon as possible, with a week's pay, fourteen shillings for each trooper, and ten shillings and sixpence for each dragoon, in their pockets. The situation was serious—Leicester had fallen, the enemy drawing towards Harborough, and "the army about Oxford was not yesterday advanced, albeit it was ordered to do so." (Carlyle, vol. i.)

The king, however, had no immediate design on the Association. On the 31st May his army, strengthened by 800 horse from Newark, had arrived before Leicester, and Rupert immediately converted a convenient stone wall into a battery and sent a summons to Sir Robert Pye, the governor. An unsatisfactory reply being received, the battery opened and in four hours effected a breach. Arrangements were made for an assault that night. Before daybreak the storming columns advanced from several points. Twice the assault on the breach was beaten off with loss, but Colonel Page, with a party of foot, supported by some of the Newark horse dismounted, carried the wall at another point, and by daylight the whole defences had been captured. (Sir E. Walker; Whitelocke). The governor and 1200 men were taken prisoners and the town sacked.

******

Gardiner says Rupert arrived on May 28th and stormed the town on the night of 30th and 31st. It is very likely that Rupert arrived a day or two before the 31st.

******

The rapid capture of such a strong town as Leicester, defended by so good a soldier as Pye, alarmed the Houses greatly. They now understood the error they had committed in allowing the king's army to roam unopposed through the country whilst their own was tied down to a tedious siege. On the 2nd June, the Commons ordered that:

> In consideration of the king being at Leicester, and the danger to the Associated Counties thereby, the Committee of Both Kingdoms should consider of such disposition of the armies under Sir T. Fairfax as may be most advantageous for the public, and that the blocking up of Oxford be left to Major-General Browne.—Whitelocke.

On the next day two regiments of the London troops were despatched to strengthen Browne before Oxford. On the 4th June the city petitioned that the army should march towards the enemy in the field, and the Scots pressed to advance south. On the 7th June further bad news reached the House. Goring, Hopton, Berkeley, and Grenvile had combined their forces in the west, driven Weldon into the fortifications, and besieged Taunton.

Meanwhile the committee had sent Fairfax his orders in the sense determined by the House, greatly to his satisfaction. On the 4th June, writing from Marston to his father, he said:

> I am very sorry we should spend our time unprofitably before a town, whilst the king hath time to strengthen himself, and by terror to force obedience of all places where he comes; the Parliament is sensible of this now, therefore hath sent me directions to raise the siege and march to Buckingham, where, I believe, I shall have orders to advance northwards, in such a course as all our divided parties may join.—*Fairfax Correspondence.*

The siege of Oxford had not been very successful so far. The garrison, by flooding the meadows, had rendered the approaches difficult. Rainsborough had indeed taken Gaunt House on the 1st June, but the next day in a successful sally from Oxford many Parliamentary soldiers had been killed and ninety-two swept off as prisoners. Skippon had been detached to take Borstal House, but had not as yet succeeded.

On the 5th June Fairfax broke up from before Oxford and marched to Marsh Gibbon. An assault was made on Borstal House, which failed, and orders were then given to raise the siege.

After the capture of Leicester, the king remained there four days, to reassemble his soldiers, disorganised by the sack of the place, and to establish his authority firmly in the town. As the surrounding country was for the most part Royalist, the occupation of the town strengthened his hold on the Midlands considerably. The communications of Derby with London were thereby blocked, and had the former place been summoned, many of Charles' advisers believed that Sir John Cell would have surrendered it on terms, so great was the terror the sack of Leicester had inspired. But Rupert refused to demand its surrender on a curious point of honour. If, he said, the summons were refused, he would be bound in honour to attack the town, (Sir E. Walker), and this would not be convenient.

The King's Council were divided as to the next step to be taken. As soon as it was known that Fairfax had abandoned the siege of Oxford and was advancing, all idea of marching against the Scots was abandoned. The risk of being caught between their army and the Parliament's was too great. The most prudent course would have been to fall back on Worcester, where Gerard could have joined the king from Wales with 3000 horse and foot. To turn against the Association would present the flank to Fairfax, whilst Cromwell now barred the way in front with 3000 local troops.

The New Model army was thought of small account by the king's officers, and its performances under Fairfax had not as yet been such as to raise it in their estimation. It was therefore determined to turn towards the south, and offer Fairfax battle. Rupert, the nominal commander-in-chief, was opposed to this scheme, and Langdale's Northern Horse objected so strongly, that they became mutinous, and were with great difficulty appeased. They earnestly desired to march into Yorkshire and their own counties, where their lands and property now lay at the mercy of the Scots and Roundheads.

On the 5th the king, having repaired the breaches and put in a garrison, left Leicester for Harborough. When the troops were mustered at the rendezvous, the foot were found to number barely 3300 men. The losses in the assault had been considerable, the garrison absorbed many men, others had disappeared with their plunder. The horse were some 4000 strong. On the 7th the march was continued to Daventry, where a halt for five days was made. The foot were posted on Borough Hill, an eminence crowned by an old British encampment about a mile to the east of the town.

No definite information had been received about Fairfax's movements, and in this uncertainty it was not deemed prudent to advance further. The best chance of success, a rapid march and an unexpected attack on Fairfax before he could call in Cromwell's forces and other detachments, was thus lost. Provisions were collected for Oxford. (Gardiner, vol. ii.; Sir E. Walker says, that provisions were received *from* Oxford). Bad news was received from the west. A force of 2000 men, gathered from the garrisons of Hereford, Worcester, Monmouth, and Ludlow, had been defeated near the latter place by a much smaller force of the rebels.

On the 6th June Fairfax was at Brick Hill, and here Skippon rejoined him from Borstal House. On the 7th he marched to Sherrington, near Newport-Pagnel. Here Colonel Vermuyden rejoined him with 2500 horse and dragoons. Vermuyden had been sent in May to reinforce the Scots, who were weak in cavalry, when it was supposed they would march southward. On the king's advance, however, Leven, weakened by the detachment sent under Baillie to oppose Montrose, considered it his first duty to defend the Scotch frontiers, especially after receiving news of the defeat of Hurry at Auldean on the 9th May. He therefore drew back his advanced troops and concentrated west of the Pennine range. Vermuyden thereupon fell back again.

At Sherrington, Fairfax called a council of war, at which a petition was drawn up, signed by himself and the chief officers of the cavalry, praying Parliament to appoint Cromwell to the vacant post of lieutenant-general (or commander of the horse). This was agreed to on the 10th of June, after some debate by the Houses, and Fairfax thereupon sent Cromwell his appointment to the post, and desired him to join as soon as possible with all the force he could raise.

******

The Lords limited Cromwell's continuance in the service to three months, and did not ratify his appointment till the 18th June, after the Naseby fight.

******

It is evident that among the officers themselves Cromwell was considered the best cavalry leader on the Parliamentary side. Fairfax's army now consisted of 12,500 men, and Skippon was ordered to draw up "the form of a Battel." (Rushworth, vol. v.). This consisted in forming brigades of horse and foot out of the various regiments, appointing the brigade commanders and staff, and, according to the formal methods then in force, assigning to each brigade its place in battle, whether first or second line, right or left wing, &c. Letters were also written to Sir John Cell, Colonel Rossiter, and the Governors of Warwick, Northampton, and Nottingham, asking them to send any men they could spare in view of the forthcoming engagement.

On the 9th June Fairfax marched to Stony Stratford, and on the 11th to Wotton, somewhat to the south of Northampton. On the 12th he reached Kislingbury. He was now within five miles of the king's army, which still occupied its camp at Borough Hill, near Daventry. His patrols brought word that many of the Royalist horses were out grazing, and that the king himself was believed to be hunting. The Royal Army, however, quickly took the alarm, and Fairfax thought it imprudent to attack.

On the contrary, he expected to be himself attacked, and spent the dark hours of early morning in visiting his outposts. He forgot the password, and was stopped by the first sentry, who refused to let him pass till the captain of the guard arrived. Having thus received practical proof of the good discipline observed by his men on outpost, he continued his rounds, and soon found that the king's troops were burning their huts preparatory to a move.

At daybreak, they were found to be in retreat on Harborough, having sent away their carriages first. At six o'clock Fairfax summoned a council of war. Just as it was about to sit, Cromwell arrived, bringing with him 600 horse and dragoons from the associated counties. He was received with shouts by the men, and took his seat in the council. Here it was determined to follow the king. The army was drawn out to a rendezvous, whence Major Harrison was despatched towards Daventry with a reconnoitring party, and Colonel Ireton with another party of horse was sent forward to hang on the king's flank and keep touch with him.

★★★★★★

When an army, as was almost invariably the case with both armies in the Civil War, billets in villages for the night, it must be reassembled the next morning before marching off. Bivouacs were very seldom adopted even when close to an enemy. Later on, Cromwell used tents.

★★★★★★

The march of the main army was so directed as, if possible, to strike the right flank of the royal army on its way to Harborough.

That night (the 13th June) the king with the head of his column reached Harborough in safety, the tail quartering as far back as Naseby. Fairfax with his main body reached Guilsborough. Late that night, after dark, Ireton with his horsemen dashed into Naseby, breaking through the guard, driving the Royalists out of the village, and taking several prisoners. This so alarmed the king that he called a council of war in the middle of the night. His plan, on retiring from Borough Hill, had been to fall back on Newark, and there reinforce his foot from the garrisons of that place, Pontefract, and other neighbouring fortresses, before offering Fairfax battle.

It was now deemed too late to carry out this scheme. Fairfax's army was so close up, that either the retreat must be unduly hurried, with the almost certain result of demoralising the army, or Fairfax would overtake the king and force him to fight at a disadvantage. It was therefore determined to offer the Roundheads battle in the morning, the ground south of Harborough being favourable to the purpose. The Parliamentary writers give Rupert the credit for this decision, but Walker, who, as secretary of war to Charles, should have had good opportunities of knowing, states that he was opposed to it. (*Historical Discourses*).

Accordingly, early on the morning of the 14th June, the Royal army was drawn up in order of battle on a long-swelling ridge about a mile south of Harborough.

★★★★★★

This is according to Sir E. Walker, and would put this, first position about East Farnden; but it is doubtful whether this first position was not really about Sibbertoft, four and a quarter miles southwest of Harborough. Leighton and Herbert, members of the Committee of Both Kingdoms with Fairfax's army, in their report to the Speaker, say, "After an hour's march we discovered their horse drawn up at Sibbertoft, three miles on this side Harborough; an hour after their foot appeared. This was about eight in the morning." Rushworth, vol. vii.

★★★★★★

The country between this and Naseby is high and open, consisting of a number of rolling heights with flat, broad valleys between. A country, in fact, very favourable to cavalry. A patrol was sent out under Scoutmaster Ruce about eight o'clock, to obtain information, but he returned presently saying that he had been two or three miles to the front, and had seen nothing of the enemy. Whereupon, Rupert himself, with a party of horse and musketeers, rode forward to reconnoitre.

Fairfax had paraded his troops at three o'clock in the morning at Guilsborough. Believing the king would continue his retreat, he sent forward his cavalry to press the rear and flanks of the Royal Army, and then followed with the rest of his forces. His line of march led him to the right or east of the village of Naseby. He had passed it about a mile, when the scouts brought back word that the enemy was no longer retiring, but, on the contrary, appeared to be advancing on this side of Harborough. Fairfax decided to draw up his forces on a ridge on which he then found himself. Accordingly, the bulk of the cavalry were brought back, and the army drawn, says Sprigge:

> Into such a posture, as that if the enemy came on we might take advantage of our ground and be in readiness to receive him, or if not, that we might advance towards him.

******

Gardiner says of this first position (vol. ii.) that Fairfax, on seeing the king's army drawn up in the distance, on Cromwell's advice, formed up on a high hill north of Naseby, with wet, boggy ground, in the valley in front. It is most unlikely that a cavalry leader such as Cromwell should have selected ground so unfavourable to his arm, especially as he knew his horse to be at least equal in numbers to the king's, which he had beaten in every engagement, and was therefore most anxious to fight. It is most probable that Fairfax, on seeing or receiving news of the enemy's advance, deployed his troops from column into their order of battle ready to move on to any ground selected.

******

For some time Fairfax, Cromwell, and the other chief commanders anxiously waited for further information. Then they themselves saw troops advancing over a high ridge at some distance off, in the direction of Harborough. These were probably the king's forces moving on to their selected ground, but the Parliamentary leaders had no doubt but that the royal army was advancing against them. Cromwell pointed out a position somewhat further to the west which offered better ground for the employment of cavalry, opposed the enemy's advance more directly, and would prevent him getting the wind of their own troops. This last was a point much insisted on by the soldiers of that day, owing to the inconvenience, in a charge and hand-to-hand fight, of having the dust blown in the men's faces.

Fairfax agreed, and the army took ground to its left on to the position pointed out. This consisted of a gentle rise with flat top a mile and a half to the northwest of Naseby. The troops were at first marshalled along the crest of the slope, but at Cromwell's suggestion were drawn back a hundred yards or so, in order to prevent the enemy, advancing in the valley below, from seeing their numbers and disposition. The army was drawn up in a large fallow field, its left protected by a strong fence which ran perpendicularly to the front, and which was lined by Okey's dragoons, its right by a coney warren and furze bushes.

A few musketeers were pushed as skirmishers somewhat down the slope. The front occupied was about a mile, the army consisting of 7000 foot and 7000 horse. Just before the battle began. Colonel Rossiter joined with his regiment of horse. The disposition of the troops is clearly shown in the sketch further on, which is taken from Sprigge's book, (*Anglia Rediviva*). It will be seen that it assumed the usual form of two lines, with the cavalry in equal halves on the wings and the foot in the centre. The third line appears to have often been dispensed with at this period. This shallow formation gave greater extension to the wings, rendered flank attacks by the enemy's cavalry more difficult, and, in this case, prevented them altogether, owing to the hedge and broken ground on the flanks.

It will be noticed that want of space induced Cromwell to modify the arrangement on the right wing, where he commanded in person. Each regiment of horse was formed into two squadrons, and whilst the normal formation would appear to have the squadrons abreast, Pye's regiment in the centre had but one squadron in the first and one in the second line. (Sir Robert Pye had been exchanged for Colonel Tillyer, but it is probable he did not command his own regiment even if released by this date). Similarly, Fienne's regiment had one squadron in the second line, whilst its other with the Associated Counties' horse formed a third line.

Rossiter's regiment, just come up, had a squadron placed between the first and second lines immediately in support of Fairfax's Life Guards, and the others in the third line. The foot were in the normal formation, each regiment having the pikes in the centre and the musketeers on the wings. It may be remarked that the three regiments in the second line, those of Rainsborough, Hammond, and Pride, were three of the best in the army. The guns were distributed as usual in groups of two and three in the intervals between the foot regiments. The baggage was parked about a mile in rear, near Naseby, under the escort of a party of musketeers.

Glancing for a moment at the formation of the king's army, as shown in the sketch, it must be remembered that Sprigge had not the same opportunity of studying it as he had in the case of the Parliament's. (The plate seems to have been originally engraved for Sprigge's book, though afterwards reproduced in others). His plan, however, agrees closely with the accounts of the Royalist writers, and may therefore be assumed to be generally correct. It will be noticed that the king's army was drawn up in three lines instead of two, and that in the second, squadrons of horse were placed in the intervals between the foot regiments.

This does not seem to have been a common arrangement, though musketeers were often placed in the intervals between the horse regiments to shake the enemy's formation when he charged. It is not evident what good these isolated squadrons could have been, and in the face of the superior numbers of the Parliamentary horse, they were much wanted on the wings. Perhaps they were intended to complete the victory of the foot if they succeeded in a charge, and protect their retreat if they were repulsed. The king's army numbered 4000 horse and 3500 foot. Rupert commanded the right wing of horse, his own and Prince Maurice's; Sir M. Langdale the left with his own and the Newark horse; Lord Astley the foot in the centre, and the king himself the reserve.

Rupert had not ridden far with his reconnoitring party when he discovered the Parliamentary forces. Riding up towards them to observe them more closely, some movement on their part induced him to believe they were in retreat. This may very likely have been the withdrawal from the crest suggested by Cromwell. Rupert sent orderlies galloping back to hurry up the main body. Cromwell's manoeuvre attained his object, for Walker, (*Historical Discourses*), says:

> We could perceive their horse in the high ground about Naseby, but could not judge of their number or intentions.

The army arrived in "reasonable order" about 10 a.m. Rupert, anxious lest the enemy should escape, and, with his usual impetuosity, without waiting to test the accuracy of his surmise, gave the order to charge. As he did so, the whole Parliamentary Army advanced and reoccupied the crest. Rupert dashed up the hill at the head of his own

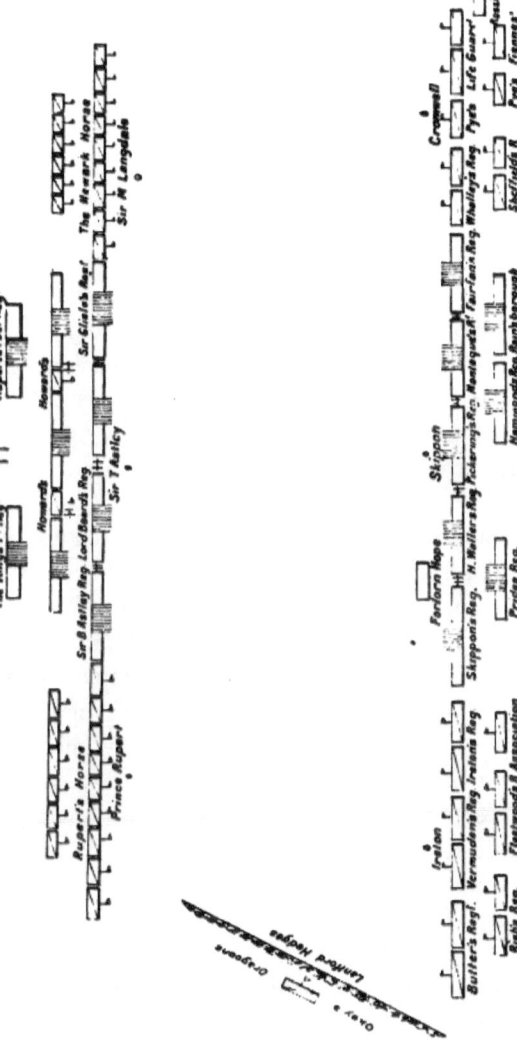

Order of battle of the two armies at Naseby, taken from a plate by I. Short, published in Sprigge, Rushworth, and other contemporary authors.

It will be noticed that this plan does not show the position of the King's horse guard. His foot regiment is called the King's regiment of foot, being his "life guard" on the original plate.

NOTE.—Okey's dragoons have been placed somewhat nearer to the Parliamentary forces than in the original plate by Sprigge, as it is impossible that they could have been from the first in a position to outflank Rupert's horse.—ED.

squadrons, against those of the Parliamentary left, which, led by Ireton, advanced to meet him. But by some error in giving or carrying out the orders, Ireton's squadrons of the second line were slow in supporting those of the first, who themselves seemed to have been somewhat disordered by their advance.

Rupert, dashing his leading squadrons against their front, flung some of those of his second line against their flank, thus routing them and driving them back on their supports. These, unable to avoid the mingled mass of flying friend and pursuing foe, were in turn broken, and in a few minutes the whole of the Parliamentary horse of the left wing was flying from the field, and Ireton was a prisoner and wounded.

But on the other flank things had taken a very different turn. Directly Cromwell recovered the crest, he sent his squadrons crashing down the hill against Langdale's Cavaliers. Whalley's regiment, charging over smooth ground, struck the enemy first, receiving a volley from their pistols at close quarters, but pressing on themselves with the point of the sword. The Life Guard and Rossiter's, hampered by the rabbit-holes and furze bushes, arrived later, but then striking into the flank of the *mêlée*, drove the northern horse back in confusion behind the king's reserve.

The second line followed in good order. Then Cromwell displayed that wonderful control over himself and his men which is the greatest, but perhaps the rarest, quality a cavalry leader can possess. Perceiving that Langdale's horsemen were sufficiently broken to prevent their charging again for some time, he refrained from completing their overthrow, and turned his attention to the battle in the centre, where the fortune of the day must finally be decided. Rapidly rallying his first line, he reformed their ranks and directed them—not to charge—but to watch Langdale's broken squadrons and prevent them from taking part in the battle again. Then with his second line he prepared to charge the Royal centre.

Just as he did so the king himself led forward his Horse Guard, a body of 500 gentlemen, from the reserve, with a view of restoring the battle on his left wing. Hardly had they advanced, when the Earl of Carnworth rode out of the ranks, and, seizing the king's bridle, turned his horse round, exclaiming as he did so, "Will you go upon your death?" At the same time the command—"march to the right hand"—was given, which the Horse Guards mistook for a signal to retire, as it led them away from the enemy. They accordingly wheeled about, and galloped off some distance in such confusion that they were not rallied till the battle was over.

In the centre the king's foot, as at Marston Moor, proved themselves of better mettle than their foes. Though out-numbered by two to one, they charged furiously at the centre of the Parliamentary line. Fairfax's regiment on the right flank was hardly engaged, but all the others of the first line were overthrown and driven in disorder back on the second. Here Rainsborough, Hammond, and Pride succeeding in checking the advance of the Royalists, and in giving time for the broken regiments to rally. The contest was raging furiously at push of pike when Cromwell's troopers wheeled round to join in it. Charged in front, flank, and rear, by horse and foot, the Royalists ranks were then broken.

The reserves were hurried up, but were unable to restore the battle. Regiment after regiment dissolved into a mass of disorganised fugitives. At last only Rupert's regiment maintained its ranks. Again and again it beat off the attacks of both horse and foot. Fairfax brought his own regiment up, which hitherto had hardly been engaged. (Whitelocke says that Fairfax brought up his Life Guard, not his foot regiment, to make this charge).

With pike and musket butt they charged Rupert's redcoats in front, whilst Cromwell's troopers fell on them again in rear. Then at last the ranks were broken, and these gallant soldiers, like Newcastle's whitecoats at Marston, died as they stood in their ranks.

Away on the Parliamentary left, Rupert, lacking Cromwell's self-possession, had loosed his squadrons in full pursuit of Ireton's flying horsemen. Galloping towards Naseby, he came across the Parliamentary baggage. Mistaking him for one of the generals on his own side, the commander of the escort stepped forward to ask how the day went. Rupert replied by asking him whether he would take quarter, but was answered with a curt "No."

Collecting a few horsemen, Rupert sent them at the train, but the musketeers beat them off. He then with great difficulty rallied his scattered troopers and led them back to the field. Arrived there, he found himself too late. Streaming away from the place where the foot had joined issue, a disorderly mass of fugitives represented the king's gallant regiments. Half a mile away Langdale and the king had succeeded in reforming their beaten troopers. Between these and the foot rode Cromwell's steel-clad horsemen, their unbroken ranks and steady movements testifying to their superior discipline.

Rupert rejoined the king, and together they formed a new line of battle with the cavalry. Of infantry and guns there were none left. Cromwell, about a quarter of a mile off, formed his squadrons into two wings, leaving a space between them for the foot, now being rapidly reformed in rear by Fairfax. Skippon had been badly wounded. Some of Ireton's troopers had rallied and joined Cromwell's horse. Ireton himself had escaped in the confusion, after he had been taken, and had rejoined the horse.

Rupert urged another charge, but in his own squadrons the horses were blown and exhausted. Langdale's men were demoralised by their defeat. Neither could be brought to charge again. For a short time the opposing cavalry stood facing each other. Then Fairfax's infantry moved forward into the space left for them by the horse, and Cromwell gave the word to charge. The Royalist troopers never awaited the onslaught. Wheeling about they galloped from the field as fast as they could spur. Then Cromwell let go his men in pursuit. No more need of serried ranks, it only remained to push the victory to the utmost. On through Harborough swept the chase, up to the walls of Leicester.

Then only, after a pursuit of twelve miles, the Parliamentary troopers were recalled. Five thousand prisoners, twelve guns, two hundred carriages, indeed, all the enemy's train and baggage, remained in the hands of the victors. Amongst the carriages was the king's, with his cabinet and all his secret correspondence. The publication by the Parliament of some of these papers, especially his letters to the queen, did the king's cause more harm than even his defeat, for they opened the people's eyes to his dealings with the Irish Catholics, and to his negotiations for foreign aid. (The account in text is collated from Sprigge, Walker, Whitelocke, Clarendon, Cromwell's letter in Carlyle, Rushworth, &c.)

The honours of the day lay principally with Cromwell. Once again Rupert and he had fought in the same battle, though they had not, as at Marston Moor, actually charged each other. Again Cromwell had proved himself the better cavalry leader. No doubt the advantage of numbers lay entirely on his side. But in cavalry actions more depends on the opportuneness of the charge than on the numbers by which it is carried out. Again and again large masses of cavalry have been defeated by far inferior numbers, when better handled. Rupert and Cromwell represented two different types of cavalry soldiers. The former was a light cavalry-man. His troopers discarded all defensive armour on account of its weight. Their charge was prompt and rapid.

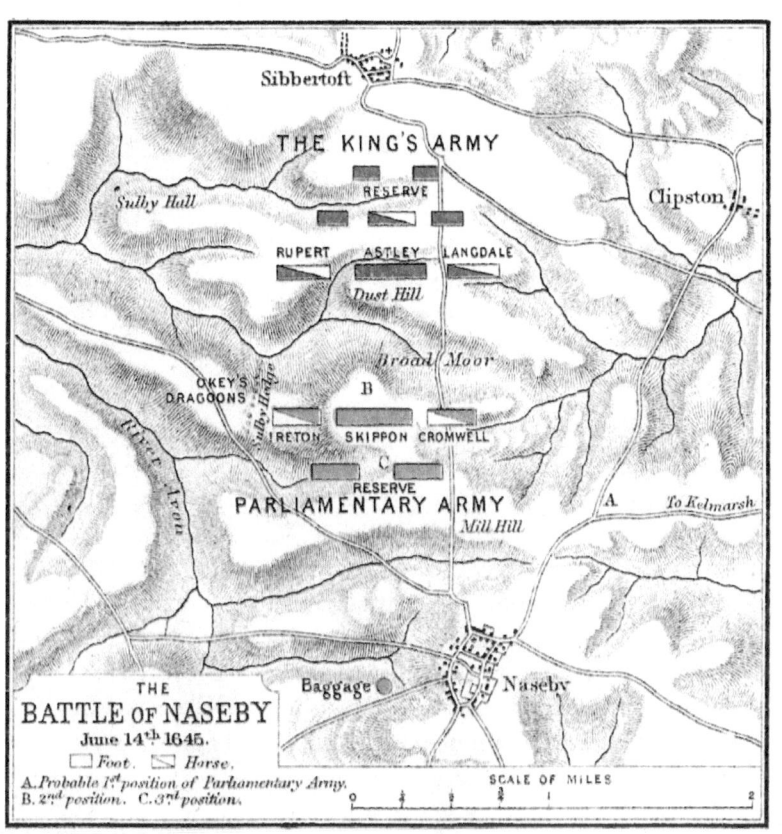

On the other hand, Cromwell's favourite troops were *cuirassiers*, big, heavily-armed men, and therefore slower. Both discarded the evil practice of halting to fire before charging. But while the former relied for momentum and striking power on pace, the latter depended on solidarity and weight. The result was not conclusively in favour of one nature of cavalry or the other in battle. For although Cromwell defeated Rupert, and every other cavalry commander he engaged, yet Rupert, defeated in turn nearly all the other Parliamentary leaders when in command of the same troops.

Therefore, the reason for the superiority of the one over the other must be sought for in the men themselves. It was undoubtedly in his extraordinary self-control, and his power of enforcing discipline upon others, that Cromwell's superiority lay. In the midst of the most furious *mêlée* he never lost his head, or his control over his men, as Rupert did. The former attribute was a gift of nature, the latter the result of infinite care and patience in training his men. It is in speaking of this battle that Clarendon says:

> That difference was observed all along, in the discipline of the king's troops, and of those which marched under the command of Fairfax and Cromwell (for it was only under them, and had never been remarkable under Essex or Waller) that, though the king's troops prevailed in the charge, and routed those they charged, they seldom rallied themselves again in order, nor could be brought to make a second charge again the same day: which was the reason that they had not an entire victory at Edgehill: whereas the other troops, if they prevailed, or though they were beaten and routed, presently rallied again, and stood in good order, till they received new orders.

The shameful flight of the 500 gallant gentlemen who formed the King's Horse Guards, merely on a mistaken word of command, and the impossibility of rallying them, testifies in the plainest manner to the loose discipline prevailing amongst the Royal horse. Want of pay had necessitated the practice of living at free quarters, and the temptation of free quarters had led to plunder, and plunder to the demoralisation of the army. The officers were no better, or even worse, than the men.

The invariable gallantry and steadiness of the king's foot in battle points to a much better state of discipline in the infantry, perhaps from fewer opportunities of plunder. The common idea about the king's

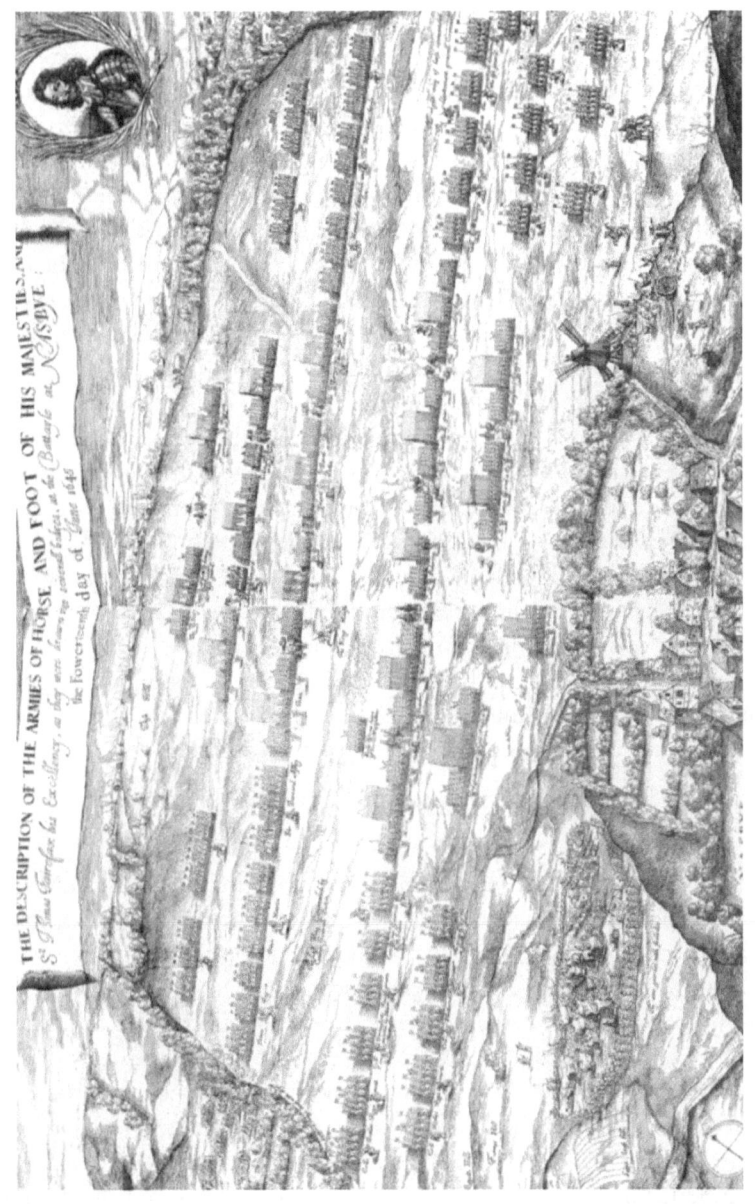

forces is that his strength lay in his high-born, well-mounted cavaliers, whose reckless charge would bear all before them till overwhelmed by numbers. The sober fact is that the king's horse often equalled that of his enemy in numbers, whilst his foot was nearly always greatly outnumbered; and though the former performed many dashing exploits, it is to the gallant peasants who trailed pike and musket in his quarrel that most of the honour acquired by his side on the battlefield is due.

On the evening of the battle Cromwell recalled his horse to Harborough, whither Fairfax also brought up his foot. The king continued his flight to Ashby-de-la-Zouch, where he passed the night. He had still a considerable body of horse, but the whole of his foot had been killed or taken. His losses among the officers had been severe, twenty colonels and senior officers had been killed, thirty-two field officers and seventy captains were among the prisoners.

Over 600 soldiers had been killed, and 4500 or 5000 taken prisoners. The Parliament, in killed and wounded, had lost about 1000 men. Skippon and Ireton had both been wounded, and Fairfax's helmet had been knocked off. The next day the king, with the remains of Rupert's and Maurice's horse, continued the retreat to Lichfield and on the 17th reached Bewdley. Langdale's horse for the most part reached Newark, narrowly escaping Sir John Cell, who with 2000 horse and dragoons, was marching from Derby to join Fairfax.

From Harborough both Fairfax and Cromwell wrote short reports of the battle to Parliament. Cromwell, in his, which was addressed to the Speaker, acknowledges the severity of the fighting.

> We, after three hours' fight, very doubtful, at last routed his army.

The victory had been even more complete than at Marston Moor, where the darkness had stopped the pursuit. The next day, 15th June, Fairfax advanced with his army to the village of Glyn, near Leicester, sending on his horse to surround the town. On the 16th he summoned the place, but the governor. Lord Loughborough, refused to surrender, and preparations were made to storm it. On the 17th the batteries opened, and the storming parties told off, when the governor offered to treat. On the 19th the town was surrendered, the garrison marching out without arms. Rossiter was then sent to join Gell and Lambert. Their combined forces amounted to 3000 fresh horse, and were sent in pursuit of the king. He, however, reached Hereford in safety on the 19th. Here he hoped to recruit his foot again, and in a few days Gerard joined him with 2000 men.

Cromwell and Fairfax

When Charles marched northward from Evesham towards Chester at the beginning of May, Leven, as we have seen, had concentrated his field army in Westmoreland. His object was to cover the siege of Carlisle, and to prevent the king attempting to break through into Scotland by the roads west of the Pennine hills, and so join Montrose. But when he heard of Charles' move eastward towards Leicester, he marched back into Yorkshire to bar the road east of the range. What with the detachments under Baillie and Hurry, the troops employed in the siege of Carlisle, and the garrisons of various places, he had with him but 4000 or 5000 men. Parliament urged him again to move south, but he replied that his men must be first paid.

The Houses, who had more troops still in the field than they could pay regularly, had neglected the Scots, and their pay was much in arrear. Leven had perforce to allow his men to live at free quarters, and this, as usual, led to a good deal of plundering. It is also said that the Scots' army was accompanied by a very large number of women and camp-followers, who also had to be fed somehow. Both Royalists and Puritans hated the Scots, and altogether they were very unpopular. Parliament took their pay into consideration after the Battle of Naseby, and then Leven consented to advance. By the 20th June he had reached Nottingham.

When Goring had left the king at Stow he had marched for Taunton. Joining his forces with those under Sir J. Berkeley, he drove Weldon, who had quitted Taunton after relieving it, back into the place and laid siege to it. He brought with him a commission to command in chief in this theatre of war. Sir R. Grenvile was appointed his Major-General; Hopton, General of the Artillery. Sir J. Berkeley was ordered to take command of the forces before Plymouth. In a few days, however, this was all changed.

On the 19th May Digby wrote to the Prince of Wales, who was in supreme command in the west, ordering Goring to march at once and rejoin the king, and appointing Hopton to command in chief. Goring, however, demurred, declaring that if he were allowed to press the siege, Taunton would be taken in a very short time, whereas, if he marched without the local troops, Weldon could reinforce Fairfax's army by as many men as he could bring to the king, and the west would be open to incursions from the Parliament's garrisons in Dorset and elsewhere. He was therefore allowed to continue the siege. Clarendon, (vol. v.), who hated him heartily, describes in full his ill-behaviour at this juncture.

He spent his time in the wildest excesses, he exacted contributions for the support of his troops, and then never paid the men. His horse were encouraged to plunder and ill-treat the inhabitants, whilst his foot soldiers, starved and unpaid, deserted in hundreds. The siege was negligently conducted, the various outposts badly selected and insufficiently held. The garrison continually worsted them in sallies, and carried off cattle and supplies into the town. Grenvile, who, on recovery from his wound, had resumed his command before Plymouth, joined Goring later as Major-General in command of the local troops.

According to Clarendon two greater scoundrels never disgraced an army by their misconduct, or mismanaged worse the operations of their forces. And in Goring's case the mismanagement was wilful, as he wished to avoid the chance of being again posted to a subordinate command on the termination of the siege. He really possessed very superior military talents when he chose to exert them. Berkeley, as ordered by the king, took command of the forces before Plymouth. Massey, with a small Parliamentary force lay at Dorchester, too weak to relieve Taunton in the face of Goring's army.

In addition to the regular forces in the field on both sides there were, in the districts where the effects of the war had been especially severe, armed bands of Clubmen. This was particularly the case in Wilts, Dorset, and Somerset, where Goring encouraged them, either with a hope of inducing them eventually to join the king's side, or for some more private reasons of his own.

Thus about the 20th June the king was at Hereford, Goring before Taunton, Fairfax at Leicester, part of the Scotch Army under Leven at Nottingham, and another part under David Leslie besieging Carlisle, which was now reduced to the last extremities. Many of the king's advisers urged him to cross the Severn and join Goring, when their combined forces would have amounted to a considerable army. However, as Wales had hitherto furnished him with a large proportion of his foot, he preferred to remain on the west bank of the Severn and attempt to raise a fresh force. He was also still in hopes of receiving large reinforcements from the Irish Catholics, and even from abroad, hopes which were, however, never realized. In spite of his large concessions on paper to the Catholics, the Irish leaders could not be brought to trust to his sincerity.

Fairfax, after the capture of Leicester, had two courses open to him. He could either follow the king into Wales and disperse his new levies, or he might march into the south-west, relieve Taunton, and attack Goring. From the king, nothing was to be feared for some time, whereas if Goring captured Taunton, the prestige of the Royal armies would be somewhat restored; Goring might then succeed in his endeavour to enlist the Clubmen into his forces, and might thus in a very short time be at the head of a considerable army.

As it was, he was much stronger than any force the Parliament could oppose to him in Wilts or Dorset. Fairfax therefore determined to join Massey in Dorset and then march against Goring. His line of march lay through Warwickshire and Gloucestershire, so that he might still turn against the king should orders be received from Parliament to do so. On the 26th, however, letters were sent him from the House permitting him "to prosecute his intentions against the enemy." (Whitelocke). Ordinances were passed empowering him to press soldiers for his army for three months longer, and another directing the Committees of Counties to proceed against deserters from his forces by martial law. Desertion was rife among the pressed men, and Gardiner says, (vol. ii.), the army was in great distress and want, although the troops had been mustered and paid on the 19th after the capture of Leicester.

On the 26th June Fairfax was at Lechdale, where a skirmish occurred, and the next day he reduced the small garrison of Highworth. Rupert, on hearing of his march, feared that his objective was Bristol; he therefore hurriedly left Hereford, and went there to see to its garrison and defences. On the 2nd July Fairfax reached Blandford, and here he first began to have trouble with the Clubmen. Some 5000 of them are said to have gathered under Captain Penruddock. They demanded that the garrisons of the counties should be placed in their hands, till the king and Parliament had settled as to their disposal, that they should be allowed to carry arms, arrest disorderly soldiers, and be put to no charge except for the maintenance of the garrisons.

They also asked that the laws should be administered by the ordinary channels. Fairfax had an interview with a Mr. Hollis, their leader, a day or two later, who demanded permission to carry a petition to the king and Parliament. Fairfax answered them in a conciliatory manner, assuring them that he would maintain discipline and severely punish any of his soldiers who molested them, but would have nothing to do with the petition. The Clubmen appeared for a time satisfied. Though asserting themselves neutral, they were for the most part more in favour of the king than the Parliament, and skirmishes had taken place between them and the garrisons of Sturminster and Lyme. They could have given a good deal of trouble by cutting off stragglers and messengers, and in the event of a reverse could have done much damage.

On the 3rd July, Fairfax was at Dorchester, having joined Massey, and on the 4th he reached Beauminster. Goring, on hearing of his approach, raised the siege of Taunton and prepared to meet him by occupying the line of the Yeo, the bridges across which at Ilchester, Loadbridge, and Long Sutton he fortified. That at Yeovil he destroyed, placing a guard on the right bank; that at Petherton across the Parrot was treated in the same way. The bridges across the lower Parrot were secured by the fortress of Bridgewater and the town of Langport, which had been entrenched. In this position he awaited reinforcements from Grenvile and Prince Charles. The banks of the streams were marshy, and though Goring faced south-west almost towards the point from which he expected his reinforcements, the position was a strong one, and was supported by the fortresses of Bridgewater and Bristol. Fairfax could not march into Devonshire without dislodging him.

On the 5th July, Fairfax reached Crewkerne. The horse of his advanced guard, under Fleetwood, skirmished with some of Goring's troops near Petherton, whereupon the outpost by the broken bridge fell back on Ilchester. Fairfax, on hearing of this, immediately ordered out three regiments of horse and two of foot, who marched to Petherton, repaired the bridge, crossed the Parrot, and advanced in two parties towards Ilchester and Loadbridge. Fairfax and Cromwell, coming up, reconnoitred the enemy's position, but finding them too strongly posted at the bridges to be forced, they fell back to Crewkerne, leaving outposts at Petherton and Martock. The next day the army rested at Crewkerne.

The strength of the forces immediately at the disposal of each of the opposing generals is difficult to arrive at. Fairfax, with the addition of Massey's troops, may have had 14,000 or 15,000 men. Goring could not have had more than 10,000. Probably the actual numbers were on both sides considerably less than these figures. Clarendon says that Goring, on his own showing, must have had almost as large a force as his enemy, but Goring's statements were not to be relied on.

On the 7th July, Fairfax drew out his forces to a rendezvous about a mile from Crewkerne on the Petherton road. Riding on with Cromwell he again examined the bridges over the Yeo. He found them still strongly held, the enemy on the alert, his troops following the movements of the Parliamentary forces on the further side of the river, the scouts and patrols constantly skirmishing in the meadows. A Council of War was held at which it was determined to force a passage at the broken bridge at Yeovil. Accordingly, the bulk of the foot marched to that town, whilst the horse remained to observe the bridges at Ilchester and Loadbridge, and prevent the enemy falling on the rear of the army.

The cavalry post at the further side of the broken bridge retired on the approach of the Parliamentary foot, and Fairfax caused the bridge to be repaired immediately. But on the next morning early (8th July) intelligence was received that the Royalists had abandoned Ilchester and Loadbridge and fallen back on Langport. Goring, in fact, finding that Fairfax had got the passage at Yeovil, and his expected reinforcements not arriving, concentrated his troops, so as still to cover his communications with Bridgewater. Fairfax thereupon, instead of crossing at Yeovil, marched down the left bank to Ilchester, where he quartered for that night.

Goring, having drawn his forces together at Langport, despatched a large force of cavalry the same day across the Parrot towards Taunton. He hoped that town might now be off its guard, and that he might thus be able to capture it by surprise, although it had resisted all his efforts during the many weeks he had lain before it. Fairfax, however, received notice of this movement, and immediately sent Massey with his Gloucester horse, reinforced by a strong detachment from the main army, in pursuit. Another strong party of horse and dragoons was despatched soon after in support.

On the 9th, Fairfax crossed the Yeo and marched to Long Sutton. Hearing that Massey was likely to engage the enemy, he sent 2000 musketeers under Colonel Montague to support him. Massey, however, overtook the enemy before the musketeers came up, and surprised him when resting in the valley of a stream with many of his horses out grazing. Charging immediately, Massey easily routed the Royalists and took a great number of men and horses. That afternoon Fairfax's patrols from Long Sutton came across Goring's outposts holding the passage of a small stream about a mile to the east of Langport. A smart skirmish ensued in which a Royalist cornet and some foreign troopers were taken prisoners.

The next morning Goring prepared to dispute the passage of the rivulet, apparently with the view of covering the retreat of his baggage on Bridgewater. Small enclosures with thick strong fences bordered the course of the stream, through which ran the narrow road from Long Sutton to Bridgewater. The right bank rose steeply and formed a hill, the top of which was more open, and on this, about a musket shot from the stream, Goring posted his horse and pikes, whilst he lined the hedges in the valley thick with musketeers. Two cannons were placed so as to command the road.

Fairfax had assembled a Council of War at which the best method of forcing the enemy to fight was being considered, when intelligence of Goring's preparations was brought him. Instantly the Council was broken up, and orders given to draw up the forces in order of battle. Messengers were at once despatched to order Massey and Montague to return. Fairfax and Cromwell rode forward to reconnoitre. Some guns were then drawn forward and opened on the enemy's two in the road, which they silenced, and afterwards fired with good effect on the Royalist main body on the hill. The foot were then ordered to advance and clear the hedges without waiting for Massey's or Montague's return. After severe fighting the banks of the rivulet were gained, and then Cromwell ordered Major Bethell "with two troops of about 120 horse" to charge, though the ford was so narrow that the horsemen "could scarcely pass two abreast." Major Desborough was ordered to support him with about three troops.

Goring's squadrons were moving forward to support their foot when Bethell, dashing up the hill, charged, and broke their two leading troops. Charged in turn by a fresh body of some 400 horse, he was surrounded, but cut his way back, and Desborough then coming up, he again wheeled about, and together they charged the enemy's main body. In spite of their greatly superior numbers, the Royalist horse were completely routed, and the Parliamentary foot and the rest of the horse now coming up, Goring's whole army broke and fled in disorder.

Some of his regiments had not even been engaged. Bethell and Desborough started in hot pursuit, but were immediately stopped by Cromwell, who, fearing lest the enemy might rally, brought up the whole of his squadrons, and then sent them on in a properly ordered pursuit. No attempt was made by the Royalists to hold Langport, but the town was set on fire, which somewhat checked Cromwell's troopers. At Aller Drove, some two miles beyond Langport, the Royalists made a stand, but seeing the Parliamentary squadrons coming on in proper order, they broke at the first charge and never rallied again. Some escaped to Bridgewater, many others got foundered in bogs and ditches in their attempt to fly across country. About 300 of them were killed and 1400 taken prisoners, including several superior, and many inferior, officers. Two guns, three ammunition wagons, and 1200 horses were among the spoils. The Parliamentary loss was insignificant. That evening the whole army advanced as far as Middlesay, five miles on the road to Bridgewater. (Authorities whence the account of the battle is taken are—Sprigge; Clarendon, vol. v.; *Cromwelliana*. Rushworth's account is taken from Sprigge's. Cromwell's report, Carlyle, vol. v.)

The Battle of Langport is one of great interest. It proves far more conclusively than Naseby the superiority of the troops of the New Model army in all soldierly qualities over their opponents. At Naseby, Fairfax's problem was an easy one to. solve. He was attacked on ground of his own choosing.by an army of barely half the numbers of his own. In the Langport campaign the numbers were less unequal, and he had first to force the passage of a river in face of the enemy, and then to attack him in a very strong position. The manner in which the first difficulty was overcome shows great military talent on the part of the commander, and thorough discipline and flexibility on the part of the troops.

In making the flank movement against the bridge at Yeovil, care was taken that the force making it should be sufficiently strong to overcome all resistance; whilst that engaged in watching the bridges at Ilchester and Loadbridge consisted of the most mobile part of the army, which could be rapidly moved round to support the rest should it be necessary. The risk of the defeat of either wing before the other could come to its support was thus minimised. When, however, it was found that the mere threat of a passage at Yeovil was sufficient to induce Goring to withdraw from the other bridges, the foot were wisely marched back to Ilchester without crossing the river, thus reuniting the wings as speedily as possible.

Goring's dash at Taunton was boldly conceived, and though very badly carried out, it induced Fairfax to make much larger detachments from his army than Goring had made from his. Consequently, at the battle on the 10th, the opposing forces must have been more nearly equal than would otherwise have been the case. But in the battle the bad discipline maintained in Goring's army made itself felt.

The horse were disgracefully beaten before the enemy had opportunity of bringing more than a few troops into action. The foot, though they probably fought well in the enclosures, caught the demoralisation from the horse, directly the latter began to waver. Very different had been the conduct of both arms under Rupert at Marston and Naseby, where defeat was not accompanied by disgrace.

Thus, within three months of its creation, the New Model Army had defeated and dispersed both the king's armies in the field. Nothing remained to him but the garrisons of his castles, and a few small disconnected bodies of mobile troops, principally horse, who had escaped from the field of battle. The victories had been achieved without the active assistance of the Scots. The justification of those was complete who, with Cromwell at their head, carried the measures for the reorganisation of the army, in spite of the strenuous opposition of its most influential leaders. Cromwell's genius as a military organiser was clearly and completely established.

How far was he responsible for the vigorous efforts in the field, which crowned the organisation and discipline, introduced by him, with victory in battle? This can never be exactly known, but it may be shrewdly surmised that his share in the leading of the army was the preponderating one. It is certainly true that its successes commenced almost from the day on which he joined it as a Lieutenant-General of the Horse, which appointment also carried with it the position of second in command. That he accompanied Fairfax on all his reconnaissances, and that the latter always gave the greatest weight to his advice is also certain. That his voice preponderated in the Council of War is rendered more than probable, when it is remembered how important his presence with the army was considered by the senior officers before Naseby. Therefore, without holding with Hoenig that Fairfax was a mediocrity who only owed his reputation to his docility in following Cromwell's advice, it may be safely asserted that a large measure of the success of the New Model in the field was due to Cromwell's genius as strategist and tactician.

The opinions of contemporary writers on the characters of Fairfax and Cromwell are interesting. Clarendon, a shrewd judge of character, says, (vol. v.), speaking of Cromwell as the author of the re-organisation of the army, that he:

> Changed a general (Essex) who, though not very sharp-sighted, would never be governed or applied to anything he did not

like, for another (Fairfax) who had no eyes, and so would be willing to be led.

Clarendon, however, only knew the two generals as opponents, and throughout his book he endeavours to portray Cromwell as a man of extraordinary genius and of extraordinary duplicity. Whitelocke, who though perhaps not so good a judge of character as Clarendon, was behind the scenes in all the intrigues on the Parliament's side, and knew both Cromwell and Fairfax intimately and who was trusted by both, says, *(Memorials),* of the latter:

> The general was a person of as meek and humble carriage as ever I saw in great employment, and but of few words in discourse or council.... But I have observed him at Councils of War that he hath said little, but hath ordered things expressly contrary to the judgment of all his Council, and in action in the field I have seen him so highly transported, that scarce any one durst speak a word to him, and he would seem more like a man distracted and furious than of his ordinary mildness and so far different temper.

This description would make him a man of strong will, but of very highly-strung, nervous, excitable temperament, and would account both for his prompt and vigorous marches and movements, and for his failures on the battle-field from want of self-control at the critical moments.

Fairfax lost no time in following up the victory of Langport by pushing on to Bridgewater. The capture of this fortress would prove of the greatest advantage to him. Situated on the Bristol Channel, and only some thirty miles from Lyme, it commanded the northern flank of the Devon and Cornwall peninsula at its narrowest part. Lyme secured the southern flank, Taunton and Langport the centre. With these four fortresses in his possession, it would be easy for him to cut the communications between Goring, Hopton, and Grenvile, in Devon and Cornwall, and Rupert at Bristol, or the Clubmen in Wilts and Dorset. Being also one of the best ports of the rocky northern coast of Devon, communication by sea between the king in Wales and his generals in Cornwall would thereby be rendered more difficult, and more exposed to interruptions from the Parliamentary fleet.

The danger from the Clubmen, should the Royalist gentry succeed in placing themselves at their head, was very considerable. Fairfax, in passing them by in his desire to close rapidly with Goring, had temporarily appeased them with fair words, but scarcely had he passed than they again began to interrupt his communications and cut off his messengers. On the morning of the 10th, before the battle began, Hollis had reappeared in Fairfax's camp with such extravagant demands, that the latter had considered it necessary to put him in charge of the provost marshal.

During the battle he escaped, and, had the day gone against the Parliamentary forces, it would have gone ill with the beaten army. The result of the battle damped the Royalist ardour of the Clubmen considerably, and those who lived in the neighbourhood of Langport and Bridgewater resented the plundering and ill-treatment they had received from Goring's dissolute horsemen. Clarendon, (vol. v.), says they killed numbers of these latter in their flight from Langport.

On the 11th, on his march towards Bridgewater, Fairfax was met at Knoll Hill by a great body of them, who received him with demonstrations of joy. That night the headquarters of the army were at Chedzoy, some two miles east of Bridgewater. Weldon's brigade, from Taunton, was sent to invest the town on the west, the rest of the army blockading it from the other side. A detachment had been sent under Colonel Okey against a work covering the bridge over the Parrot at Borough, which was still held by the Royalists. It surrendered to him on the 13th.

After the investment of Bridgewater was complete, a Council of War was held on the 14th to determine by what method the attack on the town should proceed. The place seemed very strong. Situated in a low, flat valley, surrounded by regular fortifications, with deep wide ditches filled by the tide, it presented many difficulties to every form of attack. The rise and fall of the tide was very great, and the flood came in with great violence, especially at the spring tides. Fairfax himself was nearly caught in one of these tidal waves when reconnoitring.

All this rendered the construction and maintenance of bridges a work of great difficulty and uncertainty. Yet bridges were necessary for a close investment and formal siege. The low-lying meadows, too, were liable to flood if heavy rain came on, and the trenches would then become impassable. On the other hand, the wide, wet ditches offered an almost insurmountable difficulty to escalade. The decision on this point was therefore postponed and the first few days devoted to the collection of materials, ladders, brushwood, timber, &c., which would be necessary in any case.

On the 16th, however, the immense value of time to enable the army to follow up its successes further, whilst the season was still propitious, was so impressed upon the Council of War that it was determined to attempt the place by storm. Lieut.-General Hammond, (Lieutenant-General of the Ordnance), immediately set to work to construct portable bridges, by which the stormers could cross the ditches. The town was divided into two parts by the river, which thus formed a retrenchment to whichever side was attacked. It was determined to make a false attack on the west, and the real attack on the east. On the 18th it was settled that the attempt should be made before daybreak on Monday, the 21st July. Lots were drawn to determine which troops should form storming parties, reserves, &c. No attempt to form a breach appears to have been made, but cannon were planted to play upon the works.

Sunday was spent by the chaplains in exhorting the troops to do their utmost, and after dark the various parties were drawn out to their posts. At 2 a.m. the signal—three guns fired in rapid succession—was given, and the storming parties rushed to the attack. On the east side the bridges were thrown across the moat, the troops rushed across with little loss, planted their ladders and scaled the walls, led by Lieut.-Colonel Hewson at the head of his own regiment.

Fairfax and Skippon's regiments, led by their Lieut.-Colonels Jackson and Ashfield, pressed close after. The walls were carried, the ordnance turned on the town, and the drawbridge let down. Over it dashed Captain Reynolds at the head of a troop of Cromwell's regiment. The streets were cleared, and soon resistance was at an end in the eastern part of the town. But the enemy barricaded the bridges into the western half, and further progress was stopped. The troops on the west side had, meanwhile, by a false attack, retained the garrison of that part on the ramparts, and prevented their assisting their comrades on the east side.

Thus when day broke Fairfax found himself undisputed master of the eastern town, with all its ordnance and 600 prisoners. Finding this part of the fortress irretrievably lost, Sir Edmund Windham, the governor, opened fire on it with grenades and red-hot shot, and soon most of the houses were in flames. But in spite of the blazing houses. Major Cowell, of Pride's regiment, kept a guard in the street opposite the bridge and prevented any sallies of the garrison from the western town.

A summons having been peremptorily refused, Fairfax at first intended to repeat the attack on the west half the next night, but, changing his mind, only false attacks were delivered to keep the enemy from getting any rest. On Tuesday afternoon at two o'clock he sent to the governor, giving permission to the women and children to come out by four o'clock. Lady Windham and others came out, and then Fairfax returned the governor's fire of grenades and hot shot, and soon the western part of the town was in flames. Sir Edmund Windham then sent to Fairfax to know his terms, and, after some negotiations, the fortress was surrendered on quarter at 8 a.m. on the following day, Wednesday the 23rd. The town was found to be well provisioned and supplied with arms and ammunition.

Thus, this important fortress was reduced in less than a fortnight. This alone was a remarkable feat in the days when sieges extended over many months. The garrison of 1800 good soldiers was sufficient, the governor a brave and capable man, the townspeople well affected, provisions and ammunitions ample for a long siege. The place might have been expected to make a prolonged defence. On the other hand, the besieging force was much stronger than would have usually been employed on such a service. It is, however, to the vigorous nature of the attack that the rapid success of the besiegers must be attributed.

It was also the first of a series of attacks by storm, by which Fairfax and Cromwell wrenched from the hands of the astonished Royalists their most impregnable fortresses in rapid succession. Whenever Cromwell was present, either in supreme command or as lieutenant to Fairfax, the same method of conducting the siege was employed, with only one or two exceptions A careful reconnaissance, and a careful and ample preparation for attack whether by escalade, or by breaching, or both, and then a vigorous assault by strong storming parties. Such was the almost invariable form taken by Cromwell's sieges. So similar is the siege of Bridgewater to those afterwards carried out by him when in chief command both in England and Ireland that its success may fairly be attributed to his influence on Fairfax and the Council of War.

Cromwell at Winchester and Basing

After the capture of Bridgewater Fairfax and his Council considered what should be done next. No doubt it was advisable to follow up the blow struck at Goring at Langport, and prevent his raising fresh troops. On the other hand, not only were Fairfax's communications with London open to attacks from the Royalist fortresses of Oxford and Bristol, but the posts at Donnington, Basing House, Winchester, and Sherborne, lay actually on the most direct roads, whilst the Club-

Langport & the Country between the Parrot & the Yeo

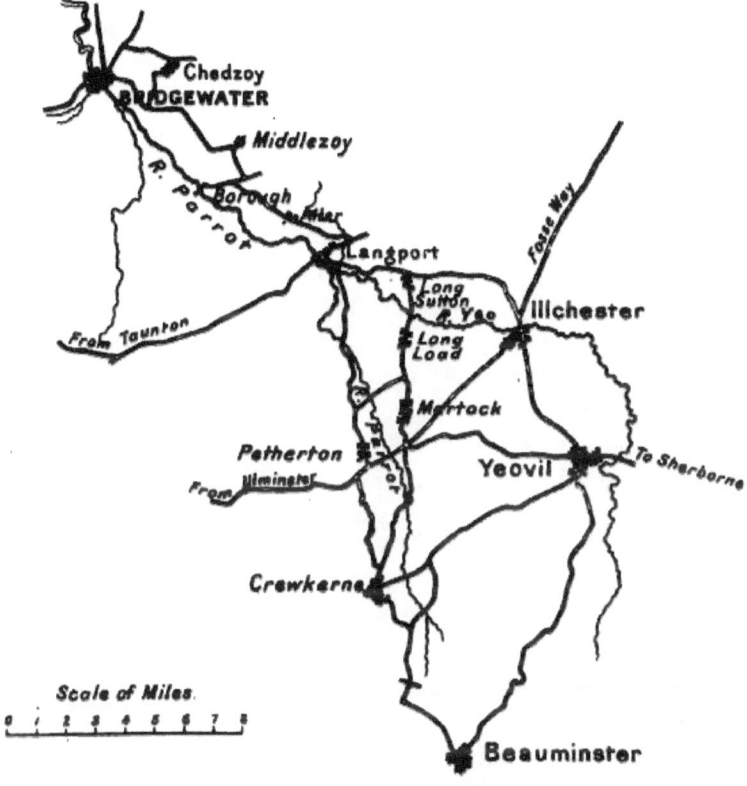

men in Wilts and Dorset were cutting off messengers and small parties. Thus provisions, ammunition, and necessaries for the army could only be brought up under strong escorts, which greatly weakened the fighting strength at the front.

The Council of War was divided, but finally the majority voted for an advance. Fairfax hesitated, but marched on the 26th to Martock, a direction which would not commit him to either course, rested on Sunday the 27th, and then feeling the pressure on his communications to be too great, wheeled round, and marched to Wells on the 28th, sending a mixed brigade of horse and foot under Pickering to invest Sherborne. By this sudden move in a north-westerly direction he hoped to seize Bath, which he knew was weakly defended, before Rupert could relieve it from Bristol. At the same time Massey with a brigade of horse was sent to Taunton and the neighbourhood, in order to keep an eye on Goring, and, if possible, prevent his advancing eastward.

On the 29th Colonel Rich, with a party of horse and dragoons, was sent forward early to Bath and summoned it. Being refused, he pushed his dragoons close up to the walls. Finding the drawbridge down, they crept across it, surprised the guard, and burnt down the gate. Hereupon the place was surrendered. A few hours after Rupert appeared with a force to strengthen the garrison, but finding the town lost he withdrew. Fairfax assembled the army on the Mendip Hills, meaning to march on Bath on the 29th, but hearing of the surrender of the place, went thither with two regiments only, sending the rest back to Wells.

Having settled the garrison at Bath, he returned, and on the 1st August, marched with the army to Queen's Camel, and on the 2nd arrived before Sherborne, which place he now determined to reduce. On this day also he sent Fleetwood with 1000 horse to Shaftesbury, having information that there would be a great gathering of Clubmen at that town. Fleetwood surrounded it with his horse and arrested Hollis and fifty ringleaders, who were placed in prison pending investigation of their proceedings. The Clubmen resented this arrest of their leaders, and the next day Fairfax, receiving information that the whole country was under arms, and that some 10,000 Clubmen were expected to assemble, who would attempt to release their leaders, determined to forestall them.

Accordingly, on the 4th August, Cromwell marched from Sherborne at the head of a strong party of horse to disperse these gatherings, of whose whereabouts he had information. The first party were found on a high wooded hill about two miles west of Shaftesbury. Cromwell went up to them accompanied by a few men only, and persuaded the people to disperse quietly. He informed them that their leaders would only be proceeded against in the regular law courts, and pointed out that if they wished to protect their homes from plunder, their best way was to stay and defend them, not to quit them. He also assured them that no plundering was allowed in the Parliament's army. Cromwell continues his report thus:

> We marched on to Shaftesbury, where we heard a great body of them were drawn together about Hambleton Hill, (in modern maps, Hamilton Hill), where, indeed, near two thousand were gathered. I sent a forlorn hope of about fifty horse; who coming very civilly to them, they fired upon them; and ours desiring some of them to come to me, were refused with disdain. They were drawn into one of the old camps upon a very high hill: I sent one Mr. Lee to them, to certify the peaceableness of my intentions, and to desire them to peaceableness and to submit to the Parliament. They refused and fired at us. I sent him a second time, to let them know that if they would lay down their arms no wrong should be done them.
>
> They still (through the animation of their leaders, and especially two vile ministers) refused; I commanded your Captain-Lieutenant to draw up to them, to be in readiness to charge; and if, upon his falling on, they would lay down arms, to accept them and spare them. When we came near, they refused his offer, and let fly at him; killed about two of his men, and at least four horses. The passage not being for above three abreast, kept us out; whereupon Major Desborrow wheeled about; got in rear of them, beat them from the work, and did some small execution upon them; I believe killed not twelve of them, but cut very many. We have taken about 300; many of which are poor silly creatures, whom if you please to let me send home, they promise to be very dutiful for time to come, and will be hanged before they come out again. Carlyle, vol. i.

Thus, partly by persuasion and partly by force, with firmness and moderation, Cromwell dispersed these dangerous gatherings. Sprigge says:

> This work, though unhappy, was very necessarie for that the

army could send neither messengers nor parties before; whereas, this done, a man might ride very quietly between Sherborne and Salisbury.—*England's Recovery*. Sprigge gives a very full account of the proceedings.

That night the troops quartered at the village of Shrawton, (apparently the modern Stourpaine), close by, where the prisoners were confined in the church. Cromwell himself returned to Shaftesbury, to be in closer communication with Fairfax, but the next day he examined the prisoners. Finding that Mr. Bravel, the Vicar of Compton, was the principal ringleader, Cromwell retained him as a prisoner with a few others. The rest he allowed to return to their homes with a caution, which they took to heart. Commissions from Prince Rupert were found on the ringleaders, removing all doubt as to the Royalist origin of these risings.

That evening, the 6th August, Cromwell and his party returned to Sherborne, where Fairfax was busy with the siege. A few days after, the 8th August, the Commons sent an Ordinance up to the Lords to continue Cromwell in his command for four months longer, which the Upper House agreed to.

The original intention had been to storm Sherborne after the manner of Bridgewater, but on the arrival of a "whole cannon" from Portsmouth it was determined to proceed by regular approaches. Miners were obtained from the Mendip Hills, and a gallery driven under the walls, whilst a large breach was made by a couple of heavy guns. Several officers and men were picked off by the enemy's marksmen stationed in two towers, but on the 14th August the towers were captured, and in turn the garrison were exposed to shots from sharpshooters posted in them.

Several summonses had been refused by Sir Lewis Dyves, the governor, and by the 15th the mine was ready to fire. The besiegers brought down faggots, &c., to fill up the ditch in front of the breach. Seeing this, and the gunners in the retrenchment being picked off from the towers, the garrison retreated into the keep. The besiegers thereupon, without waiting for orders, swarmed over the defences, and pressed on against the keep. The garrison then threw down their arms and demanded quarter, which was granted them, but the castle and all those within were plundered. Amongst Sir Lewis Dyves' papers was found much correspondence with the Clubmen. His castle had been their chief rallying point, and its loss completed their subjection.

The country people bought the plunder taken from their Royalist friends, freely, at the next market day, when, as was the custom, it was disposed of by auction by the soldiers. About 400 prisoners were taken in the castle, the walls of which were afterwards demolished.

The victory of Langport had alarmed the king at Raglan, whither he had gone from Hereford, and caused Rupert to redouble his efforts to secure Bristol. But few recruits had been raised in Wales, Gerard's exactions, when commanding the district, having alienated many of the gentry. Charles hesitated as to what to do next. A plan to join Goring in Devonshire was abandoned, on the news of the loss of Bridgewater. The local militia were discontented, though Gerard had been replaced by Sir John Astley.

News that Langhorne, the Parliamentary governor of Pembroke, had defeated the Royalists at Colby Moor on the 1st August, and had taken Haverfordwest on the 5th, made them disinclined to leave their homes. A project for the relief of Hereford, now besieged by Leven's Scots, was abandoned for want of foot. Finally the king marched northward, at the head of 3000 horse, with some vague idea of joining Montrose in the Highlands. But on reaching Ludlow, he turned eastward, and marched across England to Welbeck, lately taken by a sally from Newark, where he arrived on the 16th August.

On the 18th he was at Doncaster, where some Royalist gentry were endeavouring to raise a body of foot from among their tenants. Here he learnt that the Parliamentary Colonels, Poyntz and Rossiter, had secured the passage of the Aire at Ferry-brigg, and were close at hand with 2000 horse, whilst David Leslie was at Rotherham. Carlisle had surrendered to the latter on 28th June, and he had marched south to join Leven, who had sent him after the king with a strong party of horse. He had now received fresh orders from the Scotch Council of Estates to hurry back to Scotland and oppose Montrose, whose fresh victories had caused them much alarm.

But the king did not know this, and, fearing to be surrounded, marched to Newark. Abandoning all designs of a junction with Montrose, he marched by Stamford, Huntingdon, and Woburne to Oxford, which he entered on the 28th August. His troopers had spread themselves through the country as they marched, and committed great excesses. They reached Oxford laden with plunder, but the only permanent result of this aimless march was to exasperate the people and to further demoralize the Royal horse. Remaining only one day in Oxford, the king marched to Worcester on the 1st September. Leven, who had but very few horsemen, thereupon raised the siege of Hereford, on the 2nd September, and Charles entered it in triumph a few days after. From thence he went to Raglan, intending to raise a force for the relief of Bristol, then besieged by Fairfax.

In Devonshire Goring had rallied some of his scattered horse, assembled a few other levies, and got together some 5000 men who were quartered at Torrington and in the north of the county. But his horse plundered the country, and even seized the provisions intended for their own foot, who, starving and unpaid, deserted in numbers. Goring gave himself up to his usual debaucheries, and beyond a few skirmishes with Massey did nothing.

Thus, when Fairfax and his Council of War considered the situation on the 16th August, they knew that the king had marched northward, and was out of reach of an immediate blow. His force was not strong enough to cause any serious anxiety as to his plans. Goring and Hopton showed no signs of activity in Devonshire, the Clubmen had been suppressed, and the Royalist posts on the communications with London, Basing, Winchester, and Donnington were masked by local troops. It was desirable to press the campaign in the west, but before attacking Goring Bristol should be disposed of, as from thence Rupert would threaten the flank and rear of an advance into Devonshire.

Bristol, too, was of such importance to the king that it was determined to attack it, in spite of the plague then raging in the district.

Fairfax therefore left Sherborne on the 18th August, and, sending forward Ireton with 2000 horse to prevent the enemy burning the villages round Bristol, he reached Chew, nine miles to the south of that place, on the 20th August. By the 23rd the investment was completed on both banks of the Avon.

Thus began the most important siege of this war. Full reports both from Cromwell and Rupert are extant, (Rushworth, *Historic Collections*, vol. vii.), few other military operations of the day can be so completely studied from both sides. Rupert had great difficulties to contend with. The town lay in a hollow at the junction of the Frome with the Avon, and in view of the increased power of artillery it had been found necessary to include the space between the walls and the crest of the heights to the north, in the system of defence. This had been accomplished by running a weak parapet, five feet high and three thick, with a ditch six feet wide and four deep, strengthened at intervals by enclosed forts, from the Avon east of the town, across the Frome, and back to the Avon west of it.

The perimeter of the defences was about five miles. The garrison was very weak, and demoralised by the plague then raging. According to a report by Rupert's council of war there were, when he entered the town, but five or six hundred effective soldiers and eight hundred trained bands. By the commencement of the siege he had got together some 2300 foot, mostly raw Welsh levies, and a strong party of horse. Cromwell estimates the garrison at 2500 foot, 1000 horse, and 1000 auxiliaries.

The first step in the siege was the capture of the fort at Portshead, which allowed five Parliamentary ships, under Captain Moulton, to enter the King's Road and blockade the port from the sea. Though several councils of war were held and siege materials collected, it was not till the 2nd September that the fear of interruption from the king, now returned to Worcester, or from Goring, and the sickness in his own force, caused by exposure to bad weather, induced Fairfax to hasten matters and to attempt a storm.

The assault was fixed for the 7th September, but on the usual summons being sent, Rupert commenced to negotiate and the assault was postponed. Meanwhile the besieging force had been strengthened by 2000 Clubmen, whom Cromwell had persuaded to join the Parliamentary Army. He considered that, although they would probably be of little use, they would be kept out of mischief when employed in the siege.

The negotiations with Rupert having proved fruitless, the hour for the storm was finally fixed for 2 a.m. on the 10th September. Each brigade was to send out two or three storming parties against the works opposite which it quartered. Thus Welden's brigade, consisting of his own, Ingoldsby's, Fortescue's, and Herbert's regiments, was to attack the works south of the Avon. Montague's brigade, in which were his own, the generals, Pickering's, and Sir Hardress Waller's regiments, was to storm the works about Lawford's Gate, between the Avon and the Frome. Rainsborough's brigade, consisting of his own, Skippon's, Hammond's, Birch's, and Pride's regiments, was to attempt the works between the right bank of the Frome and Pryor's Hill Fort. This last work was of stronger profile than the majority of the others along the line, and as it occupied a commanding position from which the rest of the line could be swept, it formed the key to the defences. The rest of the line from Pryor's Hill Fort westward to the Avon was to be watched by a strong body of horse and dragoons, to prevent any attempt on the part of the garrison to break out in this direction.

Each storming party was to be 200 strong. First 40 men carrying 20 ladders, under 2 sergeants, then 5 files (15 men) musketeers and pikes, under the command of a lieutenant, then 7 files (21 men), under the command of a captain, then two parties carrying faggots to throw into the ditch. The remainder of the 200 men, under a field officer, followed by 20 pioneers, were to second the advance parties, clear the ramparts, and level them sufficiently to allow the horse to pass, or secure one of the gates and lower the drawbridge. Strong reserves both of horse and foot were to be ready to support the storming parties should they succeed in mounting the ramparts.

Gentlemen of the ordnance and gunners were to accompany the stormers and turn the captured guns against the town. These orders were drawn up by a committee of colonels of the army, and approved of by Fairfax. A few cannon had been mounted against the works, but no attempts to form breaches appear to have been made. Fairfax directed a great heap of straw and faggots to be made near a battery opposite Pryor's Hill Fort, which he selected for his post during the storm. It was agreed, to prevent confusion in the darkness, that if the outer line were captured no attempt should be made on the town walls.

At 2 a.m. on the 10th, everything being in readiness, the straw heap was lighted, and four guns fired at Pryor's Hill Fort. At this signal the stormers rushed on. Welden's brigade was beaten back with some loss, the walls on that side being too high for the ladders. Montague's brigade, however, entered the works on either side of Lawford's Gate, drove the defenders out of all the outer works, and seized the inner gate of the city itself, in Castle Street.

On the right of the Frome Rainsborough sent his own regiment and part of Pride's against Pryor's Hill Fort, Hammond's and Skippon's against the lines nearer the Frome, whilst the other part of Pride's regiment was ordered to make a false attack against a strong work called the Great Fort. Hammond's regiment at once crossed the line, and throwing down the rampart, made way for Rich's regiment of horse to enter, led by Captain Ireton, (not Colonel Ireton, Cromwell's famous lieutenant), and Major Bethell. This was necessary, for Rupert's cavalry stood ready to charge any of the Parliamentary foot who attempted to penetrate beyond the outer line. Ireton and Bethell, however, drove them back towards the Great Fort, and prevented their interfering with the foot.

Meanwhile, a furious combat was raging at Pryor's Hill Fort. The walls were high and the ladders hardly reached to the top. The assailants and the defenders under Major Price, a gallant Welshman, were equally stubborn. For two hours they fought at push of pike, whilst the four guns in the fort poured out an incessant fire of case. Hammond's regiment, having secured the entry of the horse, wheeled to its right and attacked the fort at the gorge. At last, as day was breaking, some of these men succeeded in entering through a port-hole, and in a few seconds the assailants were swarming in over all the ramparts.

Nearly all the gallant defenders, including the commander, were put to the sword. Had the fort been able to hold out, the assailants must have abandoned the rest of the line down to the Frome, as its guns would in daylight have swept the ramparts from end to end. However, by break of day the whole of the works, from the fort down across the Frome to the Avon, were in the hands of Fairfax's troops except one small work which soon surrendered.

Elsewhere Rupert still held the castle and the city itself, with the exception of the Castle Street Gate, and also two strong works called the Great Fort and Coulston's Fort. The city was now on fire in several places, and the garrison much discouraged. About four hours after sunrise, therefore, Rupert sounded a trumpet, and opened negotiations for a surrender. Liberal terms were granted him, and on the 11th he marched out at the head of the garrison, with their colours, drums, swords, and pikes, but without firearms, under escort of two regiments of horse for Oxford.

So exasperated, however, were the countryfolk in Gloucestershire against him and his plundering troopers, that he borrowed 1000 muskets from Fairfax to defend himself and his men against them. One hundred and forty cannon and quantities of arms, ammunition, and provisions fell into the hands of the victors. They had lost but 200 men in the storm, almost all from Welden's brigade and from the assailants of Pryor's Hill. It was looked upon as a special intervention of Providence that, though the plague was rife in the villages in which they quartered, the Parliamentary troops had lost but one man of that disease during the siege.

Equally with that of Bridgewater the siege of Bristol bears strong marks of Cromwell's system of war. When compared with those of Basing, Drogheda, Wexford, and others which he afterwards conducted, the inference that the same head planned them all becomes very strong, and whoever may actually. have been responsible for the conduct of these sieges, their success was only possible through the admirable organisation and discipline of the army, of which, as has been shown, Cromwell must be considered the originator. No operation in war tries the discipline and steadiness of troops more severely than a night attack, and the assaults on Bridgewater and Bristol are brilliant examples of such operations.

On the king the loss of Bristol came as a thunderbolt. He had confidently expected the place would have held out for long. Without waiting to inquire into details, he dismissed Rupert from all his commands, and gave him a pass to go beyond the seas. This led Rupert to publish a justification, in which the great difficulties of the defence are clearly and moderately set out. But though the king forgave him, he never again occupied the same position in the Royal Army and Royal Councils as before.

The blow was indeed an irreparable one for Charles, finally severing the communications between his Welsh levies and his forces in Devonshire under Goring. Always vacillating, he again determined to attempt a junction with Montrose, whose victory at Kilsyth on the 15th August had apparently laid the Lowlands at his feet. But the movement would now be difficult from the outset, for Poyntz, who had followed Charles from Yorkshire, lay with 3000 horse between Hereford, whither the king had returned, and Worcester. After some manoeuvring, however, he succeeded in getting away northward through the mountains, again followed by Poyntz, and on the 26th September he reached Chester, then besieged by Colonel Jones.

Entering the town himself, he sent Langdale with a strong party of horse to get behind Jones and attack him from the rear. On the 27th Langdale, however, got caught between Jones and Poyntz, who just then came up, and, though the king endeavoured to succour him from the town, his forces were utterly routed on Royton Heath.

Charles fled to Denbigh, where in a few days he rallied 2400 men. But here he learnt that David Leslie had totally routed Montrose at Philliphaugh on the 18th September. His prospects were now indeed gloomy; still he did not despair, but marched to Bridgenorth, ever hearing of the loss of towns and castles. Here he was joined by Maurice with 800 men, and then marched through the Midlands to Newark, which he reached on the 4th October.

Fairfax, after settling affairs at Bristol, marched to Bath, sending Rainsborough to attack Berkeley Castle on the Severn, and Cromwell to besiege Devizes. Both places were captured without much difficulty, and Fairfax moved to the latter on the 23rd September. Here a council of war considered whether Oxford should next be attacked or Goring completely crushed. It was rightly considered that to destroy the army in the field was of more importance than to capture the fortress, especially since the latter and the surrounding country had been so carefully prepared for defence that the time necessary for its capture would allow Goring to recover strength and territory.

Fairfax therefore marched on the 1st October by Dorchester to Chard, where he halted awaiting a convoy of treasure, his men being without pay, and himself suffering from wounds and exposure. At the same time he sent Cromwell to clear his communications of the fortified posts still held by the Royalists. The lieut.-general arrived on the 28th September before Winchester with a brigade of foot and three regiments of horse. What ensued cannot be more tersely described than in his own words:—

> I came to Winchester on the Lord's day, the 28th of September, with Colonel Pickering, commanding his own, Colonel Montague's, and Sir Hardress Waller's regiments. After some dispute with the governor, we entered the town. I summoned the castle: was denied; whereupon we fell to prepare batteries, which we could not perfect (some of our guns being out of order) until Friday following. Our battery was six guns; which being finished, after firing one round, I sent in a second summons for a treaty, which they refused. Whereupon we went on with our work, and made a breach in the wall near the Black Tower; which after about 200 shot we thought stormable, and proposed on Monday morning to attempt it. On Sunday night, about ten of the clock, the governor beat a parley, desiring to treat. I agreed unto it, and sent Colonel Hammond and Major Harrison in to him, who agreed upon these enclosed Articles.— Carlyle, vol. i.

Peters, who made a narration concerning these operations to the House, said that on examining the works after the surrender, he found the storming parties would have had to carry six distinct lines of defence before obtaining complete possession of the castle. On the 6th October Lord Ogle, the governor, marched out with his garrison, only the officers retaining their arms, to Woodstock. On taking possession of the castle, Cromwell found the place very well supplied with provisions of all sorts, and armed with seven cannon well furnished with ammunition.

The terms of surrender had stipulated that the inhabitants of the town should be unmolested. Complaints were, however, made to Cromwell that some of his troopers had been plundering. The accused were at once arrested, tried by a court martial, and six troopers condemned to death. One selected by lot was hanged in public, the other five sent with a trumpeter to Sir Thomas Glenham, Governor of Oxford, to be disposed of as he should think fit. He returned them "with an acknowledgment of the lieutenant-general's nobleness in being so tender in breach of articles."—Sprigge, *England's Recovery*.

Cromwell lost no time in marching to Basing House. This famous mansion, the seat of John Paulet, Marquess of Winchester, had been fortified by him as a Royal garrison at the outbreak of the war. It was a magnificent pile, fit residence for one of the richest and most powerful of the English nobility. It consisted of two main buildings, the old, and the new house, surrounded by ample courts, stables, gardens, &c. The Paulets were Catholics, and therefore expected but scant mercy from the Presbyterian and Puritan fanatics of the Parliament's army. They were men of culture and artistic tastes, who had filled their rooms and galleries with all the best art which Europe could then produce.

Everything which the science of military engineering could suggest had been done to strengthen the defences, probably under the direction of the famous architect, Inigo Jones. Ramparts and ditches, pallisades and covered walls, protected the buildings from breaching or escalade. Provisions for some years, rather than months, (Peters' Narrative to the House, Sprigge), were stored in the vaults. Situated on the main road to the west Basing had proved a thorn in the side to the Parliamentary armies employed in that direction. It had been besieged again and again without success. Waller had been foiled in at least one attempt, Manchester had failed even to cover the siege. For some time it had been closely invested by Dalbier when Cromwell arrived before it on the 7th October.

Losing no time in erecting his batteries, by Friday the 10th, Cromwell had his guns planted against the southeast angle of the works. Dalbier had previously directed his against the northern front. For the next three days a steady fire was maintained, and by Monday the breaches were considered practicable. Arrangements were then made to storm the place on the following morning. On Tuesday morning, the 14th October, at 6 o'clock, that is, just at daybreak, the signal (four guns fired in rapid succession) was given, and the storming parties rushed forward at two or three points.

With their usual determined courage, Pickering's soldiers poured over the outworks and carried the new house at the first rush. The defenders fired a train of powder which had no effect, and retired into the old house. Here they called a parley, but the assailants refused to listen. Meanwhile, Montague's and Waller's regiments had carried the works defending the guard-house, and drawing their ladders after them, clambered over a wall into the central court and joined Pickering's men in the attack on the old house. This did not long resist, but was also taken by storm, and in three quarters of an hour from the signal being first given, the whole place was in the hands of the Parliament's soldiers.

The Marquess of Winchester, Sir Robert Peak, Inigo Jones, and 300 officers and men were taken prisoners. Colonel Hammond and Major King, who had been captured by the garrison a few days before when reconnoitring the house in a mist, were released. The soldiers fell upon the rich spoils, and the house was completely sacked before night. Money, jewels, and plate fell to the share of the soldiers. The rich furniture and immovables, the provisions, and even the lead and iron from the roofs and gutters, were sold the next day by auction to the country folk, who came with their carts and carried them away. Whilst the pillage was proceeding a fire broke out, which, being neglected, soon consumed all the soldiers had left.

In twenty-four hours nothing but tottering blackened walls remained of the stateliest home in England. Such was the fate of a fortress taken by storm in those days. Lucky were the defenders to receive even quarter for their lives. About forty of the assailants and 100 of the defenders perished in the fight. Peters says that others who had fled into the cellars were imprisoned there by the falling debris and were suffocated by the fire.

Cromwell, who had thus in a few days captured a place which had resisted the attempts of all other commanders for years, in reporting its fall recommended that its defences should be razed, he says:

> I humbly offer to you, to have this place utterly slighted, for these following reasons: It will ask about eight hundred men to manage it; it is no frontier; the country is poor about it; the place exceedingly ruined by our batteries and mortar pieces, and by a fire which fell upon the place since our taking it. If you please to take the garrison at Farnham, some out of Chichester, and a good part of the foot which were here under

Dalbier, and to make a strong quarter at Newbury, with three or four troops of horse, I dare be confident it would not only be a curb to Donnington, but a security and a frontier to all these parts; inasmuch as Newbury lies upon the river, and will prevent any incursion from Donnington, Wallingford, or Faringdon, into these parts; and by lying there, will make the trade most secure between Bristol and London for all carriages. And I believe the gentlemen of Sussex and Hampshire will with more cheerfulness contribute to maintain a garrison on the frontier than in their bowels, which will have less safety in it.—Carlyle, vol. i., for Cromwell's report and Mr. Peters' Narrative; Sprigge; *Cromwelliana*, *Weekly Account*, 8th to the 15th October).

Very sound strategy for one who, according to Gardiner and other critics, understood little of that art. A fortress is only of use when it prevents attacks from the enemy on territory or communications, or threatens his. Therefore, with the exception of some few cases, such as that of London in this war, where it is prudent to render some great base or magazine absolutely secure, fortresses should be placed on the frontier. When ill placed they are an actual source of weakness to the possessors, as absorbing men, stores, and money, which would be far better employed elsewhere.

Cromwell lost no time at Basing, but having freed the main roads south of the Kennet, he left Donnington to be dealt with later by Dalbier, and turned back with all speed to rejoin Fairfax. On the 16th October he was at Wallop, a good march on his way. The next day Langford House, near Salisbury, surrendered to him at the first summons. Corfe Castle now only remained to the king between London and Exeter. Pickering's regiment was sent to besiege this stronghold. Cromwell, marching rapidly, reached Chard on the 20th October. Here he received an order from Fairfax to join him in person at Silverton forthwith. Either this order was not received till later, or Cromwell found it impossible to comply with it at once, as he does not appear to have joined Fairfax till the 24th at Crediton, by which time his brigade had reached Honiton.

Fairfax wished to consult with Cromwell as to the next steps to be taken. On the 11th October, the convoy of treasure had reached Chard and the army had been paid. On the 13th it had advanced to Axminster, where Goring's horsemen, who knew every lane and path in the country, passed through the outposts and carried off some sixty prisoners. On the 14th the army marched to Honiton, and on the 15th to Colhampton, Goring's horse falling back before it. Massey was this day sent with his horse and Welden's brigade of foot to attack Tiverton Castle, which commanded an important bridge over the Exe.

On the 17th October at a Council of War it was determined to reduce Tiverton as rapidly as possible, and therefore Fairfax marched thither on that day, leaving detachments at Bradninch, Silverton, and Columb, to secure the roads eastward and prevent Goring breaking through that way and rejoining the king. On the 18th batteries were constructed and opened fire, and on the 19th a Council of War was called to consider the method of an assault which it was determined to deliver that afternoon. Whilst the debate was proceeding, a round shot struck the chain which held up the drawbridge, and cut it, letting the bridge fall. Whereupon the soldiers, without waiting for an order, dashed across the bridge, before it could again be raised, seized the gate, drove the defenders from the outworks, and, following at their heels, entered the church and castle, whither they retired, almost at the same time. The garrison were granted quarter, but plundered and stripped.

Having secured this important post on his flank, Fairfax returned with his army the next day to Silverton. Then it was determined to invest Exeter rather than march further into Devon, leaving so strong a garrison in rear; for Exeter was believed to hold 1000 horse and 4000 foot. On the 22nd the army crossed the Exe, to Newton Siers, where information was received that Goring had marched to Okehampton with most of the horse from Exeter. The weather was now very wet and the roads well-nigh impassable. The army moved a few miles on the 23rd to Crediton, either with an idea of following Goring or of obtaining better quarters, and halted there a few days. At a Council of War on the 25th the plans were again altered, perhaps owing to the presence of Cromwell. Fatigue and exposure to the bad weather now prevailing had caused much sickness in the army, the men were becoming exhausted and needed rest.

It was, therefore, determined to withdraw them to the east of the Exe, where the villages offered good quarter and supplies were more easily available. The Parliamentary gentry of Devon had been urging Fairfax to march at once to raise the siege of Plymouth in order that traffic might be reopened with that town, and it looks as if it required the influence of Cromwell's stronger will to enable him to resist the pressure. The army recrossed the Exe on the 26th, and on the 27th was quartered about Topsham.

Here, again, the Devonshire gentry urged that a bridge might be thrown across the Exe at Topsham and Exeter invested on all sides. But the commanders were firm, and insisted on entrenching the line of the Clyst, a tributary of the Exe, joining it at Topsham, and thus make their communications on the east side of the town secure, before shutting it in on the west. Fortified posts were then established at Bishop's Clyst, Poultimore, and Stoak, whilst the headquarters were drawn back to Autree. In this position the army remained some weeks.

After the king had reached Newark on the 4th October, he remained there some days settling the garrison and reducing the excessive number of general officers, said to have been twenty-four for a force of 2000 men. But hearing a false report of a new success of Montrose, he again determined to march with his horse to join him.

Accordingly, on the 12th October he reached Welbeck and intended the next day to march to Rotherham. But on this day a trumpeter, which had some time previously been sent by him to Leven, returned, bringing with him true information about the state of affairs. Montrose, he said, had retreated to the Highlands, Leslie was in possession of the Lowlands, and Leven's army was towards Newcastle.

Hereupon the king thought he had himself better remain in England, but he sent 1500 horse under Lord Digby and Sir M. Langdale to try and cut their way through to Montrose. On 20th October Digby surprised 1000 Parliamentary foot at Sherborne in Yorkshire, but whilst he was securing his prisoners Colonel Copley arrived with 1250 horse. In the action which ensued, Digby was worsted and driven with considerable loss to Skipton. He, however, persisted in his enterprise, but on 1st November was met on Carlisle Sands by a party of Scotch horse under Sir J. Browne. He was routed, and during the next few days his troopers were completely dispersed. Himself with Langdale and a few others escaped to the Isle of Man.

Meanwhile, the king had returned to Newark with 800 horse. Here Rupert and Maurice joined him. Incessant quarrels ensued between the princes and Sir R. Willis on the one side, and the king's personal entourage on the other. Meanwhile Poyntz and Rossiter, with a strong body of horse, had arrived in the neighbourhood and closed all the roads against foraging parties and weak detachments. Finally, Rupert went to Belvoir, which was still held for the king, and demanded a pass from the Parliament to go abroad, which was refused him.

On the 3rd November the king assembled 500 horse after dark in the market-place at Newark, and, placing himself in their midst, marched that night to Belvoir. Obtaining fresh guides there, he continued without resting to a village about eight miles from Northampton, which he reached late on the afternoon of the 4th. Thence, marching mostly by night, he made his way to Banbury and Oxford, which he reached on the 6th November, in four days from leaving Newark.

The End of the First Civil War

The tide of war had now set in definitely against Charles. The campaign which he had opened with bright and not unreasonable hopes was closing in gloom and disaster. The forces of the king and Parliament were no longer evenly matched. Whilst those of the former still remained a militia, led by gallant, but headstrong and independent leaders, those of the latter had been welded by the genius of a great soldier into a regular army in which the strictest discipline was maintained. The loose disconnected efforts of the Royal commanders were shattered by the strong concentrated blows of the New Model Army. From the beginning the jealousies and quarrels of the princes, nobles, and courtiers who controlled the king's armies, which his weak, irresolute will had entirely failed to suppress, had rendered all proper strategical combination impossible.

On the other hand, once the Committee of Both Kingdoms had given the military leaders a free hand, the strategy of the Parliament had been both sound and practical. When permission to act on his own responsibility had been granted to Fairfax, he had found himself in the centre about Oxford, whilst Cromwell on the right, and Massey on the left, faced superior forces of the enemy. Turning at once against that wing of the king's army which was the most formidable and menacing, Fairfax had joined Cromwell and crushed Rupert at Naseby. Then wheeling to his left and marching rapidly, he had joined Massey against Goring, and driven him in disorder into the western peninsula. When both the armies in the field had been thus disposed of, he turned against the Royal fortresses, which fell one after another before his swift and determined attacks.

Not only had the Royalists been beaten, but they were also becoming rapidly demoralised. In those districts which had hitherto been most devotedly loyal to the king, the adherents of the Parliament were beginning to assert themselves. This was especially the case in

South Wales, where hitherto the king had recruited most of his foot. Early in October, Colonel Morgan, Governor of Gloucester, had left that town with 300 horse and 400 foot. Numbers of Monmouthshire men joined him, and with these he marched to Chepstow, where, on the 6th October, he summoned the castle. After a few days it was surrendered to him, the Welshmen of the neighbourhood showing no signs of coming to the assistance of the governor, Colonel Fitzmorris. Morgan then marched to Monmouth, which castle also surrendered on the 22nd. On the 12th October, Langhorne followed up his successes in Pembrokeshire by taking Carmarthen town and castle.

The Glamorganshire men had been among the first whom Gerard's unpopularity had alienated from the king. Whilst Charles was endeavouring, in August, to raise forces against the Scots at Hereford, they had insisted on the castle at Cardiff being placed in the hands of a committee nominated by themselves. No sooner had the king withdrawn Langdale's cavalry from South Wales and marched towards Chester in September, than this committee declared for the Parliament. Thus some of the principal castles and posts along the southern coast of Wales were in the Parliament's hands by the middle of October, and their connection with Gloucester and Bristol was cemented in December by the capture of Hereford by Colonels Morgan and Birch, the Governors of Gloucester and Bath, who succeeded in obtaining admission by a stratagem.

In North Wales Colonel Jones defeated the Royalist Sir William Vaughan, and Beeston Castle was taken. On the 5th December Lathom House, so long and gallantly defended by the Countess of Derby, capitulated.

These successes had been obtained by the Parliament in spite of the fact that Montrose's victories had drawn the greater part of the Scotch Army back into Scotland. The troops remaining with Leven had effected nothing of importance during his expedition into the west. Unpaid, they had perforce to live at free quarter, which, as usual, begat plunder. They were so reduced in numbers that Leven endeavoured to recruit in England, and even, it is said, pressed Englishmen into his ranks. For these reasons the inhabitants, whether Royalists or Roundheads, regarded the Scots as foes, and Parliament passed a vote that Leven had no power to raise forces in England. (Whitelocke). He had on his part behaved loyally enough to his allies, but, disgusted with his treatment by Parliament, he, after raising the siege of Hereford, marched away north, intending to re-enter Scotland. He had already reached Northumberland, when Parliament, by dint of paying up some of the arrears due to his men, and promising more regular pay in future, induced him to return and besiege Newark, before which place he arrived on the 2nd December.

The Royal forces in Devon and Cornwall might still amount to some 10,000 men. But they were greatly demoralised, and two at least of the commanders were unprincipled ruffians. Grenvile, who commanded before Plymouth, applied to his own use the funds intended for his troops. Goring endeavoured to negotiate with Fairfax, proposing the abdication of the king and the substitution of Prince Charles on the throne. When Fairfax would not listen, he quitted his command and went to France on the pretext of raising money and men.

All Charles' schemes for obtaining assistance abroad or from the Irish Catholics having failed, he again, in December, attempted to treat with Parliament, but in vain. He had still with him at Oxford a considerable body of horse under Rupert and Maurice, and these conducted a series of forays into the neighbouring counties. Fairfax detached three regiments of horse into Buckinghamshire, which stopped the Royalist expeditions in that direction. His own forces near Exeter had by this time been somewhat recruited by their rest, but much sickness still prevailed among them. A forward movement was now determined on. Local troops were brought up from Lyme to occupy the works along the Clyst, and the army marched on the 6th December to Tiverton.

The next few days were spent in arranging the investment of Exeter on all sides, when news was received that Prince Charles, who had still some 5000 horse and 4000 or 5000 foot at his disposal in Western Devonshire, was advancing to relieve the place. Fairfax, who was not strong enough to fight the prince and besiege Exeter at the same time, concentrated his forces on the 8th January at Crediton. Leaving a couple of regiments to watch the roads running north of Dartmoor, he marched into the tract lying to the south of it then called the South Hams, into which Lord Wentworth, now commanding the Royalist horse, had advanced.

The next day, 9th January, Cromwell surprised Wentworth's advanced guard in quarters at Bovey Tracey. The officers, who were gambling in an inn, flung their stakes out of the window, and whilst the Parliamentary troopers stopped to pick up the silver they escaped out of the back. Most of their men also got away, but 400 horses were captured.

The cold was intense, the roads bad, but on the 11th, Fairfax, who had provided pack-horses for his transport, reached Totness, and the next day he sent two regiments to reconnoitre Dartmouth, and pushed strong parties of horse in the direction of Tavistock. Such was the demoralisation of the Royalists, that on the approach of these parties they abandoned their works before Plymouth, leaving some of their artillery and ammunition in them, and retired in haste across the Tamar.

Meanwhile a summons had been sent to Dartmouth and rejected. Fairfax and his principal officers then reconnoitred the town. The defences were strong and mounted over 100 guns, the garrison numbered more than 1000 men, and the place was well provisioned. Fairfax had no cannon, the weather was extremely cold. Nevertheless, it was determined to attempt the storm of the fortress.

The next few days were spent in procuring the necessary materials, ladders, &c., and Captain Batten brought round some ships from Plymouth, and blockaded the port from the sea. Provisions were scarce, when an extraordinary take of fish in the estuary supplied both inhabitants and troops, and caused the latter to believe in a miraculous intervention of Providence in their behalf.

The assault was fixed for the night of Sunday, the 18th January. The day was spent in exhortations by the chaplains to the men to do their duty bravely. After dark the various parties were formed up in their places. The frost had broken, and the night was "very milde, as at Midsummer." (Sprigge). Three storming parties were drawn up against the town, one led by Lieut.-Colonel Pride, opposite the North Gate, a second by Colonel Hammond against the West Gate; and the third, under Colonel Fortescue, before Tunstal Church. A small party, assisted by some seamen, were to make a false attack on Kingsworth Fort, a strong work, opposite Dartmouth, on the other side of the river.

At 11 p.m. the signal was given, and the storm commenced. Little resistance appears to have been offered, for all three columns quickly mounted the works, and thus captured the town. The defenders only fired one round from their cannon. The assailants lost but one man killed, and a few wounded. The governor, Sir Hugh Pollard, retreated into the castle. The next morning, both this work and Kingsworth Fort surrendered, the former on quarter, the latter, which could have still offered a stout resistance, on good terms.

This assault, considering the strength of the works, and the absence of cannon and siege material, was a very bold one, but succeeded probably through the demoralisation of the defenders. A great many of the garrison were Cornishmen, who had hitherto proved the best infantry on the king's side. Earlier in the war their resistance would have been far more stubborn. Fairfax dismissed them all to their homes, on their undertaking not to bear arms again against the Parliament, and gave each man two shillings to pay his way.

Having thus driven the enemy back in the south of Devon, and wrested from him his principal fortress in that direction, Fairfax again turned his attention towards Exeter. He took up his quarters at Chudleigh, and sent Colonel Hammond to attempt Pouldram, now called Powderham Castle, a fortified post on the Exe, below the town. This surrendered on the 26th January. Exeter was now closely invested on all sides, and the fort at Exmouth blockaded. Some thought of storming the town was entertained, but laid aside for the time. On the 29th January Fairfax received information that the Oxford horse were raiding in Wilts and Dorset, and hoped to relieve Corfe Castle. He therefore sent Colonel Cooke with three regiments of Massey's horse to oppose them.

******

The narrative of this brilliant little cavalry raid, conducted by a Royalist, Colonel Cromwell, is given in *Cromwelliana*. Wareham was captured, and Corfe Castle relieved. On his return, towards Oxford, Cromwell was met by Cooke, and taken prisoner, his men being driven back to Corfe, whence they afterwards made their escape.

******

Meanwhile Lord Hopton, who had now assumed the command-in-chief of the Royal forces in the West, had determined to attempt the relief of Exeter from the North. For this purpose he assembled all the forces he could raise at Stratton, in North Cornwall, early in February. Fairfax, who had early intelligence of this design, determined to oppose him. By this time the line of investment round Exeter had been so strengthened by fortified houses and field works, that it could be held by comparatively few troops. A regiment had also been raised in the South Hams for the Parliament's service amongst those whom the exactions of Goring's horse had alienated from the king, and to this regiment was entrusted the duty of securing the south of the county. On the 9th February, the army was assembled at Chudleigh. Sir Hardress Waller was left to command the line of investment, with three regiments of foot and one of horse. The line east of the Exe was held by the local forces from Lyme. On the 5th February orders had been sent to Cooke to return, but he had not yet arrived.

On the 10th February Fairfax marched to Crediton, where he remained three days, awaiting treasure from Dartmouth and completing his arrangements. Here he obtained intelligence that Hopton had marched on the 10th to Torrington, with 4000 horse and 3000 foot, and was fortifying that town. On the 14th Fairfax advanced with five regiments of horse and seven of foot to Chumleigh. He was thus somewhat weaker than Hopton in horse, but stronger in foot.

The weather was so wet on the 15th that the army remained at Chumleigh, and some skirmishes only occurred between the advanced patrols. The advance was resumed on the 16th at 4 a.m., the weather suddenly clearing when the troops were on the march. Their progress, however, seems to have been slow, as it was past 5 p.m. and getting dark when the van was drawn up in Stapleton Park, about a mile from Torrington.

The park surrounded a large country house from which an outpost of the enemy had been driven by the advanced guard a few hours previously. In pursuing the enemy the horse of the advanced guard had got engaged in the enclosures which surrounded the town. The foot were, therefore, brought up to support them, or cover their retreat. The enemy then drew more forces out of the town, and Fairfax, unwilling to fall back, ordered Colonel Hammond with three regiments of foot to move forward and form a reserve to the advanced guard. The Royalists, however, contented themselves with occupying the enclosure immediately in front of the Parliamentary outposts; and Fairfax, not wishing to engage in the darkness, ordered his men to bivouac.

About 9 o'clock p.m. the Royalists withdrew some of their more advanced posts, which caused Fairfax to believe that they were about to retire, and he ordered his own patrols to follow them up. These advanced close up to the town, but were there received by a volley of musketry. Hearing the firing, the supports hurried up, and immediately afterwards Hammond brought up his three regiments and threw them into the combat. Finding his van now hotly engaged, Fairfax ordered a general advance. The town was strongly barricaded, and a fierce struggle ensued at push of pike. At last the barricades were carried. Twice the Parliamentary foot endeavoured to advance down the street, twice they were driven back by charges of the Royalist horse.

Each time, however, Hammond and the other officers succeeded in rallying their men at the barricades, and retained possession of them. Then Major Stephens came up with the "forlorn hope" of horse, and the Royalists were driven back. Their foot soldiers were a good deal scattered, but under cover of the darkness and protected by their horse, which charged repeatedly, they for the most part escaped out of the west gate of the town and across the bridge over the Torridge. By this and other passes the horse also retired. Owing to the darkness and the enclosed country the Parliamentary horse were unable to pursue. About 400 prisoners were taken, some 200 of whom were placed under guard in the church, where the enemy had placed their principal magazine.

Whilst the fighting was still going on in the streets, a terrible explosion occurred. Over eighty barrels of powder had blown up in the church. Pieces of the masonry and roof were hurled all over the town, and almost all the prisoners in the building and all the guard were killed, besides a few others in the streets. A great deal of plunder, including all Lord Hopton's personal baggage and 500*l*. in specie, was taken in the town, whilst the number of arms picked up showed that the rout of the foot had been complete.

Hopton's horse fled across the Tamar, his foot for the most part dispersed, only 400 men remaining the next day with the colours. Desertion was now rife amongst them, parties both of horse and foot coming in daily and surrendering to Fairfax.

Letters had been intercepted at Dartmouth from the queen and others in France, announcing that assistance for the king might shortly be expected from that country. As the foreign troops would most likely be landed in Cornwall, and in order to take advantage of the demoralization of Hopton's soldiers, Fairfax, with the advice of his council, determined to prosecute the war vigorously in spite of the inclement weather.

Sending off a detachment to invest Barnstaple, he ordered Colonel Butler to force the passage of the Tamar at Stratton on the 24th February. This done, on the 25th he himself crossed to Launceston, and then secured all the passages of the river down to Plymouth. Having thus prevented any attempt of the Royalists to slip past him eastward, he next drove Hopton steadily down the ever-narrowing promontory, till he had him hemmed in near Penzance. This was effected with very little fighting, for though the Royalist horse was as numerous as the Parliamentary, the men had very little heart left in them, and their excesses had at last alienated the once so loyal Cornishmen.

At Padstow a vessel from Ireland was seized in which letters from Glamorgan and Digby were found announcing that 6000 Irish Catholics were now ready to cross to the king's assistance, and that 4000 more might be expected in May. Fairfax had these letters read to the inhabitants of several parishes on Bodmin Down, and such was the horror with which the Irish rebels were regarded by Englishmen that 1000 men at once volunteered for service with the Parliament.

Hopton had now no alternative but to surrender on the best terms he could obtain. Respect for his personal character induced Fairfax to give him more favourable conditions than would otherwise have been granted. Of all Charles' generals he only had displayed any talents for organisation. His own Cornish troops had been well disciplined and trained, and had always fought with great steadiness and often with brilliant success. Yet he had been ousted by princes and courtiers, and had never been granted an important command until the Royal cause was absolutely lost. He was now in the humiliating position of having to surrender to forces hardly more numerous than his own.

******

He can hardly be said to have been in supreme command at Cheriton, since his superior, Forth, was present, on whose advice the Royalists were restricted to the defensive.

******

After some negotiations, a treaty was concluded at Tresillian Bridge, and on Sunday, the 15th March, the disarmament of the Royalists began. It was completed by the 20th, the officers retaining their horses, swords, and pistols. On taking an oath not to serve again against the Parliament, both officers and men were permitted either to return to their homes, in which case they had safe-conducts granted them by the general, or they were permitted to take service beyond the seas, in which case they were allowed to remain in England a certain time before embarking. Many of them enlisted into the Parliament's forces for service in Ireland. Prince Charles had already escaped to the Scilly Isles.

This winter campaign in Devon and Cornwall was a high test of the efficiency of the New Model Army. On leaving the cantonments east of Exeter the men's clothing was in rags, and only a timely supply of boots and stockings, which reached them at Crediton, enabled them to continue the march. The roads across the bleak uplands and down the steep combes were often well-nigh impassable, and provisions must very frequently have been scarce. Yet the men neither straggled nor loosened their discipline. The sound strategy of merely watching the enemy's fortresses whilst vigorously attacking his army in the field, was still adhered to.

The storming of Dartmouth seems an exception, but Fairfax probably had good reason to anticipate that the defence would be slack. The engagement at Torrington was also remarkable. Hitherto the battles in this war were of the formal set type, both sides being carefully drawn up in order of battle before the fight commenced. Here a general action was brought on by the successive support of the advanced guard engaged with the enemy's outposts. Success in such an action requires highly disciplined troops, and officers trained to mutual support. Much more is this so, when, as in this case, the battle is fought by night. Had Fairfax delayed till the morning his enemy might have slipped away, but, relying on the efficiency of his troops, he had no hesitation in committing them to a difficult night engagement.

After the capitulation of Hopton's army Fairfax marched back to Exeter, where he arrived on the 31st March. The governor, Sir John Berkely, immediately opened negotiations for its surrender, and whilst these were proceeding Fairfax sent Ireton with several regiments of horse to surround Oxford, and cut off its supplies and communications with the outside. Exeter surrendered on the 9th April, the garrison receiving similar conditions to Hopton's men, except that those who still wished to serve the king were allowed to repair to Oxford. A special article in the treaty secured the Cathedral from defacement. Here also the Princess Henrietta fell into the Parliament's hands. Barnstaple and Dunster Castle capitulated about the same time to detachments sent against them, and on the 18th April Fairfax marched for Oxford.

Outside the sphere of operations of Fairfax's army, the tide of fortune was also running strong against the king. In February Chester, with its surrounding castles, Hawarden, Holt, and Ruthen, were forced to surrender, whilst in the western midlands Belvoir Castle and Ashby-de-la-Zouch met the same fate. The Royalists in South Wales had for a few days in February regained possession of Cardiff town; but Langhorne quickly recovered it, and relieved the castle, which had not surrendered. Sir J. Astley had succeeded in collecting some 2000 men about Worcester, and early in March the king called him up to Oxford. He marched on the 19th, but Brereton, who, after the surrender of Chester, had moved southwards, got intimation of his movement, and, assisted by Colonel Morgan from Gloucester, fell upon his forces just as they had dispersed to their quarters at Stow on the 22nd.

Astley and many officers and soldiers were taken prisoners, the stout old knight exclaiming as he gave up his sword, "Now you have done your work and may go play, unless you fall out among yourselves," (Whitelocke), a prophecy which was soon to be fulfilled. The king, who had marched to Chipping Norton to meet him, fell back to Oxford on learning of his defeat.

Determined not to be shut up in Oxford, Charles quitted it on the 27th April in disguise, accompanied only by Mr. Ashburnham, for whose servant he passed, and his chaplain, Dr. Hudson, who was intimately acquainted with the paths and by-ways in Buckinghamshire.

After some hesitation, he opened up communication with Montreil, the French agent with Leven's army before Newark, at whose quarters in Southam he arrived on the 4th May. The next day he gave himself up to the Scots, and was taken to David Leslie's quarters at Kelham.

Fairfax arrived at Garsington near Abingdon on the 1st May. The bends of the Isis and its confluence with the Cherwell below, and other streams above, Oxford, rendered a close investment very difficult. East, south, and west of the town the meadows could be flooded for some distance.

The rampart, at which the Royalists had been working since 1642, was strong and high, and of regular trace, curtain and bastion duly flanking one another. The loss of Woodstock, lately captured by Rainsborough, and of Abingdon, had made gaps in the circle of outlying forts, but the towns of Wallingford and Radcot and the fortified houses of Faringdon, Sherborne, and Borstal, and a few minor posts, remained to render close investment and siege difficult and costly. On the north side the conditions were somewhat more favourable, as the heights there offered good positions for camps and siege works, and flooding was impossible. The spirit and strength of the garrison, which was estimated at from 5000 to 7000 men, rendered an assault too hazardous, especially as it was only on one front that such an attempt could be made, and feigned attacks on the other side were impossible.

Fairfax determined to proceed by regular approaches from the north. Skippon, who, since Naseby, had been recovering from his wounds, but had now rejoined, was entrusted with the task of conducting the siege, for which his experience and professional training made him the fittest commander. The foot were cantonned on the north in villages and tents. Large redoubts were constructed on Headington Hill and elsewhere, and connected by lines of entrenchment. The Cherwell was bridged in two places, and the communications throughout the lines improved. The investment to the south and west was conducted principally by the horse. Separate detachments were detailed to besiege Wallingford, Faringdon, Borstal House, and the other outposts. On the 6th May the investment was completed and the works already begun. On this day also Banbury surrendered to Colonel Whalley. He had besieged it for eleven weeks, and had attacked it in the formal manner of sap and gallery. His detachment was now at Fairfax's disposal, who had then under his immediate command somewhat over 20,000 men. (At a general muster on the 6th June the numbers present were 19,300. Whitelocke). With these he not only undertook the siege of Oxford, but despatched parties of horse to cut off supplies, &c., from Worcester.

On the 11th May Fairfax sent summonses to Oxford and the surrounding garrisons. Newark had surrendered on the 8th May, by the king's order, and it was thought that the governor of Oxford would see the futility of further resistance. Many persons of quality had of late quitted the town, and given themselves up to the Parliamentary outposts. Negotiations were commenced, which at first offered little hope of a treaty, but as the hopelessness of the Royal cause became daily more apparent. Sir Thomas Glenham, the governor, at last, on the 20th June, signed the articles of surrender. The garrison received very similar terms to those granted to Hopton's men, and on the 24th June 3000 soldiers, with many gentlemen and their servants, marched out with the honours of war and then laid down their arms. They were allowed to retain all their private property, even fair spoils of war. Some 2000 or more local troops were disbanded in the town.

Three hundred pieces of ordnance were captured, but not so much ammunition or provision as had been expected. For a few days before the surrender the garrison had kept up a furious cannonade to get rid of the ammunition, whilst the authorities had sold the provisions to pay the men.

The more rabid Parliamentary partisans grumbled at the easy terms granted to the headquarters of malignancy, but the relations with the Scots had already become so strained that Parliament was anxious to have its army free to act against them if necessary. The early surrender of the town, therefore, was of more importance than the terms exacted.

The outlying posts surrendered at the same time as Oxford except Wallingford, which did not fall till the 22nd July, on which day

Worcester capitulated to Rainsborough. On the 19th August the old Marquess of Worcester surrendered Raglan Castle to Fairfax. Donnington, Portland, and St. Michael's Mount had surrendered during the spring. Corfe Castle had fallen by stratagem on the 28th February, Pendennis Castle in Cornwall, the fortress of Conway, Flint Castle, and other posts in North Wales submitted during August.

The first civil war was over.

Flight of the King

As a fighting machine the New Model Army had proved successful almost beyond the expectations of Cromwell and those associated with him in his efforts to re-organise the Parliamentary forces. The work for which it had been originally intended was now finished, the king's adherents everywhere crushed. The military forces in the pay of the Parliament were more than were now required for service both in England and Ireland, and the cost of their maintenance was very heavy. £60,000 a month was voted for this purpose, but even so the pay of the men fell into arrear. Taking into consideration the incidental expenses entailed by the war in England and Ireland, and the cost of the fleet, the military expenditure of the Parliament amounted probably to double that sum. It was therefore natural and right that the government should reduce its expenditure by disbanding the troops superfluous to its needs.

But so long as the Scotch Army lay on English soil, occupied English fortresses, and retained the king, Parliament was in no hurry to cut down the most efficient part of its forces, the army commanded by Fairfax. The local troops were first disbanded, and certain corps, such as Massey's horse, which had been originally raised for service in certain localities, but had afterwards been employed on general service. Massey's men were disbanded by Fairfax in October. They mustered some 2500 men, mostly professional soldiers, men who made campaigning their business of life. Sprigge says:

> Divers of the disbanded, with a solitary attempt at humour, came from very remote countries, and had Passes some for Egypt, others for Mesopotamia and Æthiopia.

Their discipline was that of professional soldiers, strict enough in their military duties, but lax in their relations with the populace. Frequent complaints had been made of their plundering proclivities. They were disbanded without trouble, each man receiving six weeks' pay in satisfaction of his arrears.

When, however, an agreement was come to with the Scots, England evacuated by them, and the king delivered to the Parliamentary Commissioners, the Parliament began to consider how it should further reduce its military forces and its expenditure. It was not intended to disband the army altogether, the new government was not firmly enough established for that. On the 19th February, 1647, the Commons voted that 5000 horse, 1000 dragoons, and sufficient foot for the garrisons of certain fortresses, should be permanently kept on foot in England. (Whitelocke). This was the first occasion on which an English Parliament had agreed to the maintenance of armed forces in peace, that is, of a standing army.

Other forces were required for Ireland, where the Parliament was determined that the rebels should be reduced, and 3000 horse, 1200 dragoons, and seven regiments of foot were to be set apart for this purpose. The rest of the army was to be disbanded. But in carrying out this very justifiable measure the Presbyterian majority in the House endeavoured to arrange that the physical forces of the country should be placed entirely in the hands of their own party, and this brought about the political struggle between the army and the Parliament which will now be very briefly touched on.

No stronger proof of how entirely the New Model Army was Cromwell's creation can be found than in its prevailing political tone. Officers and men nearly all belonged to the Independent party of which he was the leader. Fairfax, who formally nominated the officers, was no violent partisan of either party, for although he sided with the army in the forthcoming struggle, he afterwards acted with the Presbyterians. Had he selected his officers away from Cromwell's influence, more Presbyterians would probably have been found amongst them. This army was very different from what men had hitherto been accustomed to in the armies of mercenaries of the period.

It was an assemblage of citizens, each of whom, whilst submitting to the strictest military discipline whilst under arms, believed that he carried with him into his military life all his rights and responsibilities as a citizen. They were men of a far higher social standing than the ordinary soldier of the day, more resembling, indeed, in that respect, the men whom universal service brings into the ranks of continental armies today, (1899). Political feeling ran as high as religious, and every soldier in this army of saints, as the Cavaliers sneeringly called them, was a politician. Holies and the Presbyterians in the Commons, who formed a majority, were highly dissatisfied with the tone of the troops.

The Presbyterian sect was violently intolerant, and if once the army was in the hands of its leaders, they would use their power to suppress the other sects and enforce uniformity throughout the kingdom. Not understanding the men with whom they had to deal, they thought they could take advantage of the changes in the army, necessary on reduction, to substitute Presbyterian officers for Independents in the regiments which were to be retained.

But the Independents saw through the device, and the soldiers determined to resist. It does not appear that the alarm was sounded by the superior officers; its first notes seem to have emanated from the ranks and the regimental officers. Cromwell was certainly a thoroughgoing Independent, but his reverence for the authority of Parliament was very great, and up to the end of March he seems to have attended the House regularly and to have taken no part in the agitation amongst the soldiers, though he certainly sympathized with their views, as is evidenced by his letters to Fairfax. (Carlyle vol. i.)

The soldiers had many legitimate grievances, and of these they made use to resist disbandment on the terms proposed by Parliament. The latter proposed to give them six weeks' pay on disbandment as satisfaction for their arrears; the soldiers who had served throughout the war in the horse claimed forty-three, and in the foot eighteen weeks' pay. Several cases had lately occurred in which soldiers had been indicted and imprisoned by the civil courts for acts contrary to civil law, but done by them in the execution of their duty as soldiers. They therefore demanded that an act of indemnity for acts of war should be passed before they were disbanded.

They also desired that adequate provision should be made for the maintenance of soldiers maimed during the war and for the widows of those killed; also, that men who had voluntarily enlisted for service against the king in England should not be compelled to serve in Ireland against their will. A petition to be presented to Parliament through Fairfax, embodying these desires, was started, and extensively signed by the men and regimental officers. Parliament, on hearing of this, endeavoured to treat the army with a high hand. The petition, although still unpresented, was treated as an act of mutiny. Officers were called to the Bar of the House for having countenanced it, and the Presbyterian majority succeeded in passing a declaration that whoever signed or promoted the petition was "an enemy to the state and a disturber of the public peace."

This most impolitic measure destroyed any chance the Presbyterians might have had of obtaining their aims, had they proceeded with tact and moderation. The soldiers insisted on the redress of their grievances, insisted yet more vehemently on their right as citizens to petition Parliament. The Presbyterians, who had no physical force equal to opposing that of the army, were forced to grant concessions. They did so with bad grace, and in bad faith. Commission after commission was sent down to Saffron Walden, where the army now lay, to conciliate the men, induce them to disband, and to persuade the regiments for Ireland to embark.

The men refused to do either. Cromwell, Skippon, and other superior officers were appointed members of these commissions, and were honestly anxious to find some means of putting a satisfactory end to the quarrel; but in vain. The army was thoroughly suspicious of the intentions of the Presbyterian party, and their list of grievances increased. To the council of officers which had at first represented the army at the conferences were now added agents or "agitators," men chosen from the ranks of each regiment to represent their comrades, and to give expression to the unanimity of all ranks in demanding redress of grievances.

The Presbyterians endeavoured to bribe officers and men to desert their comrades by prospects of better pay, but without success. They then intrigued with the Scots to remove Charles from Holmby House, where he now resided, into Scotland, raise an army there in the king's name, invade England, and crush the New Model army. This came to Cromwell's ears and confirmed him in the suspicions he had gradually come to entertain of the ultimate designs of Holies' party in Parliament.

One evening at the end of May a number of leading Independents assembled at his house to consider what should be done. They determined to relieve Charles' escort at Holmby, as Colonel Graves, its commander, was a Presbyterian, and to substitute men on whom they could thoroughly rely. Fairfax could not be asked to intervene, as there were no proofs of the design for removing the king which could be published. It was therefore determined that Cornet Joyce, one of the most violent of the "agitators," should be entrusted with the task. At the head of 500 chosen troopers he was first to secure the magazines at Oxford, and then to relieve Colonel Graves's regiment, as escort to the king, and hold him safe at Holmby.

Joyce exceeded his orders. He not only secured the person of the king on the 2nd June, but insisted on his removing to some spot nearer the army. When asked by Charles for his commission for so acting, he merely pointed to the lines of grim, earnest-looking troopers drawn up in the court. The king said with a smile:

> It is a fair commission, and as well written as any I have seen in my life.—Rushworth, vol. vii.

Secretly rejoicing in the dissensions, he perceived among his enemies, he was by no means loath to accompany Joyce, and when taken over by Whalley, at Fairfax's direction, a day or two later, he refused to return to Holmby. Hereafter, he was kept in touch of the army until his escape from Hampton Court.

Then followed, on the 10th June, the famous rendezvous on Triploe Heath, where Fairfax, accompanied by the Parliamentary Commissioners, rode up to every regiment, and explained to the men the latest concessions of Parliament. At each they were greeted with cries of Justice! Justice! The patience of the troops was exhausted, and the next day they commenced to advance on London. Not only the Parliament, but the City, which was for the most part Presbyterian, was greatly alarmed. The militia, the governing committee of which had already been purged of all Independents, was called out, and an attempt was made to enlist soldiers.

The superior officers now openly associated themselves with the men in their demands.

A letter, written at this time to the Lord Mayor and Aldermen of London, is signed by Fairfax, Cromwell, Lieut.-General Hammond, and ten colonels. Carlyle considers it was drawn up by Cromwell, who had been with the army since the 3rd June. In this the officers declare that their sole demands are:

> Satisfaction to our undoubted claims as soldiers, and reparation upon those who have to the utmost improved all opportunities and advantages . . . for the destruction of this army with a perpetual blot of ignominy upon it.

They warn the lord mayor that, although the army has no intention of plundering or injuring the city, they will not be responsible for the results should armed resistance be attempted. After this all the protestations, vindications, &c., of the army were issued in Fairfax's name.

On the 11th June the army reached St. Alban's, and the panic in the City was great. Shops were closed, and the militia under arms. But the advance was not resumed on the 12th, and the panic subsided. On the 15th the Houses received the reply of the army to their latest proposals, and a demand that eleven of the members who had shown themselves most hostile should be suspended, and impeached on charges that would be submitted by Fairfax. Holies, Sir W. Waller, and Massey were among those named.

The Houses hesitated; but on the 23rd June Fairfax's Council of War drew up a Remonstrance, in which their demands were categorically displayed. It ended by declaring that if satisfactory replies were not forthcoming by the night of the 1st July the army would proceed by "such extraordinary courses" as should be thought fit to enforce the demands. On the 25th June the troops resumed their advance, and on the 26th reached Uxbridge. The House thereupon gave the eleven members leave to absent themselves for a time, and during the next few days passed votes complying with the soldiers' demands.

Fairfax then withdrew his headquarters to Reading, and on the 24th to Bedford. But at this juncture, when opposition to the army had ceased in Parliament, it sprang up in a fresh quarter. The citizens of London were mostly Presbyterians, the lord mayor and the Common Council almost entirely so. Parliament, at the desire of the army, had reinstated the Independent members of the Committee for the militia of London who had previously been removed. This interference with the management of their local forces seems to have particularly irritated the citizens. An agitation was started against the reinstatement of the Independents, against the expulsion of the eleven members of Parliament, and against the taxes necessitated by the expense of the army.

Parliament at first refused to listen, but the town was full of reformadoes, as discharged soldiers were called, and adventurers. A dangerous mob assembled, and on the 26th July forced its way into the Commons during the sitting, and compelled the members present to pass votes at its dictation.

On receiving this news Fairfax immediately marched for London. The City authorities called out the militia, gave the command to Massey, and commissioned him, Waller, and Poyntz to enlist soldiers, The latter had commanded the Yorkshire horse with success in the war against the king, but when he attempted to carry out the orders of Parliament to disband the troopers they had made him a prisoner, marched him to Reading, and thrown in their lot with the New Model. Fairfax had then released him, and he had repaired to London.

When the Houses assembled on the 30th July it was found that the

Speakers, the Sergeant at Arms, with the Mace, and many members were absent. Those present reinstated the eleven expelled members, and elected fresh Speakers. Meanwhile Fairfax was rapidly approaching, and on the 3rd August reviewed his troops, some 20,000 men, on Hounslow Heath, attended by the Earls of Manchester and Warwick, a dozen peers, the Speaker of the Commons, and the members who had fled from London. The men received them with loud cheers, shouting, "Lords and Commons and a Free Parliament." That evening Rainsborough, with two regiments of horse and two of foot, occupied Southwark, and seized the gate on London Bridge.

The City now lost heart. On the 4th August Fairfax demanded the surrender of all the forts on the western front, which was at once complied with. On the 6th he entered London by Hyde Park, at the head of a regiment of foot, and three of horse, and accompanied by all the members of Parliament who had taken refuge with him. The Lord Mayor and Aldermen met him at Hyde Park Corner, with a complimentary address, and he then proceeded by Charing Cross to Westminster, where the House was restored to the condition it was in before invaded by the mob on the 26th July. This time most of the eleven members retired to the Continent. Massey and Poyntz also withdrew. On the 7th August the whole army marched in triumph through the streets, and quartered near at hand in Kent and Surrey, the headquarters being at Croydon.

Fairfax secured the Tower by garrisoning it with 300 men of Pride's regiment, and appointing Colonel Tichbourne Lieutenant-Governor.

The Presbyterians were now reduced to passive opposition to the army, which expressed itself in neglecting to pay the assessments levied for the maintenance of the troops. The City of London, in particular, was backward in this respect. In vain Parliament again and again directed the payment of arrears. Neither would the merchants supply a loan of 50,000*l.* which the House voted should be raised. The auditors of the army were without money to pay the men, and recourse was necessarily had to free quarters.

The usual results followed, loud complaints on the part of the inhabitants, and a gradual relaxing of discipline. Fairfax had to institute regimental courts-martial, the first ever convened in the English Army, to settle on the spot disputes between soldiers and civilians. The headquarters were removed to Putney, but it was considered dangerous to remove the troops too far from London, and provisions began to get scarce and dear.

Cromwell, who had resumed his seat in the House after the entry of the troops into London, represented the army in Parliament, and pressed forward the necessary votes of money. But on the troops he urged moderation. Fairfax and the leading officers behaved with exemplary patience. But the rank and file were getting out of hand. The frequent presence of the agitators at the Councils of War had accustomed them to argue with their superiors, and to consider their opinions as of equal weight. They held meetings by themselves, and no longer confined themselves to discussing their grievances, but put forward political demands, which had nothing to do with their wrongs as soldiers.

A sect of Socialists, called the Levellers, was increasing rapidly, and its doctrines were spreading among the soldiers. John Lilburne, an ex-officer, and a disputatious, though honest demagogue, was the leader of the sect, and particularly busied himself in propagating its tenets in the army. Lilburne's regiment, the colonel of which was a cousin of his, was his chief field of labour. Cromwell had once befriended him, but, having a reverence for order, was strongly opposed to the Levellers. Lilburne soon became his bitter opponent.

The "agitators" became more and more permeated with the Levellers' doctrines, and on the 17th October some of them presented to Fairfax a political tract, called *The Case of the Army*, which, they declared in a covering letter, explained how the army had declined from "its first principles of safety, what mischiefs are threatened thereby, and what remedies are suitable." They concluded:

> For Sir should you ... command our silence and forbearance, yet could not ... you discharge us of our duties to God or our own natures.—Rushworth vol. ii.

Fairfax submitted this letter to a Committee of officers for consideration, but they hesitated what to advise. On the 1st November, the agitators presented him with another paper called *The Agreement of the People*, setting forth their political demands, which they said "we declare to be our native rights, and therefore are agreed and resolved to maintain them with our utmost Possibilities against all opposition whatsoever."

Fairfax could not submit to be dictated to in this manner. On the 9th November he dissolved the Council of War, sent both officers and agitators back to their regiments, and forbade the meetings of the latter altogether. At the same time, he ordered the brigades, into which the army was now permanently divided, (mixed brigades containing both horse and foot), to rendezvous on certain dates at certain places, where he would explain to the men what steps the superior officers were taking to obtain redress for their grievances.

The first brigade consisted of Fairfax's, Rich's, and Twistleton's regiments of horse, and of Fairfax's, Pride's, and Hammond's regiments of foot, and were quartered in Hertfordshire. Their rendezvous was fixed for the 15th November, on Corkbush Field, between Hertford and Ware. But in addition to these regiments, two others, Lilburne's and Harrison's, appeared on the parade without orders. These two regiments were those most deeply tainted with the Levelling principles, and the former had expelled most of its officers and was commanded by a Captain Bray. In their hats the men of these two corps placed copies of the *Agreement of the People*, on the outside of which was written "England's Freedom—Soldiers' Rights."

Fairfax, accompanied by Cromwell and the other superior, officers, rode up to each regiment in turn. To each a Remonstrance was read, in which Fairfax expostulated with the men for their distrust of their officers, and declared his intention of supporting to the utmost the just demands of the army, as set forth in a letter he had lately written to Parliament. Always most popular with the men, the regiments of the first brigade received him with acclamations.

The soldiers expressed themselves satisfied with his efforts in their behalf, repeated their vows of obedience to his orders, and as many as could signed a paper to that effect. Harrison's regiment caught the enthusiasm of the others, tore the obnoxious papers from their hats, and joined in protestations of devotion to the general. Lilburne's regiment remained sullen. Colonel Rainsborough and one or two other superior officers, who were themselves disciples of John Lilburne, were encouraging them to hold out. They had presented Fairfax with a petition on his arrival on the ground, and refused to be satisfied with his Remonstrance.

The moment was critical, the regiment was in open mutiny, and had it been allowed to march off unscathed the authority of the officers was gone. Cromwell saw the danger, and, riding up to the regiment, ordered the men to tear the papers out of their hats. They refused. Without a moment's hesitation he then ordered Captain Bray and thirteen others, who appeared ringleaders, to step forward. They obeyed and were at once placed under the custody of the provost marshal, the regiment, overawed probably by the attitude of the others, making no resistance. Three men were selected out of these fourteen and then and there tried by a Council of War for mutiny. They were found guilty, and one of them selected by lot was shot at the head of the regiment. The rest of the fourteen were removed under custody. The regiment then gave no further trouble.

Colonel Rainsborough, Colonel Ewer, and Major Scott were also put under arrest, but, on expressing contrition for their share in the proceedings, were pardoned, as was eventually Captain Bray, after his case had occupied a Council of War for some time. The rest of the fourteen were drummed out of the army.

The other brigades gave no trouble at their rendezvous. Just previously to the first on Corkbush Field, the king had escaped from Hampton Court on the 12th November. His flight assisted the officers in regaining the confidence of their men, for amongst the ranks there was a widespread belief that the superior officers were intriguing with him to reinstate him on the throne on terms which would be exceedingly beneficial to themselves, but would leave the soldiers in the lurch. When first taken over by the army he had been very leniently treated. He had been allowed great liberty, all his family and friends were allowed to visit him, and he was always treated with great deference. Fairfax, Cromwell, and other superior officers often had interviews with him, and probably they, and most other people, anticipated that he would be eventually reinstated in some form or another.

Afterwards they found out that he was not to be trusted, and that, whilst giving them fair words, he was intriguing with the Presbyterians, the Scots, the French Government, and others. He was then treated with less ceremony, and either for this reason, or because they feared his life was in danger, restrictions were placed on his liberty and visitors. A rumour got abroad that the Levellers intended an attempt on his life, and about the 9th November Cromwell wrote to Whalley, who commanded his escort:

> There are rumours abroad of some intended attempt on His Majesty's person. Therefore, I pray you have a care of your guards. If any such thing should be done, it would be accounted a most horrid act.

Whalley showed this letter to Charles to explain the increased vigilance of the guards, and he, either really alarmed, or glad of this excuse, easily contrived his escape on the night of the 12th. After a few days, he gave himself up to Lieut.-Colonel Hammond, governor of the Isle of Wight, who held him in custody at Carisbrook Castle, where he was out of danger, and removed from temptation to intrigue.

By his presence of mind and firmness Cromwell had quelled a dangerous mutiny. With the Puritans the finger of God was to be seen in all the events of life. Cromwell and his earnest-minded officers held solemn fasts and prayer-meetings, where, with great searchings of heart, the cause of His anger with them, as displayed in their late dissensions with their men, was sought out. They found it, as they believed, in their previous intercourse with the arch-malignant—Charles Stuart. Henceforth they would have none of him. With these men religion guided every action of their lives. What they believed they acted on. Faith—stern and fanatical, but real and inspiring—drove them to resist tyranny, drove them with fierce enthusiasm against the ranks of their foes. In battle such men are irresistible.

Fairfax was convinced by the attitude of the troops that it was necessary to obtain money, not only for their current pay, but to disband those now superfluous to the establishment. For without money to pay the men's arrears they could not be disbanded. He therefore on the 18th November ordered Hewson's regiment to march into London and put pressure on the inhabitants to pay the arrears of the assessment. At the request of the House Cromwell intervened, and the movement was counter-ordered. But the officers continued to put pressure on the House, and, during December, Parliament—by sending commissioners into all the counties for the purpose—succeeded in raising the necessary money.

During the next two months the disbandment of the superfluous troops went on. The terms were arranged between the superior officers and a committee of the Commons which sat at Windsor. They were drawn up with great skill. The younger soldiers, who, having fewer arrears, required less money on disbandment, were selected for discharge. Those entitled to it were paid two months' pay in cash and were given reliable debentures for the remainder of their arrears. At the same time the army was re-organised and placed on a still more modern footing. The Independents were but a minority of the whole nation, and were surrounded by hostile factions.

The struggle might at any moment break out afresh, and it was necessary to retain the tried and very efficient officers who were the backbone of the Independent strength. In order to retain them whilst reducing the number of men, the number of regular regiments of horse was increased from twelve to fourteen, whilst the strength of each troop was reduced from one hundred to eighty. The regular regiments of foot were increased from fifteen to seventeen, the strength of each being reduced from 1200 to 800. (Thirty independent companies were also organised apparently for the garrisons of fortresses). Thus, the modern system was introduced of many weak cadres in peace, which could be readily increased in war. The local troops were altogether disbanded.

It was not long before the wisdom of organising the army so that it could be rapidly increased in strength became very apparent.

Cromwell in South Wales

The Independents, who now ruled England by virtue of their command of the army, were not popular. Both Royalists and Presbyterians detested them, and they also alienated the common people, who cared little for politics, by the strict laws they passed against all forms of sport or amusement on Sunday, hitherto the national holiday. Riots occurred at Christmas in Maidstone and London; and Parliament, no longer trusting the City militia, directed Fairfax to send a couple of regiments to Westminster. Baxter's regiment of foot was then quartered in Whitehall, and Rich's of horse in the Royal Mews.

On the 9th April, a more serious riot broke out in the City, the mob seizing the gates and remaining in possession of the streets until dispersed by the troops the next day. The disbanding of the local troops also was not accomplished without trouble. Captain Wogan's troop of Worcestershire horse, with himself at their head, marched off bodily into Scotland, where they were joined by many Cavaliers and were received into pay by the Scots. Pembroke Castle was garrisoned by local forces under Colonel Poyer, a drunken and eccentric Presbyterian.

Colonel Flemming was sent by Fairfax about the end of February to disband the garrison, and to substitute a few regular troops which he brought with him. But Poyer shut the gates and refused him admittance. Langhorne's troops also refused to disband and joined Poyer. Fairfax ordered Flemming to use force if Poyer continued obdurate. He therefore landed two heavy cannon from a ship in the harbour, and prepared to batter down the gates of the castle. But the garrison, now much stronger than he, sallied out on the 23rd March, routed him, and captured the guns. In a few weeks all South Wales was in a blaze.

Colonel Horton, who had been sent down to assist in keeping order, found great difficulty in advancing. Whichever way he went the people rose behind him, Royalist gentry and Presbyterian townsmen making common cause. His horses could not be shod, as the smiths left their forges and cut their bellows. Flemming, in another encounter with the insurgents, was defeated, himself and many of his men killed. Chepstow, Tenby, Carmarthen, and other castles were seized by the Royalists in April, and things looked so ominous that Fairfax on the 1st May arranged that Cromwell should assume command in South Wales.

Elsewhere the aspect of affairs was very threatening. A riot occurred in Norwich, the magazine was blown up, and many people killed before the troops dispersed the rioters. Another outbreak happened in Cornwall. Behind all these disturbances in England lay the threat of a Scotch invasion. The bigoted Presbyterians of that country viewed the proceedings of the English "Army of Sectaries" with holy horror. The Duke of Hamilton, who had been released before the end of the war in Cornwall, skilfully improved the occasion to urge the cause of the King and the invasion of England. During the summer of 1647 the Scotch Parliament voted a "declaration" which asserted the determination of the Scotch nation to assist the Presbyterians in England against the army, by force of arms if necessary. It based the right to interfere on the Covenant which had been sworn to by both nations.

Argyle and most of the kirk ministers were opposed to war, but were outvoted by Hamilton's faction, which grew rapidly stronger. By the spring of 1648 an army of 40,000 men had been voted, nominally for the safety of the kingdom, but in reality, as was well understood by all parties, to be employed against the English Army.

The Cavaliers of the North of England seized this favourable opportunity for an outbreak. On the 2nd May news reached London that Sir Marmaduke Langdale had surprised Berwick, and a few days later it was learnt that Carlisle had fallen in the same way to Sir Philip Musgrave. The Cavaliers now held the keys of England and could open the gates and let in their Scotch allies. Parliament had very few forces in the North to oppose them. Lambert, who had succeeded Poyntz at York, had at his disposal the Northern horse, now part of the regular forces, and a few garrisons. He occupied Appleby and strengthened the garrison of Newcastle, but the Cavaliers flocked to Berwick and Carlisle, and Langdale drove Lambert's outposts back to the northern borders of Lancashire.

On the 3rd May a letter from the Lord Chancellor of Scotland was read in the House, which demanded the reinstatement of the king, the disbandment of the army, the enforcement of the Covenant, the establishment of the Presbyterian Church, and the suppression of all other sects. In reply, the English Parliament demanded compensation for Berwick and Carlisle, captured by malignants who had harboured in Scotland. There could be no longer any doubt as to a rupture between the two nations, and Fairfax was ordered to march north with all the forces he could raise. He fixed the 15th May as the day of departure.

Cromwell left for South Wales on the 3rd May, taking with him two regiments of horse and three of foot as reinforcements. On the 11th, the welcome news reached London that Horton, with some 2000 or 3000 men, had defeated 8000 Welsh insurgents at St. Pagan's, near Cardiff. Some 3000 men were taken, but Langhorne, who commanded them, escaped, though wounded, with Powell and others to Pembroke. On the same day, Cromwell reached Chepstow, where he left Colonel Ewer to get cannon up from Bristol and besiege the castle, whilst he himself pushed on for Cardiff. Thence he marched to Carmarthen, which was evacuated by the enemy, and about the 24th May, he reached Pembroke, having detached 1200 men under Colonel Read to besiege Tenby.

He immediately set about the siege of Pembroke, where the insurgents now occupied both town and castle. He did not at first anticipate being long delayed before it. But Poyer, though intemperate and eccentric, was a stout soldier, and the officers with him, who had nearly all deserted the Parliament, knew they were fighting with ropes round their necks. The place, too, was by nature and art very strong. Cromwell had no cannon, except one or two which he obtained from the *Lion*, a Parliamentary ship in the harbour, and a siege train was ordered up from Wallingford. The place was closely invested. On the 25th May, Chepstow Castle surrendered, and on the 31st, Tenby. The detachments left for their siege then rejoined Cromwell.

In the eastern counties and in the neighbourhood of London, the old strongholds of the Parliament, the feeling against the Independents ran very high. On the 3rd May tumults broke out at Colchester, and the Grand Jury of Essex presented a petition to Parliament praying for the restitution of the king and the disbandment of the army. At Bury St. Edmunds a riot occurred about setting up a may-pole. On the 16th May a mob of several hundred persons from Surrey carried a petition through the City to Westminster and got into dispute with the guards. A soldier was killed and several hurt before the troops from Whitehall and the Mews dispersed the petitioners. The petition was to the same effect as that from Essex.

The Houses forbade Fairfax to withdraw the regiments from London for the north as he had intended. Then information arrived that all Mid and East Kent was in revolt, and that the fleet in the Downs was mutinous. On the 20th May, Fairfax, who had just started, was ordered to desist from his march northward and to crush the insurrection in Kent.

This rising was entirely popular in its origin. Its leaders were two unknown country gentlemen, Hale and l'Estrange, but several men of note soon joined them, and the command of the insurgents was given to the elder Goring, the Earl of Norwich. The discontent in the fleet appears first to have arisen from the appointment of Rainsborough as vice-admiral.

During the early part of the Civil War, the Earl of Warwick had commanded as admiral, and Captain Batten under him as vice-admiral. At the time of the self-denying ordinance, Warwick retired, and Batten seems to have exercised the chief command. But as a Presbyterian he was not trusted by the Independents, who, towards the end of 1647, superseded him by Rainsborough.

The latter had originally been a sailor, but throughout the war commanded a regiment of foot on land. The seamen resented his supersession of Batten, and his unpopularity was increased by an inquiry he instituted into the behaviour of the men on his flagship. The Kentish Royalists, seizing the opportunity of the fleet being in the Downs, stirred up the seamen to mutiny, and the crew of the flagship rose on the 28th May, and put Rainsborough and his officers ashore. The other ships mostly followed suit, only those officers who sided with the men being allowed to remain.

Immediately on hearing of this outbreak. Parliament sent Warwick to the fleet to appease the men and restore order. He arrived too late to effect anything in the Downs and repaired to Portsmouth, where he set about preparing the ships lying there for sea. Thus, at the end of May, the situation was as follows. Fairfax was near London with the larger part of the army about to operate against the Kentish insurgents. Two hundred and twenty miles away Cromwell was besieging Pembroke. In the extreme north of England, Lambert, with very scanty forces, comprising scarcely any foot outside the garrisons, was opposing very superior forces of Royalists. Behind these last lay the Scots, now arming rapidly, but as yet unready to move. The whole of

England was in a state of unrest, and small forces had to be retained in many places to overawe the inhabitants.

The prospect was a truly gloomy one for the Independents. Their forces were divided into three groups, as far apart from one another as they well could be, and opposed everywhere by superior forces. The Scotch invasion was only a question of time, and outbreaks threatened everywhere.

The worst of all was the loss of the command of the sea, for should the revolted ships place themselves at the disposal of Prince Charles, then in Holland, the Royalists would acquire all those advantages as to transport of troops and stores which had been enjoyed by the Parliament in the first Civil War, and above all, the trade of the country would be at their mercy. The best chance for the Independents lay in the fact that their army was excellently organised, its officers thoroughly efficient, and its leaders men of decision and energy. On the other hand, the forces of the enemy would be fresh levies, although many of the individual officers and men would be soldiers of experience.

Fairfax, though suffering from a severe attack of gout, acted with his usual energy. By the 29th May, he had assembled four regiments of horse and three and a half of foot on Blackheath, and by the 31st he had driven the insurgents behind the Medway, where they occupied a strong position on Barnham Down, holding Rochester on their right and Maidstone on their left, and securing the bridges from Aylesford to the sea. Swinging to his right, Fairfax crossed the Medway on the 1st June above the insurgents' position, and, falling on their left, drove them out of Maidstone after severe fighting.

Most of the insurgents then dispersed, but Norwich with a considerable party crossed the bridge at Rochester and marched boldly for London, hoping the capital would declare for the king. Fairfax sent Whalley with 500 horse in pursuit, whilst he himself turned to pacify East Kent and reduce the fortresses along the coast, which, with the exception of Dover, had fallen into the hands of the insurgents.

Norwich halted at Blackheath on 3rd June, finding that the London Presbyterians would not risk a rising, and on Whalley's scouts appearing his forces dispersed, himself and 500 Cavaliers escaping across the Thames at Greenwich to Bow.

By the 10th June, all Kent had been recovered by Fairfax, except the castles of Deal, Walmer, and Sandown, which were besieged by a detachment under Rich. The fleet was still in the Downs, and Rich sent a trumpeter on board the flagship with a message from Fairfax, offering the seamen pardon if they would submit. The answer was returned by the boatswain, all the commissioned officers having been put ashore.

He refused the proffered terms, and the next day the flagship with six others sailed for Helvoetsluys, where they were joined by Prince Charles. Other ships followed, and eventually the prince found himself at the head of nineteen sail. The last to join him was Batten in the *Constant Warwick*, then the smartest vessel in the fleet. Batten had long hesitated, but finally determined to join the Royalists.

Whalley crossed the Thames after Norwich, but was too weak to attack him as he was joined by many Royalists of note—Sir Charles Lucas, Lord Capel, and others. Finding that the Londoners were unlikely to assist him, Norwich fell back by Brentwood and Chelmsford to Colchester, followed by Whalley. On the 11th and 12th, Fairfax crossed at Gravesend, joined Whalley, who had got together some 2000 Essex militia at Coggeshall, attacked Norwich the next day before Colchester, and after severe fighting drove him into the town. He then set about the siege of the place, the investment being completed by the 24th June.

In many parts of England skirmishes occurred at this period. Pontefract Castle, an important post in South Yorkshire, was taken by a party of Royalists disguised as drovers.

In Wales, the siege of Pembroke was giving Cromwell much more trouble than he expected. The garrison consisted of 2000 foot and 300 horse, all resolute men. At first they were inclined to treat, but Cromwell would listen to no terms but absolute surrender. He had obtained two whole and two demi-culverins and two drakes from the *Lion*, but found these insufficient to form a breach. The siege train was on its way, but never arrived. (Gardiner says that the guns were eventually recovered and in position a day or two before the place surrendered).

It was shipped in the Bristol Channel to be brought round by sea, but the ship was detained by contrary winds, and finally wrecked at Berkley on the Gloucestershire shore.

As soon as he had got his guns mounted, Cromwell stormed a village close to the South Gate which had been used as an outpost by the defenders, but after that the siege made little progress. Here is his own account of the early part, given in a letter to Speaker Lenthall, (Carlyle vol. ii.):—

Leaguer before Pembroke,
14th June, 1648.

All you can expect from hence is a relation of the state of this garrison of Pembroke, which is briefly thus:

They begin to be in extreme want of provision, so as in all probability they cannot live a fortnight without being starved. But we hear that they mutinied about three days since; cried out, 'Shall we be ruined for two or three men's pleasure? Better it were we should throw them over the walls.' It's certainly reported to us that within four or six days they'll cut Foyer's throat, and come all away to us. Poyer told them, Saturday last, that if relief did not come by Monday night, they should no more believe him, nay, they should hang him.

We have not got our guns and ammunition from Wallingford as yet; but, however, we have scraped up a few which stand us in very good stead.

Last night we got two little guns planted, which in twenty-four hours will take away their mills; and then, as Foyer himself confesses, they are all undone. We made an attempt to storm him about ten days since; but our ladders were too short, and the breach so as men could not get over. We lost a few men, but am confident the enemy lost more. (The actual numbers slain were twenty-three on the Parliamentary side, and four on the Royalist. *Cromwelliana*).

Captain Flower, of Colonel Dean's Regiment, was wounded; and Major Grigg's lieutenant and ensign slain; Captain Burges lies wounded, and very sick. I question not but within a fortnight we shall have the town. Foyer hath engaged himself to the officers of the town not to keep the castle longer than the town can hold out.

Neither indeed can he, for we can take away his water in two days, by beating down a staircase, which goes into a cellar, where he hath a well. They allow the men half a pound of beef, and as much bread a day, but it is almost spent.

We much rejoice at what the Lord hath done for you in Kent. Upon our thanksgiving for that victory, which was both from Sea and Leaguer, Foyer told his men that it was the prince coming with relief. The other night they mutinied in the Town. Last night we fired divers houses, which runs up the Town still; it much frights them.

Confident, I am, we shall have it in Fourteen days by starving.
I am, Sir,
Your Servant,
Oliver Cromwell.

But Cromwell was too sanguine. Not only had he to contend with his enemies within the fortress, but the whole countryside was only waiting for a favourable opportunity of rising for the king. He greatly wished to send some horse to Lambert's assistance in the North, and had despatched a party when on the march towards Pembroke. More he could not yet spare. Provisions could only be obtained by foraging. The county militia was arming, and its officers were known to be disaffected. All through South Wales along his communications with England, the Royalists were plotting, or breaking out into rebellion. The surest way to crush the threatened insurrection was to seize the ringleaders before it had time to break out. The following letter, though long, is well worth perusal, as it shows how carefully Cromwell thought out the details of even the minor operations of war, and how clearly he expressed himself in giving orders. (Carlyle, vol. ii.) Note too the half-expressed apology for giving directions on details which might generally be left to the officer on the spot:—

> To Major Thomas Saunders at Brecknock. These (This letter was enclosed in the same packet with another. It was superscribed "For Yourself.")
>
> 17th June, 1648.
> Sir,
> I send you this enclosed by itself, because it's of greater moment. The other you may communicate to Mr. Rumsey as far as you think fit, and I have written. I would not have him or other honest men be discouraged that I think it not fit, at present, to enter into contests; it will be good to yield a little, for public advantage, and truly that is my end; wherein I desire you to satisfy them.
> I have sent, as my letter mentions, to have you removed out of Brecknockshire; indeed, into that part of Glamorganshire which lieth next Monmouthshire. For this end. We have plain discoveries that Sir Trevor Williams of Llangibby, about two miles from Usk, in the County of Monmouth, was very deep in the plot of betraying Chepstow Castle; so that we are out of doubt of his guiltiness thereof. I do hereby authorise you to

seize him; as also the High Sheriff of Monmouth, Mr. Morgan, who was in the same plot.

But because Sir Trevor Williams is the more dangerous man by far, I would have you seize him first, and the other will easily be had. To the end you may not be frustrated, and that you be not deceived, I think fit to give you some characters of the man, and some intimation how things stand. He is a man, as I am informed, full of craft and subtlety; very bold and resolute; hath a House at Llangibby well stored with arms, and very strong; his neighbours about him very malignant, and much for him,—who are apt to rescue him if apprehended, much more to discover anything which may prevent it. He is full of jealousy; partly out of guilt, but much more because he doubts some that were in the business have discovered him, which indeed they have, and also because he knows that his servant is brought hither, and a minister to be examined here, who are able to discover the whole plot.

If you should march directly into that country and near him, it's odds he either fortify his House, or give you the slip: so also, if you should go to his House, and not find him there: or if you attempt to take him, and miss to effect it; or if you make any known enquiry after him,—it will be discovered.

Wherefore as to the first, you have a fair pretence of going out of Brecknockshire to quarter about Newport and Caerleon, which is not above four or five miles from his House. You may send to Colonel Herbert, whose House lieth in Monmouthshire; who will certainly acquaint you where he is. You are also to send to Captain Nicholas, who is at Chepstow, to require him to assist you, if he (*i.e.* Williams), should get into his house and stand upon his guard. Samuel Jones, who is quartermaster to Colonel Herbert's troop, will be very assisting to you, if you send to him to meet you at your quarters; both by letting you know where he is, and also in all matters of intelligence. If there shall be need, Captain Burges's troop, now quartered in Glamorganshire, shall be directed to receive orders from you.

You perceive by all this that we are, it may be, a little too much solicitous in this business;—it's our fault; and indeed such a temper causeth us often to overact business. Wherefore, without more ado, we leave it to you; and you to the guidance of God herein; and rest

Yours,

Oliver Cromwell.

P.S.—If you seize him, bring,—and let him be brought with a strong guard,—to me. If Captain Nicholas should light on him at Chepstow, do you strengthen him with a strong guard to bring him. If you seize his person, disarm his House; but let not his arms be embezzled. If you need Captain Burges's troop, it quarters between Newport and Chepstow.

Both Sir Trevor Williams and Morgan had formerly served the Parliament, and it seems they were both taken. This letter shows how excellent Cromwell's information was. He must have done much of such work in South Wales.

Towards the end of the month a party of 500 militia were drawn together, under pretence of defending the coast against some Irish ships, but in reality to assist the garrison of Pembroke. Cromwell never waited for them to declare themselves openly, or do some hostile act, but promptly sent 250 horse, who attacked and dispersed them.

Thus the siege dragged on. The want of heavy guns and proper appliances rendered this the most tedious of all Cromwell's sieges. And never was a speedy finish more necessary, having in view the clouds gathering in the North.

> They (the garrison) have made some notable sallies upon Lieutenant-Colonel Readers quarter, to his loss. We are forced to keep divers posts, or else they would have relief, or their horse break away. Our foot about them are four and twenty hundred; we always necessitated to have some in garrisons. So wrote Cromwell to Fairfax on the 28th June. (Carlyle, vol. ii.)

On their part the besiegers gave the garrison more than one "alarm," but not, apparently, a second real attack. Cromwell adds:

> The country since we sat down before this place, have made two or three insurrections; and are ready to do it every day; so that, what with looking to them, and disposing our horse to that end, and to get us in provisions without which we should starve, this country being so miserably exhausted and so poor, and we no money to buy victuals,—indeed, whatever may be thought, it's a mercy we have been able to keep our men together in the midst of such necessity, the sustenance of the foot for the most part being but bread and water.

The siege guns had been "recovered from sinking," but were still detained by cross winds. Yet matters were beginning to look better, and the country to become quieter, since this letter opens by a report to Fairfax that "I have, some few days since, despatched horse and dragoons for the North." Four troops of horse and two of dragoons were sent. They marched by Chester, where Colonel Dukinfield had had some trouble lately, and where, if necessary, Captain Pennyfather's troop was to be retained.

At this juncture, when Fairfax and Cromwell were busy at the sieges of Pembroke and Colchester respectively, the Duke of Buckingham, the Earl of Holland, Colonel Dalbier, and one or two other Royalists and Presbyterians of influence, raised a party of horse and foot at Kingston, and marched towards London, hoping to be joined by the malcontents in the City, Surrey and Kent. On the 7th July they marched to Reigate, where Major Gibbon met them with two troops of horse, and drove them back on Kingston.

A sharp skirmish ensued near Nonsuch Park, in which the Royalists were routed, and pursued into Kingston, where their foot made good the entrance to the town. The next morning it was found that they had left, and fled into Hertfordshire. Fairfax despatched a party of horse under Colonel Scroop from before Colchester, who fell upon them early in the morning of the 10th, and killed, captured, or dispersed them all. Buckingham escaped, but Holland was taken, and Dalbier killed, and hacked to pieces by the soldiers, who considered him a deserter to the enemy.

At last, on the 11th July, the garrison of Pembroke was driven, by want of provisions, to surrender. Major-General Langhorne, Colonels Poyer and Matthews, Captains Bowen and David Poyer, old Parliamentary officers, submitted to the mercy of the Parliament. The rest had terms granted them. With the fall of the fortress, the Royalists in South Wales lost their opportunity, and the country quieted down. Cromwell lost no time in marching to Lambert's assistance. On the 14th he started, though his foot had no shoes, or stockings, and no money. He directed his march on Gloucester.

And haste was indeed necessary, for on the 8th July Hamilton, with 10,000 men, had crossed the border.

Cromwell Joins Lambert

The campaign of 1648 in the North is one of the most interesting of those in which Cromwell was engaged. To understand it properly the physical features of its theatre and their effect on roads and communications should be considered. The map shows how these ran in Cromwell's time.

The frontier between Scotland and England is divided topographically into three nearly equal parts. To the east, from Learmouth to the North Sea, it follows the course of the Tweed. In the centre, from Learmouth to the boundary between Northumberland and Cumberland, it follows the crest of the rugged Cheviot Hills, and on the west it dips down again into the valley of the Esk. A glance at the map shows that the Lothian Hills on the north of the Tweed, and the spurs of the Cheviots on the south, threw the only available road across the eastern section along the coast through Berwick, which thus dominated this section. (But did not entirely block it. Cromwell, towards the end of this campaign, crossed the Tweed further west and advanced into Scotland, whilst the Scots held Berwick).

Across the centre section there were no roads at all. In the western section, the western spurs of the Cheviots and the Pennine Range pushed the principal road across the frontier down into the valleys of the Esk, Lewin, and Eden, which last river it crossed at Carlisle. At the point where the frontiers of Scotland, Northumberland, and Cumberland meet, the Cheviot Hills bend sharp to the south to form the Pennine Range, along the crest of which runs the boundary between Northumberland and Durham on the east, and Cumberland and Westmoreland on the west.

The Pennines are continued, under different names, by a succession of wild hills and moors, which very nearly follow the boundary between the counties of Yorkshire and Lancashire. These hills form the watershed between the rivers running east into the North Sea, and those running west into the Irish Sea, and they eventually merge into the mountainous district of the Peak. Throughout the entire length of one hundred and twenty miles they were, in Cromwell's days, crossed by only three principal roads, one following the line of the old Pict Wall from Carlisle to Newcastle, another from Lancaster, by Settle and Skipton, to York, and the third from Rochdale to Leeds. Other minor roads existed, the chief of which was that through Stainmore Dale, from Appleby to Bernard Castle.

When Langdale and Musgrave had secured Berwick and Carlisle, they had opened the gates to their Scotch allies on both roads, by which the latter could invade England. The sympathies of the inhabitants were more Royalist in Cumberland and Westmoreland than in

Northumberland, and Musgrave's influence was great in the former counties.

Langdale therefore made Carlisle his headquarters, and pushed forward along the road to the west of the Pennines. He had no intention of attacking Lambert until the Scots should arrive. His objects were to occupy territory, collect supplies, and enlist recruits. He, therefore, as has been seen, advanced as far as the northern boundary of Lancashire, whilst Lambert withdrew his posts on that side of the watershed into Northumberland, Even Appleby Castle appears to have been given up. On the other hand, Lambert strengthened the garrison of Newcastle, and fortified Raby and Walton Hall. He himself took post at Bernard Castle, covering the debouch of the Stainmore Pass.

The local forces were called out. Lancashire in particular proved loyal to the Parliament and assembled her militia in strength. Yorkshire, too, contributed a considerable body of horse. At the end of May Colonel R. Lilburne joined Lambert with a regiment of regular horse. Early in June Langdale advanced through the. Stainmore Dale. He was reported to be 7000 or 8000 strong, but as later he was credited with only some 4000, this was probably an exaggeration. Lambert quitted Bernard Castle, and offered Langdale battle on Caterly Moor, five miles off. But nothing came of it, and Langdale fell back again through the pass.

The Committee of Lancashire sent two regiments of horse and four of foot, under Colonel Ashton, to join Lambert, (Rushworth, vol. viii.; elsewhere reported to be only one regiment of horse and two of foot), and thus reinforced, he, in turn, crossed the watershed. He took Brougham Castle, Penrith, and Appleby. Langdale retired before him, but was overtaken, defeated with some loss, and driven back to Carlisle. Lambert himself was at Penrith on the 15th June. He followed Langdale up, and offered him battle two miles outside Carlisle. But it was not the latter's policy to fight now, as he expected the Scotch army would arrive shortly.

Lambert therefore occupied the bridges and passes south of the town, and sent Colonel R. Lilburne with three troops of horse into Northumberland. Langdale had shortly before sent Sir R. Tempest with a strong body of horse to relieve Colonel Grey, then blocked up in Berwick by Colonel Saunderson with a couple of troops. On Tempest's approach, Saunderson fell back, and Grey joined the former at Alnwick. Sir A. Hazlerigg, Governor of Newcastle, sent the Durham horse, under Colonel Wren, to join with those of Northumberland under Colonel Fenwick, and 100 infantry mounted as dragoons, to oppose the further advance of the Royalists.

Colonel Lilburne joined these, and together they made up some 900 mounted men. The Royalists were estimated at 1200, and on the night of the 30th June were quartered in villages along the Coquet River. Early in the morning of the 1st July Lilburne surprised them, sweeping down so rapidly from village to village, that the Royalists in one had not time to alarm those in the next. Grey, Tempest, 300 prisoners, and 600 horses were taken, and the rest dispersed. This victory cleared Northumberland of Royalists up to the gates of Berwick.

Elsewhere, throughout the northern and midland counties, the Parliament was raising troops wherever men and officers could be trusted—not in great numbers, except in Lancashire and Yorkshire, generally a troop here and another there, more, apparently, with a view of keeping order, than of opposing the Scots. The Royalists, firmly established at Pontefract, whither many of the old Newark Cavaliers had repaired, were plundering the country around, and had taken possession of the Isle of Axholm. Rossiter, with some 800 mounted men, mostly local troops from Yorkshire and Lincolnshire, had been detailed to keep them in check. On the 5th July he fell upon a party of them, estimated at 1000 men, as they were returning from a plundering expedition, totally routed them, and took 500 prisoners.

But the Scotch Army was now ready to advance. In spite of Argyle and the kirk ministers, the Presbyterian Royalists had gained their wish, and an army of some 20,000 men had been assembled in Southern Scotland. These were not yet all complete in equipment and organisation, nor was the train of artillery ready; but about one-half were ready to march. The Duke of Hamilton was General-in-Chief, the Earl Callender Lieut-General of the horse, General Middleton Major-General of the foot. (Middleton afterwards took a command with the horse, and Baillie became Major-General).

Neither of the Leslies would take a command in this campaign. Hamilton had served with high rank under Gustavus Adolphus, but he had really little military talent. Callender was an influential Scotch nobleman, which constituted his principal recommendation for his post. Middleton was an experienced soldier. Under him was General Baillie, who had commanded without success against Montrose, but was a good soldier as far as training and experience go.

Hamilton had the choice of invading England either by Berwick or Carlisle. The road through the former, east of the Pennine watershed, ran after the first two marches through open, fertile, and populous country, with several alternative branches leading south. The fortresses of Newcastle and York would embarrass the advance, but, on the other hand, Pontefract would strengthen the lines of communication. It was, moreover, the most direct road to London, and had been the one adopted by the Scotch armies in 1640 and 1644. To the west of the watershed, the road through Carlisle, Lancaster, and Preston was the only one running north and south practicable for a considerable army. In Westmoreland, it crossed a mountainous district by several steep passes, and as far as South Lancashire ran through a sparsely populated country.

Advancing along it Hamilton would have the mountains of Cumberland, or the sea, close on his right, and the Pennine Range on his left. It thus formed an almost continuous defile. The Pennine Hills, whilst protecting his flank, would screen the movements of the enemy in the Yorkshire valleys beyond. But Langdale had the greater part of his force on the Cumberland side, the people were supposed to be better inclined to the Royalists, and it was part of the scheme that some of the Scotch forces under Monro in Ulster should be brought over the Irish Sea to join the army of invasion in England. Hamilton, therefore, chose the road through Carlisle.

Accordingly, he assembled such of his troops as were ready to march at Annan, and on the 8th July, at four o'clock in the morning, he crossed the border at the head of 10,000 men. He took over the fortress of Carlisle from Sir Philip Musgrave, and placed a Scotch garrison in it, contrary to the wishes of the inhabitants. His army he quartered about Wigton, some ten miles to the south-west. He wrote to Lambert saying that he had entered England, because the English Parliament had given no satisfaction to the desires of the Scotch Parliament, that he could not avoid the northern parts of the kingdom, but wished no harm either to Lambert or the kingdom.

Lambert curtly replied that, as to Hamilton's dissatisfaction with the Parliament, that was nothing to him, but that as the duke had come:

> ...in a hostile way into England, he would oppose him to the utmost, and fight him and his army as traitors and enemies to the kingdom upon all opportunities.—Rushworth, vol. viii.

The Parliament also, on receiving news of the Scotch advance, declared their forces to be "enemies to the kingdom of England."

A great opportunity was now open to Hamilton. Lambert was too weak to oppose him directly. Fairfax lay before Colchester, Cromwell before Pembroke, both engaged in sieges with barely men enough for the purpose. Elsewhere there was no force of importance on which the Independent Parliament could rely. The only English fleet ready for the sea, except a squadron in Irish waters, lay in Helvoetsluys at Prince Charles' command. A few days would suffice for its re-victualling. Money had been always the great lack in the Royal camps, but money need no longer be wanting with the trade of England at the mercy of the fleet. Presbyterians and Royalists awaited throughout the country in breathless expectancy as to what would follow.

Had Hamilton advanced at once, sweeping Lambert out of his path, the sieges of Colchester and Pembroke must have been abandoned, in order that Fairfax and Cromwell might oppose him. Such a blow to the prestige of the army would of itself have brought recruits by the thousand to the Royalist standards. The opportunity was a fleeting one. Pembroke was on its last legs, Colchester could not resist for ever without relief. The Earl of Warwick was energetically fitting out a new fleet for the Parliament. Prompt action was, as usual, necessary to military success.

But Hamilton was not the man to avail himself of such a chance. He had delayed in Scotland, and he loitered again when he had crossed the border. There were, as is always the case, a thousand excuses for delay. Only half the Scotch army was up, the train was not ready, Monro had not left Ireland, where an English squadron, under Captain Clarke, was baffling his attempts to embark. The allied English and Scotch forces required organising. Langdale, the only soldier of talent amongst the commanders, continually urged an immediate advance. At last, the friction between him and the Scotch officers grew so great that it was arranged that the English and Scotch forces should march separately. The former, composed of local men, amongst whom abundance of guides could be found, were to take the van. The Scots would follow a day's march in rear.

It was not till the 15th July that Hamilton made any forward movement. Meanwhile Pembroke had surrendered, and Cromwell was on the march to oppose him, with but a small brigade of ragged, shoeless veterans, it is true, but bringing in himself that military insight and vigour of action which, at a crisis in war, makes the presence of the right man worth more than many battalions.

Hamilton had crossed the border with 3500 horse and 7000 foot.

Langdale was reported to have 3000 men properly armed and fit to join the field army. Lambert's forces were much inferior, though their exact numbers cannot be ascertained. He had recalled Lilburne, who with his own, the Durham and Northumberland horse, had been quartered about Hexham since their action on the Coquet. The detachment Cromwell had sent on from Pembroke must have also joined him by this time. He lay at Penrith when the allies advanced on the 15th July. When they had arrived within two miles of the town, he fell back to Appleby, where his foot passed the night and his horse in the villages round about.

The enemy followed to within seven miles of Appleby. The weather was very bad, and the next day, Sunday, nothing further occurred. That night Lambert's horse lay all night in the field expecting an attack, but as none came and the morning was very wet, they were dismissed early on Monday to their quarters, only the outposts remaining. Suddenly about nine o'clock, strong bodies of the enemy appeared advancing through the rain. The alarm was given, a charge by Harrison with the horse of the outposts checked the enemy, and the foot had time to occupy the entrances to the town. Here they maintained themselves until the horse had re-assembled. Lambert then withdrew his troops in good order through Stainmore Dale to Bowes, leaving a garrison in Appleby to hold the castle. (Lambert's report of the 19th July given in Rushworth, vol. viii.)

Hamilton advanced no further for the time. Langdale's troops besieged Appleby Castle, and placed a detachment at Brough, whilst the Scots were quartered back along the road as far as Carlisle, Lambert fixed his headquarters at Bernard Castle, and held Bowes, Richmond, and the villages commanding the Stainmore Pass. In these positions the opposing forces remained till the end of the month. Hamilton had no grasp of the strategical and political position. Neither evidently had Sir James Turner, the pedantic Dugald Dalgetty, who was his Adjutant-General. In his *Memoirs* he attributes the delay to the advance from Scotland having been unduly hurried by Langdale's impatience. The Scots, therefore, halted to await the reinforcements which they should have received before crossing the border. Meanwhile Cromwell was advancing and their best opportunity was slipping away.

Very different had been Cromwell's proceedings. Quitting Pembroke on the 14th July, only three days after the fall of the fortress, he arrived on the 26th at Gloucester. From here he wrote to the Committee at Derby House for shoes to be ready to meet his barefooted infantry on their march through Northamptonshire. His horse had been sent on, except one regiment, as quickly as possible, and on the 27th more than thirty troops joined Lambert at Bernard Castle. (So Lambert reported, but this would seem almost more than Cromwell had with him in Wales).

Cromwell himself was at Warwick with something under 3000 foot and one regiment of horse on the 30th, and reached Nottingham on the 3rd August. By this time his men had received their new shoes. He now wrote to Lambert directing him to forbear fighting until he came, and he sent some local forces from Leicester-, Derby-, and Nottinghamshires, to relieve Rossiter before Pontefract, and thus set free a body of good horse for the field. On the 8th August he reached Doncaster, where his men received their first pay for months, and where he rested till the 11th, awaiting a train of artillery from Hull. His infantry had marched over 250 miles in twenty-six days, including halts, through a mountainous country with bad roads for the first ten days, and barefooted most of the way. (The distance is 250 miles measuring in straight lines from Pembroke to Gloucester, thence to Warwick, thence to Nottingham and thence to Doncaster; the real distance marched must have been much more).

Truly the English soldier of those days had no reason to be ashamed of his marching powers.

Hamilton's expected reinforcements reached him about the end of July, and on the 29th Appleby Castle surrendered to Langdale. A few days before Sir Matthew Bointon, the governor of Scarborough Castle, had declared for the king. He had only some eighty soldiers as garrison, and his revolt from the Parliament did not affect the course of the war, except that it caused some trouble to retake the Castle. But it showed how disaffected were many of the officers trusted by Parliament, and what a large accession of strength a vigorous conduct of the campaign might have brought Hamilton. The same may be said of Colonel H. Lilburne, governor of Tynemouth, who, having sent all the men of the garrison on whom he could not depend out of the castle on some duty, shut the gates and declared for the king, on the 14th August. His fortress was stormed the next day by a party sent by Sir A. Hazlerigg from Newcastle.

But even after his reinforcements had come up, Hamilton advanced very slowly. By the 2nd August he had reached Kendal, his cavalry being pushed out under Callender to Dent and Sedbergh, evidently to watch Lambert. He, however, did not obtain much information about the latter's movements. At Kendal he stayed some days, and here Monro joined him, having succeeded in avoiding the Parliament's ships. He brought 1200 horse and 1500 foot, all veterans. (Turner, *Memoirs*).

Hamilton had now concentrated all the forces on which he could count for the campaign. The Scotch forces under his immediate command may have mustered 17,000 or 18,000 men, Langdale had at least 3000, and Monro 2700. He could therefore dispose of 22,000 or 24,000 men. (Many of the estimates put his numbers higher, some as high as 27,000). Against him Lambert and Cromwell combined could not bring half his numbers. And he did not even know that Cromwell had left South Wales. The country in which he lay was poor, and supplies were difficult to obtain.

Everything therefore pointed to a rapid advance. But Hamilton's character was too undecided to allow him to act with vigour. His subordinate commanders did not respect him, each wanted his own way. At his councils of war the members disputed, but nothing was decided. Partly to avoid disputes, and partly for ease of supply, it was decided that the three contingents should march separately, Langdale's leading, Hamilton's Scots forming the main body, and Monro's Scots, with Sir Philip Musgrave's Cumberland levies, the rear-guard. An interval of a day's march separated the contingents. Even the direction of the march was not settled. Langdale's forces in advance took the road by Settle and Skipton into Yorkshire. At the latter place was a strong castle, the governor of which Langdale believed he could win over. On the 8th August he arrived at Settle, his horse being in advance at Cargrave. But the governor of Skipton proved obdurate, and Langdale again halted, waiting for the Scots to close up.

Hamilton reached Hornby on the 9th August and called a council of war to decide whether to take the road into Yorkshire on which Langdale had advanced, or that through Preston and Warrington in Lancashire. Turner says:

> Callender was indifferent; Middleton was for Yorkshire; Bayly for Lancashire. When my opinion was asked, I was for Yorkshire; and for this reason only, that I understood Lancashire was a close country, full of ditches and hedges; which was a great advantage the English would have over our raw and undisciplined musketeers; the Parliament's army consisting of disciplined and well trained soldiers and excellent firemen; while, on the other hand, Yorkshire was a more open country and full of heaths,

where we might both make use of our horse, and come sooner to push of pike. My Lord Duke was for the Lancashire way; and it seems he had hopes that some forces would join with him in his march that way, I have indeed heard him say that he thought Manchester his own if he came near it. Whatever the matter was, I never saw him tenacious in anything during the time of his command but in that. We chose to go that way which led us to our ruin. (*Memoirs*, also better spelt and punctuated in Carlyle, vol. ii. The quotation in the text is from the latter).

But, even when the route was settled, more delays occurred, and many precious days wasted.

When Lambert learnt that Hamilton had passed Stainmore Dale on his march south, he also fell back southward to Ripon, pushing his patrols along the valleys of the Ure and the Wharf, thus watching the minor passes, and the road through Settle into Lancashire. The train having arrived from Hull, Cromwell left Doncaster on the 10th or 11th August, and reached Wetherby on the 12th. Here he was joined by Lambert, who had pushed Ashton's Lancashire levies up the valley of the Aire towards Langdale's position beyond Skipton. Cromwell had now at his disposal:

> .... about two thousand five hundred horse and dragoons of your old army; about four thousand foot of your old army; also about sixteen hundred Lancashire foot, and about five hundred Lancashire horse: in all about eight thousand six hundred.—Cromwell to the Speaker, dated 20th August, 1648. Carlyle, vol. ii.

Very possibly he had also a few other levies, which were not present at the ensuing battle, and were therefore not counted by him in his report of the fighting. Lambert certainly had horse from Yorkshire, Durham, and Northumberland, but these may have been engaged in watching the passes and on other duties. Or they may have belonged to those Northern horse who had deposed their commander, Poyntz, the year before, taken part with the army in its struggles with Parliament, and had afterwards been reckoned as a part of it. At any rate, Cromwell's forces numbered but a little more than one-third of Hamilton's.

Cromwell was not, however, the man to stay counting heads. He had unlimited confidence in his troops, and was not afraid of pitting them against the greatly superior numbers of the Royalists. Leaving his train, which he had taken much trouble to obtain from Hull, at Knaresborough, "because of the difficulty of marching therewith through Craven," he marched on the 13th to Otley. Langdale says that he learnt of the junction of Cromwell and Lambert this day, and immediately sent information to Hamilton. (Langdale's letter in Fairfax's *Correspondence*, vol. ii). Turner, however, declares that he never got any information as to Cromwell's arrival, or as to the movements of the Parliamentary forces. (*Memoirs*).

At any rate, Hamilton acted as if he had heard nothing, and made no preparations to meet the threatened attack. His main body moved slowly towards Preston, which was reached on the evening of the 15th by the foot, the horse quartering in widely-scattered villages for the sake of forage and provisions. Langdale drew in his advanced parties on the 13th, and then moved towards Preston, taking the road down the valley of the Ribble past Clitheroe. He met Callender and several of the Scotch cavalry officers by the way, but information had now come in that the Parliament's forces had divided, and part had marched by Colne on Manchester to defend that important town.

Fearing no attack, the Scots took no precautions to meet one. Langdale's force, from being the advanced guard, had now become, more by accident than design, a cover to Hamilton's exposed flank. On the 16th, most of the Scotch horse were across the Ribble, when Langdale, in the evening, received certain information that Cromwell with his whole force was within three miles of him. He was then at Longridge Chapel, still north of the Ribble and east of Preston. He hurried into the town to inform Hamilton, so he says, but Turner says, (*Memoirs*):

> Want of intelligence help'd to ruin us, for Sir Marmaduke was well near totally routed before we knew that it was Cromwell who attacked us.

At any rate, Hamilton did not believe that the Parliament's forces, on his left flank, could be sufficiently numerous to interfere with his march, and ordered the advance to be continued to Wigan on the morrow. Monro and Musgrave were still a day's march, or more, behind.

Meanwhile, Cromwell was pressing on. The odds in numbers against him were great, and though Hamilton's dispositions for the march were ill-arranged and carelessly carried out, his forces could still be concentrated in a single day in the neighbourhood of Preston or Clitheroe. On the 14th August, Cromwell reached Skipton, and on the 15th, Gisburn, where he was joined by Ashton's troops. He was now across the watershed and in the valley of the Ribble, down which Langdale had just marched on the way to Preston.

On the 16th, he advanced to Hodder Bridge, which spanned, either the Ribble at its junction with the Hodder, (as in the text of Cromwell's letter), or this latter stream a little higher up. (As Carlyle says it did in his note to that letter). Here a council of war was held to decide whether the advance should be continued across the bridge straight on Preston, or by Whalley across the Calder and south of the Ribble, so as to reach the line of Hamilton's advance about Wigan, "to interpose between the enemy and his further progress into Lancashire and so southward." (Carlyle, vol. ii., Cromwell's letter to Lenthall).

The former course would probably lead to an engagement with the enemy:

> Who we did believe would stand his ground, because we had information that the Irish forces under Monro, lately come out of Ireland, which consisted of 1200 horse and 1500 foot, were on their march towards Lancashire to join them. It was thought that to engage the enemy to fight was our business.

And therefore the advance was continued across the bridge to Stonyhurst Hall, where the army bivouacked. Very early next morning the advance was resumed, and soon the advanced guard, consisting of 200 horse and 400 foot, encountered Langdale's rear-guard. Major Pownel, who commanded the foot of the advanced guard, was forming up his men when, says Hodgson:

> The general comes to us, orders us to march. We not having half of our men come up, desired a little patience; he gives out the word, 'March!'—*Memoirs*. Hodgson was a captain of the Yorkshire foot, not of the New Model Army.

Cromwell was in no mood for delay. He knew Langdale was retiring, and was anxious to force him to an engagement. The latter says in his letter already quoted:

> I drew my forces together in a field, and so marched towards Preston betimes in the morning, where I found the duke and Lord Callender with most of the Scotch foot drawn up; their resolution was to march to Wigan, giving little credit to the intelligence that came the night before, but suffered their horse to continue in quarters ten or twelve miles off within half an hour

of our meeting, and by that time I was drawn into the closes near Preston, the enemy appeared with a small body of horse; the Scots continued their resolution for Wigan, for which end they drew their foot over the bridge.

Thus, was Langdale left with his 3000 foot and 600 horse to bear the full brunt of Cromwell's attack.

Immediately round the town there seems to have been an open piece of common, and beyond that enclosures and small fields surrounded by high strong fences, until the open moor in the direction of Longridge Chapel was reached. Langdale, weak in cavalry, occupied the enclosures with his foot, lining the hedges with his musketeers. A deep miry lane led up from the moor to his position, and another led by his right flank to the bridge over the Ribble. His dispositions were skilfully made, and deceived Cromwell, who imagined that he occupied a more extended position than he actually did.

Cromwell, having driven in Langdale's horse, formed up his army for attack. The country was ill-adapted for horse, the fighting fell therefore principally on the foot. Seven troops of horse and dragoons were behind at Clitheroe, and part of Ashton's foot were at Whalley watching the bridge over the Calder.

******

See Cromwell's letter dated 17th August, Carlyle, vol. ii.; Ashton with the greater part of his forces was with Cromwell; see letter dated 20th August.

******

The remainder of the troops were disposed as follows:—Colonel Bright's and Fairfax's regiments were sent against the enclosures to the left of the lane, with Ashton's Lancashire men in reserve, the regiments of Colonels Reade, Dean, and Pride advanced on the right. Harrison's and Cromwell's own regiments of horse were ordered to advance up the lane with one regiment in reserve. Thornhaugh's and Twistleton's supported the right, the remainder of the horse were on the left. The fighting on the left and centre was very severe. The right, being too prolonged, hardly came into action at all.

> Colonel Bright's, my Lord General's, Lieutenant-Colonel Readers, and Colonel Ashton's had the greatest work; they often coming to push of pike and to close firing, and always making the enemy to recoil.... The enemy making, though he was still worsted, very stiff and sturdy resistance. Colonel Dean's and

Colonel Pride's, outwinging the enemy, could not come to so much share of the action; the enemy shogging down towards the bridge, and keeping almost all in reserve, that so he might bring fresh hands often to the fight. Which, we not knowing, and lest we should be outwinged, placed those two regiments to enlarge our right wing; and this was the cause they had not at that time so great a share in that action.—Cromwell to Lenthall, dated 20th August.

Whilst Langdale was actually engaged, Baillie marched away towards Wigan, by Hamilton's orders, who imagined he had only Ashton to deal with. He crossed the bridge over the Darwen with all his foot except two brigades. The horse had marched the night before to Wigan.

Langdale, whilst making "very stiff and sturdy resistance," was entreating Hamilton for succour, he says:

> The duke being incredulous that it was the whole army (*i.e.* Parliament's Army), sent Sir Lewis Dives to me, to whom I answered it was impossible any forces which were inconsiderable would adventure to press upon so great an army as we had, therefore he might conclude that it was all the power they could make, with which they were resolved to put all to the hazard; when I desired I might be seconded and have more powder and ammunition. The Scots continued their march over the river, and did scour (*i.e.* evacuate) a lane near the bridge, whereby the Parliament's forces came upon my flank; neither did the forces that were left to my supply (Turner says he sent some ammunition and commanded men to Langdale's assistance *Memoirs*), come to my relief, but continued in the rear of mine.

For four hours did Langdale continue to valiantly make head against odds of two to one, and against the best soldiers led by the most successful general in Europe; but the end came at last. He continues:

"When most of the Scots were drawn over the bridge, the Parliament's forces pressed upon me in van and in flanks, and so drove me away into the town," hotly pursued by the Parliament's horse; for the moment the enclosures were clear, Harrison's and Cromwell's regiments charged down the lane and fell furiously on the retreating Royalists, utterly routing and scattering them. At the same time Fairfax's and Ashton's foot, pushing forward on their left, drove the Scotch foot, which had been posted near the bridge to secure the passage and support Langdale, across, or into, the river, seized the bridge and cut off the fugitives from the rest of the army.

Hamilton and Callender with a guard of horse were in the town as Cromwell's troopers came thundering down the streets at the heels of Langdale and the flying remnants of his forces. Personally brave to extreme, Hamilton himself led two or three charges, and for a moment checked the pursuit; but when the bridge was lost, there was nothing left but to fly. He and a few superior officers escaped to the Scotch army south of the Ribble by swimming across. The beaten horse fled north, closely pursued, to Monro, who was about a day's march in that direction; the remainder of Langdale's and the Scotch troops north of the Ribble were killed, taken, or dispersed.

The Parliament's foot, passing over Ribble Bridge, pressed forward against that over the Darwen, where Callender had posted 600 musketeers for its defence. (Turner says this was at Ribble Bridge, but from his description it would appear that he confused the bridges over the Ribble and Darwen). The ground favoured the attack, and the musketeers were soon driven across and back to the Scotch main army, which occupied some rising ground about a quarter of a mile beyond. Thus, as night fell, the Darwen separated the combatants, the bridge being in Cromwell's hands.

As the results of this day's fighting Cromwell had completely defeated part of the united Scotch and Royalist army. A thousand of them were slain, four thousand taken. Monro was completely separated from Hamilton, and the latter completely cut off from his base in Scotland. Cromwell's first care was to perfect his victory. He ordered the troops at Clitheroe to reinforce the detachment at Whalley, guard the bridge there, and prevent the Scots from regaining their communications by a circuit in that direction. A considerable party of horse had already gone north to follow up the fugitives, and to observe Monro. He himself remained to deal with Hamilton's main army, which was still formidable, in numbers at least.

Formidable as it might be in numbers, the Scotch army was no longer formidable as a force. Over the soldiers hung the dispiriting influence of defeat, though but few had as yet fired a shot or struck a blow. A great part of the train and ammunition had been lost, and they were cut off from their own country and source of supply. The weather had been very wet, and the soldiers lay in the soaked fields or toiled along the miry roads. They had lost confidence in their leaders;

THE BATTLE OF PRESTON.

indeed, these latter could have had but little confidence left in themselves. During the night a council of war was held. Middleton and the greater part of the horse had been recalled from Wigan, but had not yet appeared.

The question discussed was, whether to remain in their present position until his arrival, or march immediately towards Wigan to seek him. The former alternative would have involved a battle; the latter was decided on, chiefly at the instigation of Callender. The roads were so bad and the transport so deficient that it was decided to destroy what remained of the ammunition train. Preparations were therefore made to blow it up as soon as the army had departed. The troops moved off in the dead of night and had gone some distance by daylight, but the arrangements for blowing up the ammunition failed, and it all fell into Cromwell's hands.

Thus, began this retreat in gloom and depression. It was carried out in confusion, and ended in disaster. Sir James Turner, who commanded the foot of the rear-guard, has left a most graphic description of the chaos and misery which reigned throughout. The foot, retiring in the night by one road on Wigan, missed Middleton, who was advancing to their support by another, and who thus arrived at the Darwen to find them gone, and himself in the presence of Cromwell's victorious army. He immediately followed the foot, covering their retreat, hotly pressed by Cromwell's troopers.

Turner says:

> Next morning, we (the foot) appeared at Wigan Moor, half our numbers less than we were; most of the faint and weary soldiers having lagged behind, whom we never saw again.

By the night march the Scots had gained the start of Cromwell, who says:

> In the night the duke was drawing off his army towards Wigan; we were so wearied by the dispute that we did not so well attend the enemy's going off as might have been, by means of which the enemy was gotten at least three miles with his rear, before ours got to them. I ordered Colonel Thornhaugh to command two or three regiments of horse to follow the enemy, if it were possible to make him stand till we could bring up the army. The enemy marched away, 7000 or 8000 foot, and about 4000 horse; we followed him with about 3000 foot and 2500 horse and dragoons, and in this prosecution that worthy gentle-

man. Colonel Thornhaugh, pressing too boldly, was slain.

Middleton, so Turner says, managed the retreat well. On his joining the foot:

> We began to think of fighting in that Moor, (Wigan Moor), but found it impossible—in regard it was nothing large and was environed with enclosures which commanded it, and these we could not maintain long for want of that ammunition we had left behind us. And therefore, we marched forward with the intention to gain Warrington, ten miles from the Moor we were in; and there we conceived we might face about, having the command of a town, a river, and a bridge.

The road to Warrington lay through Wigan, where it crossed a small river by a bridge, which, with the streets, formed a narrow defile through which the army must pass. Turner thus describes what ensued.

> It was towards evening and in the latter end of August, when our horse began to march. Some regiments of them were left with the rear of the foot. Middleton stayed with these; my Lord Duke and Callender were before. As I marched with the last brigade of foot through the town of Wigan, I was alarmed; that our horse behind me were beaten, and running several ways, and that the enemy was in my rear. I faced about with that brigade; and in the marketplace serried the pikes together, shoulder to shoulder, to entertain any that might charge; and sent orders to the rest of the brigades before to continue their march and follow Lieutenant-General Baillie, who was before them. It was then night, but the moon shone bright.
> A regiment of horse of our own appeared first, riding very disorderly. I got them to stop till I commanded my pikes to open and give way for them to ride or run away, since they would not stay. But now my pikemen, being demented (as I think we were all), would not hear me; and two of them ran full tilt at me. One of their pikes, which was intended for my belly, I gripped with my left hand; the other ran me nearly two inches into the inner side of my right thigh; all of them crying of me and those horse, 'They are Cromwell's men.' This was an unseasonable wound, for it made me, after that night, unserviceable. This made me forget all rules of modesty, prudence, and discretion.

I rode to the horse and desired them to charge through these foot. They, fearing the hazard of the pikes, stood. I then made a cry come from behind them, that the enemy was upon them. This encouraged them' to charge my foot so fiercely that the pikemen threw down their pikes, and got into the houses. All the horse galloped away, and, as I was afterwards told, rode, not through, but over our whole foot, treading them down.

Turner having by these drastic measures cleared the streets, beat his drums, re-assembled his men, and followed Baillie to Warrington. Skirmishes occurred throughout the night, Cromwell's forces bivouacking in a field outside Wigan.

Further on, near Winwick, some three miles from Warrington, some of the Scotch foot, under "a little spark in a blue bonnet," made a last stand the next day. They blocked the roads with pikes and lined the hedges with musketeers. Cromwell says:

> We held them in some dispute till our army came up; they maintaining the pass with great resolution for many hours; ours and theirs coming to push of pike, and very close charges, which forced us to give ground; but our men, by the blessing of God, quickly recovered it, and charging very home upon them, beat them from their standing, where we killed about a thousand of them, (including the little spark in a blue bonnet), and took, as we believe, about two thousand prisoners.

Meanwhile Hamilton, Callender and Middleton, with what was left of the horse, all of whom were now in advance of the foot, arrived at Warrington. Here they determined to leave the foot and make the best of their way back to Scotland if possible. They accordingly moved off towards Malpas and Drayton, and Baillie, on arriving at Warrington with the shattered remnants of the foot, received an order from Hamilton to make the best terms he could with Cromwell. The Scots held the bridge, which was barricaded, and might have made another stand here, but there was no longer any hope of cutting their way back to Scotland, or evading Cromwell's close pursuit. Negotiations were therefore opened with him, he says:

> Considering the strength of the Pass, and that I could not go over the river (Mersey) within ten miles of Warrington with the army, I gave him these terms: that he should surrender himself and all his officers and soldiers prisoners of war, with all his

arms, ammunition, and horses to me; I giving quarter for life, and promising civil usage.

The fine army, at the head of which Hamilton commenced his march south from Kendal, was now irretrievably ruined. With only some 3000 dispirited and starving horsemen, he was still wandering aimlessly in the enemy's country, vainly endeavouring to find a way back. Cromwell halted at Warrington to reorganise the pursuit and secure his prisoners. His own horse were wearied out, so he wrote to the lieutenants of the counties to call out the local forces to cut off Hamilton.

> If I had a thousand horse that could but trot thirty miles, I should not doubt but to give a very good account of them; but truly we were so harassed and haggled out in this business, that we were not able to do more than walk an easy pace after them. I have sent post to my Lord Grey, to Sir Henry Cholmely, and Sir Edward Rhodes, to gather all together with, speed for their prosecution; as likewise to acquaint the Governor of Stafford therewith.

Again:

> For they are the miserablest party that ever was; I durst engage myself, with five hundred fresh horse and five hundred nimble foot, to destroy them all. (Letter to the Committee at York—Carlyle, vol. ii.)

Lambert was also sent in pursuit with such of the horse as could march.

Cromwell had 10,000 prisoners. His whole force did not amount to so many. Monro, with a still intact force, might make an attempt to rescue the 4000 prisoners or so who were still at Preston.

> Cromwell left Colonel Ashton's three regiments of foot, with seven troops of horse ... at Preston, and ordered Colonel Scroop, with five troops of horse and two troops of dragoons, with two regiments of foot ... to embody with them; and have ordered them to put their prisoners to the sword if the Scots shall presume to advance upon them, because they cannot bring them off with safety.

These Preston prisoners had not been given promise of quarter. From the prisoners themselves little was to be feared. Cromwell says:

The trouble and extreme charge of the country where they lie is more than the danger of their escape. I think they would not go home if they might, without a convoy, they are so fearful of the country, from whom they have deserved so ill. Ten men will keep a thousand from running away.

Cromwell, leaving the pursuit of Hamilton to Lambert and the local levies, turned north again to deal with Monro.

With forces hourly diminishing through straggling and desertion, Hamilton wandered on through Malpas, Drayton, and Stone to Uttoxeter, aiming apparently at Pontefract. As he was leaving Stone the enemy's troopers fell on his rear and captured Middleton. Langdale and Callender left him on the road, and on the 25th August he surrendered to Lambert at Uttoxeter. Of all the generals of his army, Callender only escaped; the rest, with nearly all the surviving troopers, were taken.

The fate of the rank and file prisoners was a hard one. Hitherto, during the civil war, the common soldiers who had been taken had been exchanged or eventually released. But the Parliament looked upon the Scotch invaders and their English allies as wilful disturbers of a peace arrived at after much shedding of blood, and determined to show them no mercy. They were sold to contractors who shipped them off to re-sell them to the Virginia planters, or to the Venetian Government for service in their galleys. The Duke of Hamilton was beheaded. Langdale escaped from Nottingham Castle. None of the others were sentenced to death.

No two opinions can exist as to the combined boldness and skill with which the English armies were handled in this campaign. Hamilton's choice of a line of invasion was from a military point of view a bad one, and was doubtless decided on for political reasons. The road through Cumberland, Westmoreland, and Lancashire practically formed a continuous defile where a few men could successfully oppose many. The remarkable point in the campaign is that Lambert elected to defend this defile, not by taking advantage of the many excellent defensive positions to directly oppose the enemy in front, but by withdrawing behind the mountains on the flank, thereby threatening his communications.

The success of this indirect defence was most marked. Hamilton, for instance, dared not advance beyond Appleby until he had captured the castle, because it commanded the debouch of the Stainmore Gap.

Had he passed on whilst the English still held this position, Lambert might at any moment have come down the gap and completely cut his communications. When he did advance, Langdale was pushed into the passes leading into Yorkshire, whilst the Scotch army defiled behind him, causing great delay. Thus, without risking a battle, indeed without fighting at all, Lambert greatly delayed Hamilton's movements and at the same time secured his junction with Cromwell or any reinforcements coming from the south.

The promptness with which Cromwell availed himself of the favourable position brought about by his lieutenant's clever manoeuvring is admirable. Though so inferior in numbers, when the opportunity offered of striking his adversary piecemeal and in the flank, he seized it without losing a moment. After leaving Doncaster on the 11th August, he never halted a day till the last remnant of his enemy's foot had surrendered at Warrington on the 19th. In those nine days he had marched 140 miles and fought two fierce engagements. His attack was not only on his enemy's flank, but also at the most opportune point. For at Preston the road Hamilton was following, always hemmed in between the hills and the sea, crossed two deep rivers, each spanned by a single bridge.

If driven south across the rivers here, the only other possible road by which he could rapidly regain his communications with Carlisle, that by Whalley, was already in Cromwell's hands. Thus defeat would mean disaster, unless he could at once retire northwards. Cromwell's actions all point to his being fully alive to the advantages of the position. Mark how he hurried on the attack on Langdale, lest the allies should perceive their error and get time to rectify it. He may not have known that the Scots were already partly across the river when he attacked—he could scarcely have foreseen that they would continue to cross after that attack had begun. But he disposed his men to take the best advantage of the situation as he knew it, and also of any chances of the nature that did occur. He not only attacked Langdale in flank and forced him to form his front parallel and close to his lines of communication, but he strengthened his own right, "lest"—as he says—"we should be outwinged," (whilst his own communications were well covered by his line of advance), and thus the enemy enabled to escape northwards.

It is also clear that he hoped to surprise Hamilton and beat him in detail. He appears not to have known that Monro had already joined the Scots at Kendal, and that the separation of the three contingents that made up Hamilton's army was voluntary. But he did know that Monro was not with Hamilton, and believed that the latter would await the former at Preston. If, then, he had moved south of the Ribble, and had thrown his army across the line of the Scots' advance, he would have helped to bring on the very concentration of the enemy's forces which he wished to prevent, and would have reduced himself to the defensive, as he could not have attempted to force the passage of that river in the presence of a greatly superior force, which already held the bridges over it and the Darwen. The campaign of Dunbar proves that Cromwell perfectly understood when a position was too strong to attack. Thus, the attack on Langdale near Preston was strategically sound, and so directed as to take the greatest advantage from the situation.

******

As a further proof that Cromwell's attack on Langdale's flank and the Scotch rear was made with a thorough appreciation of the strategical advantages that would accrue if successful, take his letter to Lenthall dated the 4th August, 1651. In this he explained to the House the object of the manoeuvre by which he dislodged Prince Charles from Stirling, and which induced the latter to march into England (see Chap. 17). To reassure the public as to the results of this march, he said, "When England was much more unsteady than now, and when a much more considerable army of theirs, unfoiled, invaded you, and we had but a weak force to make resistance at Preston—*upon deliberate advice*, we chose rather to put ourselves between their army and Scotland: and how God succeeded, that is not to be forgotten."—Carlyle, vol. iii.

******

Cromwell advances to Argyle's Assistance

The effect of this decisive victory was felt instantaneously throughout both kingdoms. Those, Royalists or Presbyterians, who, in England, had been awaiting the issue of events, abandoned their schemes for joining the invaders, and quietly submitted to the existing government.

After a gallant resistance and much negotiation, Colchester capitulated on the 28th August. The principal officers surrendered at the mercy of the Lord General, the officers under the rank of captain and the soldiers on quarter for their lives as prisoners of war. Two of the officers, Sir Charles Lucas, who was accused of breaking his parole, and Sir George Lisle, were shot as a warning to insurgents; Sir Bernard Gascoigne, also sentenced to death, was reprieved owing to his foreign origin. The rest were left by Fairfax to be disposed of by the Parliament.

The discouragement spread equally to the revolted crews of the fleet. Prince Charles had not made much of his opportunity as master, for the time, of the sea. He had sailed from Holland about the middle of July, and appeared off Yarmouth on the 25th July, with nineteen ships. Here he landed some men, apparently with a view of making a diversion in favour of Colchester. But a party of horse which happened to be in the neighbourhood at once compelled them to re-embark. He then put to sea again, and appeared on the 29th in the Downs, where some Parliamentary troopers in a rowboat, assisted by a couple of seamen, surprised one of his small ships.

Here he stopped a number of merchantmen, and could have increased his funds considerably had he treated them as prizes and sold them abroad. But he was most anxious to conciliate the London merchants, whom he believed were really favourably disposed to him. He therefore allowed them to ransom their ships at a low rate. Another futile attempt to relieve Deal followed, and soon after the news of Preston battle was received. This put an end to a scheme Charles had been meditating of joining the Scots. He lingered about the mouth of the Thames some little time more, sailed up to Yarmouth again at the end of August, attempted to land, found himself opposed, and returned to the Thames.

His absence had given an opportunity to Warwick, who had got some ships manned and ready for sea up the Thames, and others at Portsmouth, and wished to join the two squadrons. He dropped down to the Nore with the Thames ships, but the Portsmouth contingent had not arrived when Prince Charles reappeared in the Downs on the 29th August. The Royal fleet was superior, but neither wished to engage among the shoals, and Warwick determined to run up the river if attacked. But on the 31st, Prince Charles weighed anchor and stood out to sea, apparently in the hope of coming across the Portsmouth ships. These, however, passed him in the night and joined Warwick the next day.

The Royal fleet then made off to Goree Roads in Holland, whither Warwick afterwards followed them. He, in time, persuaded most of the ships to return to their allegiance to Parliament. Eventually Prince

Rupert escaped with seven ships, went first to Ireland, then on a buccaneering cruise. Pursued by Blake, he lost all his ships but two, which he finally sold to the King of France. (Warwick's Report, Rushworth, vol. viii.; Clarendon vol. vi.)

Nor was the victory less felt in Scotland. Hamilton had left his brother—the Earl of Lanark—with a force in Scotland, to overawe Argyle and the Kirk party. But no sooner had news of Hamilton's overthrow reached Scotland than the latter party began to arm. With Argyle's clansmen to begin with, they soon raised a force of 6000 men. Leven and David Leslie accepted commands. They seized Edinburgh and its castle, and refused to allow Lanark admission.

Meanwhile Monro was retiring before Cromwell, doing all the damage he could in England. He gathered to his force the remnants of Langdale's horse, which had fled from Preston, and with the levies of Sir Philip Musgrave, he may have had six or seven thousand men. But they were in a demoralized condition with the exception of his own Scotch veterans. Towards the end of August, he sent a party of horse into Durham and Northumberland, who passed through the country:

> Plundering like devils, terrifying the people, wounding divers, taking away the children of others to get money for the redemption of them; besides quarter they had of divers £3 a house.—Letter from Newcastle in Rushworth, vol. viii.

Monro himself fell back to Appleby.

Cromwell followed these marauders. But the tremendous exertions of the campaign had told on his men, and more on the cavalry horses, so that he could not move with his usual rapidity. "This army's much discontented for want of pay, having received none a long time, and find no course taken to supply them; they have not a penny to shoe their horses, and have lost so many, slain, lamed, or tired out, in desperate and most difficult service against the Scots, and in the long pursuit of them; abundance of our Horse-Soldiers are on foot, and they see no Course taken to recruit them." (So, wrote one from the army on the 15th September; Rushworth, vol. viii.)

The four most serviceable regiments of horse had gone with Lambert in pursuit of Hamilton.

On the 1st September Cromwell was at Knaresborough, and on the 8th he was at Durham, where "a day of thanksgiving was held for the great deliverance of these parts."

But Monro and his marauders had already gone. On the 3rd September, he had received a post from Lanark desiring him to hasten into Scotland and assist the latter against Argyle and Leven. The Scotch and English Royalists therefore parted, the former crossing the border, in number about 3000, and marching by Kelso towards Edinburgh. The English Cavaliers under Sir Thomas Tildesley retreated to Berwick, where, however, the Scotch governor, Ludovic Leslie, refused to receive them, and they gradually dispersed. One piece of mischief intended by Monro was thus prevented. He had determined to fire all the coal pits in Northumberland and Durham. Truly their experiences in Ireland had made his veterans adepts in the art of marauding.

Cromwell was at Newcastle on the 10th September, Morpeth on the 11th, and Alnwick on the 12th, finding the country everywhere miserably plundered. Hence, on the 15th, he summoned Berwick, but the governor, not quite knowing who was then master in Scotland, returned a "fair, but dilatory answer." Meanwhile, Monro had joined Lanark, and the two faced Argyle's forces at Edinburgh. They numbered some 7000 men, of which 2500 were horse, but were not strong enough to attack Argyle in the very strong position that Edinburgh affords. They therefore turned aside and marched to Stirling, where they seized the bridge and castle and thus secured all Scotland north of the Forth. Argyle followed to Falkirk, where it is said Monro attacked his troops during an armistice and killed or took 700 of them. (Letter from the army, Rushworth, vol. viii.; Cromwell's letter of 20th September, Carlyle, appendix 13, vol. v.)

Negotiations had already been going on between the two Scotch forces, and now Argyle, feeling himself not strong enough, sent to Cromwell to ask his assistance. Cromwell on the 16th September sent Colonel Bright and Scout-master Rowe to Argyle, demanding the surrender of Berwick and Carlisle, and threatening if this request was not complied with to invade Scotland. He had already sent a strong party of horse to the border to observe Berwick from the English side. The next day he marched to Cheswick, where Lambert joined him, and was, on the 19th, sent forward across the border with three regiments of horse.

For Cromwell had received on the 17th the letter from Argyle and the Chancellor, the Earl of Loudoun, inviting him into Scotland. In his reply, he announced that he was about to advance to their assistance, and repeated his demands for the surrender of the frontier towns. (Carlyle, vol. ii.) But in spite of the miserable condition which this part of England had been reduced to by the Scots, he determined that no retaliation in kind should be allowed in his army.

On the 20th he issued a proclamation forbidding plundering under pain of the severest penalties, and ordered it to be read at the head of every company and troop in the army. (Carlyle, vol. ii.) A few days later the troopers of Colonel Wren's, a newly-raised local regiment, having taken some horses from the Scotch farmers, were paraded by Cromwell on the banks of the Tweed. He restored the stolen horses, cashiered the troopers, handed their lieutenant over to the provost marshal, and suspended the colonel. The regiment was then sent back in disgrace to Northumberland.

On the 20th, more troops crossed the Tweed by a ford, Cromwell himself being at Norham, and on the 21st, he followed with the rest of his forces. Two regiments of foot and one of horse were left before Berwick on the English side. Cromwell's headquarters were fixed at "Lord Mordington's House," near which six regiments of foot, four of horse, and some dragoons were assembled. Lambert had been pushed on with six regiments of horse and one of dragoons towards Edinburgh. He quartered on the 22nd in East Lothian, within six or seven miles of the capital. Some of the foot had also been sent on to secure the important pass of Cockburn's Path.

On the 22nd, Cromwell rode out to meet Argyle and Lord Elcho, who came to arrange for his assistance against Lanark. They sent an order to Ludovic Leslie to surrender Berwick to the English, but he refused unless he received an order from Lanark. The latter seeing the futility of attempting to oppose Argyle with Cromwell to back him, was now anxious to come to terms, and sent the required order both for that town and Carlisle. On the 29th, Berwick was evacuated by the Scots and occupied by the English, whilst Colonel Bright was sent to take over Carlisle. Cromwell went himself to the former place, left a regiment of foot there as garrison, and wrote to the Speaker urging that guns and ammunition might be sent to make it secure against any future attempt on the part of the Scots. On the 3rd October, he started for Edinburgh, where he was received as a powerful and honourable ally.

He here arranged the relations in which the two nations should stand to one another, and insisted that not only should Monro's and Lanark's forces be at once disbanded, but also that no officer who had taken part in Hamilton's "Engagement" should ever again hold an office of public trust. On the 7th October, after being feasted in Edinburgh Castle, he left for Dalhousie. One result of Hamilton's disastrous invasion was that the Scots lost the balance due to them of the £400,000 which the English Parliament had agreed to pay on their quitting England the year before. It amounted to over £100,000.

At Dalhousie Cromwell remained a day or two and then went on to Carlisle, of which he formally took possession on the 14th. Lambert had been left behind at Edinburgh to assist Argyle in maintaining order until u force of 4000 men, which was to be kept on foot for that purpose under Leven, was organised. The rest of the English troops were withdrawn.

Ashton had meanwhile retaken Appleby and dispersed a small Royalist levy, which had besieged Cockermouth. Mytton had retaken Anglesea, which the Welsh Royalists had seized upon. Deal and Sandown castles had surrendered, Scarborough town had been carried by assault. The castle, however, still held out, and Pontefract showed no symptom of yielding. Thither went Cromwell about the end of October and found it far from being at the point of surrender, as it had been represented to him. On the contrary, he writes:

> The castle hath been victualled with two hundred and twenty or forty fat cattle, within these three weeks, and they have also gotten in, as I am credibly informed, salt enough for them and more. So that I apprehend they are victualled for a twelvemonth. The men within are resolved to endure to the utmost extremity; expecting no mercy, as indeed they deserve none. The place is very well known to be one of the strongest inland garrisons in the kingdom; well watered; situated upon a rock in every part of it, and therefore difficult to mine.
>
> The walls very thick and high, with strong towers; and if battered, very difficult of access, by reason of the depth and steepness of the graft. The county is exceedingly impoverished; not able to bear free-quarter; nor well able to furnish provisions, if we had moneys. The work is like to be long, if materials be not furnished answerable. I therefore think it my duty to represent unto you as followeth, *viz.*:—
>
> That moneys be provided for three complete regiments of foot, and two of horse; that money be provided for all contingencies which are in view, too many to enumerate. that five hundred barrels of powder, six good battering-guns with three hundred shot to each gun, be speedily sent down to Hull:—we desire none may be sent less than demi-cannons. We desire also some

match and bullet. And if it may be, we should be glad that two or three of the biggest mortar-pieces with shells may likewise be sent.—Letter to Committee of Dorley House dated 15th November, 1648, from Knottingley, near Pontefract.

Cromwell did not take Pontefract. Urgent business called him off to London in December, and he left Lambert to finish the siege. Like Pembroke, it is one of the few fortresses which he thought too strong to be taken by storm after a short preparatory battering. The above extract is therefore very interesting, as it shows what artillery, ammunition, and material were considered necessary to reduce a typically strong place, well victualled and manned, in his days. Mortars were just coming into favour, and they are often mentioned in the accounts of his sieges as doing great damage.

In a letter written from before Pembroke, he asks the Committee of Carmarthen to have cast some "shells for our mortar-piece; the depth of them we desire may be of fourteen inches and three-quarters of an inch." (Carlyle, vol. v.) As he had no siege train at Pembroke, it is possible that even larger mortars were in use. Cromwell was quite right in his estimate of the strength of Pontefract. It did not capitulate until the following March. Scarborough Castle surrendered on the 19th December.

After the siege of Colchester, Fairfax had visited the principal towns of the Eastern Association, and fixed his headquarters at St. Albans. There the quarrel between the Parliament and the army broke out afresh. For the Presbyterian members had taken the opportunity offered by the employment of the troops on the campaign to reassert their superiority in the House.

The assessments were no longer enforced, the troops were not paid, the old question as to the London militia again cropped up, and in spite of the vote passed whilst the Independents were in the ascendant, that no more addresses should be made to the king, a treaty was opened with him at Newport. The troops were further exasperated, as it was known that the Presbyterians had countenanced the insurrections, if they had not always directly aided them. Petitions began again to pour in to Fairfax from the officers and the regiments, and finally a Remonstrance was drawn up and presented to the House with a covering letter from Fairfax by Colonel Ewer and some other officers.

This Remonstrance began by demanding that the king, as the chief source of the troubles and bloodshed of the last six years, might be brought to justice. Further, that the Prince of Wales and the Duke of York might be declared incapable of government, and exiled unless they submitted to Parliament. Justice was demanded on some "capital causers of the war," and many other political points were touched on principally relative to the assembly, duration, and powers of Parliament.

This was the first occasion on which it was openly suggested that the king should be brought to trial, and it may be noted that Fairfax was in command and Cromwell not even present when the Remonstrance was drawn up. The next step of the army was to secure the person of the king. This was effected by first relieving Colonel Hammond, who was considered somewhat too favourably inclined towards Charles, by Colonel Ewer as Governor of the Isle of Wight.

Then, on the 29th November, one or two companies of the regular army were landed in the island under some selected officers. These relieved the local troops, who had previously been on guard on the king's person, that night after dark, and the next morning he was transported to Hurst Castle, on the other side of the Solent. The old system of putting pressure on the Parliament by drawing the army near London was resorted to, and on the 26th November the headquarters were removed to Windsor. On the 30th November, the officers drew up a fresh declaration, or remonstrance, accusing the Parliament of treacherous or corrupt neglect of public trust, and announcing their intention of marching on London. (Rushworth, vol. viii.)

On the 5th December, in spite of the threatening attitude of the army, the Commons voted that the king's concessions at the treaty of Newport formed sufficient grounds for settling the peace of the kingdom. Next day Colonel Pride's regiment of foot and Colonel Rich's of horse marched to Westminster, relieved the trained bands on guard on the Houses, and stopped a number of members, whose names were on a list held by Pride, and who were pointed out to him as they were entering the House by Lord Grey of Groby.

This act of force, commonly known as "Pride's Purge," virtually terminated the conflict between Parliament and the army. For the members who had opposed the latter, being restrained by force from taking their seats, the remainder voted what it required. On the 8th December two regiments of foot and several troops of horse were quartered in the City; and the treasuries at the Weavers', Haberdashers', and Goldsmiths' Halls were seized by Fairfax's order, to ensure the payment of the troops. The strictest discipline was enforced. Two soldiers of Dean's regiment rode the "wooden horse" for an hour in front of the Royal Exchange, and then ran the "gantelope" of the regiment, for attempting to extort money from a citizen. Freedom of trade was maintained, a declaration to that effect being issued by Fairfax and his council of war.

The sequel to these events was the impeachment, trial, and execution of the king, to which no reference is here necessary. As a soldier, Cromwell took little part in the events which have been touched on, except that he forwarded to Fairfax on the 20th November certain petitions which he had received from the officers of the northern army, and of which he expressed his approval. They were to a similar effect as those sent to Fairfax by his own officers. Cromwell did not reach London until the 7th December, the day *after* Pride's purge. Fairfax issued all the orders by which the proceedings of the army were controlled, including those for removing Charles to Hurst Castle, his further removal to Windsor on the 16th December, and for Pride's proceedings on the 6th December.

No doubt Cromwell approved of what was done, but the orders were not his, but those of Fairfax and his council of war. When the general dissented from the king's trial under his wife's influence, he still retained the command of the army. In the proceedings in Parliament and as one of the king's judges, Cromwell acted as a member of the House and not as an officer.

One of the first matters considered in Parliament after the execution of the king was the re-subjection of Ireland. It had long been a reproach against the army that it had wasted time in the squabbles with Parliament which should have been devoted to suppressing the insurgents in that country. Also that, being the instrument of the Protestants of England, it had refused to execute their unanimous desire in respect to the Papist insurrection. As soon, therefore, as the form of future government for the Commonwealth was sufficiently settled, the questions—what troops should be sent to Ireland? and under whom?—were debated in the House, and also in the Council of the Army. The latter had declared on the 19th February that 10,000 men were required for service in Ireland.

On the 15th March the House voted that Cromwell should be asked to accept the command. He agreed, and on the 30th his appointment was confirmed. The Council of State had on the 6th March recommended that the contingent should be 12,000 strong, and this number was finally decided on. The business of furnishing means for the transport and payment of these forces was now taken in hand by the House, it having been decided that two months of arrears and a month's pay in hand should be given the troops before they started. A Parliamentary Committee, of which Cromwell was one, visited the Common Council of the City on the 12th April, and succeeded, after some debate, in obtaining the promise of a loan of £120,000 from the City. But subsequent delays in payment of this loan, however, prevented Cromwell's departure for Ireland for some months.

The Council of the Army, which sat at Whitehall, on its part, proceeded to select the regiments to be sent and to organise the contingent. The representatives of the fourteen regiments of horse and fourteen of foot, then comprising the regular forces, met at Whitehall on the 20th April. In their presence a child drew lots for four regiments of both horse and foot, and five troops of dragoons, for service in Ireland. The lots fell on the horse regiments of Commissary-General Ireton, Colonel Scroop, Colonel Horton, and Major-General Lambert; on the foot regiments of Colonels Ewer, Cook, Hewson, and Dean; and on the dragoon companies of Major Abbott, Captains Mercer, Fulcher, Garland, and Boulton. Other regiments appear to have been specially raised for the service, for says the *Perfect Diurnal* of that date:

> There are three more regiments already forming besides those of the army, *viz.*, a regiment of foot for Lieutenant-General Cromwell, Colonel Venables' regiment, and the Kentish regiment under Colonel Phaire.—*Cromwelliana*. Phayre is the usual spelling of Phaire.

But the feeling amongst the rank and file was by no means good at this moment. The mutinous sparks kindled by the Levellers, which had apparently been stamped out on Corkbush Field, had ever since been smouldering in the ranks. John Lilburne, the principal mischief-maker, though nominally under the custody of the Lieutenant of the Tower, was allowed considerable liberty. This he employed in fanning the smother into flame. Luckily for the army and the nation, the command of the former was in the hands of men equal to the occasion.

As early as the 1st March, 1649, eight troopers had presented a letter to Fairfax asserting the soldiers' right to petition Parliament without the consent of their officers. They were immediately arrested, and on the 3rd four of them were tried by court-martial and sentenced to ride the wooden horse face to the tail, their swords to be broken over their heads, and to be cashiered. The sentence was carried out, and about the same time Lilburne published his two pamphlets: *England's New Chains Discovered*, and *The Hunting of the Foxes from Triploe Heath to Whitehall by Five Small Beagles*. These pamphlets were aimed principally at Cromwell, and purported to trace the gradual imposition of a military hierarchy and despotism in place of the aristocratic monarchy overthrown with the Royalist armies. The "five small beagles" were supposed to be certain troopers of the Levellers' sect, who had sympathized with and assisted Lilburne in his denunciations of the superior officers, (probably five of the eight who had presented the petition to Fairfax). He and they were now made close prisoners.

But the mischief had already in part begun. The Levellers' tenets had spread far among the horse regiments; the foot do not appear to have been much affected. Mutinies occurred in several regiments in different places, and almost at the same time. Some of Whalley's troopers who were quartered in the City about Bishopsgate refused on the 26th April to march when ordered to do so. Scroop's and Ireton's regiments refused a few days later to go to Ireland. Some two hundred men of Reynolds' regiment, led by a Captain Thomson, broke into mutiny at Banbury.

Fairfax and Cromwell proceeded at once to Bishopsgate when the news of the mutiny reached them, with sufficient force to compel obedience. Fifteen of the ringleaders were seized and tried by court-martial. Five of these were sentenced to death, but of these only one man, trooper Lockyer, was shot in St. Paul's Churchyard, the cathedral being then a quarter for horse. But the example was hardly sufficient. On the 30th his comrades gave his corpse a funeral with all military honours. A hundred troopers went in front, six trumpeters preceded the bier, sounding a knell; Lockyer's horse followed it, clothed all over in mourning. Behind, a great multitude, soldiers and civilians, men and women, marching in rank and file, all with sea-green ribbons on hat and breast. At the churchyard in Westminster "some thousands more of the better sort" awaited the procession. (Whitelocke). Never was private trooper awarded a more imposing funeral.

When the excitement had cooled down, Fairfax ordered a rendezvous of his own and Cromwell's regiments of horse in Hyde Park on the 9th May. Here Cromwell addressed the men. He pointed out how irrevocably the fates of the Independent Parliament and army were now bound together; how the former had acquiesced in all the latter's demands, as to the punishment of delinquents, as to the duration of Parliaments, &c.; how trade had been re-established, and the navy placed on a good footing; how regular pay had now been provided for the troops. If the army were to exist at all, it must be governed by military discipline. The theories of the Levellers could have no place in a military society. Those who found such discipline a burden were at liberty to take their discharge, and would have their arrears paid them.

Cromwell, though his speeches in Parliament, as they have been transmitted to us, seem so involved and confused, never spoke to his soldiers in vain. He possessed a power of convincing and influencing them which never failed; the power of a mighty will speaking to weaker ones. Only one trooper raised objections, and was somewhat insolent. He was arrested, but then pardoned by Cromwell. It was after this parade that Lilburne and his beagles were rigorously confined.

The men of these regiments soon gave proof of their reliability. Colonel Reynolds had on the 12th May attacked, with the bulk of his regiment, Thomson's mutineers, and dispersed or taken them with the loss of but one man. Thomson, with some eighty troopers, escaped towards Northampton. But at Salisbury the mutineers of Scroop's and Ireton's regiments amounted to about 1000 men. A Cornet Thomson, brother to the captain, was their leader, no other officer being with them. They expected reinforcements from Harrison's and Horton's regiments, quartered further west, but these never arrived. On the 13th May, Fairfax and Cromwell left London at the head of their own regiments to suppress the outbreak. They marched *via* Alton, Fairfax having previously dispatched a letter to the mutineers, demanding their submission. This they received near Marlborough, whither they had gone, and in their reply, they professed their respect for the general, but refused to go to Ireland, and demanded a general meeting of the *agitators* and officers.

Hearing of Fairfax's approach, the mutineers attempted to cross the Thames at Newbridge, apparently with the view of joining Captain Thomson's men. But Reynolds from Oxford was on the look-out, and secured the bridge against them. They then crossed by a ford higher up, and reached Burford on the 14th, where they quartered for the night.

Fairfax was marching from Alton by Andover on Salisbury, when he heard, on the 14th, of the movement of the mutineers towards Oxford. He immediately turned north after them. As he went on he must have picked up certain information of their movements. That evening he arrived "within a long night's march of them." (*Cromwelliana*). Here he halted; but though he had made "a march of near fifty miles," (see note following), after the men and horses had had time for a little rest and something to eat, he ordered a detachment under Cromwell to press on.

******

Note: Carlyle, vol. ii., quoting some unnamed authority. From London by Alton to Burford is over ic» miles. If Fairfax only started on the 13th, as the account given by Carlyle infers, the whole distance was covered in two days. But I cannot find any confirmation of the date.— T. S. B.

******

It was midnight when the latter reached Burford. In the ranks of the Levellers everyone was equal; it was no one's duty to set guard or outpost, or to send out patrols. The mutineers slept securely in their quarters, their horses in their stables. No warning was received of Cromwell's approach. He first secured all the exits of the town, and then entering attacked the mutineers in their beds. Utterly surprised, the latter made little resistance. A few shots were fired, but the majority endeavoured to escape through garden gates, over walls, or anyhow, leaving their horses behind them. But one man was killed.

The prisoners taken are variously estimated in different accounts from 400 to 900. Thomson and Dean, the ringleaders, were taken. Nine hundred horses were captured. The next day a tenth of the prisoners were selected, tried by court-martial, and sentenced to death. On the 17th the prisoners were assembled on the roof of the church, whilst the doomed men were brought into the churchyard below.

The first brought forward for execution was Cornet Thomson. He admitted his fault, expressed contrition, faced the firing-party, gave them the signal, and fell dead at the volley. The next after him:

> . . . . was a corporal, brought to the same place of execution, where, looking upon his fellow-mutineers, he set his back against the wall, and bid them who were appointed to shoot— shoot! and died desperately. The third, being also a corporal, was brought to the same place, and without the least acknowledgment of error, or show of fear, pulled off his doublet (standing a pretty distance from the wall), bidding the soldiers do their duty, looking them in the face till they gave fire, not showing the least kind of terror or fearfulness of spirit.—*Cromwelliana*.

Cornet Dean was next brought forward. He expressed contrition, and, with the rest of the condemned men, was reprieved. Cromwell then went into the church, and after speaking to the prisoners, who had sent a petition to Fairfax, acknowledging that they had justly deserved death, he released them. They were then quartered apart from the other men, and eventually either sent to their homes or their regiments.

Meanwhile, Captain Thomson, who had escaped from Banbury, reached Northampton with the remnant of the mutineers. Here he seized a field-gun and some ammunition, and then marched for Wellingborough. He was pursued by a Captain Butler with a select party of troopers, overtaken, and his men dispersed or captured. He himself escaped into a wood, but was discovered on the 19th May by a party of troopers. He made a desperate resistance, and was at last shot, after killing a lieutenant and wounding several men. This was the last serious trouble given by the Levellers in the army, though a few minor outbreaks occurred later. In August some of Colonel Cooke's regiment mutinied at Minehead and refused to embark for Ireland, but were eventually persuaded or compelled to obey. In September some of the troops at Oxford mutinied, but were suppressed by their own officers, and two of them executed.

The military authorities were now able to turn their attention again to preparing the troops for Ireland. On returning towards London, Fairfax and Cromwell stayed a few days at Oxford, where they were feasted and had honorary degrees of doctors of civil law presented them. Again, on their arrival in London, they and the principal officers were entertained with great ceremony at the Grocers' Hall; the merchants of the City feeling greatly relieved at the suppression of the socialistic mutiny in the army.

The mutiny had, however, considerably disturbed the arrangements for Ireland and delayed the departure of the troops. One of the old newspapers, the *Perfect Occurrences* of the 1st June, speaks of the regiments of Colonels Stubbard, Phayer, Venables, and Hunk of foot, and of Colonel Reynolds and Major Shelborne's of horse, as being amongst those now for Ireland. The latter was now Cromwell's regiment, as in it occurred the first vacancy for a colonel. (Cromwell's original regiment, the famous "Ironsides," became Fairfax's regiment on the organisation of the New Model Army). These and some other regiments were, during the month of June, moved to Bristol and other western garrisons ready to embark.

On the 22nd June the Commons sent Cromwell his commission as Lord Lieutenant-General and General Governor of Ireland. At his request his accounts as commander in the northern campaign were audited and passed before his departure. Another cause which may have somewhat delayed him was an investigation then pending into certain forgeries of his signature by a Mr Spavan, lately his secretary. This man, together with a Captain Mitchell and a servant, had carried on a regular trade in passes, and protections to papists, delinquents, and others, to which Spavan forged Cromwell's signature. He was sentenced to:

> Ride on horseback from Whitehall to Westminster and thence through the City, with an inscription on his back and on his breast, written in capital letters, to signify his crime.—*Cromwelliana*

But the chief cause of Cromwell's delay was his determination not to leave till he had the money to pay his men.

A life-guard was allowed Cromwell by Parliament, and it proves the respect and esteem with which he was then regarded, that men of rank and position competed for admission to its ranks. At last everything was ready for his departure. Here is the account given of it by the "special reporter" of the day:

> This evening (the 10th July) about five of the clock, the Lord-Lieutenant of Ireland began his journey by the way of Windsor and so to Bristol. He went forth in that state and equipage as the like hath hardly been seen, himself in a coach, with six gallant Flanders Mares, whitish-grey, divers coaches accompanying him, and very many great officers of the army: his life-guard consisting of eighty gallant men, the meanest whereof a Commander or Esquire in stately habit, with trumpets sounding almost to the shaking of Charing-Cross had it now been standing; of his life-guard many are colonels, and believe it, it's such a guard as is hardly to be paralleled in the world... The lord-lieutenant's colours are white.—*Cromwelliana*.

On the 14th Cromwell reached Bristol.

Cromwell's Plan of Campaign

In 1642 the Protestant forces in Ireland were divided into three groups—one in the county of Cork under Lord Inchiquin, another about Dublin under the king's viceroy, Lord Ormond, and the third about Derry, Belfast, and the other ports of Ulster, which consisted of

Scotch troops under Monro. The Catholic rebels held all the centre of the country. When the Civil War broke out in England, Inchiquin and Monro sided with the Parliament, whilst Ormond remained faithful to the king.

Thus divided, the Protestants could not hope to reconquer the country, and might probably have been annihilated, had not the Catholics been equally split into factions. The great Ulster chief, Owen Roe O'Neil, held aloof from Lord Preston and the Catholics of the centre and west, whilst the Pope's *nuncio* formed a third party, which effectually prevented the others from combining.

The war lingered on, conducted in guerrilla fashion, with the usual accompaniments of plunder, murder, and rapine, until Ormond, by the king's orders, patched up a truce with the rebels. He then sent over the greater part of his forces to Charles' assistance, but scarcely had he done so, when the rebels broke the truce, and Ormond with difficulty retained Dublin itself. The truce had never been recognised by Inchiquin or Monro.

At the termination of the first Civil War the Parliament sent over some reinforcements to the Protestants, not regiments of the New Model Army, but such local troops and Royalist soldiers, who volunteered for this service rather than disband. In February, 1647, Ormond, at the king's direction, handed over the command of Dublin to Colonel Jones, who arrived there with a party of these reinforcements. Jones was one of the ablest soldiers who fought for the cause of the Parliament, and for a while matters went better for the Protestants. He defeated Preston with great slaughter at Dungan Hill, near Dublin, in August, whilst Inchiquin fought his way into Tipperary. Coote occupied Derry with English troops, and Monro, who had been defeated by O'Neil in 1646 at Benburb, near Armagh, began to recover ground. In the autumn of 1647, George Monk, who had been in the Tower since his capture at Nantwich, took service with the Parliament, and was given the command of the Protestant troops about Drogheda and Dundalk.

But when in 1648 the Presbyterian Royalist outbreaks occurred in England and Scotland, the Protestants in Ireland were again divided. On this occasion Inchiquin and Monro declared for the king, whilst Jones, Monk, and Coote adhered to the Independent party.

Prince Charles' advisers seized this opportunity to send Ormond back into Ireland. He landed at Cork on the 30th September, 1648, and went to Kilkenny, where, after infinite trouble, he formed an alliance between Inchiquin, Monro, and the bulk of the Catholics. O'Neil refused to join, and made a treaty with Monk. At this juncture Prince Rupert arrived on the coast with several sail of the ships which had mutinied in the Downs, and for a period held the command of the Irish waters. (The actual number of vessels he had with him is variously estimated by different authors from sixteen to seven.—T. S. B.) He was, however, defeated by an English fleet under Popham about the 1st May, 1649, before Ormond was ready to move.

At last, on the 1st June, Ormond advanced with some 6000 foot and 2000 horse. He drove Jones back into Dublin, and sent Inchiquin against Monk. The latter's troops were mostly Scotch Presbyterians, who deserted him, and he' had to abandon Drogheda, Dundalk, and the neighbouring towns, and fly to England. A large detachment of O'Neil's troops under Major-General Ferral was also defeated by a party of Inchiquin's horse under Trevor on the 15th July.

Thus, by the end of July, the hold of the Parliament on Ireland was reduced to the two towns—Derry and Dublin. In the former Coote was closely besieged by a combined Scotch-Irish force under Lord Ardes and Colonel Stewart, whilst Ormond and Inchiquin invested the latter. About the last of the month O'Neil approached Derry, and assisted Coote in driving off the besiegers—but O'Neil's treaty with Monk had been repudiated by the English Parliament, and he was already negotiating with Ormond. Shortly afterwards he openly joined the Prince's party,

Cromwell arrived at Bristol on the 14th July. He had appointed Milford Haven as the rendezvous for the bulk of his forces and for the fleet which was to convey them into Ireland. His intention was to have landed in Munster, where the Protestants were strong in the counties of Cork and Waterford. It was known that many of Inchiquin's officers and men were dissatisfied with his alliance with the Catholics, and Cromwell was already in correspondence with Colonels Townsend and Piggott, and other officers in the garrisons of Cork, Youghal, and the neighbouring ports. He had also gained over Lord Broghill, a nobleman whose influence in Munster was very considerable, and would be of great use to him there.

The story goes that Broghill had determined to join the prince in Holland, and had gone to London to obtain a passport for Spa on the plea of ill-health. Cromwell, who suspected, or had information of, his design, visited him privately one evening, and there and then offered him the choice between arrest or adherence to the Independent Parliament. Broghill, convinced by his arguments, chose the latter alternative. (Maurice's *Life of Orrery*). Whether this story is true or not, it is certain that Broghill accepted during the spring of 1649 a commission as Major-General in the Parliament's service.

Whilst the bulk of the forces were intended for Munster, Cromwell directed four regiments—the foot regiments of Venables, Moore, and Thurke, and Reynolds' horse—on Chester, whence they were to sail to Dublin to reinforce Jones. On receiving news of the loss of Drogheda their departure was hastened, and they landed on the 25th July. Monk visited Cromwell about this period, and probably the information which he brought determined the latter to go himself to Dublin, taking with him an extra reinforcement from Milford. The money for the troops, however, had not yet arrived, and without the money Cromwell would not sail.

The reinforcements from Chester brought Jones' forces up to 4000 foot and 1200 horse. Ormond was now pushing the siege with vigour, especially on the southeast towards the harbour. He had, however, detached Inchiquin, with two regiments of horse, into Munster, to oppose any hostile attempts in that direction, and had posted Lord Dillon with 2000 foot and 500 horse on the north of the Liffey to invest Dublin on that side. South of the river he was but little stronger than Jones, who, on the morning of the 2nd August, made a vigorous sally and utterly routed Ormond, capturing all his camp, taking many prisoners, and completely dispersing the rest.

Ormond fled to Kilkenny, whence in a week he returned to Trim, having rallied some 300 horsemen. His great object now was to delay the English advance, as he knew they were about to receive large reinforcements, until he could again collect an army strong enough to oppose them in the field. For this reason he put the best troops and best officers available as garrisons into Drogheda, Trim, and Dundalk. Many of these were English Cavaliers or Scotch veterans.

Cromwell was already on board ship in Milford Harbour when he heard of Jones' victory. The money had arrived, and he was ready to sail. This victory, commonly called the Battle of Rathmines, had completely altered the aspect of affairs, but Cromwell still adhered to his former plans. On the 13th August he sailed with twenty-five ships for Dublin, where he landed on the 15th, whilst Ireton on the 15th sailed for Munster with seventy. The latter reached Cable Island, off Youghal, when he put about and sailed up the Irish Channel to Dublin, where he landed on the 25th. Contrary winds were given as the reason of this manoeuvre, the real one probably being that Inchiquin, on his return to Munster, had discovered that correspondence was passing with Cromwell, and had removed the suspected officers from the garrison.

Ireton, therefore, on arriving off Youghal, found that the garrison would not admit him, as he had probably anticipated that it would. His promptness in sailing to Dublin shows, however, that he must have had instructions for such an emergency from Cromwell, and it is possible that the whole manoeuvre was only a feint, intended to mislead Ormond as to the real point of concentration. A few days later Colonel Horton also arrived from Milford, bringing with him the troops, for whom accommodation on the transports could not at first be found.

Thus, at the end of August, Cromwell had some 10,000 foot and 5000 horse concentrated at Dublin. Except Derry, where the English had a garrison of 900 men, the whole of the rest of Ireland was in the hands of the Catholics and their Royalist allies, and the conquest of the island must be begun afresh.

It was not men, but money, that Ormond lacked. The alliance now completed with O'Neil had set free the forces hitherto retained in King's and Queen's Counties to guard against any inroads he might make in Ormond's rear. The country was full of *banditti* called "Tories," retainers of the smaller chiefs and nobles, whom the troublous times had called forth. These men were at the call of the Catholic leaders, so that in point of numbers Ormond could dispose of a very large force. But money wherewith to organise these hordes into armies he could by no means obtain, though he spent his own fortune freely in the cause. Of officers capable of reducing these plundering ruffians to discipline he had very few.

Ireland, a country of mountain and bog, was in many parts well suited to a successful guerrilla warfare. It was studded with innumerable castles and strongholds, for even in the most peaceful times no man was safe far from his own strong walls. These fastnesses formed rallying points for the Tories when they assembled for a raid, whilst the mountains and bogs afforded them refuges when attacked. The roads were few and bad, the climate unhealthy for English soldiers, who caught ague and fever amongst the undrained swamps. After the massacres of 1641, the English Protestants regarded the native Irish as their descendants in India regarded the *Sepoys* after Delhi and Cawnpore.

Indeed, the problem before Cromwell much resembled, in its main features, that which presented itself to the English generals after the capture of Delhi. A numerous but disorganised enemy, incapable of offering serious resistance in battle, disappearing, when pursued, into bog or jungle, turning up again in some unexpected quarter; having no headquarters, and therefore nothing decisive to strike at. An enemy that was everywhere, yet nowhere, not to be found when searched for, always reappearing when the search had passed.

One great advantage Cromwell possessed which Clyde did not when the latter organised the English armies for the suppression of the Mutiny. He was engaged in an island, and held the command of the sea. Every port that he seized could be converted into a fresh base, and his communications would therefore be comparatively short. But the solution arrived at by the two generals was practically the same. Strong, lightly equipped columns were employed, moving from one base to another, striking rapid blows in all directions, hemming the enemy in from two or more sides.

The bitter race hatred, and the deplorable conditions of the country had a pernicious effect on the discipline of the English soldiers who had been some time in the country. Like the native Irish, they lived on plunder whenever they made their expeditions; plunder taken not only from the enemy under arms, but also from the wretched farmers and peasants on their line of march. Cromwell, on his arrival in Dublin, found Jones' troops incorrigible offenders in this respect. He determined to stamp out this form of crime at once. He knew that plundering greatly militates against the success of an army.

Not only does it totally destroy the discipline of the troops, but it enhances the difficulties of supply, and may thus make movement impossible. It is of the utmost importance to a general to gain the confidence of the inhabitants of the country through which he marches. Should they expect ill-treatment and plunder, they will quit their homes, hide their grain, drive off their cattle, and attack the stragglers of the army. If, on the contrary, they are well treated, they will remain at home and sell the produce of their farms to the invaders.

During the fortnight which followed his arrival in Dublin, and whilst Ireton's and Horton's detachments were at sea, Cromwell busied himself with reorganising Jones' troops. He dismissed many of the officers, and replaced them by men he could trust. He issued a proclamation against plundering, which is well worth quoting:—

Whereas I am informed that, upon the marching out of the armies heretofore, or of parties from garrisons, a liberty hath been taken by the soldiery to abuse, rob, and pillage, and too often to execute cruelties upon the country people: Being resolved, by the grace of God, diligently and strictly to restrain such wickedness for the future, I do hereby warn and require all officers, soldiers, and others under my command, henceforth, to forbear all such evil practices as aforesaid; and not to do any wrong or violence towards country people, or persons whatsoever, unless they be actually in arms or office with the Enemy; and not to meddle with the goods of such, without special order.

And I further declare. That it shall be free and lawful to, and for all manner of persons dwelling in the country, as well as gentlemen and soldiers, as farmers and other people (such as are in arms or office with or for the enemy only excepted) to make their repair, and bring any provisions unto the army, while in march or camp, or unto any garrison under my command: Hereby assuring all such. That they shall not be molested or troubled in their persons or goods; but shall have the benefit of a free market, and receive ready money for goods or commodities they shall so bring and sell.

The proclamation goes on to promise protection to all who live quietly in their homes and pay the lawful contributions, and ends by affirming:

Being resolved, through the grace of God, to punish all that shall offend contrary hereunto, very severely, according to Law or Articles of War; to displace and otherwise punish all such officers as shall be found negligent in their places, and not to see to the due observance hereof, or not to punish the offenders under their respective commands.

Having reorganised Jones' troops, and given his horses some days to recover from the effects of the sea-voyage, Cromwell was ready to take the field. Of the campaign which ensued, we have an excellent and succinct account in his own despatches to Speaker Lenthall, which were printed in the old newspapers, and have thus been retained when so many of his reports have been lost. His first object was to open communications with Coote, and send him reinforcements. To effect this, and to clear the country in the neighbourhood of Dublin, it was necessary to reduce the garrisons of Drogheda, Trim, and Dundalk.

With this view, Cromwell, on the 31st August, assembled "eight regiments of foot, six of horse, and some troops of dragoons, three miles on the north side of Dublin,"—and marched towards Drogheda.

> The design was to endeavour the regaining of Tredah (Drogheda); or tempting the enemy, upon his hazard of the loss of that place, to fight.—Cromwell to Lenthall, 17th September, 1649. Carlyle, vol. ii.

On the 13th September the army arrived before the town, which was surrounded by a strong wall with round bastions and a few outworks. It lay athwart the River Boyne near its mouth. It contained many churches and other strong buildings, and on an eminence within the walls, called the Mill Hill, was a fort which served as a citadel. The garrison was at least 2500 strong, of whom some 300 were horse, and consisted of picked men, many of them English. Sir Arthur Ashton, the governor, was a brave and experienced soldier. (Clarendon, vol. vi., says Sir A. Ashton "thought he could hold the place against any force for at least a month.")

Ormond, as has already been said, then lay about Trim.

Cromwell's forces were probably some 8000 or 9000 strong, though some accounts estimate them at a higher figure. If he had attempted to invest the place all round, he would, as he himself explains, have been too weak to resist sallies in force, as the river would greatly have hindered the communications between the troops on the north and south of the town. He therefore confined his attack entirely to the south side. His siege train had been brought up by ship, and the first week was spent in building batteries and bringing up guns, mortars, and ammunition. The garrison made several sallies, but were always beaten back.

During the delay Cromwell gave practical evidence of his determination to maintain strict discipline and to put down pillage. Another proclamation was issued forbidding soldiers to plunder on pain of death, and two were hanged for transgressing this order. ("A letter from Ireland," *Cromwelliana*). At last, on the 10th, the batteries were ready. A summons was sent to the governor, who returned an unsatisfactory answer. The guns then opened fire. They were first directed against the steeple of a church and a tower, whence the defenders kept up a galling fire from " long fowling pieces." Cromwell says:

> Our guns, not being able to do much that day, it was resolved to endeavour to do our utmost the next day to make breaches

> assaultable, and by the help of God to storm them. The place pitched upon was that part of the town-wall next a church called St. Mary's; which was the rather chosen because we did hope, that if we did enter and possess that church, we should be the better able to keep it against their horse and foot until we could make way for the entrance of our horse; and we did not conceive that any part of the town would afford the like advantage for that purpose with this.—Letter to Lenthall, Carlyle, vol. ii.

This church was at the south-eastern angle of the wall.

> The batteries planted were two, one was for that part of the wall against the east end of the said church; the other against the wall on the south side. Being somewhat long in battering, the enemy made six retrenchments: three of them from the said church to Duleek Gate, (near the western end of the south wall), and three of them from the east end of the church to the Town-wall and so backward. The guns, after some two or three hundred shot, beat down the corner tower, and opened two reasonable good breaches in the east and south wall.

This was about five o'clock on the afternoon (10th September), and the assaulting columns were ready formed for the attack. Colonel Castle's regiment formed the forlorn hope, Hewson's and one or two others the main body, Colonel Ewer's the reserve. The signal was given and the stormers rushed at the breaches. A very hot engagement ensued, but the English in a second assault carried the breach.

The enemy, however, still offered a strenuous resistance, and, bringing up reinforcements, drove the stormers out again. Colonel Castle fell mortally wounded, some other officers were killed, the men fell back defeated for the moment. Whilst the attack was proceeding at the breach, a party of the stormers, assisted by Captain Brandly and forty seamen, had attacked a *tenaille* which covered the south wall near at hand. This they carried and put the defenders to the sword. A sally port gave communication between the ramparts and this outwork, and an attempt was made to force a way in through this, but it was choked with the dead bodies of the defenders.

Cromwell, as he saw his men driven down the breach, had hurried to the reserve. Placing himself at the head of Ewer's men, he led them personally to the attack. The other regiments rallied and joined in this third attempt. This time not only the breach, but the church and the retrenchments were carried. Once taken, these proved an advantage to the assailants, as they prevented the defenders' horse from charging, until an entrance had with difficulty been made for the English cavalry. The streets were then cleared.

> Divers of the enemy retreated into the Mill Mount, a place very strong and of difficult access; being exceedingly high, having a good graft, and strongly pallisadoed. The governor, Sir Arthur Ashton, and divers considerable officers being there, our men, getting up to them, were ordered by me to put them all to the sword. And indeed, being in the heat of action, I forbade them to spare any that were in arms in the town; and, I think, that night they put to the sword about 2000 men; divers of the officers and soldiers being fled over the bridge into the other part of the town, where about 100 of them possessed St. Peter's Church steeple, some the west gate, and others a strong round tower next the gate called St. Sunday's. These, being summoned to yield to mercy, refused. Whereupon I ordered the steeple of St. Peter's Church to be fired, when one of them was heard to say in the midst of the flames, 'God damn me, God confound me; I burn, I burn.'
>
> The next day the other two towers were summoned, in one of which was about six or seven score; but they refused to yield themselves, and we, knowing that hunger must compel them, set only good guards to secure them from running away until their stomachs were come down. From one of the said towers, notwithstanding their condition, they killed and wounded some of our men. When they submitted, their officers were knocked on the head; and every tenth man of the soldiers killed, and the rest shipped for the Barbadoes. The soldiers in the other tower were all spared, as to their lives only, and shipped likewise for the Barbadoes.—Letter to Lenthall, Carlyle, vol. ii.

Such was the famous storm of Drogheda. The refusal to give quarter is condemned by modern humanity.

******

The Royalist accounts declare that the soldiers offered the garrison quarter, but Cromwell ordered them to kill their prisoners, and that Ashton, Verney, and others were killed in cold blood sometime after they had surrendered.

✶✶✶✶✶✶

No quarter was given in the Secundrabagh, and yet most Englishmen regard the fact with complacency, looking on the slaughter as an act of just retribution. More Protestants were massacred in 1641 than Englishmen were murdered in India in 1857, and if only a part of the stories then circulated in England were true, under even more horrible conditions. The well at Cawnpore was filled with the dead bodies of slaughtered women and children. The story ran in England that in Munster the rebels had filled a quarry with both dead and living, and had left all to rot together. For long no quarter had been given by either side. When an English ship captured one with Irish on board, the wretched prisoners were tied back to back and flung into the sea. Cromwell himself says:

> I am persuaded that this is a righteous judgment of God upon these barbarous wretches, who have imbrued their hands in so much innocent blood, and that it will tend to prevent effusion of blood for the future. Which are the satisfactory grounds to such actions, which otherwise cannot but work remorse and regret.

There were many English in the garrison who had taken no part in the massacres of 1641. But if they chose to ally themselves with such "barbarous wretches," they could not complain if they shared their fate. Cromwell makes no mention of any unarmed inhabitants killed, nor do the Parliamentary accounts. In a second letter he gives the names of the principal officers and the numbers of the rest killed.

Cromwell's expectations as to the effect which the fate of Drogheda would have on other garrisons were fulfilled. Reconnoitring parties of horse and dragoons found Dundalk and Trim both abandoned by their garrisons. The latter place had been held by some Scotch companies, who left so precipitately that they abandoned their heavy guns.

Cromwell had already despatched 1000 foot by sea to Coote's assistance. He now sent Venables with a strong detachment to clear the communications with Ulster and assist Coote, whilst with the rest of the army he fell back to Dublin. Ormond's army appears to have dwindled away. Venables took Carlingford and Newry after but slight resistance, and defeated Trevor, who had been sent by Ormond with a party of horse to attempt to surprise him. On the 27th September Trevor fell upon Venables before daylight, drove in his pickets, and defeated his horse. But the foot, rallying in the enclosures, drove back

Trevor's men. Then the English horse reformed and defeated the Irish with loss.

Cromwell's policy appears to have been to secure all the principal seaports, before pushing into the interior. This was certainly the right thing to do. Had he attempted to follow Ormond, the latter's forces would have evaded pursuit and the English would have been worn out by marches hither and thither, and would have died by the hundred of fever. As it was, the ravages of the disease were beginning. In his report of the capture of Drogheda, Cromwell, writing from Dublin on the 17th September, says, (Carlyle, vol. ii.):

"We keep the held much; our tents sheltering us from the wet and cold. But yet this Country-sickness, (species of fever), overtakes many; and therefore we desire recruits, and some fresh regiments of foot may be sent us. For it's easily conceived by what the Garrisons already drink up, what our Field Army will come to, if God shall give more garrisons into our hands."

The burden of his reports during this campaign is ever—more men! more men!

Cromwell before Waterford

Having secured his communications with the north, and got possession of the ports of Drogheda and Carlingford, which, with Derry, gave the English a good foothold on the north-west coast, Cromwell turned his attention to the south. Here were numerous good harbours, of great importance, because they attracted most of the trade of the country, and through them Ormond communicated with France and Holland, with Henrietta Maria and Prince Charles. Besides, in Munster assistance might be expected from the Protestants.

Accordingly the army quitted Dublin on the 23rd, and marched south, keeping near the sea-coast. The Ormond's Castle at Arklow was abandoned at its approach, the Esmond's stronghold at Limbrick was quitted and burnt. The Castles of Ferns and Enniscorthy were surrendered on summons, and on the 1st October the army reached Wexford. Ormond had thrown a garrison of regular troops into this town under Colonel David Sinnott. On the 3rd October Cromwell, having established his army before the place, summoned it. Sinnott was inclined to treat, and, after some negotiations, four commissioners were appointed to settle the terms of surrender on the 5th October.

Wexford is situated on the south shore of the estuary of the River Slaney, and is therefore very difficult to invest without the assistance of ships. A fort lower down commanded the entrance to the harbour, and whilst the negotiations were proceeding Cromwell sent a party of horse and dragoons to make an attempt on it. On their approach the garrison quitted it, and escaped to a frigate that was lying close by. The dragoons occupied the fort, and with the assistance of some seamen who arrived at this juncture from the fleet, which lay outside, turned the guns on to the frigate. She immediately hauled down her flag. Another small vessel was also captured. The Parliament's ships could now enter the harbour.

But on the 4th October the Earl of Castlehaven, who was hovering on the other bank of the Slaney with a party of Irish, threw a reinforcement of 500 foot into the town. On the 5th, when Sinnott should have sent out his commissioners, he did not do so, alleging that, as Castlehaven was his superior officer, he could not treat without his orders. Cromwell then cancelled the safe conduct to the commissioners, and proceeded to press the siege vigorously.

In the south-east angle of the town wall stood a keep which commanded the rest of the defences. Cromwell determined to attack this, for if this were taken the rest of the town must submit. Batteries were therefore constructed at this point, and were finished by the 10th. The siege guns had, as at Drogheda, been brought down by sea, and landed on the 6th. On the 11th the batteries opened fire, and after some 100 rounds had been fired, Sinnott again offered to treat for the surrender of the place. Safe conducts were given to four officers who brought Cromwell Sinnott's proposals, which the former thought unreasonable. He sent them back, proposing his own terms, which were briefly, quarter for the garrison, and immunity from plunder for the inhabitants. He concluded with these words:

> I expect your positive answer instantly; and if you will upon these terms surrender and quit, shall, in one hour, send forth to me four officers, of the quality of field officers, and two aldermen, for the performance thereof, I shall thereupon forbear all acts of hostility.—Carlyle, vol, ii.

But before the hostages came out the town was no longer in a position to treat. Captain James Stafford, one of the commissioners whom Sinnott sent out, commanded in the castle. He "being fairly treated," says Cromwell, "yielded up the castle to us." A party of English soldiers entered and took peaceable possession; but it appears that the rest, neither the English nor the garrison, were informed of what was happening. As soon as the English soldiers appeared on the castle walls, the Irish quitted the town wall. The besiegers, perceiving the opportunity, seized their scaling ladders without orders from Cromwell, rushed forward, scaled the ramparts, and poured into the town. In the town the Irish resisted bravely, and a fierce fight ensued in the market place, but they were soon overpowered. Nearly the whole garrison perished either by the sword, or by the upsetting of the boats into which both soldiers and inhabitants had crowded in their endeavours to escape. The place was sacked. Cromwell estimates the losses of the Irish at nearly 2000, whilst the English loss was barely twenty.

The assault of the town and the slaughter of the garrison, amongst whom it appears were many townsmen, took place without Cromwell's direct order. But he justifies the conduct of his men on account of the cruelties alleged to have been perpetrated there on the Protestants. In one instance, he says:

> About seven or eight score poor Protestants were by them put into an old vessel, which being, as some say, bulged by them, the vessel sank, and they were all presently drowned in the harbour.

In another instance:

> They put divers poor Protestants into a Chapel (which since they have used for a Mass house, and in which one or more of their priests were now killed), where they were famished to death.—Cromwell to Lenthall, Carlyle, vol. ii.

Besides the booty which the soldiers took, the English captured a great quantity of iron, hides, tallow, salt, pipe and barrel-staves, and three new frigates, building or preparing for sea. These were in addition to the one taken before at the mouth of the harbour.

The fate of the town was a miserable one. True or not, the soldiers doubtless believed the stories told them of the cruelties of the inhabitants to Protestants. Believing themselves the direct instruments of God's vengeance on murderers, they spared none whom they found armed on the day of the assault. Cromwell wrote:

> This town is now so in your power, that of the former inhabitants, I believe scarce one in twenty can challenge any property in their houses. Most of them are run away, and many of them killed in this service.—Cromwell to Lenthall, Carlyle, vol. ii.

Then he recommends that "an honest people" should be sent to settle there, the houses being good, and the place convenient for trade.

Whilst Cromwell was before Wexford, Ormond had collected what troops he could at Graig, (now called in the ordnance map Graiguenamanagh, a small town on the Barrow), a place some six miles from Ross. Here he was joined by Lucas Taaffe with 1000 foot and 300 horse sent by Clanricarde. Inchiquin's two regiments of horse also rejoined his army. He had with difficulty succeeded in persuading the town of Wexford to accept a garrison of regular troops, and believed that place to be secure for some time. But he was doubtful of Duncannon, a very important fort on the east shore of the estuary of the Barrow and Suir.

Therefore, sending Castlehaven towards Wexford with an Ulster regiment, he rode with a small escort to Duncannon. Castlehaven succeeded in ferrying his men across into Wexford; and Ormond, after settling the garrison at Duncannon, returned to Graig. He then placed Lucas Taaffe with his Connaught regiment in Ross, and marched himself to the relief of Wexford. Crossing the Slaney above the town, he arrived opposite it on the evening of the 9th October. The next day he arranged to send in more men to reinforce the garrison and to replace Sinnott, who was considered too young, by Sir E. Butler. The latter crossed into the town on the 11th, but hardly had he got in, than the place was stormed. He endeavoured to escape in a boat, but was shot in the head during the crossing.

Meanwhile Ormond had marched off, intending to recross the Slaney near Enniscorthy. Cromwell got intelligence of this, and sent Jones, who was now his Lieutenant-General, with a party of 1400 horse, in pursuit. When Ormond approached the ford, he found a party of horse from the garrison of Enniscorthy drawn up to dispute his advance. At the same time Jones was coming up rapidly in his rear. He therefore made a long detour through the Wicklow Mountains to Leighlin Bridge, which he reached on the 13th. Jones, unable to overtake him, returned to Cromwell.

The treaty between Ormond and Owen Roe O'Neil was now completed, and the latter was on his march to join the former. He was, however, very ill, having, as it is asserted, been poisoned. (He died on the 6th November). He sent Ferral and Hugh O'Neil in advance with 3000 or 4000 men, but so great were the difficulties of supply that they did not reach Kilkenny till the 25th October. In this respect the most marked difference existed between Cromwell's army and his opponent's. The strict discipline he enforced among his troops, and his supply of ready money, enabled him to keep open market in his camps, and, says Carte, (vol. iii.):

> All the country people flocked to his camp with all kind of provisions; and due payment being made for the same, his army was much better supplied than ever any of the Irish had been.

Thus, whilst the native armies could hardly move or be kept together, he could march swiftly and with ease.

Ormond left his horse to recruit in Carlow, whilst he went himself to Rosbereon to secure Ross, Duncannon, and the line of the Barrow generally. He reinforced Taaffe's garrison in the first-named place to 1500 men on the 18th, and sent Colonel Wogan, the English Royalist, with his own life-guard of 120 English gentlemen into Duncannon.

Cromwell was already before Ross. Having settled the garrison of Wexford, and left Colonel Cooke there as governor, he marched for Ross on the 15th October, and arrived before the place on the 17th. Ormond lay on the opposite bank of the river. Cromwell sent a summons to the governor on arrival, which the latter took in at the gate, but to which he sent no answer.

The next day Ormond, after putting the reinforcements into the place, marched off to meet O'Neil's men at Kilkenny. Neither here nor at any of the other sieges did he attempt to relieve the garrison by the only really effective way of doing so, namely, by attacking the besiegers in their camp. He contented himself with reinforcing the garrison, and sending such supplies as he was able to procure into the place. This he could easily do, because the large Irish towns were all situated either athwart, or on, one bank, of a river. Cromwell's army was not strong enough to invest such places on both banks. It is true that Ormond's forces were not fit to face the English in the field, but his cavalry, if well used, might have caused them great annoyance, stopping their supplies, cutting off foraging parties, and harassing their outposts.

Cromwell lost no time in preparing a battery for the three siege guns he had brought with him. It was ready by the evening of the 18th, and opened fire on the morning of the 19th. Taaffe then sent an answer to the summons, asking for a cessation in order to treat. This Cromwell refused, but offered to allow him to march out with arms, bag and baggage, drums and colours, and promised protection to the inhabitants. These terms sound very liberal, but Cromwell could not well help himself, for, as he remarks:

Indeed he, Taaffe, might have done it without my leave by the advantage of the River.—Cromwell to Lenthall, the 25th October. Carlyle, vol. ii.

The ramparts do not appear to have been very strong, as by this time there was "a great breach made in the wall." (*Cromwelliana*). The stormers were drawn up ready, Colonel Ingoldsby having been selected by lot to lead them. However, the governor, after a vain attempt to be allowed to withdraw his guns, now accepted the offered conditions,, and sent out hostages for his good faith in carrying them out. Another point which Cromwell refused was permission for the inhabitants to celebrate Mass. "Where the Parliament of England have power, that will not be allowed of," (Letter to Lenthall, the 25th October, quoted above), he wrote. The Irish then marched out, and the English took peaceable possession. About 500 of the garrison—Englishmen who had served under Inchiquin in Munster for the Parliament and then for the king—now joined Cromwell's forces.

The headquarters remained at Ross till the 15th November. The men needed rest, and the "country disease" was rife among them. Here it carried off its first distinguished victim, Colonel Horton, whose victory over the Welsh at St. Pagan's had saved the situation the summer before. Cromwell himself, though a native of the fen country, fell sick. But the vigour and success of the campaign had already produced great results outside the immediate theatre of operations. Broghill had gone to Munster, and partly by his persuasion, and more through the encouragement which Cromwell's successes gave them, the adherents of the Parliament, which were numerous in that province, began again to assert themselves.

About the 1st November, Cromwell received the welcome intelligence that the important port of Cork had declared for the Parliament, and had refused to admit Inchiquin, who endeavoured to enter. A Colonel Townsend then attempted to make his way by sea from Cork to Ross, but was stopped by a fort at the mouth of Cork harbour, which was still in the hands of the Irish. "General" Blake, now in command of a squadron in Irish waters, happened to be with Cromwell at the time, and the latter sent him to Cork in the *Nonsuch* frigate to open communications with the inhabitants.

A few days later:

> The *Garland*, one of your third-rate ships, coming happily into Waterford Bay, (within easy reach of Ross), I ordered her and a

great prize, lately taken in the bay, to transport Colonel Phayre to Cork; whitherward he went, having along with him near five-hundred foot, which I spared him out of this poor army, and £1500 in money; giving him such instructions as were proper for the promoting of your interest there.

As they went with an intention for Cork, it pleased God the wind coming cross, they were forced to ride off from Dungarven. Where they met Captain Mildmay returning with the *Nonsuch* Frigate, with Colonel Townsend aboard coming to me; who advertised them that Youghal had also declared for the Parliament of England. Whereupon they steered their course thither; and sent for Colonel Gifford, Colonel Warden, Major Purdeu—These appear all to have been officers in Inchiquin's Munster army—(who with Colonel Townsend have been very active instruments for the return both of Cork and Youghal to their obedience, having some of them ventured their lives twice or thrice to effect it), and the Mayor of Youghal aboard them, who accordingly immediately came and made tender of some propositions to be offered to me.

But my Lord Broghill being on board the ship, assuring them it would be more for their honour and advantage to desire no conditions, they said they would submit. Whereupon my Lord Broghill, Sir William Fenton, and Colonel Phayre, went to the town; and were received—I shall give you my Lord Broghill's own words—"with all the real demonstrations of gladness an overjoyed people were capable of."—Cromwell to Lenthall, dated the 14th November. Carlyle, vol. ii.

The importance of these sea-ports, especially of Cork, was immense. The obstructive fort at the mouth of the harbour appears to have soon been reduced. The English had now also a firm foothold in Munster, and their fleets safe harbours on the southern coast, from whence they could intercept the communications between the Irish and the Continent. Phayre landed his men at Youghal, and having secured that town with the assistance of the English malcontents in Inchiquin's army, many of whom joined him, he marched to Cork. This place was then also made safe. Other smaller towns followed suit—Baltimore, Castlehaven, and Capoquin—so that the English were now again paramount south of the Blackwater.

Cromwell's army was getting very short-handed. The captured

fortresses absorbed many men as garrisons. He writes, on the 14th November:

> It is not fit to tell you how your garrisons will be unsupplied and no field marching army considerable, if but three garrisons more were in our hands.—Cromwell to Lenthall, dated the 14th November. Carlyle, vol. ii.

The "country sickness," malarious, or typhoid fever, was decimating his ranks.

He wrote:

> I scarce know one officer of forty amongst us that hath not been sick. And how many considerable ones we have lost, is no little thought of heart to us."

He was himself very sick at this time. He therefore urged that recruits, money, shoes, and clothing might be sent as soon as possible. He also wrote to Dublin, ordering some convalescents, who had been left there sick, but were now fit to march, to rejoin the army.

These convalescents consisted of 350 horse and 800 foot under Major Meredith, and they were ordered to march by Arklow and Wexford. After they had started Cromwell learnt that Inchiquin, with some 3000 horse and foot, meant to attack them on the way. He immediately dispatched a swift messenger to warn the detachment, and sent fifteen or sixteen troops of horse to their assistance. The messenger reached Meredith at Arklow, and the next day he marched to Glascarrig, a distance of some eighteen miles. Here he found the horse Cromwell had sent to his assistance had not arrived, so he determined to push on to Wexford, seven miles further.

Inchiquin had intended to attack the detachment about Glascarrig, but arrived too late, and found that it had already passed and was some distance on the road to Wexford. Leaving the foot to follow as they could, he pushed on with the horse of Sir Thomas Armstrong, one of those who had deserted Jones in Dublin, and of Colonel Trevor, whom Venables had lately beaten in Ulster—in all some 1500 sabres. A few miles from Wexford he overtook Meredith's force on the sea shore. Cromwell says (letter to Lenthall, dated the 14th November. Carlyle, vol. ii.:

> The foot were miserably wearied, having already marched eighteen miles, and being only lately out of hospital. They immediately drew up in the best order they could upon the sands,

the sea on the one hand, and the rocks on the other, where the enemy made a very furious charge, overbearing our horse with their numbers . . . . . forced them in some disorder back to the foot. Our foot stood, forbearing their firing till the enemy was come almost within pistol shot, and then let fly very full in the faces of them, whereby some of them began to tumble, the rest running off in a very great disorder, and faced not about until they got above musket-shot off. Upon this our horse took encouragement; drawing up again; bringing up some foot to flank them.

One of the English officers. Lieutenant Warren, had got mixed up in the *mêlée* and carried along by the retreating Royalists. He saved himself by putting a token into his hat, similar to that which Inchiquin's troopers wore in theirs, and escaped back to the English. He told them that:

The enemy was in great confusion and disorder, and that if they could attempt another charge he was confident good might be done on them. It pleased God to give our men courage; they advanced; and falling upon the enemy totally routed them; took two colours and divers prisoners, and killed divers upon the place, and in the pursuit. I do not hear that we have two men killed, and had one mortally wounded, and not five that are taken prisoners.—Cromwell to Lenthall, dated the 14th November. Carlyle, vol. ii.

The reinforcement that Cromwell had sent had not arrived when the action was fought, and if the enemy's infantry had been present, "without doubt Inchiquin, Trevor, and the rest of those people who are very good at this work, had swallowed up this party."

This gallant defeat of some of the best troops the Irish party possessed, led by some of their most experienced and enterprising officers, must have greatly discouraged them—proving that even in their favourite warfare of ambush and surprise, they were no match for the steady courage of the Puritan veterans. It must also have shown them how their most secret plans came to Cromwell's ears, owing to his excellent system of gaining intelligence. However he may have obtained them, Cromwell never seems to have lacked good spies, and his wonderful military judgment sifted the wheat from the chaff in their reports with infallible accuracy.

Meanwhile an unsuccessful attempt had been made against Duncannon, whither Cromwell sent a detachment with two guns. A Royalist man-of-war lay under the fort. She had entered the bay with two rich prizes. These had been taken by the Parliamentary fleet, but she herself had got safely under the guns of the fort. The besiegers placed their cannon so that they could rake the frigate, and after a few shots she weighed anchor, ran down to the fleet, and surrendered. But the English made no impression on the fort, which held an excellent garrison and a resolute commandant.

The Earl of Castlehaven got into the fort and examined the besiegers' lines with Wogan. They then concluded that if they only had a few horse they could make a successful sally. Castlehaven returned to Waterford, where he procured boats, and that night he assembled a troop of eighty cavalry on the shore. The men were dismounted, and the horses placed in boats, saddled and accoutred, with pistols in their holsters. The boats then dropped down the Suir with the tide, and, escaping the Parliamentary fleet, got safely into Duncannon.

As soon as the horses were disembarked, Wogan mounted eighty of the life-guard on them, and immediately sallied into the besiegers' lines. The enterprise was most successful. The English, knowing that there were no horse in the fort, could not imagine whence these came, and thought that forces from abroad must have landed on the coast. In the darkness the greatest confusion prevailed, and many English were cut down. That morning, the 5th November, they raised the siege and rejoined Cromwell at Ross.

This successful sally was very cleverly planned. It was evidently much better to mount the men at the fort, who knew the country and could find their way in the dark, than to bring the troopers down from Waterford. Wogan, however, was unusually lucky in having the gentlemen of the life-guard, a body of skilled horsemen, in his garrison.

Whilst Cromwell lay at Ross he had employed the time by constructing a bridge over the Barrow. Ormond, now strongly reinforced by O'Neil's Ulster troops, gave out, to encourage his men, that he sought an engagement with the English; he advanced from Kilkenny, which lies on the River Nore, towards the junction of that river with the Barrow a mile or two above Ross. Cromwell was willing enough to take up his challenge; the difficulty was to get at him, as he held the passages of the river. Cromwell appears to have thought it would be easier to force the passage of the Nore than of the Barrow above their confluence, perhaps because an attack from that side would be less expected.

Having finished the bridge, he sent the greater part of his force across the river on the 15th November, under the command of Jones and Ireton, being himself too ill to accompany them. On the 14th a small part had been sent forward under Colonel Abbot to make an attempt on Inistioge, a small town on the south side of the Nore, where was a ford. On Abbot's party approaching with materials for burning the gates, the garrison escaped across the river, and Abbot took possession of the town. That night it rained heavily, and when Jones arrived the next day, the ford was impassable. He therefore marched further up the river to Thomastown, where there was a bridge.

The town lay on the left bank, and Jones found the bridge broken, the town strongly garrisoned, and Ormond's army on the march to Kilkenny. He had no bridging material and only two guns. To force the passage and repair the bridge would have cost many men, and taken some time. He had only a few days' provisions with him; so, he determined to fall back to Ross. But before doing so, he dispatched Colonel Reynolds with twelve troops of horse and three of dragoons against Carrick, a small town on the Suir, where there was a bridge.

Reynolds, on arriving before the place, divided his forces, and made a feint against one gate, whilst the other party rode quietly in through another. The garrison seems to have been completely taken by surprise, for the place, being strong, was capable of offering a stubborn defence, as Reynolds proved a few days after. It contained a grim old Norman castle, dating back to the first conquest of Ireland in Henry II.'s days. This also surrendered without resistance.

Though the attack on Carrick had not formed part of Cromwell's plan when he sent Jones out from Ross, he fully appreciated its immense importance, and determined at once to take advantage of its lucky capture. Waterford was now the only important port in the south of Ireland not in the hands of the English, for Kinsale and the neighbouring town of Bandon Bridge about this time declared for the Parliament. (Prince Rupert had before this escaped out of Kinsale with the loss of three ships.—Whitelocke).

Moreover, it was the most convenient port, in the south, for England; and without it Ross was of little use as a harbour, because the forts of Duncannon on the east, and Parsage on the west, commanded the Bay of Waterford below the confluence of the Barrow and the Suir. Waterford was situated on the south bank of the Suir, and to attack it Cromwell must cross that river, which was tidal, and unbridged as far as Carrick. The possession of the latter town therefore gave him the opportunity of attacking Waterford and completing his hold on the south coast. Besides this, the communications between Wexford and Ross on the east, and Youghal and Cork on the south, which before could only be maintained by sea, crossed the Suir at Carrick, and were therefore now open to the English by the most direct land route.

Cromwell determined to attack Waterford at once, though the season was very far advanced for siege operations. On the 21st and 22nd November the army marched to Carrick, Cromwell being sufficiently recovered to accompany it himself. Here Colonel Reynolds was left with 150 foot, his own regiment of horse, six troops, and one troop of dragoons. Very little ammunition could be spared him, the stock with the army being very low. On the 23rd Cromwell marched for Waterford.

Ormond understood the importance of Carrick as well as Cromwell, and, crossing the Nore, he determined to recapture it. He appeared before the place the day after the English Army had quitted it, and made preparations for an attack. He appears to have had no cannon with him, and, leaving Inchiquin to assault the place, went himself to Waterford.

Inchiquin summoned the town, and, being refused, his troops rushed to the attack from all sides. They succeeded in burning the gates, only to find that the defenders had raised stone barricades behind them. The English troopers assisted the foot and dragoons in defending the walls. Their scanty supply of ammunition was soon expended, and they then had recourse to stones, which they flung down on the assailants' heads. The latter attempted to breach the wall by a mine, but it was ill laid, and "flew in their own faces." The attack lasted four hours, and then Inchiquin drew off his baffled troops. The fighting had been severe, and at close quarters.

The assailants left forty or fifty dead under the walls, "and have drawn off, as some say, near four hundred more, which they buried up and down the fields, besides what are wounded." (Cromwell to Lenthall, undated; Carlyle, vol. ii.) Such had been the haste and fury with which Inchiquin's men had rushed at the walls, that his own trumpeter, returning from delivering the summons, was killed by them.

Both in the taking and defending of this place Colonel Reynolds, his carriage was such as deserves of much honour.—

Cromwell to Lenthall, undated; Carlyle, vol. ii.

Most of the chief Irish towns, whilst joining themselves to the Royalist and Irish alliance, had refused to accept a garrison of regular troops, considering doubtless that they risked more from the latter's propensity to plunder than from an unexpected attack by the English. Ross and Wexford had only admitted Ormond's men a few days before the siege began, and when it was quite certain it would be undertaken. When Cromwell quitted Ross on the 21st November Waterford had admitted no regular garrison. (Carlyle, vol. v.) He therefore sent a letter that day by his trumpeter to the mayor, pointing out that he would obtain much better terms for the town if he would treat at once for its surrender than if he first received a garrison from Ormond, who would compel the town to offer resistance. (Carte says, vol. iii., that Major Kavanagh, with 200 men, had been sent there about the 11th November).

The mayor replied by demanding a cessation of hostilities for fifteen days, and safe-conducts for four commissioners to treat. Cromwell did not receive this reply till after he had appeared before the town on the 24th, as his trumpeter had been sent back across the river on the 23rd, and was thus looking for him on the north bank of the Suir whilst he was approaching on the south.

He, however, received a copy of the mayor's reply in answer to a second summons on the 24th. He refused to agree to a cessation for fifteen days, but offered to observe one for five, provided the town pledged itself to receive no reinforcements during the cessation, and for twenty-four hours after. The mayor's reply to this proposal has not been kept, but he must have refused to entertain it, as Cromwell proceeded with the investment.

His first step was to send Jones with a regiment of horse and three troops of dragoons to make an attempt on the fort at Passage:

> A very large fort with a castle in the midst of it, having five guns planted in it, and commanding the river better than Duncannon; it not being much above musket-shot over where this fort stands.—Cromwell to Lenthall, undated; Carlyle, vol. ii.

In spite of the inadequacy of a party of horse and dragoons only for siege purposes, the defenders of the fort surrendered it upon quarter for life, without resistance. A battery two miles lower down, built to prevent hostile ships lying in the bay, also surrendered with its guns. The English were now in complete possession of the right bank of the estuary below Waterford.

Duncannon, a large fort on the opposite, or Wexford bank, still held out. But the bay was here sufficiently wide to enable vessels up to 300 tons to pass out of range of that fort by hugging the opposite shore. Provisions and supplies could therefore now be brought up the Barrow to Ross by ship, and one of the principal objects for investing Waterford had been attained. There were no longer any hostile ships in the estuary which could hinder vessels moving up to Ross.

Ormond, after leaving Carrick, had marched down to Waterford, where he persuaded the mayor to admit Lieut.-General Ferrall with 1500 men as the garrison. He was returning next day, the 25th November, to Carrick, which he made no doubt was in Inchiquin's hands, when he met an officer, who informed him that the latter had been beaten off, and had retired to Clonmel.

Ormond had only an escort of fifty men with him, and was therefore compelled to make a long detour to avoid the enemy. At Clonmel he received an appeal from Waterford for succour, and on the evening of the 1st December, marched down thither with a considerable force. (According to Carte's account the 3rd December. The date given by Cromwell for his retreat from Waterford has been followed here).

By the capture of Passage Cromwell had sufficiently secured the mouth of the Barrow, and prevented access to Waterford by sea. The weather was very stormy, and his men were falling fast by disease. He found that the town had accepted a regular garrison, and the siege would therefore prove tedious, and, at that time of the year, might prove disastrous. He therefore determined to abandon the enterprise, and to put his troops into winter quarters in the ports on the south coast.

He marched off on the 2nd December, "it being so terrible a day as ever I marched in all my life."—Cromwell to Lenthall, dated the 19th December; Carlyle, vol. ii. As he was drawing off Ormond appeared on a hill on the opposite side of the river. The latter wished to cross and fall on Cromwell's rear, but the Corporation of Waterford refused him passage through their town. He had therefore to content himself with sending further reinforcements to the garrison, and returned to Clonmel.

Cromwell marched that day to Kilmac-Thomas Castle. As he was marching off the next morning he received the welcome intelligence that Dungarven had surrendered to Lord Broghill, who was near that town with 1200 or 1300 horse. Lieutenant-General Jones, who had suddenly fallen sick, was taken thither, and died in four or five days. Cromwell felt his loss deeply. Originally in the king's service in Ireland, he had espoused the cause of the Parliament, perhaps, as Carte says, because he had been passed over for promotion. He therefore knew the country and the people well, and when, after doing good service in England, the Parliament sent him over as Governor of Dublin, he proved himself the most capable soldier that had ever held that difficult post. Cromwell himself marched to Youghal.

A few days after the English had abandoned the siege of Waterford, Lieutenant-General Ferrall determined to retake the fort at Passage. He therefore arranged with Wogan to send over a party, with two battering guns and a mortar from Duncannon, whilst he would send Major O'Neil with 500 Ulster foot to join with them and attack the fort. Cromwell got wind of the design, and ordered Colonel Zanchy to advance with his regiment of horse, which was quartered on the Blackwater, and a few dragoons, to prevent it. Ormond also marched down the north bank of the Suir to reinforce Ferrall.

Zanchy, who had about 320 men, found the place beset when he reached it. Cutting down a lot of stragglers he met with on the way, he charged the enemy and drove them back.

> The enemy got into a place where they might draw up; and the Ulsters, who bragged much of their pikes, made indeed for the time a good resistance; but the horse pressing sorely upon them, killed near an hundred upon the place; took three-hundred-and-fifty prisoners, amongst whom Major O'Neil and the officers of five-hundred Ulster foot, all but those which were killed; the *renegado* Wogan, with twenty-four of Ormond's *kurisees*, and the Governor of Ballihac.—Cromwell to Lenthall, the 19th December; Carlyle, vol. ii.

Whilst the fight was proceeding Ferrall marched out of Waterford to O'Neil's relief. Ormond, too, was most anxious to go to his assistance with his horse. But again the Corporation refused to allow the troops to pass through the town—the only way by which they could reach the field. Ferrall's men refused to face Zanchy's horsemen, and fell back in disorder. Ormond had about fifty of his personal escort and friends with him in the town. With these he mounted and rode out towards the scene of action. He soon met Ferrall's men retreating in great disorder, hotly pursued by the English. By cleverly availing himself of some broken ground, Ormond deceived Zanchy as to his numbers, and succeeded in covering the retreat of the foot.

Had Ormond marched by the south bank of the Suir from Clonmel, he might have arrived in time to support Ferrall and defeat Zanchy, in which case Passage would probably have fallen and the command of the estuary have been regained. But neither then, nor later, would he risk his horse on the south of the Suir, as he had no ford or bridge lower than Clonmel, the passage through Waterford being refused him. He now sent his troops into winter quarters. Only Clonmel and Kilkenny would admit regular garrisons, so the rest of the troops had to be scattered about in small villages, where they lost what discipline and knowledge of drill they possessed.

In the north Venables and Coote had by this time recovered most of the important towns, and had routed the Scotch-Irish forces under Ardes and Monro at Lisnegarvy in December. Here also both sides went into winter quarters.

Cromwell's headquarters were fixed at Youghal, and during January he visited Cork and the other English garrisons in that neighbourhood. The campaign had been very successful. Waterford alone of all the places attacked had held out, and the failure here, due to bad weather and want of time, had been minimized by the capture and retention of Passage. In every skirmish the English had proved their superiority to the Royalists. The whole of the south, east, and north coast was in the hands of the English. Cromwell had shown that it was possible to keep his forces together and subsist them in a country devastated by plunder and inhabited by a hostile population.

This Ormond, the head of the Irish confederation, had never been able to do. It is true he had great difficulties to overcome. As the head of a confederation composed of many distinct and even hostile parties, it was very difficult to maintain connected action in their armies. Money and supplies must be drawn through the commissioners of the counties assembled at Kilkenny. But the commissioners neglected to perform their duty, and money and supplies were not forthcoming.

Indeed, the wretched inhabitants were in no condition to pay taxes or supply provisions *gratis*. Plundered and illtreated by this army and that, by the Catholics, old Irish, English, Scots, and Tories, the peasants had not the wherewithal to pay contributions, and hid such of the produce of their holdings that escaped the marauders. Cromwell's system solved the problem how to induce the peasants to part willingly with what they could spare; but then he was in possession of ready money, which Ormond was not.

Cromwell Returns to England

Cromwell did not leave his men long in winter quarters. As soon as their health had recovered he again took the field. He had received considerable reinforcements from England, amongst them his son Henry, who commanded a regiment of horse. His cadres were now full, and his men in good health and spirits. The season (end of January) was still unsuitable for siege operations, and, therefore, though the reduction of Waterford was of great importance, he determined first to clear the country inland of the many castles and strongholds which in the counties of Kilkenny, Tipperary, and Limerick still held garrisons of Irish. By doing so, he would enlarge the territories from which he could draw supplies, and improve his communications with Dublin, which now lay along the east coast.

The rivers Suir and Blackwater, with the mountains which rise on their southern banks, form, as it were, a double moat and rampart, cutting off the harbours of Youghal, Cork, and Kinsale, on the south coast, from the rest of Ireland. The Blackwater rising near Killarney, and flowing due east, cuts all the communications between the harbours and the interior of the island.

But the course of the Suir, from its sources near Templemore to Cahir, is north and south, and it is not until it reaches the latter town that its bed forms the ditch to the rampart. Its tributary, the Aherlow, backed by the Galtee Mountains, continues the line westward from Cahir for some distance, and further on other streams and the mountains of North Kerry prolong the defences to the sea. Beginning from the west, the first gap or gate in the ramparts occurs at Buttevant, the road through which crosses the Blackwater at Mallow, and thence over a pass in the Nagles Mountains to Cork. This is the route now followed by the railway.

The next gate is at Mitchelstown, whence the roads inland cross the Suir at Cahir and Ardfinnan, and those to the coast cross the Blackwater at Mallow and Fermoy. Mallow is, therefore, a point of , great strategical importance, directly blocking the principal roads through the Buttevant and Mitchelstown gates, and threatening the flank of the subsidiary one by Fermoy. From Cappoquin there is a road leading past the Knockmealdown Mountains to Newcastle and Ardfinnan, and this road was of considerable importance to Cromwell, because supplies could be brought as far as Cappoquin by water from Youghal.

There does not, however, appear to have been any bridge over the

Suir at Newcastle in his days. The third and last gate is at Carrick, the road from Cork, Youghal, and Dungarven sweeping round the eastern foot of the Comeragh Mountain. Midway between the second and third gates, the Suir was bridged at Clonmel, but no pass leads directly hence across the mountains. A good road, however, leads from this place along the south bank of the river to Newcastle, and there joins the road to Cappoquin. Below Carrick the Suir was not bridged.

Away beyond the Suir, forming the glacis, as it were, of the fortress, lie the fertile lands of South Tipperary, broken, by several ranges of rugged hills. The walled towns of Callan, Fethard, Cashel, and many smaller castles formed the outworks or detached forts of the fortress.

The situation in January, 1649, was briefly this. Cromwell held the harbours on the south coast, and the line of the Blackwater. He held the bridge over the Suir at Carrick, but no other, and he had command of the mouth of that river through the fort at Passage. Beyond the Suir he held Ross with the bridge over the Barrow, over which his land communications with Leinster ran.

Ormond had nowhere an army which could oppose the English in the field. The few troops which still hung together at the end of the previous campaign had been dispersed for the sake of subsistence all over the country, and could not be got together again. The mere rumour that Cromwell would take command in Ireland had made Prince Charles waver in his determination to go thither, and the English successes had decided him finally to abandon that project.

He now turned to the Scots, who, throughout the summer of 1649, had been endeavouring to persuade him to take the Covenant and join them as the nominal head of their nation. Real power they never intended to grant him; but should he comply with their conditions, they were quite ready to raise an army to invade England, and compel that country also to accept Charles as king, provided he would undertake to establish the Presbyterian religion. The negotiations had lasted long. Charles detested the terms offered, but, when all other schemes failed, he had to accept them in the end.

By January it was well known in England that the Scots were again threatening an invasion, which the Parliament was by no means inclined to await. It was wisely considered bad policy for the English, who had still a powerful army afoot, to wait until the Scots had time to raise and organise fresh forces and invade England at their pleasure, thus making that kingdom once more the scene of a bloody war. If the Scots were determined again to interfere in the affairs of England, the inconveniences arriving from the presence of hostile armies might fairly, on this occasion, be thrown on Scotland.

When, however, Fairfax was sounded as to his views, it was found that he was unalterably opposed to an invasion of Scotland. Since the execution of the king, he had, under his wife's influence, inclined more and more to the Presbyterian party, who were in politics, as in religion, sympathizers with the Scots.

Baffled by Fairfax's obstinacy, the Independents again had recourse to Cromwell; and on the 8th January the Commons voted that:

> The Lord Lieutenant of Ireland be desired to come over, and give his attendance here in Parliament.—*Commons' Journals,* vi.

The letter which the speaker accordingly wrote to Cromwell on the 8th January did not reach him till the 22nd March, and though he knew of the vote from private letters and newspapers, he did not consider himself justified in moving in the matter until he received the official communication. (See his letter to Lenthall, dated the 2nd April; Carlyle, vol. ii.) But the rumour of his speedy removal to England may have induced him to accelerate matters in Ireland. On Ormond it had the opposite effect. Knowing of the prince's intention to join the Scots, he foresaw that their quarrel with the English Parliament would create a diversion in his favour.

When he heard that Cromwell would be recalled to take command against them, he considered that it would be best to desist from action in the south as much as possible, trusting that the resistance of the garrison towns and castles would delay Cromwell so long that he would have to leave the country before completing its subjugation. Meanwhile, with such forces as he could raise, he would attack the English in Ulster, where the Scots were numerous and inclined to assist him.

Cromwell, however, gave Ormond no time to mature his plans. He determined to move in two columns. One under Reynolds should cross the Suir at Carrick, advance into Kilkenny, clear the south of that county of the enemy's garrisons, and secure the passage over the Nore and the Barrow leading towards Dublin. The other column, under his personal leading, should first clear the country lying between the Blackwater, the Suir, and the mountains running westward to the sea, and then, crossing the Suir, should advance to join Reynolds, sweeping the Irish garrisons out of South Tipperary. Ireton with a reserve was to support the other two, and at first to follow Reynolds' column.

This latter consisted of fifteen or sixteen troops of horse and dragoons and 2000 foot. Cromwell's own force, intended for rapid movement, was made up of twelve troops of horse, three of dragoons, and 200 or 300 foot. (Cromwell to Lenthall, the 15th February; Carlyle, vol. ii.) Ireton's numbers are not given.

Cromwell left Youghal on the 29th January and marched to Mallow, apparently following the south bank of the Blackwater. He reached this important point on the 31st. Here he left Lord Broghill with a force of 600 or 700 horse and 500 foot, which had accompanied the column, to protect the approaches to Cork through the gap described above as the westernmost or first gate in the rampart. Inchiquin was known to be about Limerick and North Kerry, and might make an attempt down this line.

Cromwell himself turned eastward, marched through the second gate, and took Clogheen and one or two other castles which cannot now be identified. He was now fully in possession of all the country south of the first line of the rampart. Broghill strengthened his position greatly by advancing through the first, or Buttevant, gate, and taking Old Castletown and another castle commanding the approach to it in the county of Limerick. The whole of this county now submitted right up to the walls of Limerick itself, and agreed to pay contribution in lieu of being plundered.

The bridges over the Suir in front of Cromwell at Cahir, Ardfinnan, and Clonmel, were blocked by castles in the hands of the enemy. He, however, succeeded in crossing the river by a ford or by boats "with very much difficulty," marched to Fethard on a very tempestuous day, and reached that town at night.

> After a long march we knew not well how to dispose of ourselves; but finding an old Abbey in the suburbs, and some cabins and poor-houses—we got into them, and had opportunity to send a summons. They shot at my trumpet, and would not listen to him for an hour's space; but having some officers in our party whom they knew, I sent them to let them know I was there with a good part of the army. We shot not a shot at them; but they were very angry, and fired very earnestly upon us; telling us it was not a time of night to send a summons.
> But yet, in the end, the governor was willing to send out two commissioners,—I think rather to see whether there was a force sufficient to force him, than to any other end. After al-

most a whole night spent in treaty, the town was delivered to me the next morning upon terms which we usually call honourable; which I was the willinger to give because I had little above 200 foot, and neither ladders nor guns, nor anything else to force them. That night, there being about seventeen companies of the Ulster foot in Cashel, above five miles from thence, (real distance is 9 miles), they quit it in some disorder; and the Sovereign and the Aldermen sent to me a petition, desiring that I would protect them, which I have also made a quarter.—Cromwell to Lenthall, dated the 15th February; Carlyle, vol. ii.

Reynolds, after crossing the Suir at Carrick, marched into Kilkenny, as Cromwell had intended. After defeating a party of the enemy's horse, he advanced to Callan, where the enemy held three castles. Two of these were stormed and their garrisons put to the sword, the third surrendered on articles. Cromwell joined Reynolds here. Ormond was in Kilkenny, expecting an attack. One small success had lately befallen his troops. Some of the gentry of Wexford had succeeded in surprising the castle of Enniscorthy. It is said they invited the garrison to a feast, made them drunk, and then slaughtered them all. Ormond had discovered a plot by which a Colonel Tickle, one of the senior officers in Kilkenny, had agreed to surrender the place to Cromwell. Tickle was executed, and the English did not at that moment attack the town, but Cromwell sent Reynolds to reduce Knocktofer Castle, and himself fell back to Fethard.

Meanwhile the inconvenience of having no bridge over the Suir above Carrick was much felt, and Ireton was send to reduce Ardfinnan Castle, as the bridge at that place was on the most direct road to Mallow, and also the nearest to the pass through the mountains to Cappoquin. Ireton took the place with little loss. This was during the first week in February. On the 9th Cromwell directed Colonel Phayre, who had been left in Cork, to send up what reinforcements he could spare, as the garrisons of the captured towns were absorbing his men.

> If you can send two companies more of your regiment to Mallow do it. If not, one at the least; that so my Lord Broghill may spare us two or three of Colonel Ewers's, to meet him with the rest of his regiment at Fermoy.—Cromwell to Phayre; Carlyle, App. No. 18).

On the 24th February Cromwell appeared before Cahir, which surrendered on summons. About the same time the Castles of Golden, commanding a bridge across the Suir higher up leading towards Limerick, was also taken, as were the castles of Dundrum, beyond Golden, and Kiltinane, near Fethard. All the strongholds in South Tipperary and the bridges over the Suir were now in Cromwell's hands, except Clonmel, which, as it commanded no particular pass over the mountains, might for the moment be neglected. The county of Tipperary submitted to a contribution of £1500 a month, and this where Ormond could raise nothing. Indeed, Cromwell found supplies plentiful in Tipperary, "having plenty both of horse meat and man's meat for a time."—Cromwell to Lenthall, the 16th February; Carlyle, vol. ii. The letter is dated from Castletown, near Mallow, whither he had gone on some business, probably about reinforcements.

His views on the eventual economy of keeping an army well supplied with money are well expressed in this letter:—

> Sir,—I desire the charge of England as to this war may be abated as much as may be, and as we know you do desire, out of your care to the Commonwealth. But if you expect your work to be done, if the marching army be not constantly paid, and the course taken that hath been humbly represented—indeed, it will not be for the thrift of England, as far as England is concerned in the speedy reduction of Ireland. The money we raise upon the counties maintains the garrison forces; and hardly that. If the active force be not maintained and all contingencies defrayed, how can you expect but to have a lingering business of it? Surely we desire not to spend a shilling of your Treasury, wherein our conscience do not prompt us.

About this time, the 14th March, Lord Broghill, who had been joined by Henry Cromwell, fell upon a party of Inchiquin's horse near Limerick and defeated them, taking 160 men, among them several senior officers, and 300 horses. As was usual, those officers who had previously deserted the Parliament's service were shot. There was now no longer any fear of interruption from Inchiquin in the west, and Cromwell determined to clear the county of Kilkenny and the bridges across the Nore and the Barrow. For this purpose Colonel Hewson, who was quartered at Dublin, was ordered to advance from Ballysonan, a castle he had lately reduced, towards Leighlin Bridge. Colonel Shilbourne was ordered to support him with a party of horse from Wexford.

Ormond was at this time vainly endeavouring to organise an army out of Monro's Scots, O'Neil's Ulster men, and Clanrickard's Connaught forces, to take the field against Coote and Venables in the north. Castlehaven was, however, in North Tipperary with his own forces, and to prevent his holding the passes over the Barrow against Hewson and Shilbourne, Cromwell directed Colonel Reynolds, with about 800 horse and dragoons and 500 foot, to attack him in rear. Reynolds crossed the Nore and moved up towards Leighlin Bridge, where he offered battle to Castlehaven, which the latter did not accept.

Hearing no tidings of Hewson, Reynolds fell back to Thomastown, out of which he drove the garrison, who fled to a castle near at hand, where they surrendered in a day or two. Thomastown was of importance, as there was a bridge here over the Nore, and here Cromwell and Ireton joined the force. They waited another day or two to obtain tidings of Hewson, and soon heard that he had reached Leighlin Bridge, which was commanded by a strong castle. Castlehaven had fallen back to Castlecomer, so Cromwell sent Hewson orders to attack the fort, and if successful, to march southward to join him.

Leighlin Castle fell, and the two forces joined at Gowran, where was a strong fort commanding the town held by Colonel Hammond, "a Kentish man," with Ormond's own regiment. Cromwell sent him a summons, and offered him terms, which he refused. Thereupon a battery was erected and a breach made, when Hammond demanded a treaty. This Cromwell refused, but told him that if he surrendered, the soldiers should have quarter, but the officers must surrender at mercy. These terms Hammond accepted.

All the officers but one were shot, apparently a needless act of cruelty. Some of them were English, and Cromwell appears throughout this campaign to have treated such English as took service against the Parliament in Ireland with a severity he never used towards any class of prisoners elsewhere. Having cleared the communications with Dublin, Cromwell determined to attack Kilkenny, until lately the headquarters of the Irish Confederacy. The commissioners had fled at his approach. The place was strong, well-fortified, with a good garrison, under Sir Walter Butler, much reduced in numbers by the plague. Cromwell arrived before the place on the 22nd March, and that evening sent a summons to the governor, mayor and aldermen. The next morning Sir W. Butler sent a laconic refusal. Thereupon the English commenced a battery for the three siege guns they had with them.

The town of Kilkenny lies, for the most part, on the south or right bank of the Nore, but there was a suburb on the other bank which was also fortified, and formed a bridge-head. At the north-western end of the principal town, and outside the walls, lay the Irish town, which was not fortified. The point selected for the breach was near the south-east angle, at the end of Ormond's stables, between the castle gate and the rampart. (Carte, vol. iii.) By Monday the 25th the battery was ready, and between five and six o'clock the guns opened fire, for, though negotiations had continued, the town did not seem inclined to come to terms. During the morning arrangements for the assault were made, the storming parties told off for the breach, and Colonel Ewer, with 1000 foot, was directed to attack the Irish town.

At twelve o'clock the signal for the attack was given; Ewer captured the Irish town without much difficulty or loss. The stormers "fell upon the breach; which indeed was not performed with usual courage or success; for they were beaten off with the loss of one captain, and about twenty or thirty men killed and wounded"—which certainly does not point to very severe fighting. The breach was not so practicable as it seemed.

> The enemy had made two retrenchments or counterworks, which they had strongly pallisadoed, and both of them did so command our breach, that indeed it was a mercy to us we did not farther contend for entrance there; it being probable that if we had it would have cost us very dear.—Cromwell to Lenthall; Carlyle, vol. ii.

That evening Cromwell sent a party of eight companies of foot to assault the suburb on the left bank of the Nore. This was captured with the loss of only four or five men. (Cromwell does not say whether scaling ladders were used, or how the ramparts were surmounted). The officer in command attempted to cross the bridge, fire the gate at the further end, and enter the town itself; but he was beaten back with the loss of forty or fifty men. Cromwell then set about constructing a fresh battery, but Butler considering that further resistance was useless after the loss of the Irish town and the suburb, agreed to surrender the place on terms. Accordingly, on the 28th March, the garrison marched out with the honours of war, but laid down their arms two miles out of the city. They were then permitted to rejoin their friends, being allowed 100 muskets and 100 pikes to defend themselves against the "Tories." Cromwell himself complimented the garrison on its gallant defence.

The town paid a ransom of £2000, and escaped plunder. A party of Royalists, attempting to enter Kilkenny during the siege, got into a neighbouring stronghold called Cantwell Castle, whence they asked Cromwell's permission to go beyond the sea to take service with a foreign State. This he allowed, and even furnished them with money to enable them to travel. Afterwards this method of dealing with Irish officers and soldiers was extensively employed by the English.

Cromwell now marched to Carrick. He had already sent Colonel Abbot to reduce Ennisnag, "where were gotten a company of rogues which revolted from Colonel Jones," and Adjutant-General Sadler to attack some castles forming outposts to Clonmel and Waterford, which places he now intended to attempt. Ennisnag surrendered, the men being given quarter, and "their two officers hanged for revolting." Sadler stormed and burnt a castle called "Pulkerry," now unrecognisable, (perhaps Kincor Castle, on the Suir, which tradition says was destroyed by Cromwell), near Clonmel; the whole garrison perishing by the sword, or in the flames, having refused to surrender. Then, marching down the river, two or three castles near Waterford were surrendered to him, their garrisons marching off without arms. The most important of these was the grim old stronghold of Granny commanding a bend of the Suir.

From Carrick Cromwell wrote his report to Lenthall on the operations in Kilkenny. Again, he had to urge that more money be sent.

> Sir, I may not be wanting to tell you . . . that, I think in my conscience if moneys be not supplied, we shall not be able to carry on your work. . . . Sir, our horse have not had one month's pay of five. We strain what we can that the foot may be paid, or else they would starve. Those towns that are to be reduced, especially one or two of them, if we should proceed by the rules of other states, would cost you more money than this army hath had since we came over. I hope, through the blessing of God, they will come cheaper to you.—Cromwell to Lenthall, the 2nd April; Carlyle, vol. ii.)

Ready money was the basis of his system of supply. Except in garrisons, and then only on emergencies, the soldiers were not supplied with food or provisions by the commissariat. They bought their own in open market, for which money was necessary. If there was none forthcoming, the inhabitants were forced to supply them with food, generally getting some sort of receipt for it, on which they might afterwards recover the value from Parliament.

Cromwell had by this time received the Speaker's letter, formally inviting him to attend Parliament. But since that letter was written under the impression that it would find him in winter quarters, instead of in the field, and since a second and subsequent letter, dated the 26th February, making no mention of what he was required to do in the matter, had also reached him, he asked for further instructions.

Meanwhile, he determined to prosecute the campaign vigorously.

Recruits were still wanted. In his above quoted letter Cromwell says: "I do not know of much above two-thousand of your five-thousand recruits come to us." Parliament had apparently informed him that the latter number had been sent. Meanwhile castles and strongholds were falling continually into the hands of his troops, and many of these required garrisons, Carlow and Enniscorthy for example. He therefore appears to have remained at Carrick until the end of the month of April, resting his men, and awaiting reinforcements, but at the same time he. despatched troops to invest Clonmel, and cut off its supplies.

During this month George Monro, disgusted at the appointment of the Catholic Bishop of Clogher to command the confederated forces in the north, surrendered Enniskilling to Coote, and quitted the country.

On Saturday, the 27th April, Cromwell himself appeared before Clonmel with a siege train. On the evening before the *President*, a Parliamentary frigate, had left Milford, bearing letters to him, again requesting his return to England, and with orders to await his pleasure. These letters reached him whilst before Clonmel. Perhaps they induced him to hasten the siege unduly. The place was held by 2000 Ulster men, under Hugh O'Neil, who had given evidence of their determination to make a vigorous defence. It was built on the north bank of the Suir, and covered a bridge. Roads ran on either bank to Waterford. It was the largest town in Tipperary, and a place of considerable trade.

Ormond fully understood its importance, and had made considerable efforts to raise a force for its relief. At last Lord Roche and the Bishop of Ross succeeded in collecting some forces in Kerry, and advancing as far as Macroom in the County of Cork. Lord Broghill, however, met them on the 10th May, (Carte, vol. iii. the date is doubtful, it was probably earlier), and drove them back, capturing the Bishop of Ross, whom he hanged the next day, under the walls of a castle held by the Irish. Roche attempted to rally his men at Killarney, but they were easily dispersed.

Cromwell got his guns in position against Clonmel on the 30th April, (*Perf. Diur.* the 6th to 13th May, *Cromwelliana*), but there seems to have been unusual delay in effecting a practicable breach. The place selected was the north-east angle of the rampart near St. Mary's Church. It was not till the 9th May that the order for the assault was given. The stormers poured over the breach, but after hard fighting were driven out. Again they rushed forward, and again the breach was carried. But the assailants were by no means inside the works yet.

> The enemy had made themselves exceeding strong, by double works, and traverse which were worse to enter, than the breach; when we came up to it, they had cross-works, and were strongly flanked from the houses within their works.

These retrenchments the assailants could by no means pass, and when night came they were still untaken.

But the Ulster men had had enough of it, and during the night they slipped out over the bridge, and made for Waterford. The mayor, deserted by the garrison, put on a bold front, and sent out to Cromwell offering to treat. The latter, believing he would still lose many men if the fighting were continued, consented, and gave him good terms. It was not till the town was entered that the true state of affairs was discovered. A party was then sent in pursuit of the Ulster men, but only some 200 stragglers were overtaken and cut down.

The English losses had been severe. A colonel, two captains, and some inferior officers had been killed, two lieutenant-colonels, and some other officers wounded. What the losses were among the soldiers is not stated, but they must have been considerable. (In St. Mary's Churchyard stands an old headstone, on which is roughly cut *NL et comes*. Tradition says that fifty of Cromwell's soldiers are buried beneath).

Whitelocke says:

> They found in Clonmel the stoutest enemy this army had ever met in Ireland; and that there was never seen so hot a storm, of so long continuance, and so gallantly defended, either in England or Ireland.

After the capture of Clonmel Cromwell handed over the command in Ireland to Ireton, and sailed for England. He landed at Bristol on May 28th, and proceeded straight to London, where he arrived on the 31st. He was given a public entry, with considerable state, Fairfax himself, though his superior officer, coming out with many other officers, and members of Parliament, to meet him on Hounslow Heath. Not only were his services in Ireland such as merited the gratitude of his party, but they also looked to him to defend the nation against a renewed attack of the Scots.

Never had an English Army done so much for the pacification of Ireland in the same time, as that under Cromwell had done during the nine months he remained in the country. The task before him on landing required an administrator, as well as a soldier, and the Parliament had happily made him both civil and military chief. Side by side with the defeat of his foes went on the re-establishment of order. Often the military operations were directed with a political, rather than a strategical object, though those for the most part coalesced, as indeed they usually do.

Cromwell fully understood that in an island with the physical properties, and in the stage of civilization, of Ireland of his day, the rivers form the principal lines of communication, and the ports contain the principal wealth of the country. Therefore he first seized the ports, and when his hold on the coast was secure he proceeded to master the basins of the rivers—the Blackwater, the Suir, the Barrow, and the Nore. He left before he had time to take in the basin of the Shannon with the port of Limerick at its mouth, which would have completed his command of the country.

Even his possession of the Suir was not complete since Waterford still held out. In the north his lieutenants, following the same principles of action, had already seized all the ports, and were pushing inland along the rivers. And before he left the work was so far advanced that his successors in command were able to complete it. In June Coote broke in pieces what remained of the northern confederacy, under the Bishop of Clogher, near Letterkenny. In August Waterford surrendered to Ireton, after making a good defence. The valley of the Shannon was not dealt with till the following year, 1651. Limerick surrendered in October, and the subjugation of Ireland was then practically complete.

Cromwell Crosses the Border

Cromwell took his seat in the Commons on the 4th June, and received the thanks of the House for his services in Ireland. The government were determined to invade Scotland. The Juncto of the Council of State resolved, says Whitelocke, on the 25th June,—

That having a formed army well provided and experienced they would march with it forthwith into Scotland, to prevent the Scots marching into England, and the miseries accompanying their forces to our countrymen.

They had not yet despaired of inducing Fairfax to accept the command. On the same day Cromwell, Lambert, Harrison, St. John, and Whitelocke were ordered to meet Fairfax in Whitehall, and endeavour to persuade him to reconsider his decision. At this meeting, according to the evidence of Ludlow, who was by no means a favourable witness, Cromwell did all he could to induce Fairfax to accept the command of the army in Scotland. But in vain; he remained obstinate in his refusal, though he professed himself willing to command should the Scots first invade England.

★★★★★★

Fairfax declared that it was contrary to the covenant to take up arms against the Scots, unless they first did so, and therefore he could not, in conscience, accept the command. He acknowledged that it seemed very probable that they would invade England, and that it would be a great military advantage to forestall them.

★★★★★★

The next day, the 26th June, he sent in the resignation of his commission as commander-in-chief, and Cromwell was at once appointed in his place.

Cromwell lost no time in making his preparations in London. The army was collecting about York, and thither he went on the 29th June. Lambert was appointed major-general, Whalley commissary-general, and Fleetwood lieutenant-general. As Cromwell left London news was received that Prince Charles had landed on the 24th in the Cromarty Firth. (According to Sir E. Walker, at Barmouth, on the River Spey; *Hist. Discourses*). It was with great reluctance that he had decided to put himself in the hands of the Scotch Presbyterians.

Montrose had been sent before to attempt once more to raise the Highlands to the old Royalist war cry; with the hope that he might muster such a force amongst the Highland clansmen and cavaliers of the Lowlands, as would render Charles independent of Argyle and the Kirk party. But in vain; Cromwell had dealt the Scotch cavaliers a blow at Preston, from which it would take them long to recover. Montrose had landed in the Orkneys in March, and then crossed over to the mainland. He was soon met by David Leslie, who completely routed his forces at Carbisdale.

★★★★★★

Leslie did not command in person in this action, which, as far as numbers are concerned, was a mere skirmish. The Scotch Parliamentary forces consisted of only a few troops of horse under Colonel Strachan.

★★★★★★

Montrose escaped from the field, but was taken a few days later. Little mercy could he expect from the Presbyterians, though they, like him, professed to be ready to support Charles. He was hanged at Edinburgh on the 21st May.

Charles had now no alternative but to accept the conditions offered by Argyle's party. Before he landed he was forced to take the covenant, and most of his friends and advisers were removed from him. He was preached at by the ministers, and his father's misdeeds held up before him as a warning. In short, he was treated much more as a prisoner than a king.

The Scots were rapidly increasing their forces. In spite of Hamilton's defeat at Preston, they were still confident in the superiority of their army over the English, remembering the king's futile attempt to oppose them in 1640. David Leslie was appointed commander-in-chief. Trained under Gustavus Adolphus, he was the best soldier of the old school which the civil wars had produced, prudent, cautious and skilful in handling his men. Cromwell and he knew each other well, and had fought side by side at Marston Moor, of which the Presbyterians were wont to assert they had saved the former from destruction. Now they were to meet as enemies under conditions which promised a fair test of strength and skill. The old style and the new were to fight out the battle on a fair field.

The armies which the two generals were to lead were also good representatives of the older and the newer methods of war. Under Cromwell a regular standing army, which, since he had first organised it in 1645, had been kept on foot, in peace as well as in war. The regiments had been kept together; officers and men mutually knew and trusted each other. The training and exercising of the men had never been allowed to slacken. The promotion of the officers and non-commissioned officers had been carried out systematically. Everyone knew his place, his duties, and his prospects. On the other hand, Leslie commanded an army got together for this particular war.

There were doubtless plenty of good officers glad of the chance of employment, and plenty of good material from which to recruit the ranks. Many of the soldiers had served before, and knew their discipline and the use of their arms. But for all that, the regiments were newly raised. Officers and men were not accustomed to each other, did not form part of a unity which had existed for some years, with its own history, habits, and prejudices. In these newly-raised regiments one man felt as good as another, and shaped his ideas according to his own individual experience. Though all might obey the orders of their superiors, theirs would be the obedience of a number of separate entities, not of a corporate whole.

In fact, there would be no *esprit de corps*. In Cromwell's older regiments each recruit, as he joined its ranks, would adopt the ideas, tone, and customs of the regiment, and the obedience of such a body is that of a firmly welded mass. The determination of the ruling party in the State not to admit any Cavalier or "Engager", (men who had served under Hamilton in 1648), into the army, either as officer or soldier, also debarred the Scots from making use of much of the best material in the country.

In fact, Sir Edward Walker, who was himself refused permission to serve, expresses much contempt for Leslie's army, especially for the officers; the authorities, he says:

> Placing, for the most part, in command, ministers' sons, clerks, and such other sanctified creatures, who hardly ever saw or heard of any sword but that of the Spirit.

Leslie was too capable a general to trust such troops in the field against Cromwell's veterans. He decided to occupy and entrench some strong position, covering the capital, and as much territory as possible, and there to await the English attack. If attacked in such a position the odds would be greatly in his favour. If the English refused to attack he would wait until difficulties of supply and the approach of winter forced them to retire. Then, when his own men were fresh and well fed, and his opponents harassed, wearied, and demoralised from sickness and the futility of their attempts, he would sally out and attack them in their retreat. It was a strategy he had been accustomed to on the Continent, and suited well the cautious, methodical practice of the old school of officers.

Such a position was to be found in the vicinity of the capital itself. Immediately to the east of Edinburgh rises the high, steep hill called Arthur's Seat, a northern spur of which, running down to Leith, formed the watershed between the Leith Water and the Braid Barn. The former stream, rising to the west of the Pentland Hills, runs in a fairly direct north-easterly direction. The latter, rising in the northern slopes of the Pentlands, close to the bed of the Leith Water, south-west of Edinburgh, runs first nearly east to Nidery, and then turns north-east to Musselburgh.

It thus encloses the capital on two sides. West of Edinburgh some hills follow the shore of Firth, broken by gaps formed by the Leith, Cramon, and other streams, and south of these hills lies a low and marshy tract, through which tributaries of the streams run eastward or westward. Therefore, by occupying the hills about Edinburgh, Leslie would have the advantage of lying on high ground, whilst his adversary, whether he attacked from east or south, must advance across low, marshy land.

The question of supply, too, in such a position would be exceedingly simple, as Leslie would have all the resources of the capital, its port of Leith, of Lothian, and Fife, at his immediate disposal.

As has been explained in Chapter 19, a Scotch Army invading England, or an English Army invading Scotland, was obliged in the seventeenth century to advance either by Berwick or Carlisle.

The Cheviot Hills, which form the border, run from their south-western, or Carlisle end, in a north-easterly direction towards Berwick. Thus, whilst Berwick is forty-five miles from Edinburgh in a straight line, Carlisle is seventy. Nearly half way between Edinburgh and Carlisle, and half way between the sea to the east, and the sea to the west, the Tweed and the Clyde rise in the same hills. The former runs nearly east to Berwick, the latter north-west to Glasgow and the Firth of Clyde. The country in the angle between the Tweed and the Cheviots was, for the most part, rough, wild, and mountainous, inhabited by a lawless race, who had not yet forgotten the delights of moss-trooping in the days before the crowns of England and Scotland were united on one head.

Therefore Cromwell, or any other English general, invading Scotland, and aiming at Edinburgh, would choose the Berwick route as the shortest, and as avoiding the rough, wild country south of the Tweed. North of the Tweed and Clyde again, a range of rough, high moorlands, (not always moorlands now), extends from near Glasgow to Dunbar, just south of which place they drop abruptly into the North Sea. These hills, which are called by different names in parts—

the Pentland, Moorfield, and Lammermuir Hills, form the southern watershed to the Firth of Forth.

Thus, early in July, 1650, Cromwell was collecting an army about Newcastle to invade Scotland, whilst Leslie was preparing to defend the capital. It was not his intention to dispute the English advance by force, but to render their march as difficult as possible through want of supply. With this view the inhabitants of the south-eastern counties were ordered to carry off their corn and forage, and to drive their sheep and cattle to Edinburgh. Cavalry parties were sent through the country to enforce these orders. Most of the able-bodied men were taken for the new levies. Stories of the awful cruelties practised by the English soldiers were industriously spread about in order to induce all the inhabitants to leave, and to render the country as much a desert as possible.

The point of assembly for the English Army being in Northumberland, Leslie could make sure they would advance by the Berwick road. He therefore fortified the line between Edinburgh and Leith, as the attack must almost certainly come from the east.

Cromwell, on his part, was anxious to push on. Not only was it his nature always to act with energy and vigour, but in this case there were many other reasons which rendered haste advisable. Every day added to the numbers of the Scotch army, every day improved their new levies in drill and discipline. Sir E. Walker says that when the king landed, the Scots had but 2500 horse, and 3000 foot, (*Hist. Discourses*), but that their forces increased very rapidly. He says:

> As the Scots increased in numbers, so they did in courage and discipline.

Cromwell pushed his men up towards the border as quickly as he could. Bright's regiment, which was the leading foot regiment, quartered at "Sir Wm. Fenwick's, four miles beyond Morpeth," (Hodgson's *Memoirs*), on the 11th July. The rest were echeloned back to Newcastle and Durham. Some of the horse had pushed on to the border. Cromwell himself was at Newcastle. He now found that Leslie's orders relative to supplies had been so well carried out that it would be impossible to subsist his men in the ordinary way on the country.

It was therefore necessary to halt to bake biscuit to take with the army. Further supplies would have to be obtained by sea, and the strategy adopted in Ireland of seizing some seaport, and there forming an advanced base, would have again to be practised. Between Berwick and Leith there was only one port where stores could be landed in all weathers, and that was the small and somewhat inconvenient port of Dunbar. Dunbar must therefore be Cromwell's first objective.

Whilst the army was thus halted in order that the necessary arrangements for supply might be made. Colonel Bright threw up his commission, because, it is said, the general refused to give him a fortnight's leave. Cromwell was anxious that a colonel should be appointed to this regiment, and it appears to have been the custom to allow the soldiers a voice in the matter. George Monk was one of the officers who had returned from Ireland with him and had accompanied him to the north. He therefore sent some of the senior officers to the regiment to propose Monk as their colonel.

Now it so happened that this regiment had been with Fairfax when he had defeated the Royalist troops, brought over from Ireland, at Nantwich, in January, 1644. Monk had there been taken prisoner. When he was proposed as their colonel, some of the soldiers cried out:

> Colonel Monk! what! to betray us? We took him not long since, at Nantwich, prisoner; we'll have none of him.—Hodgson's *Memoirs*.

The next day the officers proposed Lambert as colonel.

> At which they all threw up their hats, and shouted a Lambert! a Lambert!

Lambert had already a horse regiment, but it was customary to allow the senior officers of the army a regiment of each arm. Monk was thus still without a command, but about this time a new regiment was being raised on the border, and this was given to him. It has never since been disbanded; for at the Restoration, Monk, who had been the principal instrument in bringing Charles back, was allowed to retain his own regiment as part of the guards then raised for the defence of the king's person. It has ever since been famous as the Coldstream Guards, so named from the village where it was first mustered.

About the 16th July the army resumed its advance, and Cromwell was at Alnwick the next day. By the 21st the troops were concentrated in the neighbourhood of Berwick, and on the 22nd they crossed the border and encamped at Mordlington. As in Ireland, tents were carried with the army. It mustered 5415 horse, 10,249 foot, and 690 train: total, 16,354 men. (Cromwell to Lenthall, Carlyle, vol, iii.) As they crossed the border Cromwell harangued the men, pointing out the difficulties to be encountered, and exhorting them to be doubly, nay trebly, vigilant.

The army halted at Mordlington on the 23rd and 24th, whilst the arrangements for the march were completed. On the 25th it marched to Cockburn's Path, a narrow rugged pass between the Lammermuir Hills and the sea, "where ten men to hinder are better than forty to make their way." (Newspapers in *Cromwelliana*). It was, however, unoccupied by the Scots, and the army quartered that night at a village of the same name. The tents do not appear to have been up, probably they were sent on to Dunbar by sea. Leslie's orders had been well carried out, all the men had gone, and the supplies had been hidden or carried off.

> In the march between Mordlington and Copperspath we saw not any Scotchman, in Eyton and other places we passed through; but the streets were full of Scotch women; pitifull, sorry creatures, clothed in white flannell, in a very homely manner; very many of them much bemoaned their husbands, who they said, were enforced by the lairds of the towns to gang to the muster.—*A Large Relation of the Fight at Leith*, printed with *Hodgson's Memoirs*, &c.

Some of these women consented to bake and to brew for the English, but the troops do not appear to have got much out of the country. They had to rely principally on what they brought with them. Even cooking utensils were not always to be had, as armies in those days did not carry them with them. The men were often put to curious shifts to prepare their food. "Some of our soldiers brought a little raw meat with them, and became excellent cooks, a back makes a dripping-pan, and a head-piece is a porrage-pot." (*Perfect Passages,* the 26th July; *Cromwelliana*). So, says an old newspaper. Perhaps "our special reporter" was only joking, but at any rate the absence of the inhabitants caused great inconvenience to the troops.

Cromwell did everything he could to reassure the people and induce them to return. He published stringent orders relative to the maintenance of discipline, and caused them to be read at the head of every regiment with sound of trumpet and drum. No man was to straggle over half a mile from his regiment under pain of death. A proclamation was published throughout the country assuring the inhabitants of protection, if they would return to their houses. A few prisoners were taken by the horse. These Cromwell allowed to go home on their promising not to appear again in arms against him.

On the 26th July the English reached Dunbar. Here also the *Amity* and some other ships arrived that evening or the next morning, and landed some provisions for the army—a small pittance Cromwell calls it. (Letter to the Lord President of the Council of State, Carlyle, vol. iii.) On the 27th Haddington was reached. Rumours had been rife since the opening of the campaign that the Scots intended to dispute the English advance on Gladsmoor, an open piece of ground beyond Haddington, and later information seemed to confirm the rumour. The next morning, therefore, "we laboured to possess the moor before them; and beat the drums very early in the morning." (Letter to the Lord President of the Council of State, Carlyle, vol. iii.)

Only a few small parties of the Scotch horse, however, appeared. Cromwell then ordered Lambert to press on with 1400 cavalry to reconnoitre towards Musselburgh, whilst he himself followed with the rest of the army. Lambert drove in some parties of horse, and discovered the Scots in position between Edinburgh and Leith, "entrenched by a line flankered from Edinburgh to Leith, the guns also from Leith scouring most part of the line so that they lay very strong."' (Letter to the Lord President of the Council of State, Carlyle, vol. iii.; an account bound with Hodgson's *Memoirs* says that the Scots "had entrenched themselves very strongly, drawing their line from the Leith to the foot of Cannygate Street, in Edinburgh.")

The English rested that night at Musselburgh, about four miles from the Scottish position, "encamped close," that is, concentrated and ready for action. Here there was an open beach on which stores could be disembarked in fine weather, but not if the sea was rough.

The next day (the 29th July) the English advanced, and drew up in order of battle on the plain below the hills held by the Scots, hoping to tempt them to fight. They were now on the ground on which, a hundred years before, the Battle of Pinkie had been fought, but the Scots showed no sign of attempting to reverse the fortune of that day. A Scotch outpost held Arthur's Seat and lined the wall of the Royal Park in front of their right. Cromwell sent some musketeers, supported by a party of horse, who drove the Scots out of this position and occupied it. A gun was then brought up and opened fire on their main line.

At the same time four of the English ships, under Rear-Admiral Hall, cannonaded Leith. (*A Large Relation of the Fight at Leith*). But the position was too strong to be attacked in front, the Scots having at least as many men as the English, and the flanks were so well protected that they could not be turned. Nothing further occurred except a little skirmishing between the horse. The English remained all day on the field and bivouacked on it, their left occupying the village of Lang Niddery. That night proved very wet, "so sore a day and night of rain as I have seldom seen"—says Cromwell. (Carlyle, vol. iii.) The English soldiers rose from their sodden bivouacs, weary, soaked, and hungry. The provisions brought with them were expended, and Cromwell gave the order to fall back on Musselburgh, where shelter could be obtained and food got from the ships.

The retreat began at ten or eleven o'clock, Lambert commanding the rear-guard. Whilst the English had been drawn up before Edinburgh, some 500 of the country people got into Musselburgh and commenced barricading the streets. These were easily driven off by a party of Fleetwood's regiment under Major Haines. As the English marched back, the leading regiments, eager probably to get food and shelter, neglected to keep touch with the rear-guard, but marched too fast "as if we had been at a great distance from the enemy," as Hodgson, (*Memoirs*), says. The Scotch horse, seeing their opportunity, poured out of Leith on their left, and the Cannongate in Edinburgh on their right, and fell upon the English rear-guard, which was for a time very hard pressed.

The right column fell upon 200 English horse under Captain Evanson, who were guarding the extreme rear, and drove them back. Cromwell's own regiment came to their support, and repulsed their assailants, but the Scotch bringing up fresh forces, the English were in turn forced to retreat after severe fighting. Just at the critical moment Whalley brought up four troops of his own and Lambert's regiments, who fell fiercely on the Scots and routed them. The English troops got into disorder in the pursuit, which was continued up to the Scotch entrenchments. Leslie therefore sent out a fresh body of horse, hoping to retrieve the day.

But at this moment an intact troop of Whalley's regiment arrived on the scene, under Captain Chillenden, in good order. It immediately charged the advancing Scots, routed them, and finally determined the day. Lambert, who had displayed great courage, and had been throughout in the thick of the fight, was twice wounded—in shoulder and thigh—by lances. His horse was shot under him, and at one time he had been taken prisoner, but was very soon released. The other Scotch column had been defeated and driven back to Leith by

Colonel Hacker. (This smart cavalry action is well worth the study of cavalry officers. One of the best accounts is in *A Large Relation*, &c., with Hodgson's *Memoirs).*

The English arrived, wet and weary, at Musselburgh that evening. For this reason, and from information he had received, Cromwell expected an attack that night or the next morning. And, indeed, the Scotch cavalry, smarting under their defeat of the morning, determined to redeem their credit. A strong party of their best horse was therefore selected. Its numbers are estimated in different accounts at from 800 to 1500. Major-General Montgomery took the command, and under him were Colonels Strachan, Lockhart, and Kerr. Many English Cavaliers rode in the ranks, for in spite of the dislike felt for them by the Scotch Presbyterians, their experience and skill as cavalry soldiers had induced the Scotch colonels to overlook the orders against enlisting them.

The party started at night, having as guide a Mr. Hamilton, whose house—Stoney Hill—lay near Musselburgh, and was occupied by the English. That night Lilburne's and Fleetwood's regiments of horse, which had not been seriously engaged on the 30th, furnished the outposts on the English side. Lambert's regiment of foot lay at Stoney Hill, and formed a support to the horse. At three o'clock on the morning of the 31st the Scotch horse approached an outpost of Lilburne's regiment. The alarm was given, and the men mounted ready for action. Two Englishmen then approached from the enemy, and called out that it was a false alarm. Lilburne's troopers, deceived by the accent, and believing they had been addressed by some of their own patrols, dismounted.

The Scots then dashed in, rode over the dismounted troopers, but not waiting to take prisoners, galloped on towards Musselburgh. On their way, they encountered some troops of Fleetwood's regiment, forming a support to the outposts. These they defeated, but on passing Stoney Hill they received such a volley from Lambert's musketeers, that they were thrown into disorder. A fresh party of English horse, probably the reserve to Lilburne's regiment, then came up and charged, scattering the Scots in all directions. Most of them fled towards Edinburgh, and on the way, were intercepted by a party of dragoons, who had been on outpost, and whose fire emptied more of the Scotch saddles. Others were taken in the streets of Musselburgh.

On the whole, the Scots lost forty or fifty killed, and three field-officers, several inferior officers, and some eighty troopers taken. The

Scots are described by Whitelocke to have been "completely armed, (meaning wearing armour), and having all lances, pistols, and swords." The prisoners were well treated, the wounded sent back to Edinburgh in Cromwell's own coach, the rest released on parole.

These two sharp lessons taught Leslie that his troops were no match for Cromwell's veterans in the field, and made him more than ever determined to adhere to his cautious tactics. The Kirk party attributed the defeat of their men to God's displeasure at the number of profane malignants in their ranks. Prince Charles, who had arrived in Leith on the 27th July, and had witnessed both the fights, was compelled to return to Stirling. Walker, (*Historical Discourses*), says that some 4000 Cavaliers were dismissed from the Scotch forces at this time.

Nothing further happened for several days, the Scots remaining in their lines, the English in camp or quarter about Musselburgh. An exchange of declarations and letters commenced between Cromwell and Leslie, who were both honestly anxious to bring the war to an end. These declarations were considered by the councils of war on either side, and even meetings between the officers of both armies took place later. At these meetings the representatives of each army endeavoured to convince those of the other of the justness of their particular view of the points in dispute. For in these strangely constituted armies the officers were equally ready to support their cause by argument or by the sword.

These declarations and conferences produced no effect; but whilst argument was being tried, military action was not neglected. The weather proved very tempestuous. Boats could no longer land supplies on the beach at Musselburgh, and Cromwell found he could no longer feed his men there. On the 6th August, therefore, he retired to Dunbar. Even there provisions were very short, as the supply in the ships was becoming exhausted. Foraging parties searched for hidden grain, and Hodgson, (Memoirs), says that the discipline of the army was becoming relaxed. However, some fresh ships arrived from London, and landed their stores at Dunbar. Those of the inhabitants that had remained were nearly starving, and Cromwell had to issue corn and peas to them.

Under these circumstances almost any other general of this period would have entrenched himself at Dunbar, secured his communications through Cockburn's Path by suitable posts, sent out his cavalry to reconnoitre and forage, quartered his men in buildings and huts, collected all possible provisions, and settled himself into a leaguer, as it was called. There he would have awaited events, ready to follow Leslie shoul4 he quit his position; content to keep the war out of his own country, and to throw the burden of it on the Scots. Not so Cromwell. Disliking war in itself, his keen, eager nature always longed to bring it to an end. The defeat of his enemy's army was, he knew, ever the surest and speediest way to bring about peace. Therefore now, as ever, he was most anxious to force on a battle, and would leave no chance untried to bring this about. This was always the key to his strategy—the strategy of every great commander confident in himself and his troops.

As soon, then, as he had re-provisioned his army, Cromwell again advanced to Musselburgh, which he reached on the 12th August. Here he found the only change which had occurred was that even the women were gone, and the town and neighbouring villages more desolate than ever. He now determined to try whether Leslie could not be induced to fight if his communications with his sources of supply west and north of Edinburgh were threatened. On the 13th August, therefore, Cromwell marched towards the Pentland Hills and occupied a position south of Braid House, threatening the roads to Queensferry and Stirling.

During the next few days part, or all, of the army had to return to Musselburgh for supplies, but by the 17th all the troops had been drawn up to the Hills. To cover the landing-place at Musselburgh a garrison of 140 foot and forty horse were put into Stoney Hill, and the western outskirts of the village of Dalkeith were fortified and garrisoned to secure the communications of the army. Leslie, noting these dispositions of Cromwell's, contented himself with drawing some of his cannon to the west of Edinburgh and occupying Costorphine Hill. He had an outpost at Redhall, near the English camp, to counteract which Cromwell posted two troops of dragoons at Collington House.

In these positions the armies remained for some days. Leslie would not be tempted to move, though Cromwell on the 26th drove his picket out of Redhall, and appears after this to have advanced his camp to Braid House. He then determined to move westward and interpose more directly between Leslie and Stirling. The next morning (the 27th) the English Army was drawn up, and then marched off for the Edinburgh-Stirling road. Leslie immediately put his army in motion in the same direction, keeping to the high land near the Forth. The armies marched in view of one another, and the direction of their movements brought the vanguards into collision about the village of Gogar.

Both then halted and formed up in order of battle. The ground looked fair, and the English confidently expected a battle, but on their advance they found that there was a bog in front of each wing, which effectually prevented the horse from engaging. A few rounds from the English cannon drove the Scots out of some sheepfolds which they had occupied by an advanced party, but nothing further could be effected, though the cannon on both sides kept up a fire the whole afternoon. The result of the expenditure of some hundreds of rounds was that the English had twenty killed and wounded, and claimed to have inflicted a loss of some eighty or a hundred on the Scots. That night both armies bivouacked on the ground.

The next morning Cromwell, having no more bread, determined to return to Musselburgh, and marched off about ten or eleven o'clock to his old camp at Braid, where he halted for the night. Leslie also marched back to Edinburgh.

Now was Leslie's chance if he had been quick enough to have availed himself of it. He possessed an outpost on some high ground at Craigmillar, almost immediately on the line between Cromwell's camp and Musselburgh. The English were very short of provisions—many of them having, according to one account, thrown away their biscuit on the prospect of a fight. (*A Letter from a Colonel of the Army*, &c., with Hodgson's *Memoirs*)

The night of the 28th was very wet and stormy, and the English rose the next morning, hungry, weary, and drenched. They were also encumbered by a large number of sick, the cold and exposure having proved very detrimental to their soldiers. Had then Leslie occupied the ground about Craigmillar with his army he could have forced the English to fight under very disadvantageous conditions. Cromwell had foreseen this, and had, during the night, sent on a party with two guns to occupy Niddery, opposite Craigmillar. The next morning the Scots did appear on Arthur's Seat, moving towards Craigmillar, but on the guns opening from Niddery they halted. Under the cover of this fire Cromwell was able to file all his army past the threatened point, and reached Musselburgh in safety.

It appears, from a letter written on the 31st August at Musselburgh by a colonel serving with the army, (*Memoirs*), that a council of war, held on the 28th, had already favourably considered a project of retiring to Dunbar, fortifying that and perhaps one or two other posts, and there awaiting events. At another council held at Musselburgh on the 30th this arrangement was finally decided on. The season was advancing and the weather was becoming very bad. The landing of supplies on the beach was precarious, and there was nothing to be got out of the country.

The shelter afforded about Musselburgh was insufficient, and the men were rapidly falling sick. Every attempt to induce Leslie to quit his unassailable positions round Edinburgh had proved fruitless. The Scots' Army was daily increasing, whilst the English was decreasing. There was nothing for it but to form a fortified camp and retire into it, either for the winter or till Leslie offered a favourable opportunity to fight him. Nothing is said either in the account given by the colonel of the first council of war, or in Cromwell's account of the second, of any idea of shipping, (*Memoirs*), the forces and retiring to England.

The former says that:

> The council inclined generally to fall upon garrisoning of Dunbarre, and other considerable places nearer Tweed; and after one garison compleated (if we have no better complyance) to proceed to some more severe course than hath bin yet taken.—*Memoirs*.

Cromwell in his letter to Lenthall, dated the 4th September, says:

> And upon serious consideration, finding our weakness so to increase, and the Enemy lying upon his advantage, at a general council (on the 30th August) it was thought fit to march to Dunbar, and there to fortify the town. Which (we thought), if anything, would provoke them to engage. As also that the having of a garrison there would famish us with accommodation for our sick men, would be a good magazine—which we exceedingly wanted; being put to depend upon the uncertainty of weather for landing provisions, which many times cannot be done though the being of the whole army lay upon it, all the coasts from Berwick to Leith having not one good harbour. As also. To lie more conveniently to receive our recruits of horse and foot from Berwick.—Carlyle, vol. iii.

It may be assumed, therefore, that Cromwell had no intention of retiring further than Dunbar.

Cromwell's Preparations for Battle

During the 30th the boats of the ships had been busily employed in embarking the sick and wounded men. Nearly 500 were put on board, and the impedimenta to the army thus considerably reduced. On the 31st August everything was in readiness, but in order to conceal his intentions to the last moment, Cromwell postponed the retreat until the afternoon. About two o'clock the ships off Musselburgh hoisted sail, and stood off for Dunbar. (Caldwell's relation, Carte's Ormonde Papers). Somewhat later the army commenced its march to Haddington under cover of a strong rear-guard of horse. Leslie immediately sent out a strong party of horse in pursuit, and shortly afterwards followed with his whole army.

So cleverly had Cromwell deceived his enemy by showing a bold front, and withdrawing his forces unperceived, that it was night, and the English main body had already reached Haddington, before the Scots had brought up sufficient forces to attack the rear-guard seriously. There was a bright moon, and:

> The enemy had marched with that exceeding expedition that they fell upon the rear-folorn of our horse, and put it in some disorder; and indeed, had like to have engaged our rear-brigade of horse with their whole army—had not the Lord, by His Providence, put a cloud over the moon, thereby giving us opportunity to draw off those horse to the rest of our army. Which accordingly was done, without any loss save three or four of our aforementioned folorn; wherein the enemy, as we believe, received more loss.—Cromwell to Lenthall, 4th September, Carlyle, vol. iii.

That night the English quartered in the town. Colonel Fairfax's regiment of foot, and Fleetwood's of horse were on outpost duty outside the walls. About midnight an attack was made by some dragoons and Highlanders, but the pickets drove them back. The next morning, the 1st September, Cromwell drew up his army to the south of Haddington on the right bank of the Tyne, which runs past the town. Leslie deployed the Scotch army on Gladsmoor on the opposite side of the stream. In these positions, the opposing armies remained until ten o'clock, when Cromwell resumed his retreat on Dunbar.

★★★★★★

The direct road to Dunbar leaves Haddington at the north end, and follows the left bank of the Tyne for some miles. Cromwell, however, distinctly states that he drew out on the south side of Haddington, which would put him on the right bank. He may have recovered the direct road, or continued his march by tracks on this bank.

★★★★★★

His prediction that the retreat would draw Leslie out of his works had been fulfilled, and on this morning the armies faced one another away from all artificial support in the shape of entrenchments and field works. Had Cromwell drawn out to the west end of Haddington he might have attacked Leslie on Gladsmoor. But the approaches to that position were difficult, and gave the defender great advantages. It will be remembered that on the occasion of the first advance to Musselburgh there was a rumour that the Scots intended to fight on this same position, and that Cromwell was very anxious to get first on to the ground.

We laboured to possess the moor before them; and beat our drums very early in the morning.

At that time the armies were not very unequal, both having some 15,000 men, and the English were fresh. Now, however, Leslie had some 22,000 men under his command, whilst the English barely mustered 12,000. They, too, were weak from exposure and bad food, "a poor, shattered, hungry, discouraged army"—Hodgson, (*Memoirs*), calls them. It was, therefore, not considered advisable to attack the Scots, and as the latter showed no inclination to attack Cromwell's seasoned veterans, even under advantageous conditions, the retreat to Dunbar was resumed.

The Scots pursued close, pressing round the English rear so "that our rear-guard had much ado to secure our poor weak foot, that was not able to march up." (*Memoirs*). But no disorganisation showed itself among the troops, and Dunbar was reached in safety, the fire of a couple of guns covering the approaches to the camp.

The position at Dunbar was in many respects well adapted for a fortified camp. A modern map explains the situation clearly enough, for the physical features of the ground are strongly marked, and not such as would be much altered by advancing civilization. The roads run along much the same lines as in the seventeenth century. The town itself stands on a rounded rocky promontory. On its west is the Bay of Belhaven, formed by the estuaries of the Tyne and the Beil Water. It is shallow and mostly bare at low spring tides.

On its eastern shore, close to the town of Dunbar, lies the fishing village and port of Belhaven, where the Beil Water scoops itself a channel through the sand and mud to the sea. The herring fishery is, and was, the principal trade of the place, and plenty of boats and boatmen would be available for landing stores, &c. The port, though indifferent and exposed, appears to have been available to a certain extent in all weathers. From Dunbar, the rocky coast runs south-east to Berwick, twenty-seven miles away. About half-way the rugged Lammermuir Hills, running east and west, strike the coast north of St. Abb's Head, and here the road is forced through a rough and narrow pass called Cockburn's Path. The spurs of the Lammermuir Hill run out towards Dunbar in an irregular fashion, but generally following a south-west to north-east direction.

Many streams run in the deep glens between the spurs to the sea. Two of these streams, the Beil Water and the Brock Burn, running in a north-easterly direction, empty themselves into the sea, the former at Belhaven, a mile west, and the latter at Broxmouth, a mile east of Dunbar, the spur between them flattens out as it approaches the sea, and forms the rough uneven promontory on which the town stands. Immediately south of the Brock Burn and between it and another called the Dry Burn, a spur from the Lammermuir rises into a sharp ridge called Doon Hill, with very steep declivities towards the brooks, and a gentler but still sharp descent towards the sea.

The road from Haddington to Dunbar crosses the Beil Water somewhat less than a mile from its mouth; that from Dunbar to Berwick crosses the Brock about the same distance from the sea. The latter stream is insignificant of itself, but above the road its bed forms a harrow glen some forty feet deep, with sides too steep to allow infantry or cavalry to cross it in formation. In this part of its course it can only be passed by vehicles, or troops in close order, at a point about a mile and a half above the Berwick road, marked "outpost" on the sketch, where a cart track crosses and leads up into the hills.

There was a small house here at the bottom of the glen. Below the main road the banks of the burn are shelving and passable for both horse and foot in close order on a broad front. Immediately to the north of the road and on the left bank of the burn lies Broxmouth House, surrounded by a park. Very probably in 1650, the road ran to the north of the house instead of as now to the south of it. The rest of the promontory was for the most part uncultivated.

Cromwell, when he retired to Dunbar on the evening of the 1st September, occupied a position across the promontory, resting his extreme left on Broxmouth Park, his right on the Beil Water near its mouth, and holding the house in the glen as an outpost. The position was evidently a strong one, at a date when cannon planted on the Doon Hill and other spurs of the Lammermuir Hills had not sufficient range to molest his position.

An enemy attacking along either the Haddington or Berwick road would have to cross a deep glen in face of the defenders; whilst if he attempted to advance down the spur, between the brooks, the rough, roadless ground would hamper his movements, and he would have to make a frontal attack on a strong position, both flanks of which were secure. A little field fortification would have rendered the camp, with the port and the communications by sea to England, safe from attack. The weak point lay in the land communications. These lay by the coast road to Berwick, almost in a prolongation of the left flank of the position, and therefore not well covered.

Cromwell, on his advance into Scotland, had neglected to secure the important pass at Cockburn's Path. Nor did he now take any steps to occupy it, apparently under the impression that Leslie would follow him from the west. But the latter, who knew the ground well, on approaching Dunbar, quitted the main road, and moving south occupied the Doon Hill during the night of the 1st and 2nd. He also sent a party which seized the pass at Cockburn's Path.

Thus, on the morning of the 2nd September, Cromwell found himself completely cut off from England by land. For even had he wished to do so he could not have marched close past the front of the Scots on Doon Hill and attacked their detachment at Cockburn's Path. Besides, he particularly desired to retain his hold on Dunbar, as his position there prevented an invasion of England by the Scotch army. He was, however, quite aware of the difficulties of his position, entirely dependent as he was for his supplies and recruits on what he could obtain by sea, the winter coming on, and only an exposed anchorage on a rocky shore, a small indifferent port at his disposal. He immediately wrote to Sir Arthur Hazlerigg, Governor of Newcastle, a letter worth quoting, as showing his grasp of the situation and of the best way of meeting it.

> We are upon an engagement very difficult. The enemy hath blocked-up our way at the pass at Copper's path, through which we cannot get without almost a miracle. He lieth so upon the hills that we know not how to come that way without great difficulty; and our lying here daily consumeth our men who fall sick beyond imagination.

I perceive your forces are not in a capacity for present release. Wherefore, whatever becomes of us, it will be well for you to get what forces you can together; and the South to help what they can. The business nearly concerneth all Good People. If your forces had been on a readiness to have fallen upon the back of Copper's path, it might have occasioned supplies to have come to us. But the only wise God knows what is best. All shall work for Good. Our spirits are comfortable, praised be the Lord, though our present condition be as it is. And indeed we have much hope in the Lord; of whose mercy we have had large experience.

Indeed, do you get together what forces you can against them. Send to the friends in the South to help with more. Let H. Vane know what I write. I would not make it public lest danger should accrue thereby. You know what use to make hereof. Let me hear from you.—Carlyle, vol. iii.

Evidently the best way to clear the communications should Leslie continue where he now was, would be to attack the detachment in the pass in rear, whilst Cromwell held the Scotch army in front. And note well it is not to enable himself to retire into England that he wishes the communications cleared, but to enable supplies to reach him. No doubt one of the great reasons his men were falling sick was that they were accustomed to fresh meat and bread, whereas from the ships they only obtained salt junk and biscuit.

The morning of the 2nd September broke stormy and wet. The English, unable to pitch their tents, suffered from the exposure. But the Scots on the bleak Doon Hill suffered still more. The horse of their right wing had been brought down on to the plateau between the Doon Hill and the sea, over which runs the Berwick road. All that day the English stood to their arms expecting an attack, the. regiments occupying the positions assigned to them in order of battle. They now mustered but 7500 foot and 3500 horse fit to bear arms, whilst the Scots amounted to 6000 horse and 16,000 foot at least. (Cromwell to Lenthall, the 4th September, Carlyle, vol. iii.)

About 4 p.m. a movement was apparent in Leslie's army. He was bringing his men down from the hill on to the lower ground towards the sea, and along the glen. This movement has often been attributed to the influence of the kirk ministers, who believed and declared that the Lord had delivered their enemy into their hands. There is, however, no good reason for supposing this story to be true. (See, however, Mr. Gardiner on this point, *History of the Commonwealth*, vol. i.)

In that tempestuous weather the Scots could not have remained without shelter on the bare hill-top. Leslie also appears to have believed that Cromwell had already shipped his guns and meant embarking the rest of his force. He contemplated attacking him, and wished to be within striking distance.

He therefore brought about two-thirds of the horse of his left wing to join that of his right, which was at the same time moved further down the plateau towards the sea. The train also was brought down, the hill, and the foot closed to their right, and moved down to the plateau and to the bank of the burn.

A couple of troops of horse were sent to attack the outpost at the bottom of the glen, where the cart track crossed it, which was held by twenty-four English foot soldiers and six horse. These were driven back and two or three prisoners taken. The post, however, was soon recaptured. One of the prisoners taken here, a one-armed veteran, was taken to Leslie:

> Who asked him if the enemy did intend to fight? he replyed—what did he think they came there for? they came for nothing else. 'Soldier,' says Leslie, 'how will you fight when you have shipped half your men and all your great guns?' The soldier replyed. 'Sir, if you please to draw down your army to the foot of the hill, you shall find both men and great guns too.'—Carte's *Ormonde Papers*. The soldier was released and came to Cromwell, who, after hearing his story, gave him two gold pieces to replace some money of which he had been plundered.

This story, which seems probable enough, shows what was passing through Leslie's mind when he drew his men down from the hill. He evidently believed that the English were far more bent upon escaping out of Scotland than on fighting his army.

Cromwell and Lambert were at Broxmouth House watching the movement of Leslie's forces. They concluded that he meant to attack the next morning. Cromwell noticed how the Scots crowded down on to the plateau, and on to the steep slopes of the hill towards the burn on their left. The hillside was there so steep that the troops once down could move only with difficulty. If then their right wing were attacked, the left could not come in time to its support. He pointed this out to Lambert.

I told him I thought it did give us an opportunity and advantage to attempt upon the enemy. To which he immediately replied, That he had thought to have said the same thing to me. (Cromwell to Lenthall, the 4th September, Carlyle, vol. iii.) Monk was called and concurred in their opinion.

The train of artillery, which had been parked in the churchyard at Dunbar, was brought up to the position held by the troops to be in readiness, and on Cromwell's return to his quarters a council of war was summoned. According to Hodgson, (*Memoirs*), who, however, was probably not present, some of the colonels wished to ship the foot for England and break through with the horse, but the arguments of Lambert and those who were for fighting prevailed. Cromwell says—

> Coming to our quarters at night, and demonstrating our apprehensions to some of the colonels, they also cheerfully concurred.—Cromwell to Lenthall, the 4th September, in his report on the battle.

The arrangements for the attack were then made. As the Scots also appeared to be bent on assuming the offensive, it was determined to forestall them and to commence the attack at daybreak. Six regiments of horse under Fleetwood and Lambert, with a brigade of three and a half regiments of foot under Monk were ordered to open the battle. The remaining two brigades of foot, under Colonels Pride and Overton, together with two regiments of horse, were to follow in support, and to protect the guns. (Cromwell to Lenthall, the 4th September, in his report on the battle). These latter were to direct their fire on the left wing of the Scots, thus increasing the confusion which would be caused by the steep ground over which the regiments posted there would have to move. (*Memoirs*).

The night of the 2nd and 3rd was again stormy. At intervals the moon shone out brightly, but driving squalls of rain swept continually across her face and obscured her light. The Scots stood for the most part on cultivated ground. The corn had been cut and stood in shocks. The soldiers cowered amongst the sheaves, which afforded them a little shelter. According to Sir E. Walker, Major-General Holbourne, who commanded the Scotch foot, ordered the musketeers to extinguish their matches all but two in a company. (*Historical Discourses*. He also says the horse were unsaddled and some away foraging. The latter is unlikely at that hour. Walker was not present).

About four o'clock on the morning of the 3rd the English troops detailed to lead the attack marched down to Broxmouth House, and formed up there awaiting the signal. How the regiments' were brigaded that day is not clear, the various accounts being contradictory. Lambert's, Whalley's, Lilburne's, and Packer's regiments of horse, with Lambert's and Cromwell's regiments of foot, appear to have been amongst those who formed the van. The hour appointed for the attack had come, but Lambert, who was to lead it, had not yet arrived. He was away on the right marshalling the guns. Drawing up an army in darkness is a difficult operation, conducive to delays. Standing there in the gloaming the troopers consoled each other with prayer and exhortation.

> As our regiment was marching in the head of the horse, a cornet was at prayer in the night, and I appointed one of my officers to take my place. I rid to hear him, and he was exceedingly carried on in the duty. I met with so much of God in it, as I was satisfied deliverance was at hand. And coming to my command did encourage the poor, weak soldiers, which did much affect them.—*Memoirs*.

The faint light of dawn was rapidly strengthening, daylight was coming on amidst the squalls, and still no Lambert. Cromwell was impatient, scarcely constraining himself to wait for his lieutenant. A trumpet sounded in the Scotch bivouac—were they, too, about to attack? At last, at six o'clock, Lambert arrived, and immediately ordered "Packer, major to the general's regiment," (*Memoirs*), to lead on. The day had broken now, but the sun had not risen clear of the clouds. The column wheeled to the left, and skirting the north side of Broxmouth House, descended into the bed of the Brox Burn between the house and the sea. Opposite, on the right bank of the burn, which here commanded the left, stood the Scotch infantry in serried ranks. And now the trumpets rang out the charge, a great shout arose from the English ranks—The Lord of Hosts! The Lord of Hosts!—and fiercely echoed back the Scots' war-cry—The Covenant! The Covenant! The cannon opened on both sides, and the tumult and confusion of battle had begun.

Fiercely the English horse spurred up the burn side, and stubbornly the Scottish foot resisted the charge. After the horse pressed the English foot, Cromwell, riding behind Lambert's foot regiment, with which was Hodgson, ordered it to incline to its left, to get round the Scots' extreme right, and charge them in flank. Meanwhile the heavy masses of Scotch cavalry had advanced to support their foot. Down a gentle incline they charged with level lances, driving the English horse, disordered by the contest but still fighting furiously, into the bed of the stream. (The front ranks of the Scotch horse were armed with lances. Caldwell's narrative in Carte's *Ormonde Papers*).

The leading regiments of English foot were also thrown into disorder, and commenced to fall, back. Just at this moment, Gough led forward Cromwell's own regiment of foot at the charge. Crashing into the *mêlée* it drove back the Scots at push of pike, giving the disordered regiments time to rally. With these veteran soldiers but a few movements sufficed to reform the ranks. Fresh regiments of Pride's and Overton's brigades pressed forward in support, and horse and foot, the English again swept forward.

"I never saw such a charge of foot and horse," wrote Rushworth. At this moment the sun burst through the clouds and lighted up the scene, his rays glittering on lance point and pike, on breastplate and sword.

"Let God arise, and His enemies shall be scattered," shouted Cromwell, and then a few minutes later, "I profess they run." (*Memoirs*).

All along the brink of the burn the Scots were giving way. But one brigade of foot held their ground, "though at push of pike and butt end of musket, until a troop of our horse charged from one end to another of them, and so left them at the mercy of the foot." (*Memoirs*).

Now ensued a scene of the wildest confusion. The Scotch horse, broken and disordered, had no room to rally, pent in between the sea and the steep Doon Hill. This space, already overcrowded, was still more packed by the troops of the Scots' left wing endeavouring to support their defeated right. In their desperate efforts to free themselves from the throng the horse rode over their own foot. Close at their heels followed the English horse, cutting down their enemies in all directions. In a few minutes, the whole Scotch Army was in utter rout.

Hodgson wrote:

> They had routed one another, after we had done their work on their right wing, and we, coming up to the top of the hill with the straggling parties that had been engaged, kept them from bodying; and so the foot threw down their arms and fled towards Dunbar, our pinfold, and there they were surrounded and taken.

The horse fled in all directions, to Cockburn's Path, to Haddington, to Edinburgh. The English squadrons were scattered in chase. Cromwell, knowing the advantage of a properly conducted pursuit, spurred forward, and, sounding a halt, collected the troopers.

Rapidly they rallied, and as they reformed their ranks they broke out into the old Hebrew song of praise, the hundred and seventeenth psalm—

O, give ye praise unto the Lord
All nations that be.

As soon as order was restored, the squadrons were launched in pursuit. Right up to Haddington they chased the flying Scots, breaking up any groups which still remained together, frustrating all attempts on the part of the officers to rally their men. Hackers regiment followed the pursuit almost to Edinburgh, whither Leslie escaped by the speed of his horse. (Carlyle says he reached Edinburgh at nine o'clock. If he left the field of battle a little before seven he must have done at least twenty-five miles in a little over two hours). Cromwell remained on the field, securing the prisoners and the booty. Though the fighting had lasted barely an hour, the slaughter among the Scots had been great, principally during the pursuit. The early hour at which the battle had been fought allowed the chase to be followed long and far.

Consequently, the actual numbers of the Scots killed could not be closely computed. Cromwell, a day or two afterwards, estimated them at 3000. Some 10,000 prisoners were taken, many of them wounded. (Amongst the prisoners were thirty officers of general or field rank, forty captains, and over 200 of the lower commissioned ranks). The next day, the 4th September, Cromwell issued a proclamation, permitting the inhabitants to search the field for wounded soldiers, many of whom were still believed to be lying there. All the baggage of Leslie's army, 10,000 stand of arms, thirty cannon, the ammunition train, and 200 colours were captured by the victors. The English loss was trifling. Some forty were killed or died of their wounds, amongst them Major Rooksby and a cornet. A good many received minor injuries.

Such was the Battle of Dunbar, the most dramatic of all Cromwell's battles. There can be little doubt that he made a grave mistake in neglecting to secure Cockburn's Path as the most important position on his lines of communication with England. His own army was, even at the opening of the campaign, hardly strong enough for the task set it, and could ill spare men to garrison posts along the line of advance.

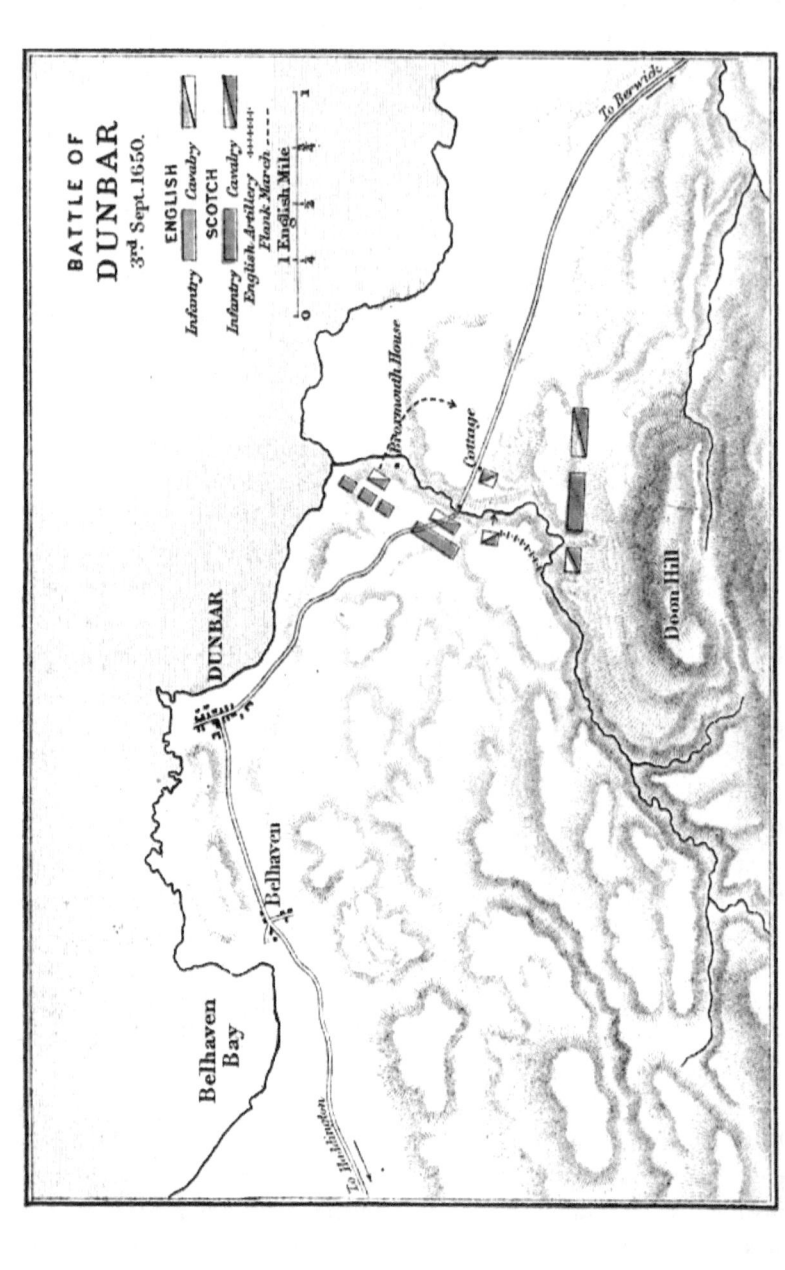

But arrangements should have been made for troops to be brought up from Berwick or Newcastle for this duty.

Cromwell, always eager for battle, prepared his plans solely with a view to that end. If successful at the front the lines of communication would look after themselves. To ensure success in the fight every available man should be brought into it. Victory rests with him who is strongest at the decisive point. By keeping this maxim clearly in view Cromwell had now twice beaten Scotch armies outnumbering his own by at least two to one. At Preston, Hamilton, by his ill-arranged march, had offered Cromwell the strategical advantage of fighting one part of his army unsupported by the rest, owing to the distance between them. The latter had immediately availed himself of the chance, crushed Langdale's English levies, and then turned on the Scots.

In 1650 Leslie, avoiding Hamilton's error, kept his forces always concentrated. But in a careless moment he allowed his troops to occupy a piece of ground on which his wings could not support each other. Cromwell immediately flung his whole force on the Scots' right wing, and routed it before the left wing could lend any help. Thus, by a strategical error on his opponents' part in one case, and by a tactical error in the other, he had been stronger at the decisive point, although his total numbers were far weaker than his foe's. So simple does this appear after a great victory is won, that success is often attributed far more to the blunders of the vanquished than to the genius of the victor.

As a matter of fact the problem is far more complicated, and only very great generals can take advantage of these fleeting opportunities. The view of a general in command of an army is not that of a historian calmly reviewing past events. It is obscured by much contradictory and false information, by uncertainty about his enemy's numbers, dispositions, and intentions, often his insufficient acquaintance with the ground. Such opportunities are very fleeting. Half an hour more at Dunbar and Leslie's dispositions might very probably have been entirely changed.

This Cromwell thoroughly appreciated. Hodgson happened to be near him at the crucial moment before the attack began in both battles, and testifies to his impatience to begin. (*Memoirs*). Mr. Gardiner, in criticizing Cromwell's strategy at Preston, says:—

> In war, as in politics, Cromwell never rose above the simple strategy of finding out the enemy wherever it was most easy to give him battle.—*Great Civil War*, vol. ix.

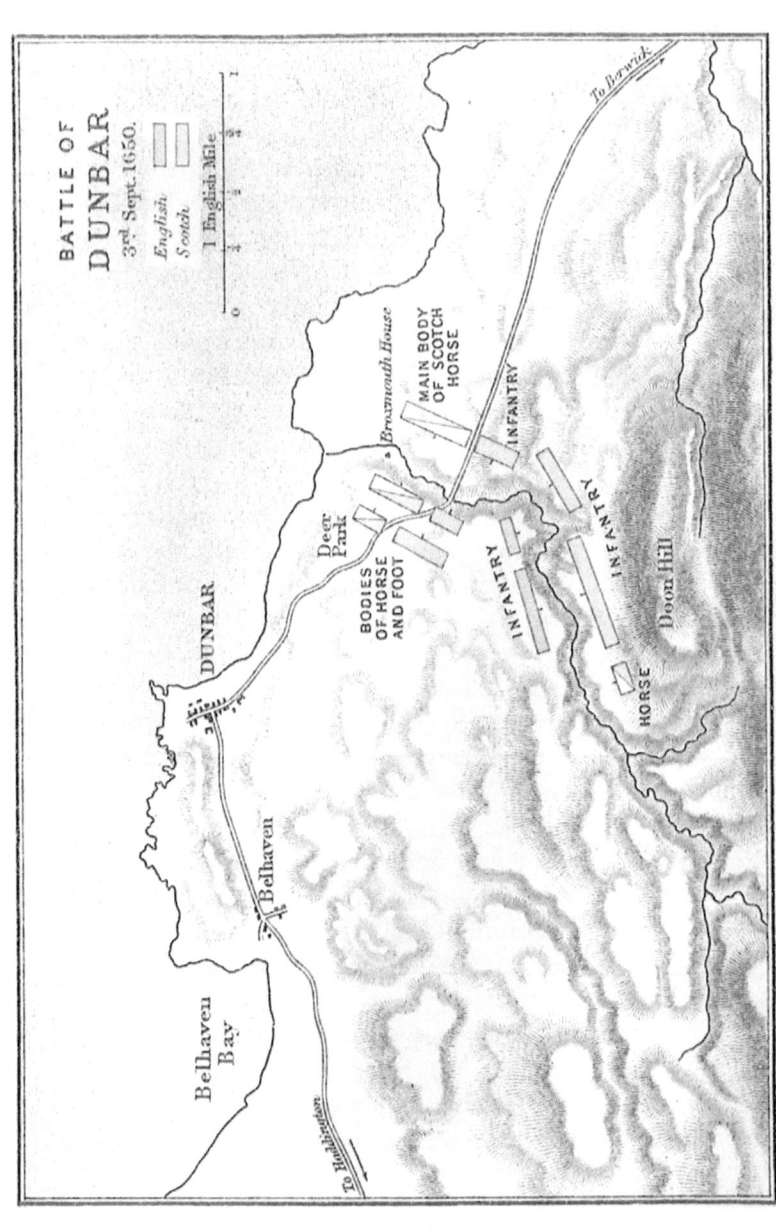

If by this be meant where it is most easy to defeat him this criticism is perfectly true, and is itself the highest praise that could be given to any general, though the historian probably did not so intend it.

Yet although Cromwell's principle of bringing every available man to fight at the critical point was sound, and achieved such brilliant results, neither he, nor any other general, can afford to neglect his communications. In this case he trusted to his ships to form fresh bases, as he advanced, close at hand. But his armies depended principally, not only for supplies, but also for transport on the country through which they passed. By Leslie's precautions Scotland afforded him neither. Consequently, directly he attempted to move away from the coast, he was brought back again, not so much from want of bread, which the ships could probably have supplied in large quantities, but from lack of means of carrying it.

Every endeavour should therefore have been made to keep the land communications open, if only to get up a sufficiency of land transport. There seems to have been no lack of forage for the transport animals, as there was much unripe and uncut corn in the fields. There was, therefore, no difficulty on that score. Without sufficient land transport the English Army was sadly hampered.

As to Leslie, his error is very evident. Not only did he dispose his men on the evening of the 2nd so that the wings could not support each other, but by crowding horse, foot, and guns on to the space between the Doon Hill and the sea, he prevented even the troops of the right wing from properly supporting each other. They had no room to manoeuvre, and only got in each other's way. They also appear to have been badly drawn up. Hodgson says that one of the arguments Lambert used at the council of war on the night of the 2nd, in favour of attacking was:

> Fourthly, they had left intervals in their bodies upon the brink of the hill, that our horse might march a troop at once, and so the foot; and the enemy could not wheel about, nor oppose them, but must put themselves into disorder.—*Memoirs*.

It is not very clear what the worthy captain means, but it is evident the Scots' formation was such as would hamper their movements. Both from the story of what he said to the prisoner, and from his dispositions, Leslie clearly meant to attack Cromwell on the 3rd, before the latter could have time either to embark his men, or fortify his position. Therefore he massed his men on his right, where they could cross the burn,

He intended to attack in strong heavy columns, whose momentum would crumple up the English. He believed the latter to be demoralised and desponding, and never anticipated the possibility of their assuming the offensive. His error arose from the old, old mistake of acting on a preconceived idea, and not according to the actual circumstances.

Edinburgh Castle Surrenders

No sooner was the battle over than Cromwell took the steps necessary to complete the victory. He felt sure the Kirk party would be crushed by this defeat, but he foresaw he would still have to deal with Prince Charles and the Cavaliers. Writing to Hazlerigg on the 4th he said:

> Surely it's probable the Kirk has done their do. I believe their king will set-up upon his own score now; wherein he will find many friends. Taking opportunity offered,—it's our great advantage, through God.

Therefore he urged Hazlerigg to send forward all reinforcements ready under Colonel Thomlinson, as soon as possible. That morning Lambert was sent on with six regiments of horse and one of foot to Edinburgh. Both the capital and Leith surrendered without resistance, but the castle held out.

One great difficulty Cromwell experienced was in disposing of his prisoners. With barely enough food for his own army, how was he to subsist an additional 10,000 men? Besides, the necessary guards to them would employ so many men, that with the numbers he then had sick, he would not have been able to follow up his victory.

Therefore, on the 4th, "between four and five thousand Prisoners, almost starved, sick and wounded," were released, and "the remainder, which are the like, or a greater number, I am fain to send by a convoy of four troops of Colonel Hacker's to Berwick, and so on to Newcastle southwards." In spite of a letter from Cromwell to Hazlerigg, praying that humanity might be exercised towards them, these unfortunate wretches suffered all the horrors of starvation and pestilence.

At Morpeth they broke into a garden and devoured all the cabbages raw, roots and all. Before they reached Newcastle a pestilence broke out among them, and many died daily. At Durham they were put into the cathedral, where the pestilence raged amidst filth and bad food, until Sir A. Hazlerigg, writing on the 31st October in reply to a letter from the Council of State, stated that out of 3000 who arrived there, but 600 remained unscathed. One thousand six hundred had been buried, the rest were all sick, and probably dying. Such was the fate of prisoners of war.

On the 6th September Cromwell left Dunbar for Edinburgh, where he arrived the next day. The Scots were re-assembling at Stirling, where there was already a considerable force. Leslie had retired thither the day after his defeat at Dunbar with such horse as he had been able to collect, amounting to some 1300. Thither, too, flocked the Cavaliers and the Royalist chiefs from the Highlands with their clansmen. The army now collecting already wore a different aspect to that swept away at Dunbar, although the leaders were for the present the same. Instead of regarding the defeat of the Kirk army as a blow to their hopes, Prince Charles and the Cavaliers received the news with delight.

The arrogance of the leaders of the Kirk and the humiliations they had inflicted on the prince had exasperated the adherents of the old monarchal party to such a degree, that they preferred the open hostility of the English Puritans to the nominal friendship of the Scotch Presbyterians. For the latter had made no secret that a king established under their auspices would be merely a puppet, without even much of the outward dignity of royalty. The Cavaliers foresaw that now either the Kirk party must submit unconditionally to Cromwell, which national pride would forbid, or it must make terms with them, as they were able to command by far the most efficient military forces left in the country.

The strategical situation, too, was now entirely favourable to them as against the Kirk party. The only road fit for the movements of an army which in those days connected the north with the south of Scotland, crossed the Forth at Stirling Bridge. The position here was strong, both by nature and art, and was held by all the force the Scots could collect. Thus while the south was open to Cromwell's attacks, the north was closed to him as long as Stirling held out. The Lowland south was Presbyterian, the Highland north was, with the principal exception of Argyle's Campbells, Royalist. Thus the recruits which could be brought to the Scots' Army would be mostly Royalists.

Cromwell appreciated the situation perfectly. He knew that the prince's army, with the warlike clans of the Highlands to draw on for recruits, and the fertile lands of Fife, Aberdeen, and the east coast available for supplies, would rapidly become more and more formidable. It was most desirable that the bridge at Stirling should be captured, and the army collecting there dispersed before it had been largely increased, and whilst the moral effect of the defeat at Dunbar was strong upon its leaders.

But his own army was very weak for the task. Although the towns of Edinburgh and Leith were in his possession, the castle at the former place was not. It was strongly built and garrisoned, contained the largest arsenal in Scotland, and was well supplied with provisions It was placed on a rock and very difficult to approach. Its reduction would therefore probably be a work of time.

Meanwhile it was absolutely necessary to retain the capital and its port of Leith, and the population was still hostile. Therefore, in advancing on Stirling a large detachment must be made to hold Edinburgh and observe the castle.

Nevertheless, Cromwell determined to make the attempt. It has already been seen how on the 4th, the day after the battle, he had written to Hazlerigg urging him to send up any reinforcements he could raise. These demands he reiterated on the 5th and the 9th. Now that Leslie's army had been annihilated, there was no use in keeping a strong force on the frontier in the garrisons of Berwick, Newcastle, &c. The most to be guarded against would be a casual raid of moss-troopers.

Hazlerigg appears to have acceded to Cromwell's demands as well as he was able, for 1000 horse and 1500 foot reached the army about this time. (Whitelock). But even so the total available could barely have reached 13,000, and probably amounted to less than 12,000 effective men. Cromwell made every endeavour to conciliate the inhabitants of Edinburgh and induce them to re-open their shops and markets. In this he was fairly successful, but not so in persuading the Kirk ministers to quit the castle, whither they had taken refuge, and again to preach in their churches. Neither did Dundas, the governor of the castle, show any signs of yielding. Thus, when on the 14th September he marched towards Stirling, Cromwell had to leave three regiments of foot to garrison Edinburgh and Leith and to continue the siege of the castle. Overton was selected to command, and his own brigade furnished the garrisons.

Thus weakened, Cromwell, with the field army, marched to a village six miles on the Stirling road. The army carried with it seven days' provisions for the men. The roads were found to be so bad that a couple of heavy guns intended for the siege of Stirling had to be sent back. The next day, in a downpour of rain, the troops reached

Linlithgow, where they quartered for the night. On the 16th they reached Falkirk, and on the 17th they advanced over the historic field of Bannockburn to within a mile of Stirling. The day was very wet, and quarters were found with difficulty.

The downpour continued on the morning of the 18th. A Council of War was held. Ladders and materials for a storm were provided, and orders given for the assault that afternoon. This was, however, countermanded, the final decision arrived at being that the town was now too strong and too strongly garrisoned to make it prudent to risk an assault. Even if it were taken, it was Cromwell's opinion that it could not have been retained, being too far in advance of his base. The troops were therefore dismissed to their quarters, and on the 19th fell back to Linlithgow. This town Cromwell determined to fortify and hold as his most advanced post. Leaving five troops of horse and six companies of foot under Colonel Sanderson and Major Mitchell to form the garrison, he retired to Edinburgh on the 21st September. (Cromwell to the Council of State," Carlyle, vol. iii.; *A Diary of the Proceedings of the Army*, bound with Hodgson's *Memoirs*).

The expedition against Stirling having failed, Cromwell set to work to establish himself securely south of the Forth before winter set in. Immediately after Dunbar he had written to Hazlerigg to send him "three or four score masons" as soon as possible by sea. These were to be employed in strengthening the fortifications of Edinburgh, Leith, and other important towns which might fall into his hands. Miners were also sent for from Derbyshire, it having been determined to attempt the reduction of Edinburgh Castle by mines.

The advance of the army had been by the east coast, and the whole of the interior and western coast had been untouched. The land communications were therefore still much exposed. After Dunbar, Colonels Strahan and Ker, two of the principal officers of the Kirk Army, had fled to Glasgow. Thence they had gone south, and were endeavouring to raise fresh forces in the south and west. The gentry and peasantry in this part of the country were strict Presbyterians and rigid Covenanters, and were therefore antagonistic to the Royalist Army, now beginning to collect in the Highlands, and to a less extent to the forces under Leslie at Stirling, which consisted principally of the broken remnants of the Kirk Army, but which were now also receiving recruits from the Highlands. Nevertheless, these western levies constituted a serious danger to the English Army at Edinburgh. They must be got rid of, either by force of arms or by persuading them that their sympathies should be more with the English Puritans than with the king.

Charles, who was now at Perth, still surrounded by the partisans of Argyle and the Kirk, made an effort about this time to rid himself of these uncongenial advisers and to put himself at the head of a purely Royalist Army. With this view it was arranged that he should one day ride out of Perth, as if bent on amusement or exercise, and go to a spot in the Highlands about forty miles off, where the Marquess of Huntly and other chieftains would join him with what horse they could raise. For some reason the scheme fell through. Charles did ride out of Perth on the 4th October on the pretence of hawking, and went to the appointed spot, but found no one there.

Sir E. Walker says, (*Historical Discourses*), that he told the scheme to the Duke of Buckingham and Wilmot, who were then with him, and who persuaded him at first not to make the attempt. Later he again determined to go, but started a day late, as according to the arrangement with Huntly he should have been at the trysting-place on the 3rd October. On the 5th he was overtaken by messengers from Argyle and persuaded, by the offer of better treatment, to return to Perth. Argyle was now afraid that he might find himself crushed between the English and the Royalists, and came to terms with the latter. Charles was then admitted to all the councils and treated with far greater respect. The preparations for his coronation were also pushed on. This alliance between Leslie's and the Royalist forces was cemented none too soon. Fighting had already occurred between them. Sir J. Browne's regiment of horse was surprised in its quarters by a party of Royalists, who were in turn pursued by some of Leslie's other regiments.

This compact between the malignants and the commissioners for the Kirk was specially distasteful to the southern and western Covenanters. Cromwell endeavoured to enlarge the split amongst his foes, with the hope of inducing the Presbyterians to remain at least neutral whilst he attacked the Royalists. Having made all the necessary arrangements for the siege of Edinburgh Castle he marched with a strong column to Linlithgow.

From thence, on the 9th October, he sent a letter to the Committee of Estates of Scotland. In this he pointed out that the quarrel of the English was with Charles and his party, but that they desired to live in peace with the Scotch Presbyterians. He therefore invited them to dismiss the prince, and to give some guarantee to the English nation that they would not again attempt to interfere in politics or support its enemies. This done he felt confident that a lasting peace could be secured. A copy of this letter was also sent to Ker and Strahan, who were now at Dumfries collecting a considerable force. Both in the northern and southern Scotch camp this letter was read and considered, but at first with little result. On the 17th October the chiefs of the western army at Dumfries issued a "remonstrance," in which, whilst they rejected the conditions under which Charles was acknowledged at Perth, and refused to admit him as king, they still maintained their quarrel with the English "sectaries," as they called the Puritans, and determined to resist them.

The position of this force, so near the border, was a nuisance to the English counties of Cumberland and Westmoreland. Whalley was sent to Carlisle with Colonel Hacker and the troops of his regiment which had formed the escort of the Scots' prisoners after Dunbar. Other forces were also collected there with a view of securing the frontier, and of eventually moving into Scotland. In conjunction with detachments of the main army they would then undertake the reduction of the southern and western counties.

Cromwell himself moved to Glasgow. Here, although the leaders of the Kirk party fled at his approach, the majority of the inhabitants remained at their usual business. The soldiers were specially warned to treat the citizens with civility, and, even by Baillie's admission, could not have conducted themselves better. (Baillie was a great upholder of the Kirk, once one of the Scots' commissioners to the English Parliament) Cromwell entered the town peaceably on the 18th, but, after a stay of two days, marched back to Edinburgh.

After the hostile declarations of the western army he was afraid that Strahan might slip past him and interrupt the siege of the castle. He was desirous to return, also, before the weather broke up. For the roads were already so bad that if much rain and snow had supervened, it would have been difficult for even the foot to get along, and impossible for the carriages.

Glasgow was too far from his other posts to make it desirable to garrison it, and it was an open town which would require considerable expenditure to render secure. The whole force therefore returned to Edinburgh. Whilst it lay at Glasgow an officer had been cashiered for holding blasphemous opinions, perhaps with a view of proving to the Scots that this army of "sectaries" was not a nest of atheists, as many of their ministers would persuade them. The correspondence between Cromwell and the leaders of the "Western Army" continued after the former's return to Edinburgh.

In answer to certain "queries" as to the meaning of some phrases in his letter to the Committee of Estates, he reiterated his assertions that the English desired to establish dominion over no part of Scotch territory, or to interfere with their religion or government. All they required was a sufficient guarantee against any future attempts of the Scots to meddle with them. Strahan eventually came over to Cromwell, but Ker and the rest remained obdurate.

Meanwhile the unsettled condition of the country had resuscitated the lawless bands formerly known along the border as moss-troopers. These bandits, who corresponded to the Irish "Tories," like them based their operations on the castle of some laird, from whence they cut off small parties of English, stragglers, foragers, or recruits on their way to join the army.

On the 5th November Cromwell issued a proclamation, in which he declared that his men were robbed and murdered "by a sort of outlaws and robbers, not under the discipline of any army," and that the leniency shown to the country had only resulted in its protection being afforded to these ruffians. As the inhabitants must know who these marauders were, and whence they came, and as their movements were generally based on intelligence obtained from the inhabitants, he would in future require life for life in those parishes where such acts were committed, and full reparation for robberies and loss. At the same time he determined to destroy the principal resorts of these bands. Borthwick Castle near Dalkeith was the first attacked. As the owner, Lord Borthwick, appeared to have held his castle under some more or less regular commission, he was allowed to march off, instead of submitting to a storm.

Lambert was then sent with some 3000 horse into the south and west to reduce these marauders, and Whalley was called up from Carlisle, where he had collected a considerable force.

Cromwell now determined to attack Ker, against whom forces could be directed from south, east, and north. The latter had about 5000 men. Cromwell expected that he would attempt to escape towards Stirling. He therefore directed Lambert, who was at Peebles towards the end of November, to march by the south bank of the Clyde to Hamilton, whilst he himself marched directly to the same place from Edinburgh. Both were to reach the appointed place by the 29th. Whalley should co-operate from the south.

******

This appears to be Cromwell's meaning in his letter to Lenthall of the 4th December, when speaking of Whalley's movements, though it is not very clear, and might mean that the latter had joined Lambert at Peebles.

******

Ker would thus be caught between the three forces, probably in the neighbourhood of Hamilton. Cromwell arrived at the latter place at the time agreed on; but Lambert had not come, and he could hear no tidings of him. He therefore concluded that he had been unable to cross the swollen torrents which lay across his road, and himself fell back towards Edinburgh on the 30th. That evening, however, Lambert did arrive and quartered in the town. Cromwell's surmise had been correct. Ker was endeavouring to reach Stirling, and was that day at Carmunnock, not very far from Hamilton. It had been arranged that on his approach Colonel Montgomery should sally out of Stirling with four or five regiments of horse, and make a diversion in his favour.

Ker, finding himself on the 30th within striking distance of Lambert, unsupported by Cromwell, determined to attempt to surprise him the next morning. Accordingly he marched that night and fell upon the English quarters before daylight. The picquets were driven in, but offered such a resistance at the entrance to the town that the remainder were enabled to get mounted and to form up. A sharp fight then ensued in the streets and enclosures which surrounded the town, in which the Scots were completely routed. Ker himself was badly wounded and taken. About 100 of his men were killed, and about the same number taken. The rest fled, pursued by Lambert, and were eventually completely dispersed by him and Whalley. The English loss was trifling. Montgomery had meanwhile moved out of Stirling as arranged, but, hearing of Ker's defeat, retired again.

The Western Army now disappeared, but Edinburgh Castle still held out, and Cromwell could not feel his hold on the south of Scotland complete until it was in his hands. In all his movements since Dunbar he had been hampered by the necessity of protecting the siege. Mining had failed, and recourse was now had to battering by heavy ordnance. Two large mortars had been brought by sea from Hull, and other suitable ordnance procured. Batteries were constructed, and were ready to open fire on the 12th December. Cromwell, as was his custom, sent a summons to the governor before opening fire. Hereupon followed a rather lengthy correspondence.

Dundas, a strict Covenanter, viewed with great suspicion the ever-increasing "malignancy" of the army and Committee of Estates at

Stirling and Perth. Yet he felt bound by his oath not to surrender the castle except on extremity. Strictly invested by the English, he received but little news from outside, and wished to assure himself of the relapse of the committee from the principles it professed when he was appointed governor. He therefore asked for a ten days' suspension of hostilities, in order to communicate with Perth. This Cromwell naturally refused, but offered to send into the castle any two persons on whom Dundas could rely to give him information as to the events in the outer world.

Dundas asked that Mr. Jaffray and the Rev. John Carstairs might be sent in to see him. But these gentlemen, who had been taken at Dunbar, and were on parole in Edinburgh, refused to act in the matter. They alleged that since Dundas would probably act on the information received from them, they would hereafter be held responsible for what he should do. This was on the 14th, and, the negotiations having come to a standstill, Cromwell ordered the batteries to open fire that morning. One of the defenders' cannon was dismounted after a few shots, and the cannonade was kept up that day and the next, the mortars doing considerable damage. On the 16th a snowstorm hid the castle and stopped operations, but on the 17th the fire was renewed.

On the 18th Dundas again commenced to negotiate, suggesting a truce for a certain number of days, at the end of which, if no relief came in the meantime, he would surrender the place. Cromwell replied by informing him, that if he liked to send out commissioners to treat at once, he might have honourable conditions On no other terms would a suspension be agreed to.

Dundas then sent out Major Abernethy and Captain Henderson, who soon agreed with Colonels Monk and White, representing Cromwell, as to the terms of surrender. These were liberal, and somewhat peculiar. The castle was very strong, amply supplied with provisions, and contained a large arsenal full of warlike material of all sorts. It might therefore hold out for an indefinite time, since from its position it was difficult to storm. It also contained an immense amount of plate and other valuable property which the inhabitants of Edinburgh had carried thither for security. Had the place been taken by storm, or on unconditional surrender, all this would have fallen as booty to the soldiers.

Now Cromwell was most anxious in the first place to get possession of the place as soon as possible, and in the second, to propitiate the inhabitants. He therefore agreed to a suspension of hostilities for four days during which the inhabitants were allowed to carry off their property. He issued a proclamation forbidding any soldier to interfere with any one so doing on pain of death. The conditions were strictly observed, and the people peaceably recovered their property. It speaks much for the discipline of the English soldiers that no case of plundering, or attempt at plunder, appears to have been reported.

At the end of the four days, on the 24th December, Dundas and the garrison marched out with the honours of war, Cromwell agreeing to protect any property of private persons still remaining in the castle. All the warlike stores fell into his hands, including sixty-seven pieces of ordnance, most of them small, and a great quantity of ammunition and provisions. The archives of Scotland were sent to the Committee of Estates at Stirling. (Carlyle, vol. iii. *The Articles of the Rendition of Edinburgh Castle*—with Hodgson's *Memoirs*).

All organised resistance of the Kirk party had now ceased south of the Forth. North of that firth, the forces, civil and military, still opposing the English, were daily becoming more purely Royalist or "Malignant." In dealing with this party, Cromwell felt none of the scruples which had led to so much exchange of correspondence, explanations, and declarations when the foe was one with whose aims, both civil and religious, he had much in common. Now the enemy was again the old one, the representative of absolutism and episcopacy. With him he could deal with a light heart.

But the moss-troopers were still numerous, and for the security of the communications with England it was necessary to suppress them before any attempt was made to attack the Royalists. At Jedburgh some of these bandits had even succeeded in capturing a Captain Dawson of the English Army and some eight of his men, whom they murdered in cold blood. Therefore, for the next few weeks, flying columns were employed in chasing these bands, and in reducing the strongholds from which they issued. Colonel Fenwick took Hume Castle, a party from Dumfries reduced Kinmore Castle. Hacker from Peebles destroyed the nests of several bands in the neighbouring hills.

A rather notorious troop under one Watt was rooted out of the Pentland Hills. A German officer named Augustin, however, who was particularly active in leading cavalry raids from Stirling or Fife, appears to have eluded the vigilance of all Cromwell's officers, and to have done a great deal of mischief in the shape of cutting off stragglers, &c. This form of warfare, which can never affect the course of a war, Cromwell regarded as inhuman, and he addressed letters both to Leslie and the Committee of Estates, asking that Augustin's raids should be stopped; but in vain. After the final defeat of the Royalists, Augustin escaped to the Continent.

Cromwell Decides to Cross the Forth

The south of Scotland being now under English control, Cromwell's restless spirit urged him on to make some attempt against the Royalist position at Stirling, in spite of the inclemency of the season. Indeed, disregard of the old system of winter quarters was one of the points in which he departed from the military traditions of his day. During the previous winter in Ireland he had granted his troops some six weeks' repose, and had resumed operations before January had closed. A good deal of the success which had followed in his campaign in Tipperary and Kilkenny, might fairly be attributed to his taking the field so early before his enemy was ready to resist him.

But the conditions here in Scotland were very different. To begin with, the climate was far more severe than that of the South of Ireland, as he was to find to his cost. And the condition of his opponents was entirely different. In Ireland they were dispersed, unorganised, deficient of money and supplies, and without any definite plan of campaign. In Scotland they were concentrated in a strong entrenched position, well officered and disciplined, with a sufficiency of supplies at any rate, and with the simple and definite object before them of defending their position and preventing Cromwell from penetrating north of the Forth. However early the campaign might open, therefore, the Royalists would be found ready.

But Cromwell, ever impatient to terminate the war, braved the difficulties, and, on the 4th February, sent nine regiments of horse and eight of foot to Linlithgow. The next day he overtook them and marched to Falkirk, amidst a tempest of snow, hail, and rain. The 6th, the troops reached Kilsyth, the afternoon proving as bad as the day before. The men already began to fall sick rapidly, and Cromwell saw the inadvisability of persisting in the attempt. On the 7th the force returned to Linlithgow, and on the 8th to Edinburgh.

In the then existing state of the roads and want of organisation in the transport and commissariat departments of the army, which were not equal to keeping it supplied under such conditions, the attempt was probably ill-advised. Still it showed Cromwell's audacity in the face of difficulties and eagerness for decisive action, which made him throw aside the dilatory tactics then in vogue. Had half the advantages in the way of good roads and organised supply departments been at his disposal, which any general operating in Europe can now reckon on, he would have succeeded in opening the campaign in spite of the weather. The worse consequence of the expedition was that Cromwell himself fell seriously ill from the effects of the exposure.

The inclemency of the season and their general's illness prevented all serious attempts on the part of the English for many weeks. The time, however, was not altogether wasted. Parliament forwarded recruits and supplies from England. The former were mostly pressed men, and service in Scotland was most unpopular with them, doubtless owing to the tales of the hardships to which the army had been exposed, which were spread by the news-prints and by other means. Whitelock says of one batch of recruits which were sent from London, that one-half deserted before they crossed the frontier, and, for the most part, re-enlisted into various garrisons.

Having assured himself of the strength of the position occupied before Stirling by the Royalists, and the difficulty of forcing a passage there, Cromwell already contemplated crossing the river elsewhere. For reasons that will be given hereafter, such a crossing would be most advantageously made east of Stirling—across the broad firth, in fact. But to cross an arm of the sea, such as this was, with horse and train, required special appliances. Large flat-bottomed boats were therefore ordered in England, and arrived in Leith early in April.

The Parliament was indeed making strenuous endeavours to bring the war to an end. As early as January Whitelock mentions rumours of an intention on the part of the Royalists to slip past Cromwell, invade England, rally the old Cavalier party to Charles' standard, and once more fight out the quarrel on the original lines of King versus Parliament. To prevent any insurrection on the part of the English Royalists, during the absence of the regular army in Ireland and Scotland, three new regiments had been raised in London during October. Other troops were collected, and when, in March, information of Royalists' plots in the north reached the Council of State, Harrison was sent towards the frontier with a considerable force. A very large number of men were now in the pay of the English Parliament in the three kingdoms, the monthly vote for their maintenance being £120,000.

Some ten miles west of Leith, and twenty-five east of Stirling, a promontory on either shore of the Forth causes it to bend slightly southward and to narrow suddenly to a width of barely a mile and a half. An island called Inchgarvie and some adjacent rocks stand about halfway between the two promontories. Inside this point the Forth becomes a land-locked loch or estuary, and just within the island lies an old-established ferry, which connects the village of Northferry, in Fife, with that of Queensferry, in Linlithgow. This ferry forms the most direct route between Edinburgh and the fertile country along the east coast.

Further to the east, on the north shore of the open Forth, and nearly opposite Leith, lies the port of Burntisland. It is evident that both the ferry and the port were of great importance to an army operating from Edinburgh towards the north. The Royalists held the island of Inchgarvie, and, on the south bank, the fort at Blackness, some five miles nearer Stirling. Cromwell determined to seize both these posts, which would give him command of the ferry, before he opened the campaign against Stirling. On the 27th March, four ships of war sailed out of Leith, passed Inchgarvie, and captured a vessel which the Royalists had stationed behind it as a guard ship. They then sailed up to Blackness, which they invested from the sea. At the same time Monk was sent with a force, consisting of a company from each foot regiment, to attack the fort from the shore. Cut off from all hope of relief, the garrison surrendered after a day or two, and by the 1st April the place was in Monk's hands. (*Cromwelliana*). The island of Inchgarvie was then closely invested by small warships.

Meanwhile, the Royalists had not been altogether idle. Charles had been crowned at Scone on the 1st January, and given the command of the army. Leslie was made second in command, Middleton Lieut.-General of the horse, Massey Major-General of the English contingent. All these were good officers, of much experience and considerable ability, but with different views and sympathies in matters civil and religious. It was unlikely that they would pull well together. The Duke of Buckingham, as the king's favourite, and one of the most influential of the pure Cavaliers, possessed great weight in the Council of War; but neither he, Wilmot, nor any of that party appear to have received any important command at first.

From the very beginning their advice was antagonistic to Leslie's, as were their interests. For whilst the re-establishment of the king on the English throne, and the restoration of the rights and property of the English nobility, were the objects they had in view, Leslie looked in the first place to driving Cromwell out of Scotland. Thus, whilst the former urged an immediate incursion into England, avoiding Cromwell's army, the latter advised that the old waiting tactics of August should be played over again at Stirling, until a favourable opportunity of defeating the English forces presented itself.

At first the necessity for raising more recruits, for drilling and disciplining them, and for organising the new army generally, gave irrefutable reasons for adopting Leslie's scheme. No better man could have been entrusted with such a task. The defences of Stirling were carefully improved, and the outposts gradually pushed more and more south, both with the object of delaying the enemy's advance and of covering as much territory as possible. Provisions were by no means abundant, but sufficient for the time. Dutch ships were employed in landing supplies on the Fife coast. The standard of discipline enforced in the army was very creditable, when it is considered that the majority of recruits were wild clansmen.

By the beginning of April Cromwell, whose life had been almost despaired of, was sufficiently recovered to think of again taking the field. Provisions were still a difficulty, most of the food being brought by sea. Dutch ships also were used in this service by the Parliament. But, unlike the previous autumn, the chief difficulty was now forage for the horses. Until the new crops were high enough to be used, nowhere could sufficient forage be found to enable the powerful English cavalry to keep the field. Horse food is so bulky that the transport arrangements of those days could not grapple with the task of bringing it from the base to the army.

But Cromwell determined to renew his attempt to bring the Royalists to battle, or to force their position at Stirling. On the 16th April, he held a review at Musselburgh, at which some "8000 or 9000 horse and as many foot" were present. (Old newspaper, *Cromwelliana*). He was received with "shouts and acclamations" by the soldiers. After the review the troops took the road towards Hamilton, their destination being Glasgow. At the same time some of the foot took ship and sailed for Burntisland with the fleet. Apparently the boats lately arrived from England were taken with them, as a landing was contemplated. This expedition effected nothing of consequence. The ships bombarded the port, but no impression seems to have been made on it, nor any landing attempted.

Why the army marched to Glasgow is not very clear. None of the contemporary accounts explain the reasons for the move satisfactorily. Possibly the idea was to establish a fresh base nearer to Stirling than Edinburgh. The army advancing thence would bar the roads from Stirling towards England more directly than from Edinburgh, and rumours of the king's intention to slip past Cromwell had been current for months. But the latter, as the sequel showed, never feared such a move, being convinced it would end in disaster.

Whatever the reason, the army, after spending one night in the open, and the next two at Hamilton, reached Glasgow on the 19th or 20th. The Royalists, hearing of this move westward, sent out a party of horse along the Edinburgh road. Availing themselves of a morning fog, they fell upon the English quarters at Linlithgow. After a severe struggle, in which the English commander, Major Sydenham, was wounded, they were driven back.

The English Army remained some ten days at Glasgow, Cromwell and the officers quietly listening to wordy attacks on themselves which the Scotch ministers thought fit to make from their pulpits. Meetings were held in which the Puritan officers contended with the Presbyterian ministers on knotty points of doctrine and church discipline. These meetings, which were conducted with due decorum, no doubt did good in bringing the two sides into personal contact. The strict discipline always preserved in the English army had done much to conciliate the Scots, who, on this occasion, mostly remained at home. The troops also quelled a riot amongst the citizens themselves, which occurred whilst they were in the town.

At the end of April, Cromwell, contrary, as far as can be judged, to the original plan, marched back to Edinburgh, where the army arrived on the 2nd May. Want of forage, and indications of a movement in that direction by the Royalists, are hinted at in the old papers and elsewhere as the cause. Perhaps also it had something to do with the discovery of a very wide-spread plot amongst the English Royalists and Presbyterians to assist the army in Scotland in reinstating the king, which was made about this time. A small vessel bound for the Isle of Man was driven into Ayr harbour, seized by the English garrison, and letters addressed to the Earl of Derby were found in her, which disclosed the whole affair.

Cromwell might have considered it advisable to stay his attack on the Royalists of Stirling until he was sure that the Parliament could deal with conspirators in England without his assistance. In the army itself it would appear that the necessity of procuring fresh supplies was believed to be the cause of the move. A contemporary newspaper says:

> From Edinburgh, the 3rd May thus: Yesterday his Excellency and the officers, with their train, horse, and foot, came to Leith

and Edinburgh, and this day received a week's provisions, so a few days will produce a second march.—*Perfect Passages*, 9th to 16th May; *Cromwelliana*,

On the 3rd, after his arrival in Edinburgh, Cromwell wrote to Harrison, who had advanced with some newly-raised forces through Lancashire towards the border,, directing him to draw nearer Carlisle. Penrith was suggested as suitable for his headquarters. At Carlisle there were already twelve troops of horse, six old and six new, and five or six of dragoons. These, and any other troops on the border, were to be ready to act with him, and stop any incursions of the Royalists into England. Harrison's levies seem to have been indifferent. Cromwell writes:

> Although your new militia are so bad as you mention, yet I am glad that you are in the head of them; because I believe God will give you a heart to reform them; a principal means whereof will be by placing good officers over them, and putting out the bad, whereunto you will not want my best furtherance and concurrence. I have had much such stuff to deal withal, in those sent to me into Scotland; but blessed be the Lord, we have, and are, reforming them daily, finding much encouragement from the Lord therein, only we do yet want some honest men to come to us to make officers."

He thoroughly understood that, with raw troops especially, their value depends on their officers.

Whether Cromwell intended to proceed with operations, at once or not, a serious relapse of his illness prevented his doing so. This was the third since he had first contracted it on that winter's march. Parliament became much alarmed. It could ill afford to dispense with his services, yet for every reason it was most desirable to prosecute the war with vigour, as soon as supplies and forage were available in sufficient quantities. The more time Charles was given, the stronger and better trained his army would become. The expense, too, of keeping up the various armies was causing much discontent in England. On the 26th May:

> The Parliament in tenderness and respect to the health of the Lt.-Gen. Cromwell have voted that his Lordship be desired to retire himself into some convenient place where he may enjoy the benefit of English air, till it shall please God to perfect his

recovery, and in the meantime to entrust the affairs of the army into such hands as his Lordship shall think fit.—*Mercurius Politicus, Cromwelliana.*

At the same time Doctors Bates and Wright were sent especially from London to attend on Cromwell, Fairfax lending them his own coach.

But before the votes, or the doctors, reached him, the patient had begun to mend. A letter dated Edinburgh, 20th May, to the *Perfect Diurnal* states that the ague from which he had been suffering had left him, but he was still too unwell to take the field.

> All thoughts of his marching with the army at their first going out is laid by; and the officers provide accordingly to manage their business without his personal presence. And truly I see neither want of courage nor unity in them, so much as in any measure to retard their action, when the growth of green oats will give us opportunity to march with our horse.—*Cromwelliana.*

Whatever the real cause of delay, the want of forage was evidently given out as the reason; the old newspapers constantly refer to it. Cromwell, in a letter of thanks to the Council of State, dated the 3rd June, speaks of himself as convalescent, and he now made rapid progress towards complete recovery.

About this time some changes were made in the chief commands in the army. Fleetwood appears to have left for England. Lambert obtained the command of the horse; Dean, equally efficient ashore as afloat, became Major-General of the foot, and Monk Lieut.-General of the train.

During June the Royalists continued to push their outposts southward. They occupied Falkirk and fortified Callander House, which lies at its eastern extremity on the Edinburgh road. A party of horse under Colonel Augustin penetrated as far as Dumfries and "alarmed" the country round Carlisle, but were defeated by the English troops on the border. (Carlyle, vol. iii.) Another foraging party carried off the horses belonging to some English dragoons at an outpost called "Bogge Hall." On the 28th, the main body marched out of Stirling to Torwood. (Gardiner, *History of the Commonwealth*).

This looked like a movement preparatory to the march into England which had been so long threatened. At any rate, the Royalists had now quitted their fortifications and might be attacked in the open.

Cromwell, who was now fit again to take the field, had, on the 25th, assembled his army in camp on the old site in the Pentland Hills. It consisted of thirteen regiments of horse, twelve of foot, six troops of dragoons, and sixteen cannon. (Whitelock, and *Cromwelliana*).

These may have amounted to 6000 or 7000 horse and 9000 or 10,000 foot, supposing the cadres to have been fairly full. About this time, a large provision fleet of 120 vessels reached Leith. (Whitelock. He is always unreliable as to dates; probably this fleet did not arrive till after the army marched).

On the 30th June, the army marched to Linlithgow, Cromwell hoping to meet the Royalists in the field. At the same time he wrote to Harrison, who was now on the Border with 5000 or 6000 troops, to send parties into the passes leading into Scotland, in order to delay the Royalists should they attempt to march in that direction. With the bulk of his forces he was to be ready to march according to the instructions he might receive. (*Several Proceedings in Parliament*, 3rd to 10th July, in *Cromwelliana*. Harrison's exact position cannot be fixed. Whitelock mentions him as in Cumberland early in June. On the 6th August, he was at Newcastle).

On the 2nd July, the English marched out of Linlithgow towards the enemy. His vedettes were first encountered about Callander House. These fell back on their main body, which was found drawn up about Torwood. To Cromwell's great disappointment the position was too strong to attack. Leslie had chosen it with his usual skill. Behind the Bonny, or Carron brook, whose banks were boggy and in many places impassable for cavalry, rises a range of hills on which Torwood lies. Here Leslie had posted his troops and strongly entrenched them. The Forth on one side and rough hills on the other protected his flanks. What his numbers were cannot be ascertained with certainty. Whitelock puts them at 15,000 foot and 6000 horse. Lord Wentworth, writing after the army had entered England, puts them at the same figure. (Cary's *Memorials*, vol. ii.)

Skirmishes during the afternoon of the 2nd July only served to convince Cromwell of the strength of his enemy's position. The brook was found unfordable except at a few places. There seemed no way of getting at his foe. That night the English camped within gunshot of the Royalists, who next morning opened fire on them at three o'clock. More desultory skirmishing ensued. About ten o'clock a council of war was held, when it was decided to fall back, under hope that the enemy would pursue. Accordingly the English retired through Falkirk to near Callander House, but Leslie did not so much as follow them up with his horse. After waiting for some three hours, the English retired to Linlithgow, where better accommodation for the troops and forage for the horses could be procured. (*Perfect Account, Cromwelliana*).

After this, Cromwell made an expedition to Glasgow, probably with a view of tempting the army to advance on Edinburgh, but Leslie refused to budge. On the 13th July, the army returned to the neighbourhood of Linlithgow, (*Several Proceedings in Parliament, Cromwelliana*), and on the following day a Scotch outpost was driven out of Falkirk. On the 15th, two battering pieces were brought up and planted against Callander House, the garrison of which had caused the English some annoyance. At eleven o'clock they opened fire, but it was seven in the evening before the breaches were practicable. Storming parties were then drawn out—ten files from each regiment—and were given faggots to throw into the moat.

Cromwell then sent in a drummer with Captain Moss, who took a summons to the commandant offering quarter to the garrison if they surrendered. The commander asked till eight the following morning, when, if not previously relieved, he would surrender. This Cromwell refused, and the house was stormed, the commandant and sixty-two men being killed, only thirteen of the garrison receiving quarter. Leslie could from his position see his outpost stormed, but made no effort to relieve or withdraw the garrison.

Cromwell now determined to carry out a measure which he had considered for some time, and which would force Leslie to quit his position and fight. This was to cross the Forth and cut his communications. The principal sources of supply for the Royalists were Perth, Fife, Aberdeen, and the eastern counties, whilst their recruits came to a large extent from Argyleshire and the western Highlands. To cross the river west of Stirling would do them but little harm, whilst Cromwell's own communications would be seriously exposed. Besides, in that direction there were no roads fit for the use of an army. To cross the Forth east of Stirling would bring him at once into the country whence the Royalists drew most of their supplies, and close up to their communications with Perth, the seat of Charles' government. It would also threaten Stirling from the rear.

Here the Forth was no longer a fresh-water stream, but a navigable arm of the sea. Cromwell would have to cross his army in boats, and this would take a considerable time. The enemy from Torwood could, if he got information in time and marched promptly, arrive at the spot chosen for disembarkation more quickly than Cromwell could concentrate them, and could crush that part of the army which landed first. Or Leslie might wait till part of the army was embarked, then move out, southwards, crush what remained behind, cut the communication of the rest, and invade England, flushed with the prestige of victory.

But the move into Fife promised the most decisive results, and Cromwell determined to run the risks. There were also some conditions which were favourable to the enterprise. The promontory on which Northferry lies is connected to the mainland by a narrow neck of land. If the first troops thrown across could seize this neck they might keep much superior forces at bay until the rest of the army had time to cross. The garrison of Inchgarvie, which, to a certain extent, commanded the passage, was reduced to great straits, and not in a position to interfere.

Leslie, having advanced to Torwood, was thirty miles from Northferry, whilst Cromwell was only ten from Queensferry, and the former must, if he wished to oppose a landing in Fife, march back over the bridge at Stirling, a narrow defile, which would somewhat delay his movements. If he attacked part of the army at Linlithgow whilst the other part was across in Fife, it could fall back on the very strong position at Edinburgh. Lastly, Cromwell having the command of the sea, need not be over anxious about his land communications.

Cromwell therefore sent orders to Colonel Overton at Leith to take Daniel's regiment, two companies each from Fenwick's and Syler's, with four troops of Colonel Lidcot's regiment of horse, and to march on the 16th July from Leith to Queensferry, thence to cross over in the boats, already provided, to Northferry, and to entrench himself on the promontory. In this he succeeded, apparently without opposition, during the night of the 16th and early morning of the 17th, Thursday; Cromwell meanwhile drew out his army as if to attack Leslie at Torwood. The latter seems to have heard of Overton's landing either on Thursday or Friday morning.

At any rate, he sent off Sir John Browne with 4000 men to oppose him. Cromwell then hesitated whether or not to attack Leslie thus weakened, but finally decided not to, and sent Lambert on Friday evening with his own and West's regiments of foot, and his own and Okey's regiments of horse to reinforce Overton.

★★★★★★

Cromwell in his letter of the 21st July (Carlyle, vol. iii.), says Thursday evening; but I think this must be a mistake. Lambert in his letter of the 22nd (Whitelock) says he arrived at the waterside very early on Saturday, the 19th. As he had only some fifteen miles to go at the most, he could not have taken over twenty-four hours on the march. Friday, too, seems to fit in better with the rest of the story. It is, however, quite possible that the boats were not ready when he reached the neighbourhood of Queensferry, and he may have halted for the night, and commenced to embark the next morning.—T. S. B.

******

Lambert reached the waterside very early on Saturday, the 19th, and at once commenced to embark. It took him, however, all that day and the next night to get his foot across. The horse did not commence to pass till Sunday morning. About 4 p.m. on Saturday he discovered Browne's troops at Dunfermline, where they quartered for the night.

On Sunday morning Browne advanced to near Inverkiething at the neck of the promontory. Lambert disposed his foot and Overton's troops to cover the disembarkation of his horse, and remained on the defensive. Browne does not appear to have made any serious attempt to attack, although he had been reinforced by some 500 men during the morning. Only some desultory skirmishing took place.

At last Lambert's horse were all across, and then he assumed the offensive. Symptoms were observed of a contemplated retreat on the part of the enemy, some of his troops wheeling about. Okey was immediately sent forward to open an attack on the rear-guard should the retreat be continued. Browne, finding himself too close to the English to retire without great risk, then drew up his forces in order of battle. Lambert did the same. Opposite the left wing the ground was very unfavourable to the action of cavalry, and there was a "pass" there lined by the enemy's musketeers. Therefore only four troops of Okey's regiment and two of Lidcot's were stationed on the left under Lidcot. The rest of the horse, Lambert's regiment, two troops of Okey's, and two of Lidcot's, were posted on the right under Okey. The centre was, as usual, made up of the foot—Lambert's and Daniel's regiments in the first line—West's and Syler's in reserve—all under Overton. Lambert had some 5000 men in all, Browne some 4500.

For an hour and a half the opponents faced each other in order of battle. Browne's troops stood on ground favourable to the defence, and Lambert hesitated to attack them. At last he heard that reinforcements were coming for Browne, and that Cromwell was falling back towards Linlithgow, which would permit Leslie to send the bulk of his forces to crush him. He therefore determined to delay no longer, and gave the order to advance. The English attacked with their usual spirit, and after a short struggle the enemy were completely routed. Two thousand were killed on the spot, "the Highlanders getting ill quarter"; 1400 were taken. The broken remnants fled to Stirling. Amongst the prisoners was Sir J. Browne, who was wounded.

Lambert had been misinformed when he heard that Cromwell was falling back. The report probably arose from the movement of two regiments of foot—Ingolsby's and Ashfield's, and two of horse—Lilburne's and Alured's, which he had sent to Lambert's assistance. These joined the latter on the 21st, the day after the fight, and brought his forces up to 7000 men. Cromwell, on the contrary, was watching Leslie closely. The latter, on hearing of Browne's defeat, determined to abandon the Torwood position, and by a rapid march through Stirling to fall on Lambert with his whole force. But Cromwell was too quick for him. Writing to the Council of State on the morning of the 21st from his headquarters at Linlithgow to report Lambert's victory, he mentions Leslie's retreat, and hastening to the front, he ordered an immediate advance. If he found that the latter was, as he expected, marching towards Lambert, he resolved to pass by Stirling and to cross the Forth by a ford, thereby avoiding the delay which would be incurred in storming the defences of the bridge. Lambert could well be trusted to hold the neck of the Northferry promontory until at least Cromwell's powerful cavalry could come up with the Royalists and attack them in rear.

Leslie felt the danger. He had got through Stirling, and was some five or six miles towards Dunfermline when he remarked Cromwell's advance. He at once wheeled about, and returned in time to re-occupy the park and his other works immediately covering the bridge, which had been first constructed and held after Dunbar. He could not have had much time to spare, as Cromwell, Dean, and a reconnoitring party had reached Bannockburn, within a mile of the suburbs of Stirling. (Cromwell to President of Council of State, dated the 24th July, Carlyle, vol. iii., *Perfect Diurnal*, the 28th July, *Cromwelliana*).

Leslie must now have been considerably stronger in numbers than Cromwell, but, though the latter deliberately offered him battle, he refused to put his forces against the English veterans, and remained within his defences. Cromwell had now gained his object. His crossing into Fife was now secure. Rapidly countermarching, he moved down to Queensferry, and immediately commenced passing the army across. By the 24th he had 13,000 or 14,000 horse and foot in Fife, leaving "somewhat better than four regiments of horse, and as many of foot," on the south of the Forth. (Cromwell to President of Council of State, dated the 24th July, Carlyle, vol. iii., *Perfect Diurnal*, the 28th July, *Cromwelliana*).

With these he continued to face the enemy. He dates a letter as late as the 26th from Linlithgow. He expected the Royalists would now base themselves on the west of Scotland, and would at least make incursions into England. The precaution he had taken to prevent this last he described in the above-quoted letter, but Vane, who read the letter in the House, omitted this part, obviously to prevent the enemy gaining information, and it thus did not get into the newspapers, and has been lost.

Before himself crossing into Fife, Cromwell wrote on the 26th a letter, (Carlyle, vol. iii.), to the Lord President of the Council of State, describing the situation and the condition of the army and of the magazines. It is a very interesting letter, throwing a light on to the wants of an army at that period.

> The enemy is at his old lock, and lieth in and near Stirling, (where he is too strongly entrenched to be attacked). Whither we hear he hath lately gotten great provisions of meal, and reinforcement of his strength out of the North under Marquess Huntly.... Our forces on this side the River are not very many, wherefore I have sent for Colonel Rich's; and shall appoint them, with forces under Colonel Saunders, to anybody close upon the Borders, and to be in readiness to join with those left on this side the Firth, or to be for the security of England, as occasion shall offer; there being little use of them where they lie, as we know.
> Your soldiers begin to fall sick, through the wet weather which has lately been.

He then asks that recruits may be hastened.

> For the way of raising them, it is wholly submitted to your pleasure; and we hearing you rather choose to send us Volunteers than Pressed-men, shall be very glad you go that way. Our Spades are spent to a very small number; we desire, therefore, that of the five-thousand tools we lately sent for, at the least three-thousand of them may be spades—they wearing most away in our works, and being most useful. Our horse-arms,

especially our pots, are come to a very small number; it is desired we may have a Thousand backs-and-breasts and Fifteen-hundred pots. We have left us in store but four-hundred pair of pistols; two hundred saddles; six-hundred pikes; two-thousand and thirty muskets, whereof thirty snaphances. (flintlocks) . . . Our cheese and butter is our lowest store of victual.

Money, as usual, was badly wanted. Cromwell, like all good generals, looked carefully after his stores at his advanced base. In this letter also he announces that the garrison on the island of Inchgarvie had surrendered their post at last. They marched out on the 24th, with swords and personal baggage only.

Meanwhile Burntisland, an important port on the Fifeshire coast, had been invested. It surrendered on the 29th. Cromwell says:

The town was pretty strong but marvellous capable of farther improvement in that respect, without great charge. The harbour, at a high spring, is near a fathom deeper than at Leith; and doth not lie commanded by any ground without the town.— Cromwell to Lenthall, the 29th July; Carlyle, vol. iii.

Whalley was then sent with a force along the shore, whilst a detachment from the fleet coasted along abreast of him. In this way several ships were captured, and "a great store of great artillery." Cromwell was now himself across the Forth, and entered Burntisland shortly after its surrender.

Cromwell's Pursuit

Having now secured a base in Fife where supplies could be landed direct from the fleet, Cromwell lost no time in attacking the Royalists' communications. Perth was the headquarters of Charles' government, and the centre of the country from which his army drew most of its supplies. Against Perth, therefore, Cromwell marched on the 30th July. Leslie had been completely outmanoeuvred. He must now either fight or give up all the eastern coast of Scotland, on which he had hitherto based himself. The western Highlands could not supply him with sufficient food or forage for his troops. Nor could he hope to feed them from the country round his immediate position, which had already been swept by the foraging parties of both armies for months.

In the face of the powerful English cavalry he could not collect supplies from the country dominated by them. Isolated parties of horse, such as those led by Augustin, might slip past their opponents and do damage in their rear; but they could not escort back long provision trains, or droves of cattle, sufficient to feed an army. Therefore the waiting game must be abandoned and decisive action taken. Either he could turn against the English in Fife, and fight them, weakened as they were by the detachment left south of the Forth, or he could march south and in turn invade England.

He could not cut the communications of the English south of the Firth, as they had cut his north of it, because from Edinburgh the roads spread out, eastwards to Berwick along the coast, and southward to Carlisle. They were not therefore confined, as his communications were, to a narrow slip between the mountains and the sea. Besides the English depended for their supplies on their fleet, and this he had no means of attacking. But by marching straight into England the Royalists might hope to create a panic among the peaceable civilian population, and to rally to the king's standard the old Cavalier party and the Presbyterians who were most discontented with the present state of affairs.

Judging by Leslie's usual cautious tactics, it is most probable that, if left to himself, he would have adopted the first alternative. He would have marched out of Stirling and taken up some position between the English at Perth and the passages of the Firth at Burntisland and Northferry. Cromwell must then have returned and attacked him in position. For, although in course of time the English fleet might have established a fresh base on the Tay, this could not be done in a moment, and meanwhile their communications would be broken.

Besides, Cromwell would never submit to be cut off from Edinburgh, it would be tantamount to a defeat. Therefore Leslie, with 20,000 men or more, would have forced Cromwell, with only 13,000 or 14,000, to attack him on ground selected by himself. He would also be fighting in a country he knew well, and of which many of his men were natives. That Cromwell risked having to fight such a battle shows that his confidence in his men was such that he did not care to count heads once he could draw his enemy out of his entrenchments.

But no doubt owing to his inaction, his failures when opposed to Cromwell, and the ever-increasing Royalist element in Charles' army, Leslie was rapidly losing weight in the Council of War.

Buckingham was intriguing to supersede him, and though Charles refused to listen to this, his own wishes coincided only too well with those of the English Cavaliers. Their desire was to use the Scotch army to invade England, raise the English discontents, seize London, place

Charles on the throne, and then crush the Puritans by overwhelming numbers. They were willing that Charles should agree to what conditions the Scotch Presbyterians demanded, provided the latter gave him a free hand in England. Cromwell's movement to Perth seemed to offer a most favourable opportunity to carry out their scheme. They believed that once over the Border thousands would join them, eager to shake off the heavy yoke of the Parliament, with its accompaniments of high taxation, and repression of all the old country amusements. Scotland and Ireland had absorbed for the time all the Parliament's regular army, that New Model Army which had been the cause of the king's defeat in the first Civil War.

Only militia and newly-raised regiments were left to oppose them, and against these they had no fear of pitting brawny Highlanders and stalwart Scotch yeomen. Such were the hopes of Buckingham's party, but Cromwell knew better. He felt that when the weather-bound coaster had been seized at Ayre, all those who could lead a rising in favour of Charles had been secured. He knew that on the Border, Harrison and Rich lay ready to oppose an invasion of England, and at least to delay the march of the Royalists.

At Perth he was but very little farther from London than Charles was at Stirling. The latter might steal a march or two and so get a start of him, but if the Royalists marched by Carlisle and Lancashire, as they probably would, his own route by Berwick and Yorkshire would be better and easier than theirs. Before crossing into Fife, he had made his arrangements for this emergency Harrison, one of his best officers, had been given the command of all the troops in the south of Scotland and on the Border.

The bulk of these latter were disposed about Berwick, and the detachment left at Linlithgow would, on Charles' advance, fall back on Edinburgh. Therefore any attempt of the latter to take the eastern route would be strongly disputed. Cromwell's own recrossing the Forth was secured by the fortifications of Leith and Edinburgh. He had therefore no fear that Charles would reach London before him.

But in the Royalist camp the hopes were high. The opportunity was fleeting, Cromwell might at any moment return to Linlithgow. Therefore directly the English advance on Perth was known for certain, Charles, on the 31st July, broke up his camp and ordered a march for England. Leslie seems to have foreseen the dangers and difficulties, and it was with a heavy heart he took direction of the march. The Scots generally did not approve of the movement. They must have seen that it was undertaken far more in the interests of the English Cavaliers than in their own.

Although they had furnished the sinews of war, their own country was left entirely at the mercy of Cromwell's troops. The Highland noblemen with their clansmen remained with Charles and shared in the march, but many of the kirk party deserted it.

The Earl of Lauderdale wrote to his wife from near Penrith on the 8th August:

> All those that were unwilling to hazard all in this cause with their king, have on specious pretence (most of them) left us.— Cary's *Memorial of the Civil War*, vol. ii.

The march was directed by Biggar on Carlisle, and proceeded rapidly. By the 5th August the Royal army was close to the Border, some 100 miles by road from Stirling. Some hopes had been entertained that the Galloway and Nithsdale men would join it, but not a man came.

Cromwell had heard of Charles' move either on the 31st July or the 1st August, but he was not certain that the information was correct. He continued his march on Perth, before which place he arrived on the 1st August.

The next day the town surrendered. (A garrison of 1300 men had been placed in the town only the day before; Whitelock). By this time, he must have been pretty certain of the object of Charles' march, which he had all along thought probable. Making no stay in Perth, he left a garrison there of one regiment of horse, one of foot, and four troops of dragoons under Overton, and left again with the army on the 3rd August. At the same time he sent Monk with 5000 or 6000 men to besiege Stirling Castle, still garrisoned by the Royalists. Cromwell marched rapidly, and by the 4th August had got his foot and most of his horse across the Forth. Here he organised the pursuit of the Royalists.

Lambert, with some 4000 horse, was ordered to march independently as rapidly as possible, join with Harrison and Rich on the Border, overtake Charles, hang on his flank, intercept and delay his march, and prevent recruits joining him. Cromwell himself with the foot, train, and the rest of the horse, would follow as fast as possible. The old regiments had been selected for the pursuit, veterans whose marching powers had been well tested, the newer regiments were sent with Monk.

By the 5th August Lambert was ready, and wrote to Harrison, informing him that he was then starting, and would march by Jedburgh or Kelso. With his lightly-equipped force he could cross the Cheviots in many places. He also wrote that Cromwell desired Harrison would march "with all convenient speed" against the flank of the enemy, taking with him his horse and dragoons, and sending Rich with his seven troops on in advance.

Harrison received this letter on the 7th August. He had been to Leith or Linlithgow to see Cromwell and take his orders about the 23rd July, and on his return ten troops, or nearly two regiments of horse, had been ordered to follow him out of the four regiments left south of the Forth. On the 6th August he was at Newcastle, with the bulk of his troops. Rich and Wharton were at Hexham, twenty miles further west. This day he wrote to the Committee for Yorkshire to raise some foot, of which he had but two companies, and to drive off all horses and cattle and to remove all provisions should the enemy approach. He says:

> The enemy mount their foot upon all the horses they can get; wherefore it will be necessary the foot you raise should be also mounted to answer them, they being a flying party.—Cary's *Memorials of the Civil War*, vol. ii.

Similar letters were sent to Lancashire, Cheshire, Staffordshire, Salop, Nottingham, Derbyshire, and the six counties of North Wales. He was about to march by Richmond to get before the enemy if possible. The next day he wrote to the President of the Council State. (Cary's *Memorials of the Civil War*, vol. ii.):

> I have with me about three thousand horse, whereof but four troops are dragoons.

★★★★★★

> Cromwell, in his letter to Lenthall, dated the 4th August, says, "About three thousand horse and dragoons besides those which are with Colonel Rich, Colonel Sanders, and Colonel Barton."

★★★★★★

He had intended to mount his two companies of foot as dragoons, but gave up the idea on Sir Arthur Hazlerigg's advice, who considered "that a hasty and irregular taking up of horses ... would more provoke the country than their service would be considerable." They were therefore left behind at Durham. The enemy were reported, he said, to have some 5000 or 6000 foot. He asked permission to raise "four or five thousand godly men, well mounted," for a month or two. He also suggested that any forces that could be spared out of the west should be sent to Gloucester, foreseeing that Massey, who was with Charles, would endeavour to reach the town with which he had been so intimately connected during the first Civil War.

Meanwhile, Charles had crossed the border on the 6th August. A summons to the Governor of Carlisle was rejected, and he had no time to lose besieging fortresses; therefore he crossed the Eden higher up. The army was then paraded, and Charles was proclaimed King of England by a Mr. Jackson, an Englishman created king-at-arms for the occasion. Trumpets sounded, drums beat, and cannon thundered a salute. Hopes were high with the Cavaliers. The next day the army reached Penrith, where it halted on the 8th, a foraging party only being sent on to bring in provisions to Kendal.

Letters from the Earl of Lauderdale and Lord Wentworth give optimistic descriptions of the Royal Army at this time.

Wentworth wrote:

> By God's grace we are come as far as Penrith in Cumberland, with a good army of fourteen or fifteen thousand foot and about six thousand horse, all absolutely at the king's command, as much as any army I ever saw under the command of his father.—Cary, vol. ii.

Lauderdale wrote:

> His Majesty is thus far advanced into England with a very good army.... This is the best Scots Army that I ever saw, and I hope shall prove the best.—Cary, vol. ii.

And again:

> Never were men more hearty for all their toil, you would not know this army.... Trust me we have not taken the worth of a sixpence, and the country are kind to us. We might have men enough if we could get arms: some we get.—Cary, vol. ii.

Hamilton was not so sanguine, he wrote to Mr. Crofts:

> We are all now laughing at the ridiculousness of our condition. We have quit Scotland, being scarce able to maintain it; and yet we grasp at all, and nothing but all will satisfy us, or to lose all.—Cary, vol. ii. This Duke of Hamilton was the brother of him who had commanded the Royalists at Preston.

Certainly, the army had marched very rapidly, near 150 miles in eight days. The errors of 1648, delays, hesitation, slack discipline, plundering, internal squabbles, and an ill-arranged order of march, were avoided in 1651. Captain Howard, the son of Lord Howard of Escrick, who apparently commanded a troop of the local militia, came over to the Royal Army with his men. He was knighted by Charles, and hopes were entertained that many others would follow his example.

However high the hopes may have been among the English nobility with Charles, his army was already in a very precarious situation. Lambert was already across the border, Cromwell approaching it. Harrison had advanced a march from Newcastle. The authority of the Parliament was far more firmly established than in 1648. The organisation of the militia was better. In Cheshire the local forces were assembling, ready to dispute Charles' advance. Lord Fairfax, true to his promise, again took up arms when the Royal Army invaded England. He was now gathering the Yorkshire militia.

Fleetwood was collecting those of the counties nearer London at Banbury. In Shropshire, Staffordshire, and the surrounding counties, the militia readily answered the summons to muster. London again called out her trained bands. In the Eastern counties similar preparations were being made. Against all this the English Royalists could, on their part, do but little. Their leaders were in exile, in prison, or so closely watched that they dared not move. The Earl of Derby, once all-powerful in Lancashire, was in the Isle of Man, whence the Parliament had not, as yet, ousted him. With difficulty he raised a boat-load or two of men and a few score of muskets and pikes.

Sir Philip Musgrave, once so powerful in Cumberland, was with him, with scarcely a man. Very few recruits joined the Royal Army. Wentworth's estimate of its numbers, 14,000 foot and 6000 horse, was probably too high. The Parliamentary reports usually give 12,000 horse and foot as its strength. Probably this was below the mark. Wentworth might exaggerate from ignorance, or a desire to reassure his friends. Harrison and the other Parliamentary leaders could only give a guess at the numbers with Charles' army, and would give a low estimate to allay the fears of their own party, and to discourage the Royalists in England. Probably the true numbers may have been somewhere about 16,000 or 17,000.

On the 9th August Charles resumed his march to Kendal. By the 15th he was at Wigan with his advanced parties near Warrington. The Cheshire foot, 3000 strong, under Colonel Birch, had been posted on the south bank of the Mersey to dispute the passage of the bridge. On this day they were joined by Lambert and Harrison. The former must have traversed over 200 miles since he left Leith on the 5th, a fine performance even for cavalry. Both appear to have been falling back before Charles for a day or two previously. The latter's advanced parties were so close on them that they had not time to destroy the bridge properly. The united Parliamentary forces on the south bank of the Mersey now amounted to 9000 horse and 3000 foot. (Some 2000 Staffordshire appear to have joined Lambert and Harrison about this time. See *Several Proceedings in Parliament*, August 7th to 14th, *Cromwelliana*).

But Cromwell's orders were—not to fight a battle without more foot. The country south of the river was, besides, much enclosed and unsuited to the action of cavalry. Therefore, only one company of foot was drawn down to the bridge, and when Charles attacked on the morning of the 16th he gained the passage after a short dispute. His horse then crossed and pressed hard after the retreating Parliamentary forces. They were, however, checked two or three times in the narrow lanes by charges of parties of Colonel Rich's regiment, which formed the rearguard. Harrison and Lambert then fell back to Knutsford Heath, on the direct road to London through Coventry, their object being to "amuse the enemy, flank and front him until the general arrive." But if necessary, their numbers were sufficient to offer him battle on suitable ground. (See the letters from Harrison and Lambert; Whitelock).

Charles' men were beginning to get discouraged. They had met with no serious opposition as yet, though large forces of the enemy were falling back before them, and they had maintained the strictest discipline and injured none; still there were no signs of a general rising of the English to join them, as they had been led to expect. On the contrary, the militia was everywhere obeying the orders of the Parliament. At Warrington, the Earl of Derby joined the army, bringing but a couple of hundred foot and fifty or sixty horsemen from the Isle of Man.

It was determined that whilst Charles should continue his march with all speed, Derby should remain behind in Lancashire and raise recruits. Massey was to assist him by opening negotiations with the Presbyterians of Manchester, he being himself of that sect, whilst Derby was an Episcopalian, and during the first Civil War had been their bitterest foe. As soon as the negotiations were fairly started, Massey would overtake Charles as quickly as possible, as great things were hoped from his influence in Gloucestershire.

For Charles had now relinquished the idea of marching straight on London. He knew that Lambert directly barred his path at Knutsford, and that Cromwell was already in Yorkshire. He also probably knew that behind Lambert lay Fleetwood at Banbury. To force his way through Lambert's and Fleetwood's forces and across Cromwell's front was more than could be expected of his army, for their united forces would more than double his. His own march had been so rapid that even the wiry Highlanders were weary and dispirited and needed rest. Therefore, it was thought best to occupy some good strategical position, between them and the Parliament's forces, where he might find food and forage were plentiful and where the population were inclined to be loyal, there to rest, refresh, and recruit his forces.

The position should cover the approaches to Wales, where the inhabitants throughout the first Civil War had given good proof of their devotion to the Royal House, and whence he might hope to rally to his standard the sturdy foot soldiers who had formed the mainstay of his father's armies. Meanwhile Derby would gather the Cavaliers and Presbyterians in Lancashire, Massey could rally Gloucestershire, and time would be gained to open negotiations with the discontented throughout the country. In Leslie he had a general of tried ability in a war of positions.

Therefore, avoiding Lambert at Knutsford, Charles marched due south towards Shrewsbury, having some hopes that the Governor would declare in his favour. A summons, however, was refused, and the Royal army passed on towards Worcester. This town had been one of the most loyal during the first Civil War, and had been the last important place in England to surrender to the Parliament. When taken at last by Whalley in July, 1646, its fortifications had been demolished. In many respects it was very well suited for Charles' purpose. Lying astride of the Severn, it blocked an important road into South Wales. Should Massey succeed in persuading Gloucester to declare for Charles and in seizing or destroying the intermediate bridges, the Royalists might rapidly gain strength behind the river.

The country round was fertile, and supplies abundant. The population was believed to be still loyal. Tactically, also, it was a strong position (see map). About a mile below the town the Teame, coming from the west, joined the Severn. A brook, large enough to hamper the movements of cavalry, ran southwards to join the Teame some half a mile to the west side of the suburb of St. John, which lay on the right bank of the Severn. Investment would therefore be difficult, and would require a very superior force.

The Parliamentary Committee of Worcestershire determined to attempt to hold the town, enlisted men, and, began to repair the broken walls. A Colonel James was appointed to command. But on the 21st August news was received that Charles' army was approaching. Thereupon the mayor, sheriff, and aldermen came to the committee and informed them that they had determined to offer no resistance to the entry of the Royalists. Most of the men already enlisted then deserted their colours.

The next morning, early, four troops of horse, sent by Harrison, entered the town. A few men were then again collected, but no foot arrived, as had been expected, from the militia of the neighbouring counties. Charles' advanced troops were now close to the walls, and the Committee decided that without more foot the place was untenable. They therefore withdrew to Gloucester after a slight skirmish, and that evening, the 22nd August, the Royal forces entered the town and were well received by the mayor and inhabitants.

Charles determined to rest his tired troops some days here. His foot regiments were quartered in and close to the town, the horse in the villages west of the Severn. Warrants to raise forces were immediately issued to the neighbouring gentry, who were supposed to be loyal. Labourers were collected to repair the fortifications, especially a large fort at the eastern entrance to the town, called the Royal Fort.

The major-generals—Lambert and Harrison—had meanwhile continued to interpose between Charles and London. They were now at Coventry. Fleetwood was still at Banbury, Cromwell was coming rapidly up. On the 13th August he was on the Tyne, at Newcastle and Newborne, with nine regiments of foot, three of horse, and a train of artillery. Lilburne, with his regiment of horse,, was about this time sent forward to join Lambert. Every endeavour was made to hasten the march of the foot. The sick were left behind at the towns through which the army marched. The weather was very hot, the men marched in their shirts; their heavy coats, arms, and accoutrements being carried stage by stage by the peasantry.

On the 19th the headquarters were at Ferrybridge. News had been received that the Earl of Derby and Sir Thomas Tildesley were raising forces in Lancashire, whilst Charles had passed on with his army. Orders were therefore sent to Lilburne to remain in that county and suppress the Royalist levies instead of joining Lambert. On the i8th he reached the neighbourhood of Manchester, just in time to anticipate Massey, who was approaching with a view of opening negotiations with the Manchester Presbyterians. Massey fell back to Catished Green, near Warrington, whilst Lilburne went on to Stockport. Here he learnt that considerable levies were being raised by Lord Derby's party, and wrote to Cromwell for the assistance of a regiment of foot. Massey meanwhile followed Charles.

On the 22nd August Lilburne, having obtained a company of foot from Manchester, two more from Chester, and fifty or sixty dragoons, marched to Wigan, where he heard the enemy were gathering, hoping to surprise them. But he found they had moved off to Chorley. The next day he marched to Preston, whither he heard the Royalists had gone, and bivouacked within two miles of it. That night he sent in a patrol to beat up their quarters and annoy them. The next afternoon the enemy retaliated.

> A party of the enemy's horse fell smartly amongst us, where our horse was grazing, and for some space put us pretty hard to it: but at the last it pleased the Lord to strengthen us, that we put them to the flight, and pursued them to Ribble bridge (this was something like our business at Mussleburg) and killed and took about thirty prisoners.—Lilburne to Cromwell, Cary, vol. ii.

Lilburne now heard that Cromwell's own regiment of foot was approaching Manchester. Cromwell had detached it with a troop of horse to his assistance, from Rutherford Abbey in Nottinghamshire on the 20th or 21st. Lilburne therefore halted on the Ribble, thinking the foot would join him there. But these, though they had marched very rapidly as far as Manchester, were now obliged ta advance with great caution, the enemy being reported to have 500 men in Manchester, and some of Derby's levies lying between them and Lilburne. The latter heard the next morning, the 25th, that the enemy was marching towards Wigan, retiring, he supposed. He therefore followed.

In reality, however, it was Derby's intention to fall on Cromwell's regiment before the horse could join it. When, therefore, Lilburne reached Wigan he found the enemy in considerable force, both horse and foot, marching out of the town towards Manchester. Being very short of foot, and the country being much enclosed and very unfavourable for the action of cavalry,, he determined to avoid a fight, and by a rapid flank march join the foot regiment before the Royalists could attack. The latter, however, seeing his inferiority in strength, wheeled about and marched back through the town ta attack him.

In spite of the unfavourable nature of the ground, Lilburne now decided to accept the proffered battle. A fierce fight ensued in the same lanes through which Cromwell had chased the Scots in 1648. After an hour's fighting the Royalists were completely routed. Lord Witherington, Sir W. Throgmorton, Sir T. Tildesley,. and Colonel Baynton were killed or died of their wounds, with sixty others. Four hundred prisoners were taken, Cromwell's regiment, which was advancing to join Lilburne, picking up many stragglers. Derby himself escaped badly wounded, and joined Charles at Worcester with but thirty horsemen. (See Lilburne's Letters to Cromwell and the Speaker, Cary, vol. ii.; Hodgson's *Memoirs*).

This defeat was a sore blow to Charles. Elsewhere his endeavours to raise forces had also ended in failure. Gloucester had proved deaf to Massey's persuasions, and held firmly to the Parliament. The militia of the counties west of the Severn showed little inclination to join him, and to raise and arm the tenants of such loyal gentlemen as were inclined to rise would take time. Besides, arms were not to be procured. Charles could not bring large quantities with him on his rapid march, and the Parliament had taken good care that none remained in the hands of gentlemen suspected of Royalist sympathies.

On the other hand, the ease with which the Parliamentary forces were mobilised surprised even their leaders. Whitelock, who was himself a member of the Committee of Safety, writes under date on the 19th August—

> It could hardly be that any affair of this nature could be managed with more diligence, courage, and prudence than this was; nor peradventure was there ever so great a body of men so well armed and provided got together in so short a time, as were now raised, and sent away, to join with the rest of the forces attending the king.

The end could not be far off now. On the 22nd August Cromwell reached Nottingham, and on the 24th Warwick. Here Fleetwood and other superior officers met him to settle the plan of attack. On the 25th 14,000 men of the trained bands of London assembled on Tuthill Fields. On the 27th Cromwell, with Lambert, reached Evesham, whilst Fleetwood advanced to Shipston. They were now within striking distance of the Royal Army at Worcester. Charles had, during the five days he had been there, succeeded in repairing Fort Royal to some extent, but the city walls did not present a serious obstacle to an attacking force. He had sent parties of horse towards Gloucester and Hereford, endeavouring to rally the old Cavaliers and the Presbyterians to his standard, but in vain. His only hope of prolonging the war lay in the advantages given him by the configuration of the rivers. Massey had broken the bridge at Upton, about six miles below Worcester. This Cromwell determined to seize and repair.

Early on the morning of the 28th Lambert was sent with a party of horse and dragoons to make the attempt. On arriving, about nine o'clock, near the bridge he found a plank flung across the gap where it had been broken. The Royalists' guard was negligent and not on the lookout, having gone into the village a little way off on the western bank of the river. Lambert dismounted eighteen of his dragoons, who crept across the plank and got into a church near the further end of the bridge, before the enemy took alarm. But the Royalists, who numbered some 300 horse and dragoons in the village, then saw what had occurred, and attacked the church.

Lambert's dragoons defended themselves bravely, and meanwhile some of his horse got across, partly by fording, partly by swimming the river. On perceiving these fresh assailants, the Royalists retired without awaiting a charge. Only Massey, who was himself present, faced the troopers, and was badly wounded by a musket shot. Lambert's men did not press the pursuit, but immediately set to work to repair the bridge, encouraged by their commander, who himself lent a hand. He also sent word back to Evesham, and Fleetwood immediately mounted 300 foot behind troopers and sent them on to secure the bridge. Later he followed with the rest of his force and two guns. (*Cromwelliana*).

That so experienced a soldier as Massey should have allowed the important bridge at Upton to be taken so easily seems to point to considerable demoralization in the Royal Army. Cromwell could now operate on either banks of the Severn, and his forces were sufficient for the purpose. Recruits had not joined Charles' forces in any number whilst he held command of the west bank, still less were they likely to come in now that the Parliamentary horse could act on the other as well. A day or two later Lord Derby rode into the town with the remnant of his levies, and the Scots learnt that the communications with their own country were cut, and that no help was to be expected from the north. The rank and file began to be restless and mutinous, and were with difficulty kept in order.

Both at Preston and Dunbar Cromwell had defeated an army twice as numerous as his own by a sudden vigorous blow. Now, on the contrary, his forces were double those of his opponent. With admirable skill he suited his tactics to the altered conditions. Whilst there was no unnecessary delay in bringing about a decisive battle, every precaution was taken to ensure that the victory should be complete. On the 28th he had examined the enemy's position. Worcester lay on the left or east bank of the river—a suburb called St. John's lying opposite, and connected to it by the bridge.

Up the river there was no bridge nearer than Bewdley, fifteen miles away. A range of hills sloped down towards Worcester, their summit being about a mile from the city. On the 29th guns were brought up, planted on the slopes of these hills, and fire opened on the town and the Royal Fort. Reconnaissances were pushed up the left bank from Upton. The enemy were found to have retired behind the Teame, the bridges over which, at Powick and a place about a mile further west, he held in force. A strong house called Maxfield House, between Upton and the Teame, was occupied as an outpost. On this day a Council of War was held on the hill overlooking Worcester, at which Fleetwood and Lambert were present, and the plan of operations was decided on. Cromwell had nearly 30,000 men with him altogether; Charles 14,000 or 16,000.

It was determined to attack on both sides of the river at once, Fleetwood to advance from Upton up the west bank; force the passages of the Teame, and attack the suburb of St. John, whilst the forces with Cromwell were to attack the Royal Fort and the town itself. To connect the two attacks a bridge of boats would be constructed over the Severn near the junction of the Teame and another across the latter river. To cut off the retreat of Charles' army towards the north, Lilburne was ordered to march his horse with all speed to Bewdley Bridge, and bring Cromwell's foot regiment also in that direction. The date of the attack was fixed for the 3rd September, the anniversary of Dunbar. Meanwhile, boats, bridging materials, and artisans were to be collected at Upton. On this day—the 29th—the Royalists made a sally, which was easily repulsed.

For the next few days but few alterations took place in the positions of the contending armies. Major Mercer, who commanded the local Worcestershire horse on the Parliament's side, had been with Lambert at the capture of Upton bridge, where his men had behaved well. He was now sent with the dragoons (five troops) and horse of his own command and two troops of Colonel Rich's regiment, of the regular army, to Bewdley Bridge. On the 1st September a party of the Royalist horse broke down the bridges over the Teame. Fleetwood sent out some troops to oppose them, in case they attempted to cross the river, but no action took place.

By the evening of the 2nd September everything was ready. The boats, bridging materials, and workmen had been collected and pushed as far up the river as possible. Fleetwood was reinforced by two regiments of foot and two of horse under Dean.

Between five and six o'clock on the morning of the 3rd his forces advanced in two columns. That on the right, in which were Blake's, Gibbons', and Marsh's regiments, was directed towards the junction of the Teame and Severn, where it was intended to throw the bridge of boats. That on the left, consisting of Haines' and Cobbet's regiments, moved towards the broken bridge at Powick, near which the Teame was fordable. Lord Grey's and Colonel Matthews' regiments formed a reserve.

The march was timed so that the troops should keep abreast of the boats, but as the latter had to be towed against the stream, or for some other reason not explained, there was considerable delay, and it was not till between two and three o'clock that the columns reached the Teame and the boats the junction of the rivers. The Royalists do not seem to have noticed the advance at first, but by the time the Parliamentary troops reached the Teame the hedges on the other side were thickly lined with musketeers. The left column endeavoured to force its way across about Powick, but for some time without success, whilst the right column awaited the completion of the bridges.

Cromwell, on the approach of the boats, sent a "forlorn" or advanced party across the Severn, who established themselves in the angle between the two rivers, and covered the construction of the bridges. That across the Severn was made first, just above the confluence of the Teame, and as soon as it was finished Cromwell himself led across a strong brigade of horse, consisting of Ingoldsby's, Fairfax's, Hacker's, and part of his own regiments, with his Life Guard. These were supported by Goffs and Dean's regiments of foot. (In Mr. Downing's account, Cary. vol. ii., these two regiments are said to be those which reinforced Fleetwood the evening before).

The Royalists were pushed back after a sharp fight, and the bridge across the Teame constructed "within pistol shot of the other." Fleetwood's right column then crossed with Lord Grey's regiment. Under the pressure of this attack the Royalists gave way all along the line, and retreated fighting from hedge to hedge towards St. John's. Fleetwood's left column then crossed at Powick, but the advance was still slow, the Royalists fighting with great gallantry and often coming to push of pike. The thick high fences favoured the defence and rendered the action of the horse very difficult.

Charles and his staff had been watching the battle from the tower of Worcester Cathedral. It had now been raging for two hours, and it seemed that Cromwell had drawn most of his forces across the river. The Royalist horse had as yet been hardly engaged, and was ready at hand. Charles, therefore, determined to collect what foot was still available, and, with it and the horse, make a resolute attack on the Parliamentary forces still on the east of the Severn. Sallying out of the Sudbury Gate, and deploying under the protection of the Royal Fort, the Cavaliers and Highlanders made a vigorous assault on the troops of Cromwell's right wing. These consisted chiefly of Cheshire and Essex Militia, stiffened by Pride's and Cooper's regiments of regular foot, and supported by the horse regiments of Lambert, Whalley, Tomlinson, part of Cromwell's, those of Harrison's brigade, and a few local troops from Essex and Surrey.

At first the foot wavered and gave way a little, but the horse coming to their help the battle was restored. A fierce fight lasted for three hours on this part of the field, both sides fighting with great gallantry. Cromwell wrote that evening:

> Indeed this hath been a very glorious mercy, and as stiff a contest for four or five hours, as ever I have seen.—Cromwell to the Speaker, dated the 3rd September (ten at night), Carlyle, vol. iii.

Seeing how things were going; on the east bank, he returned to that side, bringing several regiments back with him. Thus reinforced, his right wing began to force the Royalists back. The latter wavered, gave way, and finally broke. They fled to the town, but the Parliamentary troops pursued them so closely that they entered the gates along with them. A frightful scene of carnage and confusion then ensued in the streets. Charles vainly attempted to rally his broken squadrons, who in mad panic rode over everything that came in their way, as they galloped through the narrow streets towards the north gate, now the only one they could escape by. With his Life Guard he was swept along with the fugitives.

Darkness coming on added to the terror and confusion of the

Royalists, but somewhat checked the pursuit. Outside the Sudbury Gate Cromwell had summoned the Royal Fort. He received no answer but a volley. In a moment the Essex Militia, who, "but the day before, were so amazed at the shot from the cannon, that some of them fell flat on their faces," had mounted the defences, put the garrison to the sword, and planted their colours on the ramparts. The guns of the fort were now turned on to the town, and added to the confusion and terror there.

No time was lost in organising the pursuit. As far as the Royalist foot was concerned none was necessary; for whilst the struggle was raging on the east bank, Fleetwood had advanced steadily on the west, and about nightfall had carried the suburb of St. John. No escape was therefore possible for the defeated foot, the northern gate being choked by the flying horsemen and their pursuers. They, therefore, laid down their arms. Six or seven thousand prisoners were taken in the town, including the Duke of Hamilton—mortally wounded—and the Earls of Rothes and Lauderdale. But the majority of the horse escaped at first. Harrison was appointed to command the pursuit, for which 4000 horse were detailed. He sent forward Colonel Blundell with 1500 troopers that night or very early next morning, and followed with the rest shortly after.

Whilst the battle was still proceeding, messengers had been sent to Mercer and Barton at Bewdley, to Lilburne, and the local forces of Shropshire and Staffordshire to be on the look-out for fugitives. Therefore, whichever way the Royalists turned they found the roads and bridges barred against them. Charles was one of the first to separate himself from the ruck. His subsequent romantic adventures and final escape to France are too well known to be told again here. Harrison conducted the pursuit with remorseless energy, taking hundreds of prisoners. The unfortunate Royalists were too dispirited to make any resistance when overtaken.

The Earls of Derby and Lauderdale, with some twenty others, surrendered near Nantwich to Captain Edge of Cromwell's own foot regiment, who was by himself reconnoitring in front of his men. It will be remembered that this regiment was with Lilburne, and had moved south after the fight near Wigan. They had stopped a bridge against some 600 fugitives from Worcester, Derby's party being some of them. Hodgson writes, (*Memoirs*):

Our soldiers had pleasant work with them while they marched

by. They were, by computation, about five or six hundred men, and our musketeers would have gone into the lane, and taken by the bridle the bestlike person they saw, and brought him out without a stroke, so low was the Scot brought.

Harrison pursued the remnants that still held together through Warrington and Lancaster, sending a detachment along the road through Derby and Yorkshire under Colonel Saunders, and another under Colonel Barton through Manchester. All along these routes prisoners were taken in great numbers. (Harrison to the Speaker, the 7th September. Cary, vol. ii). Massey surrendered to Lord Grey, (Lord Grey to the Speaker, the 7th September. Cary, vol. ii.). Leslie and Middleton "were taken on Blackston edge in the moors, betwixt Karsdale and Halifax." (Colonel Birch to the Speaker. Cary, vol. ii.) Hardly a Scot returned. Those who were not taken by the troops were captured and brought in by the country people.

Worcester presented a terrible scene during the days following the battle. The prisoners taken there were driven into the cathedral:

> And what with the dead bodies of men, and the dead horses of the enemy filling the streets, there was such a nastiness that a man could hardly abide the town.—Whitelocke.

But the struggle was over, the last scene of open war between king and Parliament had been enacted. The victory was complete and overwhelming, for the Royal Army at Worcester contained all—English or Scotch—who, from social standing or previous training, were capable of organising or leading the king's forces in the field. With the exception of Charles himself, all the nobles and generals of note were killed or taken. Whitelocke, who, as a member of the Council of State, had access to the official reports, states that 3 English Earls, 7 Scotch Lords, 640 officers, and 10,000 men were taken prisoners, whilst the spoils included all the colours, arms, baggage, &c., of the Royal Army.

Immediately after the battle the militia were dismissed to their homes. Five thousand from Norfolk and Suffolk had marched in the morning after. The ease with which these local forces had been mobilized and their admirable behaviour in the battle was one of the most remarkable features in the campaign. Cromwell wrote to the Speaker on the 4th September:

> Your new-raised forces did perform singular good service; for which they deserve a very high estimation and acknowledge-

ment; as also for their willingness thereunto,—forasmuch as the same hath added so much to the reputation of your affairs.—Carlyle, vol. iii.

After arranging for the disposal of the prisoners, and ordering the demolition of the works round Worcester, Cromwell set out for London, which he entered in great state on the 12th September. It was the last campaign which Cromwell conducted in person, and one in which his military genius shone as brightly as ever.

Monk completed the work of subjugating Scotland. On the 14th August Stirling Castle surrendered to him with the regalia and records of Scotland. On the 1st September he took Dundee by storm. A day or two previously Colonel Alured had surprised and taken the elder Leslie, Earl of Leven, Lord Crayford, Lord Ogleby, and some 300 others, who were endeavouring to raise forces to relieve the town. Montrose and other towns surrendered in rapid succession, and the following year Monk subdued the Highlands. No foothold then remained for Charles in Great Britain, no spot where a nucleus of troops landed from abroad might be developed into an army.

Cromwell's illness, the want of fodder, the desirability of replenishing the magazines, and probably the necessary precautions against a possible Royalist rising in England, delayed the opening of the campaign of 1651. But once commenced, it was conducted with all the great leader's usual vigour. It is a campaign which deserves careful study, one remarkable feature being Leslie's attempt to defend the line of a river from the further, that is, the enemy's, bank, with the defile of the bridge behind him. Had he retained the bulk of his forces behind the river, he would have been in a far better position to crush any attempt to cross, whilst his fortified bridge-head secured him the power of crossing and attacking the enemy should a favourable opportunity present itself. By remaining on the defensive on the far side, he gave Cromwell the opportunity, which he so skilfully seized, of holding the bulk of the Scotch Army on that bank, whilst he threw a detachment across to the other, thus securing his own passage.

Few generals would have had the nerve to deliberately offer Charles the opportunity he desired of marching into England, when the number of the Royalists and the unpopularity of the Independents throughout the country is considered. The success of the manoeuvre thoroughly justified the risks run.

The remainder of the campaign was a triumph for the military organisation of England, under the Independent Parliament, an organisation which, as has already been pointed out, was due to Cromwell's initiative. Never had the mobilization of the militia been accomplished with such rapidity and precision. Never had they been so rapidly concentrated. Though gathered from far and near, the contemporary accounts mention no hesitation on the part of the men to serve out of their own county. The Parliament had now not only a regular army, but also a militia "entirely their own."

His Claims to be Ranked among the Greatest Commanders

The campaign of 1651 was the last Cromwell conducted in person; the crowning victory of Worcester was the last battle in which he drew his sword. The army he had trained and organised continued to carry its standards to victory in Scotland, Ireland, and on the Continent; but it was under the immediate command of other leaders. Cromwell's part hereafter was more that of the statesman than the soldier. From his cabinet he continued to direct the general movements of the English fleets and armies, with the same genius for the art of war, till every state in the civilized world sought his alliance and listened to his demands. But as a leader in the field his part had been played.

For nine years only Cromwell's career was that of a soldier. In those nine years the army had developed from an ill-trained militia into the most perfect military force in Europe. In organisation, discipline, mobility, and tactics, in everything but numbers, it was superior to the armies of all other states. Turenne and Condé looked on in astonishment as the English regiments poured over the ramparts of Dunkirk, and stormed a fortress considered impregnable except by long and wearisome siege.

Some great genius was necessary to organise such perfection in so short a time, for a national army is usually slow of growth. That genius was Cromwell. Those who have studied the history of the Parliamentary Army of the Civil War, which became the National Army of the Commonwealth, must admit that nearly every step it advanced towards efficiency was due to his initiative.

Cromwell's career as a soldier stands apart in many respects from those of other famous generals. Alone amongst them he was a civilian by training and inclination, until the pressure of events forced him to draw the sword. In the American Civil War soldier and civilian fought side by side, with equal chances of distinction and promotion. Those who rose to eminence as great commanders. Grant, Sherman, Lee, Jackson, and others, were all soldiers by education, though some of them had since exchanged the sword for the pen. Yet Cromwell won his victories by sound military method. Great victories have been gained by undisciplined mobs excited by intense enthusiasm, or by an overpowering desire for revenge. Not so Cromwell's armies. Stern fanatics as were his troopers, their victories were won, not by superior enthusiasm, but by superior organisation and military training.

Cromwell lived in what may be called the Renaissance period of the art of war. When wars were undertaken principally to satisfy the ambition of princes, there was little popular sentiment involved. As the feudal system declined the forces of the European potentates became more and more armies of mercenaries, fighting merely for pay and plunder. With the new ideas of religious and civil liberty, which sprang from the revival of secular learning in the sixteenth and seventeenth centuries, popular sentiment was again aroused. Whole nations caught the enthusiasm for an ideal; every man felt that here was something worth fighting for.

Wars were no longer left entirely to mercenary soldiers. *Burghers* and peasants sprang to arms and fought for religion or freedom. With the new class of men in the ranks came a new system of war. The mercenary soldier, living by war, sought to prolong it. The *burgher* soldier, craving for peace, and looking on war as only a necessary evil, longed to finish it. Hence the former loved dilatory campaigns, the strategy of positions and leaguers, and, above all, lengthy sieges with the prospect of rich plunder at the end. The latter, on the contrary, longed for decisive battle, and speedy release from the burden of his arms.

But old customs change slowly. The professional soldiers had crystallized the art of war into a series of dogmas and maxims. Shakespeare's Captain Fluellen, the typical soldier of the day says:

> I will be so bold as to tell you, I know the *disciplines* of war.—
> *Henry V.*, Act iii., Scene ii.

These disciplines included everything connected with a military force and its operations. Round the kings of Europe stood their professional armies, led by soldiers trained in that school. Tilly and Wallenstein, and even to a certain extent Turenne and Condé, were generals of that type. William the Silent and Gustavus Adolphus were the first to avail themselves of the new spirit, and adapt their strategy and tactics to its needs. But neither even of these developed to its fullest extent this! new system of war. Both were born in courts, and trained to arms from childhood under instructors of the old school.

The physical features of Holland tempted, or almost compelled, the Revolted States to assume a strategy of defensive positions, of open sluice gates, and strong walled cities. In his championship of Protestantism, Gustavus Adolphus commanded heterogeneous armies, and defended the territories of widely-scattered allies. Thus, whilst his strategy was bold and far-reaching, and the improvements he effected in tactics all tended to increased mobility and increased decision in battle, be still often resorted to the old system of fortified positions and delaying action.

With Cromwell the conditions were different. Unfettered by prejudices, the result of early training, gifted with a marvellous military genius, teaching himself practically the art of war in the field, beginning at the lower ranks and working steadily but rapidly up to the highest, he understood the new conditions, and stands out as the first great exponent of the modern method of war. His was the strategy of Napoleon and Von Moltke, the strategy which, neglecting fortresses and the means of artificial defence as of secondary importance, strikes first at the enemy in the field. The soldier of the old school sought how to avoid defeat; the modern leader seeks to crush his enemy.

To break in pieces some hard material the hammer employed should be of the finest temper. Cromwell saw at a glance that "old decayed serving-men and tapsters," however numerous, could never constitute an army with which to crush the Cavaliers. Organisation, discipline, skill in the use of arms, and a suitable system of tactics, were required to weld the Parliamentary recruits into troops and companies. A simple captain at the time, he could hardly at first have contemplated the reorganisation of the whole army which he afterwards effected.

But from the first his troop was a model upon which other Parliamentary officers could base their efforts. The care and the sound practical common sense with which he selected his officers and men, and then armed, mounted, trained, and disciplined them, very soon made his troop the best in the army.

The same success followed when his troop was increased to a regiment. If indeed the *Squire papers* contained a narrative of the early life of that famous regiment, showing its interior economy, its system of raising and training men and horses, its method of performing outpost and convoy duties, the manner of subsisting men and horses, its drill, and the pace and formations in manoeuvre and the charge, then the modern cavalry officer has indeed lost an inestimable fund of practical information.

✶✶✶✶✶✶

The *Squire papers*, said to contain a diary of Samuel Squire, auditor of Cromwell's regiment, besides many letters from Cromwell and others to him, were burnt in 1847, except Cromwell's letters, by the possessor to prevent family feuds which might rekindle on publication. See Carlyle, App. vol. ii.

✶✶✶✶✶✶

Cavalry was the principal arm in Cromwell's days. The fate of a battle generally hung on the issue of a charge. Yet cavalry had of all arms suffered most, since the introduction of firearms, by the crystallization of tactics brought about by the professional soldier of the day. It had lost mobility, initiative, and dash, and was incontinently afraid of the wretched flintlock muskets with which part of the infantry was armed. More and more it assimilated its tactics to those of the dragoon or mounted infantryman. Gustavus Adolphus had done much to improve the mobility of his cavalry, and had taught his troopers to fire without halting and then charge in with the sword. Rupert and Cromwell carried the improvement much further. Something on the contrast of the tactics pursued by these two famous cavalry leaders has already been said in Chapter XIII. Rupert relied on dash and pace; Cromwell on precision and cohesion.

In his earlier engagements Cromwell's success was due more to the care with which he had raised, organised, and disciplined his men, than to superior tactical skill. Thus at Grantham the opposing parties faced each other for half an hour waiting for the fire of the dragoons to throw the enemy's ranks into confusion. But Cromwell's charge, when at last it was undertaken, was made with determination, at a good pace, and without halting to fire. Learning from experience, he threw off the old system of delay, and henceforth charged as soon as his formation was complete.

His success at Gainsborough was due to his promptitude in charging and the skilful manner in which he handled his reserves. Whenever he commanded the Parliamentary cavalry, at Marston, Naseby, or Langport, he was ever the first to charge, the last to exhaust his reserves. It has been said of a cavalry fight that the commander who can throw last a fresh unused squadron into the fight will almost certainly win. More depends on the opportuneness in time and direction with which the various lines are sent into the contest, than on the numbers of men employed. On this principle Cromwell always acted. He never let go his last reserve until the last of his enemy's squadrons had been broken and dispersed.

However successful a charge had been, he always rallied the troopers before launching them in pursuit. Note his action in this respect after Dunbar and at Langport. His pursuits were fierce and carried far, and supported by properly formed bodies, to crush any attempt of the enemy to reform, as the Royalists attempted at Aller Drove after Langport. However fierce the charge, however confused the *mêlée*, Cromwell never lost control over his troops. His was that combination of nerve, decision, and military insight which makes a great cavalry leader, and which is so rare that Napoleon said but one such man appears in a century.

When Cromwell commanded forces of all arms the combined audacity and prudence of his operations are no less admirable. In the first place, he made sure of the weapon with which he would afterwards have to fight. The study of his quarrel with Manchester leaves no doubt that he was the originator of the reorganisation of the army in the spring of 1645. (See Chapter 11, and more fully, *Quarrel between the Earl of Manchester and Oliver Cromwell*, Camden So. N. S. No. 12). That quarrel was not with Manchester personally, but, as his letters, speeches, and actions prove, with his feebleness and delay, dilatory counsels and half-hearted actions.

The war spirit in the nation must be made use of. Petty local interests and personal jealousies must be thrown aside. The separate armies of the individual general or of the different associations must be amalgamated into one united army of the Parliament. The war must not be conducted in the interests of a few individuals or a class, but for the benefit of all who supported the cause. It was for the interest of all that it should be finished. It must be prosecuted with vigour, "casting off all lingering proceedings like soldiers-of-fortune beyond the sea, to spin out a war." (Cromwell's speech on December 9th, 1644).

In that sentence lies the difference between the old style and the new, between war as carried on by professional mercenaries and as carried on by nations under arms.

The New Model Army became during the Commonwealth the national army, the first standing national army England ever possessed. It was Cromwell's creation, called into existence by his energy and perseverance, based and modelled on the troops he had himself trained. Differing from the Continental armies in its origin and organisation, it was taught by Cromwell to fight on a new and more vigorous method. Never forgetting the maxim he had laid down, to cast aside all lingering proceedings, he ever struck fiercely and rapidly at his foe. His was essentially an offensive warfare, both in strategy or tactics. Never did he defend a leaguer, still less ever stand a siege. Never did he besiege a fortress whilst there was an unbeaten enemy in the field.

Of all the great commanders of his day none understood so thoroughly as he that the value of a fortress depends on the support it can give to the army in the field. If the field army is thoroughly routed, the fate of the fortress is sealed. Even in his attacks on strong places the old rules were generally cast aside. He seldom resorted to trench and sap, galleries or mines. A battery of heavy guns, a sustained cannonade, and a fierce assault on the breach, such was his usual method of dealing with a fortress that refused his summons. Not that he underrated the value of defensive works when properly applied. Read again his remarks as to the retention of the works round Basing House.

Having a properly organised and well-disciplined army, Cromwell never hesitated to use it with great vigour and boldness. Almost from the very first the operations of the New Model Army presented a marked contrast to the dilatory and disconnected proceedings of Essex, Manchester, and Waller. Whoever was in fact the author of the plan of campaign in 1645, it followed, after the first blunders caused by Parliamentary interference had been rectified, the method always pursued by Cromwell.

The blow first delivered at the king towards the north at Naseby, followed by the rapid march south and the defeat of Goring at Langport, savours strongly of his strategy. Oxford and Bristol and other Royalist fortresses lay on either side of that march, but they were not allowed to cause a day's delay. Not till both the king's armies in the field had been crushed was any notice taken of the fortified towns. Then, however, one after another, they fell rapidly before the vigorous strokes of the New Model Army.

Even when surrounded by all the turmoil of a cavalry fight Cromwell never lost his presence of mind or his control over his troops, and in conducting a campaign he never lost his grasp on the situation of affairs. With unerring judgment he suited his strategy to the conditions of the case. He knew when to dare, when to forbear. Possessing the utmost confidence both in his army and in himself, he seldom stayed to count heads if the circumstances of the case were favourable to attack. And his blow was struck with his full force—no uncertain sparring, no half measures. Yet he was no rash, reckless Hotspur, driving headlong against his enemy wherever met. When in 1648 he advanced to meet Hamilton's invading army, the fate of the Parliament was trembling in the balance.

All England watched with eager eyes the result of the conflict. Defeat or even delay meant the ruin of the Independent party. Opposed by odds of two to one, Cromwell, without a moment's hesitation, flung his small force against his enemy's flank and rear, forcing him to fight a decisive battle. When in 1651 Prince Charles brought another Scottish army across the border, Cromwell knew that the danger was comparatively small. Having brought the prince to bay by a vigorous pursuit, he deliberately waited till all avenues of escape were closed before advancing to the attack. So, too, in the Dunbar campaign, so long as Leslie refused him a fair chance of fighting, he restrained his impatience for battle. But the moment the opportunity offered for closing with his enemy, no thoughts of inferior numbers checked the swiftness and force of his blow.

Like all great commanders, Cromwell was well served by his staff and his subordinate generals, because he knew how to select the best men. Ireton, Jones, Lambert, Harrison, and Monk were all men of first-rate military abilities. A peculiarity in the conditions under which the supreme command was held in the Parliamentary armies has led some people to believe that Cromwell owed his successes more to the advice of his inferiors than to his own ability. The commander-in-chief was directed by the terms of his commission to act in accordance with the advice of his Council of War. Fairfax in his *Short Memorials* states:

> My commission as general obliged me to act with council.

Cromwell, before any serious action, as at Hodder Bridge before Preston, and before Dunbar, always summoned a Council of War. He also in writing his reports always made use of the plural, and said "we considered," "we agreed," &c. But the results of the deliberation of a Council composed of many individuals of different natures and different views must necessarily be so opposed to vigorous, concentrated action, that the saying, "*A council of war never fights*," has passed into a proverb.

Now, the operations of Cromwell's army were vigorous in the extreme, and bear all the impress of being the outcome of the working of a single, very vigorous, brain. Cromwell's influence over his officers is known to have been very great, and probably the use of these councils was to explain and discuss a line of action he had already determined on. Indeed, in the case of Dunbar we know from contemporary evidence that this was so, and that Lambert was deputed to explain to the officers his chief's views and intentions, and to persuade those who were at first inclined to advise the embarkation of the army.

Swift and accurate intelligence of the movements and intentions of the enemy are the grounds on which every general must base his plans. In this respect, the New Model Army was as highly organised as it was in others. Neither Fairfax nor Cromwell ever lacked speedy and reliable information as to the enemy's actions. The duties of the modern "Chief of the Intelligence Department" were then performed by an officer of high rank, who enjoyed the far more compact title of "Scoutmaster." Watson and Roe, who successively filled this office under Cromwell, were men of great ability, and were sometimes employed on diplomatic missions of importance. By spies and scouts, country-folk and prisoners, reconnoitring patrols and intercepted letters, they kept their chief well informed of all the enemy did and intended.

It is upon the creation of this army that the claim of Cromwell to stand amongst the very greatest soldiers of all ages should rest. When the backward military organisation of England at the outbreak of the Civil War is considered, it is perfectly marvellous that in seven or eight years one man, himself an untrained civilian at the outset, should have brought the national forces to such a high degree of perfection. No doubt he had the assistance of very able men, both in the Parliament and in the army, to push the work on. But he had also to contend with a powerful and interested opposition.

That he succeeded was due to a soundness of judgment and an iron will unrivalled even among the great names of history. Mr. Gardiner points out how, in all the great crises of his life, Cromwell hesitated long before he determined on the course he should pursue. Once, however, the mental struggle was over, and his decision made, he was as inexorable as death himself. If hero-worship is the worship of all that is manly and strong, Carlyle was fully justified in selecting him as one of the greatest heroes of history.

Politicians may differ as to the polity he as Protector developed. Soldiers can have nothing but praise for the military organisation which he introduced. The army he created was far beyond those of his day in organisation, tactics, discipline, and especially in the class from which its ranks were recruited. In this respect it was superior to the British army at any subsequent period. Never since have farmers, tradesmen, and artisans pressed so eagerly into the ranks.

This is no doubt due to the fact that never since then have Englishmen of that class felt compelled to take up arms in the defence of any cause which was more to them than life. But the army of today is, nevertheless, the direct descendant of Cromwell's New Model Army. One regiment at least has never since been disbanded, and since the Commonwealth a standing army has been maintained in one form or another. When on Charles II.'s accession all the regiments but Monk's were disbanded, a force of Guards for the king's person was immediately raised. No doubt many of the old soldiers found their way into the new regiments. An officer seeking recruits would hardly refuse a veteran from the best trained army the world then knew, provided he was willing to take the new oaths of allegiance.

And an army the success of which has been so undeviating as this one's was, must leave an indelible mark on the military polity of the country. Its successes will induce its enemies to copy its organisation and tactics. After the Napoleonic wars, every other army in Europe took its model from the French; again, after 1870 the Prussian became the ideal. So the victories of the New Model must have impressed the Cavaliers with the superiority of all its methods of war. Thus, Cromwell's army would become the model on which Charles II.'s Cavalier officers would mould their regiments.

What are the characteristics which have ever since marked the British soldier in the field? Devotion to duty and great coolness and steadiness amidst the tumult and horrors of battle. That spirit is Cromwell's teaching, the spirit of Marston, Naseby, and Dunbar. As he taught his troopers to keep control over themselves in the fiercest charge or in the flush of victory, so ever since have English officers taught their men to go coolly and steadily forward in the face of danger and death. Cromwell was essentially an Englishman, and fostered and developed the best qualities of his English soldiers. His system of fighting was adapted to the genius of the English nation, and has therefore lived in its army. It is the spirit he engendered that has carried the British flag to the four corners of the world.

ALSO FROM LEONAUR
AVAILABLE IN SOFTCOVER OR HARDCOVER WITH DUST JACKET

THE FALL OF THE MOGHUL EMPIRE OF HINDUSTAN by *H. G. Keene*—By the beginning of the nineteenth century, as British and Indian armies under Lake and Wellesley dominated the scene, a little over half a century of conflict brought the Moghul Empire to its knees.

LADY SALE'S AFGHANISTAN by *Florentia Sale*—An Indomitable Victorian Lady's Account of the Retreat from Kabul During the First Afghan War.

THE CAMPAIGN OF MAGENTA AND SOLFERINO 1859 by *Harold Carmichael Wylly*—The Decisive Conflict for the Unification of Italy.

FRENCH'S CAVALRY CAMPAIGN by *J. G. Maydon*—A Special Correspondent's View of British Army Mounted Troops During the Boer War.

CAVALRY AT WATERLOO by *Sir Evelyn Wood*—British Mounted Troops During the Campaign of 1815.

THE SUBALTERN by *George Robert Gleig*—The Experiences of an Officer of the 85th Light Infantry During the Peninsular War.

NAPOLEON AT BAY, 1814 by *F. Loraine Petre*—The Campaigns to the Fall of the First Empire.

NAPOLEON AND THE CAMPAIGN OF 1806 by *Colonel Vachée*—The Napoleonic Method of Organisation and Command to the Battles of Jena & Auerstädt.

THE COMPLETE ADVENTURES IN THE CONNAUGHT RANGERS by *William Grattan*—The 88th Regiment during the Napoleonic Wars by a Serving Officer.

BUGLER AND OFFICER OF THE RIFLES by *William Green & Harry Smith*—With the 95th (Rifles) during the Peninsular & Waterloo Campaigns of the Napoleonic Wars.

NAPOLEONIC WAR STORIES by *Sir Arthur Quiller-Couch*—Tales of soldiers, spies, battles & sieges from the Peninsular & Waterloo campaingns.

CAPTAIN OF THE 95TH (RIFLES) by *Jonathan Leach*—An officer of Wellington's sharpshooters during the Peninsular, South of France and Waterloo campaigns of the Napoleonic wars.

RIFLEMAN COSTELLO by *Edward Costello*—The adventures of a soldier of the 95th (Rifles) in the Peninsular & Waterloo Campaigns of the Napoleonic wars.

AVAILABLE ONLINE AT **www.leonaur.com**
AND FROM ALL GOOD BOOK STORES

ALSO FROM LEONAUR
AVAILABLE IN SOFTCOVER OR HARDCOVER WITH DUST JACKET

THE 9TH—THE KING'S (LIVERPOOL REGIMENT) IN THE GREAT WAR 1914 - 1918 *by Enos H. G. Roberts*—Mersey to mud—war and Liverpool men.

THE GAMBARDIER *by Mark Severn*—The experiences of a battery of Heavy artillery on the Western Front during the First World War.

FROM MESSINES TO THIRD YPRES *by Thomas Floyd*—A personal account of the First World War on the Western front by a 2/5th Lancashire Fusilier.

THE IRISH GUARDS IN THE GREAT WAR - VOLUME 1 *by Rudyard Kipling*—Edited and Compiled from Their Diaries and Papers—The First Battalion.

THE IRISH GUARDS IN THE GREAT WAR - VOLUME 1 *by Rudyard Kipling*—Edited and Compiled from Their Diaries and Papers—The Second Battalion.

ARMOURED CARS IN EDEN *by K. Roosevelt*—An American President's son serving in Rolls Royce armoured cars with the British in Mesopatamia & with the American Artillery in France during the First World War.

CHASSEUR OF 1914 *by Marcel Dupont*—Experiences of the twilight of the French Light Cavalry by a young officer during the early battles of the great war in Europe.

TROOP HORSE & TRENCH *by R.A. Lloyd*—The experiences of a British Lifeguardsman of the household cavalry fighting on the western front during the First World War 1914-18.

THE EAST AFRICAN MOUNTED RIFLES *by C.J. Wilson*—Experiences of the campaign in the East African bush during the First World War.

THE LONG PATROL *by George Berrie*—A Novel of Light Horsemen from Gallipoli to the Palestine campaign of the First World War.

THE FIGHTING CAMELIERS *by Frank Reid*—The exploits of the Imperial Camel Corps in the desert and Palestine campaigns of the First World War.

STEEL CHARIOTS IN THE DESERT *by S. C. Rolls*—The first world war experiences of a Rolls Royce armoured car driver with the Duke of Westminster in Libya and in Arabia with T.E. Lawrence.

WITH THE IMPERIAL CAMEL CORPS IN THE GREAT WAR *by Geoffrey Inchbald*—The story of a serving officer with the British 2nd battalion against the Senussi and during the Palestine campaign.

AVAILABLE ONLINE AT **www.leonaur.com**
AND FROM ALL GOOD BOOK STORES

www.ingramcontent.com/pod-product-compliance
Lightning Source LLC
Chambersburg PA
CBHW021955160426
43197CB00007B/144